AF772340

THEIR FUTURE

MICHAEL GUBSER

Their Future

A HISTORY OF AHISTORICISM IN INTERNATIONAL DEVELOPMENT

Yale
UNIVERSITY PRESS
NEW HAVEN & LONDON

Published with assistance from the Mary Cady Tew Memorial Fund.

Copyright © 2025 by Michael Gubser. All rights reserved. This book may not be reproduced, in whole or in part, including illustrations, in any form (beyond that copying permitted by Sections 107 and 108 of the U.S. Copyright Law and except by reviewers for the public press), without written permission from the publishers.

Yale University Press books may be purchased in quantity for educational, business, or promotional use. For information, please e-mail sales.press@yale.edu (U.S. office) or sales@yaleup.co.uk (U.K. office).

Set in Scala type by Integrated Publishing Solutions.
Printed in the United States of America.

Library of Congress Control Number: 2024945267
ISBN 978-0-300-27581-0 (hardcover : alk. paper)

A catalogue record for this book is available from the British Library.

This paper meets the requirements of ANSI/NISO Z39.48–1992 (Permanence of Paper).

10 9 8 7 6 5 4 3 2 1

Dedicated to my teachers, especially
Margaret Anderson, Martin Jay, Jerrold Keilson,
Rhea Lindstrom, Victor Rohr, and Gwyn Osnos

CONTENTS

THEIR FUTURE

1

International Development and Historical Amnesia

> What we need, and I am afraid it is but a truism, is a clear perception of past trends and of conditions under which they occurred, as well as knowledge of the conditions that characterize the underdeveloped countries today. With this as a beginning, we can then attempt to translate the elements of a properly understood past into the conditions of an adequately understood present.
>
> Simon Kuznets, "Economic Growth and Income Inequality," *American Economic Review* 45:1 (1955), 26

FOREIGN AID PLANNERS RARELY CONSIDER the history of the societies in which they work, an oversight noted in the development literature but little explored. In *The White Man's Burden*, former World Bank economist William Easterly argues that the "lack of historical memory in the aid community inhibits people from learning from their mistakes." Anthropologist Thomas Dichter issues a similar charge, regretting "how little [development professionals] have taken from the history of the world's actual development." And aid advocate Jeffrey Sachs, who heralds the declining share of people living in extreme poverty, notes that development workers do a poor job recognizing their past successes. Historians, too, complain that their expertise is ignored: Frederick Cooper and Randall Packard's lament that aid programs "repudiate" the past even as they "imagine" the future echoes a grievance of many scholars whose knowledge of developing societies goes unheeded.[1] As these commentators aver, aid programs costing billions of dollars operate largely in a historical vacuum. Practitioners design projects based on universal assumptions about poverty that overlook particular historical and cultural conditions, often transferring activities from one region to another with minimal adaptation to local circumstances. Many aid workers leave for foreign assignments with only a cursory awareness of precedents in their sector and the barest knowledge of their host country's history. Needs assessments that inform project planning rarely go back more than five to ten years—the typical life of a donor-funded aid project. Even when what is called 'background context' appears in proposals and reports, it is generally confined to a handful of cultural truisms or political facts.

This ahistoricism is not new. Not only were development programs in twentieth-century Asia, Africa, and Latin America frequently conceived in Western institutions, but they also took European and American modernity as normative, mapping the patterns of Western industrialization onto poorer countries seeking to 'catch up.' As a result, local solutions to development problems gave way to imported models, with tradition and experience severed from emerging plans. The past was simplified, schematized, rendered static—as either a set of age-old anthropological characteristics or a pattern of premodern behaviors to overcome. Furthermore, aid programs since the Marshall Plan treated development largely as a technical enterprise—like fixing a car or healing a sick body—that could ignore history in favor of universal scientific solutions. Development, in this regard, is a quintessentially modernist enterprise, dismissing the past in the name of a brighter future.

This short-sightedness had political implications. The waning of colonialism during the early Cold War sparked intense competition over who would shape the future of millions of newly independent people. Development, as scholars have demonstrated, was central to this contest—indeed, it was one of the twentieth century's dominant aspirations, shared by East and West, elites and peasants, donor and recipient countries alike. This book considers the struggle over non-Western futures in paradoxical fashion by examining the widespread tendency of aid planners to ignore the past. I argue that the narrowing of history to abstract formulae and the concomitant loss of a nuanced, long-term perspective on development forecloses the many possible futures contained in the historical record and available to citizens of developing countries.

Their Future chronicles the varieties of ahistoricism in international development theory and practice since 1945. This is an essential task if we hope to move beyond commonplace admonitions to pay more attention to the past when designing aid programs. Only after understanding ahistoricism's multiple forms—a presentism fostered by social-scientific and technical approaches, for example, is different from one born of bureaucratic deadlines or moral imperatives—can we devise appropriate strategies for cultivating greater historical and contextual sensitivity. The most salient work in this regard is James Ferguson's *The Anti-Politics Machine: Development, Depoliticization, and Bureaucratic Power in Lesotho,* which argues that aid projects convert political disputes into technical problems amenable to bureaucratic solution.[2] Yet the question of ahistoricism is not the same as that of depoliticization: History extends beyond politics, and many political programs are overtly presentist. More so even than depoliticization, development ahistoricism induces aid planners to turn away from local experience and precedents.

Recent histories of development show how programs born in the West were implemented and at times undermined in other regions.[3] Those who launched what Joseph Morgan Hodge calls "the first wave" of development history in the 1990s concentrated on the metropolitan elites who crafted theories and policies of development to support the Western Cold War. Since the turn of the millennium, a "second wave" of historians has expanded and deepened their insights, challenging initial assumptions that development was a monolithic Western imposition by examining the contributions of Third World citizens and the ways that local implementation altered metropolitan plans. *Their Future* adds to this literature by considering not only development theories and policies but also aid practice, stitching together a scholarly literature that is split between political analyses focused at the top of the foreign aid hierarchy and anthropological accounts of project beneficiaries. As a consequence of this bifurcation, development scholars and aid practitioners often proceed in mutual disregard—and at times open mistrust—of one another.[4]

My analysis of development ahistoricism employs three broad strategies. The first, de-silencing, as expounded by the Haitian historian Michel-Rolph Trouillot, involves the elevation of trends overlooked in dominant narratives of global or regional history.[5] As we will see in the following pages, local development efforts were frequently marginalized in favor of agendas pushed by international donors. Recovering these efforts is necessary historical spadework. A second task, provincializing, as deployed by the Indian historian Dipesh Chakrabarty, involves tracing the local and regional roots of allegedly universal development models back to the historical soil (often, but not always, Western) that nurtured them.[6] Chapter 2, for example, shows how proposals for Central European and Caribbean industrialization were elevated into universal programs for Third World uplift. By unearthing their regional origins, historical analysis can clear the way for alternatives. A final strategy is localizing—akin to, if not precisely tracking Argentinian theorist Walter Mignolo's decoloniality. It involves tapping neglected knowledge from non-Western societies to promote a more pluralistic understanding of development's methods and goals.[7] While a book on the history of development necessarily considers the many Western sources that shaped it, I also incorporate non-Western perspectives in several ways. Not only does my discussion highlight programs that emerged from the Global South; it also draws on writings, archives, and interviews with non-Western scholars and practitioners, especially in my case-study countries.[8] Where possible, I seek to illuminate knowledge available outside the halls of power, including novel development strategies based in local experience and tradition. The marginalization of developing-country insights, after all, profoundly impoverishes our understanding of development's history and potential.

The two levels of analysis employed in *Their Future*—development theory/policy and development practice—reflect my professional background as an intellectual historian and a development practitioner. Parts of the book trace the intellectual history of international development ahistoricism by analyzing key theoretical and policy statements. In these discussions, I rely on the tools of my academic subfield, undertaking textual and contextual analyses to explore the theories and assumptions of aid planners.[9] But since ahistoricism is promoted through practice as well, I also examine aid programs in several developing countries. The most potent influence on these chapters is my years of experience as a proposal writer, needs assessor, and project evaluator for various foreign aid agencies, work that granted me insight into the international development trade; skills at conducting research interviews; and access to officials, practitioners, and project beneficiaries in several countries. The book's structure reflects this two-tiered analysis, alternating between chapters on the intellectual history of development ahistoricism and case studies of projects that illustrate ahistoricism in practice.

While this book includes case studies from several countries, I do not claim expertise in all of them. Although the discussions are based on in-country interviews and archival research as well as the available academic and practitioner literature, I do not purport to offer exhaustive accounts of Bangladeshi microfinance, Zambian structural adjustment, or Guatemalan cooperativism. Instead, I hope to show—with some contextual specificity—the existence of overlooked historical experiences and marginalized bodies of knowledge that bear on development programming. From there, I hope that future Africanists, Asianists, and Latin Americanists—not to mention Africans, Asians, and Latin Americans—will carry the explorations further.

Nonetheless, it felt crucial, in a book about global development, not to focus on only one country, since doing so would beg a central question of the project—whether and how programs established in one location can be exported elsewhere. It would also consign the book to a narrow readership, likely those interested only in the society under consideration. The three case studies were chosen to reflect a range of environments, my particular choices actuated by a mixture of practical and conceptual concerns. Logistically, I had professional connections in all three case-study countries that allowed me to undertake meaningful research. Methodologically, my cases stood out as both representative of broader development trends and unique enough to provide analytic focus. Guatemalan cooperativism (Chapter 5) brought together the dominant midcentury themes of modernization, community development, and dependency—allowing me to investigate the contradictions and oversights of development theory when translated into practice. Similarly, 1970s Bangladesh (Chapter 7), *the* locus of recent microfinance innovation, exemplified both the decade's pro-poor concerns and the neoliberal push for market-friendly development. Zambia, too, stood out (Chapter 8). It was one of the most orthodox structural adjusters on the African continent, described in the 1990s as a model IMF partner. And it had the further intrigue of having implemented a previous adjustment program that was aborted in 1987 amid social and economic chaos, setting up a natural historical comparison between its two free-market experiments. Each of these chapters, while specific in time and place, evoked wider aid concerns in the decades under consideration.

Part of the challenge of undertaking a global history of this sort is being caught between different notions of expertise: For academics, development expertise seems like a dubious, even risible form of instant knowledge born of simplistic models imposed on complex national and local circumstances. For development professionals, by contrast, it is academics who are unrealistic—willfully self-isolating, unconcerned with worldly application, and dismissive of the need to act with imperfect information in the face of want and constraint. "I can't even get a bucket from Addis Ababa to the village, and I'm being asked to consider my postcolonial mindset," one exasperated practitioner-academic told me. In this book, I hope to strike a balance between local specificity and general relevance that appeals to at least some readers in both professions.

Historical Activism, Historical Amnesia

We live in an age of historical activism, one in which technical and administrative fixes for longstanding social ills have ceased to calm tempers or settle grievances. Instead, activists demand a reckoning with the past. In today's United States, racism can no longer be redressed by denouncing overt prejudice while overlooking the legacy of structural harm. On the contrary, it requires a public accounting and, for many, some kind of reparation after centuries of systemic discrimination.[10] Global inequality also necessitates retrospective justice. As Thomas Piketty instructs us, it cannot be alleviated unless one acknowledges and rectifies disparities that were centuries in the making.[11] Climate change, too—while it needs cutting-edge science and technical expertise—demands a confrontation with decades-old energy dependencies and entrenched corporate power that contributed to our looming crisis. After all, global warming is a cumulative—that is, historical—threat in which the greatest polluters are not the ones who suffer the most.[12] And for all the problems of historical analogy and comparison, fears about eroding democracy and creeping authoritarianism cannot be understood without reference to earlier political choices and past examples of democratic backsliding.[13]

Development is not immune to these calls. In the 1990s, a post-development literature cast aid not as a program for poor-country uplift but as a tool for neocolonial exploitation.[14] Starting in the 2010s, a related call to 'decolonise aid' galvanized activists, scholars, and professionals.[15] As both critics and sympathizers pointed out, these literatures tend to present development as monolithic, ignoring its internal contradictions and its varied applications in communities around the globe.[16] Nonetheless, they were instrumental in placing historical accountability at the center of aid scholarship. Also in the 1990s, a more nuanced literature on development history, noted above, posed difficult questions about the longstanding relations between purportedly humanitarian development assistance and Western foreign policy.[17] These works exposed underexamined narratives—many told from Southern perspectives—of aid's Cold War role and impact.

The recent emphasis on historical accountability follows a long retreat from history in social policy that dates back at least to the post–World War II era. Ahistoricism intensified with the 'end of history' triumphalism that followed the collapse of the Soviet Bloc, the conviction that political and economic liberalism marked the *summum bonum* of human political and economic organization. Structural incentives add to short-term thinking. "[P]oliticians plan only as far as their next bid for election," wrote historians Jo Guldi and David Armitage in 2014. "They invoke children and grandchildren in public speeches, but electoral cycles of two to seven years determine which issues prevail."[18] As a product of the postwar zeal for technocratic politics, development policy relies on short-sighted growth models and yearly budget justifications. Today's historical activism is a chance for rethinking and recalibration.

All the same, the insistence that foreign aid practitioners should be aware of history can sound rather banal. Most would agree, after all, that knowledge of the past is important to the design and implementation of successful aid programs. Yet superficial concurrence rarely translates into practice. "Most [development] plans contain a formulaic bow to the previous plan period," remarked the aid scholar Jonathan Crush in the mid-1990s, "[b]ut prior histories of the object of development—the people, country, region, sector, or zone—are deemed irrelevant."[19] Crush describes this erasure as a twofold process. First, development problems are stripped of their past: they are no longer seen as products of historical trends. And then they are transformed into abstract models amenable to technical rather than political fixes.

An occasional writer states what these practices imply: perhaps history is not terribly pertinent to development, despite calls to the contrary. With some embarrassment, the economist Eugene Staley, an early booster of the New Deal as an international model, warned that historical analysis might provide little insight for development planners. The examples of success are few and their complexity immense, and since the nature of development itself evolves continuously, lessons from the past may simply be inapplicable.[20]

More recently, the economist Paul Collier expressed doubt that historical analogues could help us understand conflict in today's developing societies.[21] But these are outliers in a field that typically acknowledges the importance of history, even if planners do not engage seriously with the past around policy and programming tables.

There are at least four categories of history that are routinely overlooked by development planners. Perhaps foremost, there is a tendency to ignore local history in the design and assessment of aid programs.[22] Despite frequent lip service, aid documents typically consign the history of beneficiary countries to perfunctory background sections before turning to the details of project design. While ahistoricism is common in many policy arenas, the suppression of local experience is particularly egregious in a development industry that often involves wealthy Western donors promoting social change in non-Western societies—and thereby recapitulates colonial patterns. The danger is not only the marginalization of non-European histories or the monopolization of expertise by the West, but also the misunderstanding of domestic socioeconomic trends and the ignorance of local experiences that might usefully inform program activities.

Another category of missing history is the history of foreign aid itself. In recent decades, the burgeoning subfield of development history has chronicled many trends in the aid industry's first seventy years that are little-known to most practitioners. The upshot of this lack of awareness is a tendency to reinvent the wheel, to offer as new interventions those that were tried before, but without reference to earlier attempts. No doubt this contributes to a hopeful optimism, unburdened by hindsight, in the compensatory powers of development—a potent asset in an industry dedicated to social improvement. But greater historical awareness can provide important services, not only by imparting the useful (if often undesired) leaven of skepticism, but also by uncovering forgotten strategies to stimulate the programmer's imagination.

A third category of missing history concerns global development trends and experiences. Not only do local initiatives frequently get lost in aid program design, but relevant activities elsewhere often go unnoticed (unless designers happen to have been involved in them). Here, the picture is more mixed. While some development programs become portable models for regional and global transfer—we will see multiple examples in the ensuing chapters—many are forgotten, forming a subterranean trove of development experiments that historians are just beginning to explore, country by country, project by project. This historical bounty can immeasurably enrich our understanding of development's possibilities and limitations.

Finally, a fourth category of missing history is the historical nature of development itself. What, after all, is development but historical change in action, an effort to improve countries' social, political, and economic destinies through deliberate, concerted change? Modern development is, in effect, an attempt to orient history toward accelerated progress—"history in a hurry," as Michael Woolcock recently quipped.[23] In this sense, development ahistoricism is a contradiction in terms—a tendency among planners to forget the very nature of what they do. To cut off the past is to deny an essential resource for envisioning change and possibility.

Varieties of Ahistoricism

Ahistoricism has taken various forms in international development policy and practice. One of them is bureaucratic. Political pressures and annual budget cycles have turned development into a high-intensity, deadline-driven industry in which practitioners work on multiple projects simultaneously. The invariable scheduling crunch contributes to a culture of haste, with the time and effort required for deep historicization and contextualization rarely available.[24] This neglect produces some surprising lapses. For example, aid organizations generally do a poor job of cataloguing and maintaining their own history, often discarding documents related to past projects in under a decade. This author worked for a contractor that kept old proposals in a remote lower-floor cabinet before recycling them after five years. Even when records exist they are commonly ignored: USAID's library in Washington D.C.'s Ronald Reagan Building is consistently one of the loneliest places on the premises. The Development Experience Clearinghouse, USAID's online archive, is underused, and many practitioners do not know it exists. As a result, much of the documentary history of development is either lost or forgotten. The same is true in other countries. While researching five- and ten-year-old projects in Uganda, this author once prompted the incredulous query,

"Why are you interested in ancient history!?" In many places, no one knows if records exist at all. Disregard of the past, in other words, has clear bureaucratic inducements: no time, no resources, no interest.

Development administration—the managerial routines that structure programs around the world—also encourages an ahistorical outlook. Many project activities are designed less for the purposes of policy alignment than to encourage 'buy-in' among implementing agencies. Unified messaging around a singular understanding of methods and goals—one project, one narrative—facilitates management and teamwork, but it can also discourage the examination of local context and alternatives that might confuse the narrative.[25] The drive to 'harmonize' donor activities in particular countries—especially strong after the 2005 Paris Declaration on Aid Effectiveness—has a similar effect. While the coordination of in-country programming helps to prevent redundancy and avoid overtaxing host-country agencies, it also delinks aid practices from competing local experiences and accounts.[26]

Historical knowledge is also devalued in hiring and education. Few historians are recruited into development practice, and their expertise is seen as eccentric (if it is noticed at all). Instead, most development experts draw on social and technical sciences that marginalize historical thought.[27] The academic training of aspiring aid professionals reflects the same presentism: it concentrates almost entirely on technical and social-scientific fields, with historical study barely touched. This was not always so. Some of development's most capacious thinkers—Albert Hirschman, Gunnar Myrdal, and Ester Boserup spring to mind—exhibited a broad historical-mindedness in their writings. Earlier, many colonial officials prided themselves on an active interest in local culture and history—an indication that development was not always exclusively technocratic, if also a warning about history's potential misuse. Yet the fact that historical knowledge could flatter colonial agents does not mean that it should be dismissed outright: science has been used for devastating harm, though no one would propose its abandonment.

Furthermore, development is imbued with an ethical and emotive ahistoricism, an activist yen to meet urgent needs with a forward-looking sense of purpose and immediacy. "Faced with the pressing human and political problems of the underdeveloped countries," wrote the pioneering Burmese economist Hla Myint in the 1960s, international agencies and academics "become impatient with impartial systematic inquiry and have taken on the role of champions and spokesmen for the underdeveloped countries." Though "morally admirable" and sometimes practically necessary, this humanitarian ardor has pitfalls. There is "a considerable amount of loose, ambiguous and emotive argument," Myint observed, "shifting the basis of the argument from economic analysis to various types of value judgement ranging from humanitarian considerations to notional self-interest."[28] This laxness holds doubly for practitioners, who confront the poor directly in their work. Standing at the coalface of poverty, it is hard to stop and consider how one got there. Yet the task of development cannot simply be accomplished through an upswell of activism. It depends upon clear analysis of the circumstances that entrenched poverty in the first place, a lucidity that must inform any sustained solution.

Similarly, lessons learned and best practices—ubiquitous in the aid world—offer abstract, decontextualized tips for project operation that can be shifted from place to place. There are sound managerial reasons for adopting them, but they nonetheless contribute to an epistemological ahistoricism that discounts the complex interaction of local context and project activities. As University of Sussex anthropologist David Mosse puts it in his excellent study of an aid project in India, "[t]he development policy models through which resources and political support are so successfully mobilised are rarely those best suited to understanding the social and historical context of development action. Indeed, standard intervention models and project cycles are designed to take out history, to exclude wider economic and social analysis, and to isolate project action from 'the continuous flow of social life.'"[29]

This leads us to the form of ahistoricism most widely canvassed in the scholarly literature: the development industry's technical bias, its penchant for presenting social change in measurable charts and logframes—what Tania Murray Li calls the "rendering technical" of local problems and contexts.[30] This technical ahistoricism divorces development problems from specific social contexts so that they become amenable to regularized administrative oversight. Since Ferguson's classic account of development in Lesotho, a scholarly consensus has emerged around the view that aid programs discount the politics of development in favor of generalized technocratic models. According to Ferguson, the World Bank mischaracterized Lesotho as an undeveloped country, ignoring an established scholarly literature showing that it was a modern labor reserve deliberately impoverished to induce the flow of migrant workers to South Africa's mines. The Bank's rendition, Ferguson explained, was self-serving: The institution did not have the clout to confront labor exploitation, but it did have the technical expertise to promote development. To label Lesotho as undeveloped was to create a field in which the Bank's portfolio could apply.[31]

"Rendering development technical," according to the influential political theorist Timothy Mitchell, is a three-step process. First, experts organize knowledge around experimental sites—pilot projects, design boardrooms—that exalt quantitative data and disembodied models. Second, they meet the inevitable project hiccups and design flaws—including social disputes—by improvising technological and administrative workarounds. And third, they conceal this improvisation behind a narrative of program adaptability. In other words, development projects, far from epitomizing the calibrated application of scientific remedies for poverty, entail a mixture of trial and error, planning and guesswork, with the latter often leading the way. Yet these vulnerabilities disappear in self-assured summative reports. As a tool for obfuscation, then, ahistoricism is integral to the enduring faith in technical solutions for poverty and development.[32]

Ironically, this mode of operation is historically conditioned. Development was a product of mid-twentieth-century social science, whose rise to prominence involved the creation of generalizable policy models. There is no denying the efficiencies of this approach. But it is also crucial to recognize that models allow experts to frame and manage problems by stripping away social distinctions, by extracting them from context and history. *Their Future* argues that development too often gets caught in a kind of template thinking, relying on decontextualized models that ignore the history of local communities and development practices. Models are not purely objective or neutral, although the temptation to treat them so is great. Moreover, they convey a sense of false familiarity: transplanted from place to place, they reassure program managers that challenges found in one location are similar to those found elsewhere, despite vast differences in time and geography.[33]

This technocratic predilection can be found among postwar development planners. As historian Michele Alacevich put it, what remains of early economists' descriptions of development in the Italian Mezzogiorno, the site of a seminal World Bank program starting in the late 1940s, has been "so well digested" that the "specific regional analysis [has] disappeared altogether from the increasingly stylized analyses of ever more varied case studies in vogue in the following decades." What survived was a "theoretical precipitate" applied in later development programs, with generalizations undergoing "thorough reformulations to adhere to new environments" or "misapplied to quite different conditions without the necessary adaptation." This process, he opines, may be considered "an important yet forgotten origin of the 'one-size-fits-all' approaches that have characterized the global development discourse in subsequent decades."[34] The historian Nick Cullather issues a similar charge: "For the development specialist, the only point in studying micro-lending in Bangladesh is to discover how a similar program might work in Ecuador. . . . In the process, history gets lost."[35]

While the chief goal of *Their Future* is to examine the varieties of ahistoricism in international development and the ways they have affected programming, the book's Conclusion offers a brief reflection on how greater historical awareness might alter development practice. I wrote this ending with some trepidation. Many books purport to explain what will make development succeed or fail. This is not one of them. I do not purport that historical awareness can guarantee project success. What I do argue is that it can have practical significance by excavating the origins of development problems and identifying possible remedies found in the historical record. But powerful histories do more than this. Like good literature, they offer breadth and proportion, increasing our appreciation of cultures and experiences beyond our own. This is especially crucial for a development industry that labors across vast cultural and socioeconomic divides. Historical thinking can also have the salutary effect of destabilizing assumptions carried into project planning. Like science, economics, or any technical field, historical analysis can be used for good or ill, to weaken or harden prejudice—with the colonial past supplying copious examples of the latter.[36] Though some argue, perhaps with this danger in mind, that history should not serve as a guide or preceptor, most commentators are not so austere, especially in our activist age.[37] History must be examined and reexamined, they argue, for it suffuses the present and future. This book proceeds in that spirit.

Historical investigations can also broaden the circumference of development possibilities by revealing strategies tried and untried that planners might consider in their programs. To examine history is to ponder not only the paths taken, but also those bypassed and what potential they still hold. Multiplying options can, of course, complicate the aid disbursement process. In a culture of client 'responsiveness' to donor requests, it is not easy to question reigning development truths or propose ideas athwart mainstream thinking. Nonetheless, while ahistoricism may boost a kind of naïve self-assurance, it also limits our ability to devise effective solutions to poverty, many of which, in one form or another, lie buried in records of the past. In this regard, historical awareness can temper excessive development hopes and enthusiasms announced boldly at almost every project launch. Ahistoricism also limits our ability to imagine the unexpected consequences a project might engender—the ways it can succeed, the ways it may fail. It thus countenances the unfulfilled aspirations that litter the aid landscape, programs inaugurated with great fanfare but little accounting for plausibility. The result: a festering disappointment found among many beneficiaries and captured in much of the development literature.

Yet I am also skeptical of the stridency of counter-proclamations that dismiss development *tout court* as neocolonial. They caricature a complex historical record. In fact, after almost eighty years, we have only limited knowledge of what development success actually looks like. Projects that appear successful (or unsuccessful) in a final assessment may reveal quite different legacies ten or twenty years on. Here, historical study can play a valuable role, since a long perspective may turn up deeper impacts than do standard short-term evaluations. Historical analysis can also offer services germane to project design: insight into sectoral trends, information on institutional relationships, valuable strategies tried in the past. And since past projects are often less politically sensitive than ongoing ones, interlocutors may be more open to sharing their views.

Development Theory, Development Practice

Development is one of modernity's incantatory terms. In common usage, it designates the transformation of a society from poor to rich, agrarian to industrial, often as part of a planned and managed process. It is also one of the twentieth century's primary utopias, promising a better future, greater prosperity, and increased opportunity. It was a central concern of Chinese nationalists trying to unify the Middle Kingdom; global leaders forging the Bretton Woods system; African politicians navigating independence; American officials courting Cold War allies; Central American peasants caught in civil wars; and many more besides.[38] "Development," as Deng Xiaoping put it in his 1992 tour of southern China, is "the only hard truth. If we do not develop, then we will be bullied."[39] Indeed, development can be regarded as *the* story of the century—a stirring global aspiration that could be bent toward "different ends by a Nehru or by an ambitious young man in a remote village."[40] As this list indicates, its meaning varied immensely, an ambiguity and suggestiveness that invited many comers. Development served as a loose and evocative framework for a range of beliefs: "that history moves through stages; that leaders and/or experts could guide or direct the evolution of societies through these stages; that some places and people in the world are at more advanced stages than others."[41] A "hosting metaphor" that accommodated "hundreds of definitions," development seemed to be "everyman's road to utopia."[42]

The verb underlying the term *development* has both an intransitive and a transitive meaning. On the one hand, it denotes the process of transforming societies from poor to prosperous, agrarian to industrial, pre-modern to modern. This is its intransitive usage: Guatemala develops. But development also denotes a program of aid and assistance provided by wealthy nations to the impoverished to help them grow and modernize. In this case, development is something done to, for, or with the poor, ostensibly to assist them in achieving their own desire to develop: The United States helps to develop Guatemala. Much (but not all) of this book focuses on the second sense of the term—development as a program of aid and assistance from donor nations and monied organizations to poor communities. However, it is impossible to understand the second definition without appreciating the appeal of the first, without realizing that many people yearned for the development of their societies and communities. Moreover, 'transitive' development was not only done by Western nations. It was global. Throughout Africa, Asia, and Latin America, postcolonial governments sought to develop (transitive) their own lands and people; some of these programs—from Latin America, from East Asia, and from (as we will see in Chapter 7) Bangladesh—became international exports. Though development doctrine was heavily influenced by Western thinkers and finances, it is impossible to make sense of the history of development without appreciating non-Western initiatives. The interaction among all these understandings of development—and the collaboration and conflict they engendered—is an essential feature of the historical landscape.

While this book examines the evolution of development theories and policies, it also grants considerable space to the work of development practitioners—those who design, implement, and evaluate aid programs. If this concern is an outgrowth of my own professional experience, it also fills a significant gap in the development literature, which tends to concentrate on either policymakers or aid beneficiaries. The result is a missing middle, with those who design and manage programs largely ignored.[43] This invisibility has several causes, including an understanding of aid work as "mere policy implementation" or as "as something other than work, such as tourism or charity."[44] In fact, the categories of policymaker, practitioner, and beneficiary overlap considerably, since aid professionals frequently shift positions during their careers, rising up the ranks from implementation to policy or taking a faculty post. Furthermore, many practitioners come from developing countries, blurring the distinction between aid donor and aid recipient.

Development, in fact, is a field "dominated by practice," with practitioners acting as midlevel intellectuals, translating policy and technical expertise into program operations around the globe.[45] As always, translation is never a simple conveyance. Practitioners carry their own beliefs and convictions into their work, and they interpret directives through experiential lenses. Thus, policy that seems straightforward on paper may get amplified, undermined, alloyed, or reversed when implemented on projects. This is especially evident at the inflection points of development history. As the pro-poor policies of the 1970s shifted to growth and market advocacy in the 1980s, projects in countries around the world continued to exhibit the pro-poor convictions of their implementers, even if the language of reports was adapted to new demands from Washington or London. Not infrequently, new policy simply provides a changed rationale for persistent practices, wrapping old strategies in new justifications. Development practice, in other words, is regularly out of sync with theory and policy, a discordance that presents some complication for the historian. While this book is organized chronologically, with case studies linked to neighboring chapters on theory and policy, each chapter has its own internal chronology that at times escapes the overall continuity of the book.

Ahistoricism among practitioners, it is important to stress, does not generally indicate a lack of local interests. In my experience, practitioners are steeped in local concerns, working and circulating with officials and beneficiaries in developing countries, hiring local colleagues onto their implementation teams, reading local books and news, cultivating lifelong friendships. They are, in sum, deeply invested in the societies where they work. (This is not necessarily the case for home office staff visiting the field on quick junkets.) Project decontextualization, therefore, does not bespeak staff segregation from the surrounding society.[46] Instead, it results from a split personality common among overseas professionals: personally invested in local affairs, but operating in a professional 'black box' when it comes to project activities, which must heed political objectives, financial dictates, and donor requirements set in distant capitals. The project becomes a self-contained mechanism, with contextual influences relegated to the outside. In this sense, the design and implementation process generates its own kind of decontextualization—a self-referential automatism that does not emerge from the constituent components, let alone staff preferences. Yet in trying to shut out external 'noise' and focus on contractual activities alone, managers, often unintentionally, isolate their project from the society it is meant to serve.

On History

At some level, history and development are synonymous in that both designate social evolution over time. If history is a general term for this process, development marks a form of hopeful, progressive, managed history. This overlap makes development ahistoricism all the more curious. Like aid practitioners, historians are chary theoreticians, preferring to practice their craft rather than elaborate its philosophy. And like the term *development*, the word *history* is multivalent. In common usage, it means both what happened in the past (in Latin: *res gestae*) and what is written about the past (*historia rerum gestarum*).[47] Forms, styles, topics, and approaches to historical analysis vary immensely, and there are longstanding debates over historical methodology that lie beyond the scope of this book. In this introduction, however, I want to acknowledge the complexity of three concepts that appear in the following chapters.

First, *Their Future* calls for greater historical analysis in development planning and practice. Yet historical analysis is not a singular thing. In his 1988 account of the American historical profession, Peter Novick chronicled nineteenth- and twentieth-century debates among historians about the concept of objectivity, exposing the changing standards and unresolved disputes over what constitutes proper historical evidence.[48] Three decades later, we are no closer to a professional consensus; indeed, historical writing today encompasses such a panoply of topics and methods that it is hard to identify any coherent pattern.[49] Although the requirement to base claims on primary-source material remains a disciplinary norm, the interpretation of evidence is hotly contested. Fortunately this book does not need to settle such thorny epistemological problems. Yet it is important to insist that my call for greater historical analysis in development planning is not issued in the hope of finding definitive solutions to poverty. What history can offer, I believe, is broad perspective, an enhanced sense of possibility, and increased respect for local experiences. These are not minor services.

Second, historical analysis is crucial for development planning because people and societies understand their experience historically.[50] The claim that human experience is fundamentally historical is easy to accept at face value. Yet people frequently forget or ignore the past as they attend to professional affairs. We are, in this sense, beings of the present, of the now—an urgency acutely felt among development practitioners who confront long- and short-term humanitarian crises. Yet inattention to the past does not mean that attitudes and behaviors are unaffected by it. History-blind, after all, is still history-bound. Indeed, even when we are 'in the moment' or focused on a goal, our assumptions, reactions, and behaviors are patterned by years of past experience. As the historian Margaret Macmillan put it, "History is something we all do, even if, like the man who discovered we are writing prose, we do not always realize it."[51] Ignoring this 'historicity' of experience blocks our social understanding—especially in development, where imported strategies confront local tempos of life.[52] Development inventories are stocked with models quarried from Western history and applied to non-Western societies in ways that both ignore their own historical specificity and deny the validity of other pasts, a phenomenon I call 'historical ahistoricism.' Yet the historically conditioned attitudes of beneficiaries shape their acceptance or rejection—and hence the success or failure—of development projects.

Finally, historical practice—the use of history in the design, implementation, and evaluation of development programs. The belief that history should serve the present is of ancient provenance: the Roman orator Cicero described history as *magistra vitae*, a guide to life. By contrast, the separation of history from politics came about in the modern era as historians professionalized and defined their primary responsibility as service to truth alone, not social or political utility. While almost no one today would argue that history should simply serve present ends, there *is* renewed appreciation for the importance of historically grounded public debate and political activism. As Piketty put it, history is "too important to leave to historians."[53] For how can we make sense of pressing global problems unless we understand the past? History, after all, is not inert. Its inescapability mandates that we return again and again to sort through complex legacies. This holds especially for cross-cultural engagement. "If you do not know the history of another people," MacMillan warns, "you will not understand their values, their fears, and their hopes or how they are likely to react to something you do."[54] Development professionals ought to heed this injunction, avoiding easy assumptions about the societies where they work.

A final paradox: In noting the prevalence of development ahistoricism, I make frequent reference to the historical attitudes evinced by aid theoreticians. Chapter 4, for example, examines 1960s modernizers who adopted an explicitly *historical* model of Western industrialization that was then transported to non-Western lands as a development framework. One could thus claim that my thesis—that development is plagued by ahistorical thinking—is prima facie false. Whereas modernizers espoused a Whiggish development narrative based on European templates—one in which nations advance toward rationality, industry, and democracy—1970s equity advocates took a bleaker view, seeing European industrialization as a traumatic process and questioning the relevance of Western experiences for postwar development. These claims are all historical in their way. Yet the application of simplified historical models to countries whose past experience is very different entails its own brand of amnesia. For development theories, even when they explicitly interpret the past, are designed primarily to enable programs of real-world change in societies across the planet today. If the rejection of precedent and the universalization of a singular experience amount to historical theses in a literal sense, in practice they often mean no concern for history at all. As I hope to demonstrate, both theory and practice contributed to development's ahistorical proclivities.

One response to the prevalence of development ahistoricism is the recounting of development history. This book takes up that task. There is of course no way that one book can summarize the whole of development's past. Many of the programs and policies considered in these pages come from American donor agencies, reflecting both my own expertise and the outsized role played by the United States in postwar development. Yet the United States was far from the only country shaping the development agenda, and *Their Future* shows that, even if Washington exercised tremendous sway, it had many partners, both North and South, in determining aid policy and practice. Indeed, development is best viewed as a global mission, shaped by unequal and shifting power dynamics, over who gets to arbitrate the future of millions of people worldwide. These questions of power, destiny, and agency stand at the heart of the international development enterprise and, accordingly, of this book.

2

The First Third Worlds: Modeling Ahistoricism

"MODELS ARE A FORM OF SELECTIVE forgetting," writes Nick Cullather in his history of the Green Revolution.

> When an analyst refers to the Taiwan model of expert-led development or the Chilean model of monetary reform, history is displaced by a capsule narrative, part fact, part fiction, designed to convey a formula for development. Context and motives are stripped away, leaving an image of outside experts isolating problems and then introducing sharply focused solutions.[1]

In a 1967 article, the British economist Paul Streeten parsed the ways that modeling accomplishes this simplifying work.[2] First, it isolates one or more causal parameters seen as sufficient to explain development (class in the case of Marxism, markets in classical economics); then it assumes away other factors as so much contextual noise, insignificant to the growth process. From there, model-builders engage in "misplaced aggregation," lumping and homogenizing complex phenomena for ease of conceptual manipulation. 'Employment,' 'capital,' and 'income' are umbrella concepts that cloak enormous internal variety. Models, Streeten acknowledged, helped to professionalize development economics, giving it scientific credentials based on the ability to present "economic facts" in quantitative form. But they also embedded false simplifications in aid theory and policy, with the messiness of social reality buried under an efficient, streamlined veneer. Streeten described the problem as a kind of forgetting: small contingencies—a local economic pattern, a unique cultural norm—often have large historical and developmental effects. By ignoring them, models miss crucial details.

The twentieth century was a century of modeling, and the prominence of development in the postwar decades was part of the broader enthronement of economics as the preeminent language of public policy. If nineteenth-century political economy treated politics and economics as conjoined, the twentieth saw the emergence of 'the economy' as an analytically distinct field—"the totality of the relations of production, distribution and consumption of goods and services within a given country or region," to use Timothy Mitchell's definition. Separate and superior, economics was esteemed over other social sciences: more precise in its findings, more neutral in its analyses.[3] Indeed, by the late twentieth-century, it became common to subordinate politics to the supposedly fixed laws of the market, as if economics were simply a hard representation of reality, a 'bottom line' beyond political or ethical dispute.

The "superiority of economics," as one historian remarked, was fortified by new quantitative measures that governments could use to analyze populations under their control.[4] While the economic discipline had embraced greater mathematization starting in the late nineteenth century, the more recent revolution came in the 1930s, when the Great Depression lent the work of economics an extreme urgency. John Maynard Keynes's monumental 1936 volume *The General Theory of Employment, Interest, and Money* capped an era in which management of the economy became the sine qua non of good governance. Keynes's work not only sanctioned government intervention to correct market disequilibria; it also promoted a wave of econometric innovation. New tools such as national income accounting, measures of gross national product, and longitudinal studies of income and inequality lent increased credibility to the arts of planning and prediction.[5] In development economics, a model pioneered by the British Roy Harrod and the Russian Evsey Domar, both Keynesians, was particularly influential in yoking growth to capital accumulation and a high savings rate (usually over 10 percent).[6] The wider development profession took note. "Developmental planning," wrote the University of Chicago economist Bert Hoselitz in 1952, requires "a procedure of analyzing social and cultural change and transforming its variables, wherever possible, into magnitudes that are quantifiable and hence measurable in economic terms." This would allow the study of development to "break the bounds of traditional economics and spill over into the realm of general sociological analysis."[7]

If new quantitative standards burnished the image of neutral expertise, they also suppressed historical and economic variety, especially in developing economies.[8] "As soon as attempts were made to apply [National Income Accounting] to countries in Central Africa in the late 1940s and early 1950s," explain two economists, "it became clear how difficult it would be to transpose a framework based on the experience of Western economies to economies whose social and cultural norms were very different from those of the West."[9] The exclusion of unpaid labor, for example, ignored not only work undertaken largely by women, but also the informal sector and subsistence farming, which occupied most of the population in poor countries.[10] Yet one cannot say that development statisticians ignored the past. On the contrary, they sought to elaborate techniques for inter-temporal and longitudinal comparison that would make sense of, as the British economist Colin Clark put it in the title of his influential 1940 study, the "conditions of economic progress."[11] Clark's income accounting tools, honed during sixteen years in Australia, eventually landed him a post at Oxford and a place among the pioneers of development economics. His authoritative volume is filled—as are those of statisticians such as Simon Kuznets, Richard Stone, and others—with time series charts that track economic magnitudes over decades, country by country, sector by sector, providing a detailed topography of midcentury global economies. The picture that emerged was one of great variety and great inequality—with vast regions unaccounted due to paucity of data.

The accounts of Clark and colleagues provided a quantitative map of national and sectoral economies that facilitated policymaking. To support the practicalities of aid programming, however, planners required still further distillation: Numbers had to be presented in sectoral rankings and aggregate country profiles, snapshots that necessarily simplified, and at times distorted, the economies they were meant to encapsulate. To take one example: The British economic historian Phyllis Deane, working out of the Rhodes-Livingstone Institute in Lusaka, acknowledged problems in translating national accounting categories, devised for industrial economies, to the largely rural African societies of northern Rhodesia and Nyasaland. For one thing, the standard division of income into "rents, profits, interest, wages and salaries, a division which has positive significance for an industrial economy, introduces concepts which are largely inappropriate to one consisting largely of peasant producers."[12] A further difficulty was attaching numerical values to the range of activities found in the rural sector. Deane's estimates were restricted to "cash incomes" and ignored the "barter trade and the output which never enters into trade at all but is produced by the villagers for the use of themselves and their families."[13] This was a substantial oversight, and Deane acknowledged that her findings provided little more than "a pointer" toward economic trajectories.[14] Furthermore, despite the spate of longitudinal studies, statistics reinforced atemporal models of development, depicting a "frozen history" in which time is "decomposed" or slowed down into a sequence of snapshots—or a row of 'stationary states,' to coopt an economic term.[15] Unlike historical time, each point in a series is fixed and excerptable. In this regard, the statisticalization of development contributed to ahistoricism and decontextualization.

Streeten's observations are apt for analyzing the impact of two pioneering economic development programs for the industrialization of agrarian regions: the Polish economist Paul Rosenstein-Rodan's big push model, which emerged from his studies of interwar East European economies; and the two-sector model of St. Lucian economist W. Arthur Lewis, whose 1954 essay "Industrialization with Unlimited Supplies of Labour" remains a talisman of development economics. Their approaches were different: If Rosenstein-Rodan engaged in explicit model-building, proposing his East European plan as a template for application across the developing world, Lewis devised a strategy for industrialization applicable in *some* developing countries—notably his Caribbean home—only to see it elevated into a universal schema. In the decades after the publication of his legacy-making essay, Lewis found himself both endorsing and battling his model.

Paul Rosenstein-Rodan and the East European Model of Development

Many terms have been used to designate the economically impoverished regions of the globe: backward lands and poor lands; undeveloped, underdeveloped, and developing societies; modernizing countries, Third World states, and, recently, the Global South or Majority World. These are not synonymous, and each has its own semantic history. But in popular usage, what unites them is the reference to an immense region—the vast swath of humanity—that faces conditions of widespread material poverty. Since World War II, development has been presented as an antidote to this condition.

The notion of 'development' as a managed process of social and economic advancement dates back well before the midcentury, though World War II pressed it into wide circulation. Prior to that, perhaps the most renowned use of the term was Sun Yat-Sen's 1920 book *The International Development of China,* which urged Western support for an international organization to foster Chinese growth.[16] The German-Australian economist H. W. Arndt traced the concept's prehistory—if not the term itself—back further still, to nationalism, colonialism, and Marxism in the nineteenth century.[17] His foraging for conceptual roots anticipated a subsequent literature, notably the works of economist Michael Cowen and historian Robert Shenton, who found the basic development framework in post-Enlightenment social theory, with its belief in the ability of rational administrators to manage and supervise human progress.[18]

The term *Third World,* by contrast, was a postwar coinage, minted in 1952 by the French demographer Alfred Sauvy to denominate the decolonizing non-Western peoples, the "ensemble of those that one calls, in the style of the United Nations, the under-developed countries."[19] Evoking France's prerevolutionary Third Estate, *le tiers monde* had both a political and an economic significance: it named those regions for which Cold War development aid might help secure political and ideological allegiance.[20] When postcolonial leaders such as Nehru, Nasser, or Sukarno spearheaded Third World solidarity by refusing alignment with either Cold War bloc, support for shared development was a central plank of their agenda.[21] In this regard, the Third World's economic needs as "underdeveloped countries" permeated even its political sense: it comprised the impoverished lands of Asia, Africa, and Latin America, many of them just emerging from colonial rule, all in need of growth and development.

Whatever their origins, these terms did not, for most of the development era, include Eastern Europe.[22] This may seem obvious, but for wartime economists it would have been surprising. Eastern Europe—or what was then often called Southeastern Europe, despite the inclusion of Poland—was central to development's earliest wartime iterations.[23] It was the cynosure of the first generation of development economists writing in the mid-1940s, the regional backdrop for their economic ruminations. And the earliest global development doctrine—the call to use surplus rural labor to fuel industrialization—originated in wartime proposals aimed at Europe's eastern tier.[24]

To be sure, the East European experience was not the only source of economic development doctrine. Matthew Connelly has mapped the widespread population concerns of the midcentury West, some of them feeding into eugenic research. It was not incidental, he shows, that the Third World moniker came from the pen of a demographer.[25] Joseph Morgan Hodge has demonstrated the shift among British colonial officers from worry about underpopulation in their African colonies to fear of overpopulation, with its consequent threat of health and environmental degradation.[26] And we will see the role that Caribbean experiments played in shaping ideas about industrial growth. But the East European program was a direct forebear of the earliest aid and industrialization templates exported to the decolonizing world—and though the geography of development shifted, the blueprint did not. Arndt is correct that postwar development ideas carried forward the "Europocentrism" of wartime economists.[27]

Geopolitics and genealogy assured the centrality of Eastern Europe in the plans of early development economists. After years of bloodletting, postwar aid efforts focused on the European recovery, and the status of Central and Eastern Europe—Poland and Germany in particular—was especially fraught, since the Allies blamed its autocratic politics and weak economies for destabilizing the continent. Many of the inaugural figures of development economics—Paul Rosenstein-Rodan, Kurt Mandelbaum, Ragnar Nurkse, Alexander Gerschenkron, Hans Singer, Albert O. Hirschman, and others—were born and raised in the region. For these pioneers, the predicament of their homelands exerted an obvious pull that left its imprint on the subdiscipline they founded. From their wartime exile in London and elsewhere, they proposed large-scale public interventions designed to overcome an agrarian backwardness that they saw as the seed of wartime vulnerability. Not only were these economists personally attentive to the needs of the region; they also exported its intellectual perspectives and debates.[28] The discourse of rural overpopulation, which preoccupied early development planners, had decades-old Central and East European roots, part of the wider Malthusian fears percolating in Europe and beyond.[29] Elite debates over whether and how to modernize poor agricultural societies took place against the backdrop of active peasant and agrarian movements that roiled East European politics in the pre- and interwar years.[30] Yet these debates have been largely forgotten. "With the end of the Second World War, and the installation of communist regimes in all the countries of eastern Europe in which the peasant parties had been important, they ceased open political activity and their ideas found no public expression," wrote development scholar Gavin Kitching. "In the west, despite or perhaps because of the cold war, little was known about them, and what had been known was forgotten by all but a handful of scholars."[31]

Economists in fin-de-siècle Austria-Hungary worried that rural overcrowding constituted not only a misuse of human resources but also a root cause of economic backwardness in areas such Galicia and Bukovina. A leading proponent of this view was the oil magnate and Polish patriot Stanisław Szczepanowski, whose widely remarked 1888 treatise *The Poverty of Galicia in Figures and a Program for the Energetic Development of the Economy of the Country* made the case that only industrialization, not revolution (a popular cause among Polish nationalists after the partitions), would reduce agrarian poverty.[32]

The concern for rural development intensified in the monarchy's successor states, especially during the depression decade of the 1930s.[33] In Poland, the early years of economic distress brought plummeting agriculture prices and increased farm indebtedness, aggravating existing problems of population density and land fragmentation. Participating in a discourse on peasant farming that led back to nineteenth-century Russian populism, Polish economists renewed fin-de-siècle debates about modernizing agriculture, publishing works on agrarian penury that contained striking anticipations of later wartime proposals for boosting 'backward' areas.[34] From his post at the journal *Gospodarka Narodowa* (National Economy), Józef Poniatowski led a group of economists who advocated industrialization as the best solution for Poland's slump. "Poland must go very fast towards industrialization, because there is no other way," he advised in 1931. "Poland today, industrio-agricultural [*przemysłowo-rolnicza*], must be, and will be in the near future, agriculturo-industrial [*rolniczo-przemysłowa*], and one cannot exclude the possibility that it will become an industrial country."[35] These themes appeared in his 1936 book *Overpopulation in the Village and Agriculture,* which argued that land overcrowding led to entrenched un- and underemployment. Yet industry offered a solution: "[D]emographic conditions allow one to count on cheap work as a permanent and powerful factor in Poland's economic development until the entire excess of the population"—a number he estimated at 8–9 million—"is absorbed."[36]

Similarly, Wincenty Styś, in three books written between 1931 and 1939, decried southern Poland's peasant surfeit and land fragmentation. A historian and economist, Styś charted the diminution of Galician farm sizes from the late eighteenth century through the early Depression, blaming demographic growth for the economic deterioration. The result was the proliferation of sub-subsistence or 'dwarf' farms, incapable of supporting a family. Like Poniatowski, he saw industrialization as the only cure for agrarian backwardness, a view he articulated fervently in his 1936 book *The Impact of Industrialization on the Agrarian System*.[37]

The socialist and economic statistician Ludwik Landau was also influential. Drawing on his own formalized accounting of interwar Polish income inequality, Landau's 1938 *World Economy* projected his country's dual economy—"islands of urban centres with modern factories surrounded by a sea of small towns and villages"—onto a "world scale," presenting it as a microcosm of global capitalism, "a miniature of the world."[38] In the context of economic depression (and on the eve of a Nazi conquest that cost the Jewish Landau his life), he charted a planned, socialist industrialization as the path out of economic disorder. Other economists took note: While Landau was little known in the West, Rosenstein-Rodan admired his work, and at a 1947 talk in Warsaw, he channeled his late colleague by asserting that "capitalism did not level out the gap between the rich and the poor countries." Poor countries "should industrialise" to make up for this imbalance.[39]

As these examples suggest, Polish interwar debates were not merely academic, nor did they remain exclusively Polish. Poniatowski advocated for his views at high official levels after his 1936 appointment to Poland's Council of Ministers. Styś traveled widely in the early 1930s, working out his proposals while studying on a Rockefeller Fellowship in Vienna, London, Cambridge, and Paris. His British advocate, the development economist Doreen Warriner, amplified the ideas of East European economists in her own volumes on the peasantry; she described southern Poland as "one of Europe's blackest spots in respect to over-population" and saw the "only remedy" as industrialization, a prospect ideally managed by a "Tennessee Valley Authority for the Danube Basin."[40] Polish economist Michał Kalecki, who later worked at the

International Labour Organization (ILO) and the UN, also adapted Landau's national income accounting as a tool for assessing poverty and inequity during his wartime stint at the Oxford Institute of Statistics.[41] In the late 1950s, after his return to Poland, he advised Nehru's India, basing his recommendations for the peasant subcontinent in part on a mental map of the interwar Polish economy.[42]

This was not the first time Eastern Europe supplied the West with an image of backwardness. The historian Larry Wolff has shown how eighteenth-century travelers, writers, and cartographers "invented" a Europe of two halves, the Enlightened West and the half-orientalized East, "provid[ing] Western Europe with an early model of underdevelopment."[43] Immanuel Wallerstein, renowned for his world systems theory, placed the continental division further back, in the fifteenth and sixteenth centuries, when societies on the previously remote Atlantic littorals fledged a new economy based on manufacturing and overseas trade, while the eastern half sank into a "second serfdom," with rural lands and bonded laborers supplying raw materials to the flourishing West. According to Wallerstein, this division formed a new continental economic system that anticipated the modern global economy of core and periphery, First World and Third.[44] In the late nineteenth century, the Balkans became a byword for political and social instability among Western statesmen, who fretted over the "Eastern Question:" what to do with the impoverished lands breaking free from the crumbling Ottoman Porte. While the modern denotation of 'development' had multiple origins, twentieth-century 'modernization' grew directly out of this episode: after World War I, the term was used to define Mustafa Kemal's political, social, and economic ambitions for raising Turkey from the ashes of Ottoman defeat.[45]

It was, however, the interwar disputes that bore most directly on development pioneers such as the Cracow-born Rosenstein-Rodan, the Estonian Ragnar Nurkse, and the German Kurt Mandelbaum. Born between 1899 and 1907, all of them did their training partly in Central Europe, where they confronted debates over agrarian poverty that they would reproduce in proposals for postwar development. In London as in Warsaw, diagnoses of Eastern Europe's economic ills stressed the overreliance on agricultural employment, rural crowding, un- or underemployed labor (often called 'disguised unemployment'), and limited markets and resources. Rural overpopulation, they feared, contributed not only to national economic stasis but to political instability and authoritarianism as well. In a 1943 book, the Odessa-born, Austrian-trained Alexander Gerschenkron warned that impoverished rural masses could be exploited by populist demagogues. Politics and economics, in other words, were tightly braided.[46]

Central European émigrés made wartime Britain a hub of economic development research. The most influential proponent of early development economics, and the quintessential example of a leap from Eastern Europe to the non-Western world, was Rosenstein-Rodan.[47] Having emigrated to Britain in 1930, the University of Vienna–trained economist became the leader of an economics working group at London's Royal Institute of International Affairs that helped to define postwar development doctrine. Founded in 1920 to promote the policy-oriented study of international affairs, the Royal Institute (known as Chatham House, after the building it occupied) opposed the punitive reparations associated with the Versailles Treaty, adopting a line similar to that of Keynes, who argued that the treaty would destabilize Europe. In the 1930s, under the directorship of historian Arnold Toynbee, Chatham House went further still, contending that Hitler's aggression was a reaction to his country's earlier mistreatment and advocating policies resembling Chamberlain's later appeasement. It took *Kristallnacht* in 1938 to make this position untenable.[48] Of more direct relevance to postwar development, in 1931 the Royal Institute became the home of the British Africa Survey that ran throughout the decade. Members Joseph Oldham and Frederick Lugard spearheaded the Survey through the Institute's "Africa Group," founded in 1924.[49] Lugard, in particular, brought with him years of colonial service as a mercenary and later governor-general of Nigeria, where he famously defined the dual human and resource development mandate associated with British overseas rule. He was, in other words, a consummate imperialist.

When World War II began, Chatham House took up a new research agenda focused on postwar reconstruction. As one facet of this effort, it recruited British and exile scholars to form an economics team linked to multiple scholarly institutions. Then a relative unknown teaching at London's University College, Rosenstein-Rodan joined in 1941 to lead the Economic Group, whose task it was to map out a postwar European economic order. Soon, his team set the pace for other centers.[50] It was here that Rosenstein-Rodan wrote his seminal 1943 essay "Problems of Industrialisation in Eastern and South-Eastern Europe," frequently cited as the founding text of modern development economics.

From its opening sentence, "Problems of Industrialisation" presented Eastern Europe as a proxy for other developing regions. "It is generally agreed," Rosenstein-Rodan wrote, "that industrialisation of 'international depressed areas' like Eastern and South-Eastern Europe (or the Far East) is in the general interest not only of those countries, but of the world as a whole."[51] A representative agrarian space, Eastern Europe provided an ideal canvas for drawing up a working model of this program. The region's advantage, in Rosenstein-Rodan's eyes, was that it was prototypical: it revealed in sharp focus the problems of rural overpopulation and disguised unemployment found in many impoverished lands. Even its differences enhanced its value as a case study: Eastern Europe had the basic infrastructure needed to foster growth—railroads, power stations, and the like. This positioned it far ahead of places such as "China and parts of Latin America," where investors would have to build core infrastructure before they could mount an economic push.[52] The demographic glut was also more "intensive" in Eastern Europe than in the Middle East, the Far East, or Latin America, all of which still had sufficient land to expand farming. Sooner or later, however, these societies would run out. Thus, far from setting the region apart, Eastern Europe's distinctions meant that it provided an extraordinary test case for a more general solution—a regional growth and development program that could be applied elsewhere. It was, in other words, the most advanced case of the general plight of 'backwardness'—the region most likely to graduate from the Third World *avant la lettre* and thus to light the way for others.

Rosenstein-Rodan laid out two possible paths for Eastern Europe's industrial advance: The first—an autarkic model—eschewed the international division of labor and emphasized growth through self-reliance; the resulting process would be slow, arduous, wasteful. Many Central European states had erected trade barriers between the wars, and their political and economic failings were often recalled as lessons in bad policy. Rosenstein-Rodan, however, cited the most recent example of rapid industrialization—Stalin's Soviet Union—as the premier instance of inefficient autarkic growth. His dismissal of the Stalinist model was not as uncontroversial as it might appear today, given the international—including Western—appreciation for Soviet industralization, the "romance," to use Russian expert George Kennan's term, of planned economic development, with its immense potential for human improvement.[53] But there was concern that leaders might once again opt for an autarkic national capitalism that had destabilized Europe in the recent past.[54]

Rosenstein-Rodan's preferred model relied on external assistance and government planning to launch an accelerated growth trajectory that would fit Eastern Europe into the global economy. Building on the American economist Allyn Young's work on the increasing returns that accrued to simultaneous investments across sectors, Rosenstein-Rodan advocated what came to be known as the "big push": a raft of investments, public and private, designed to launch a region-wide industrial boom.[55] Market forces alone would not suffice: Like industrial economies in recession, 'backward' economies were trapped in a permanently suboptimal (or bad) equilibrium in which slack demand for local products impeded industrial advance and left many people un- or underemployed. Nothing innate to the play of supply and demand would correct this inefficiency as long as societies lacked the capital needed for growth.

Instead, Rosenstein-Rodan adopted the prevalent Keynesian view that economic planning could guide the growth process—along with the concomitant fear (eloquently traced by Karl Polanyi) that unregulated markets would sabotage it.[56] Keynes's influence was felt less in specific doctrines than in the insistence that economic policies had to be tailored to particular circumstances, an insight that allowed economists to accept that market laws operated differently—and less efficiently—in conditions of underdevelopment. In regions where local capital could not be mustered, international resources had to step in. Yet like Keynes himself, Rosenstein-Rodan remained committed to core premises of classical economics. In particular, he considered it crucial to observe the principles of open trade and comparative advantage by integrating Eastern Europe into an appropriate market niche, a liberal view that recommended his program to Western policymakers. "The aim of industrialization in internationally depressed areas," he assured, was not to destabilize the fragile postwar system, but "to produce a structural equilibrium in the world economy by creating productive employment for the agrarian excess population."[57] Like his fellow émigrés, he thought this best done by cultivating East European light industries—"processed foods and light industrial articles"—rather than the primary products ("cereals") that had been a regional staple or the heavy industry favored by Stalin.[58] Advanced industries in the West, after all, could already supply all "the needs of the internationally depressed areas."[59]

The need to boost a vast, multistate, multilingual zone demanded a new funding approach. While nineteenth-century industrialization relied on market forces, "[e]xperience from the past is partly irrelevant," Rosenstein-Rodan insisted, "where the whole economic structure of a region is to be changed."[60] The coordinated application of preexisting techniques across many sectors and societies outstripped the capacity of prewar institutions, even as capital costs and political risks had risen, discouraging all but the most reckless entrepreneurs from gambling on a war-ravaged economy. And "even Eastern Europeans," he opined, "are not as tough to-day as they used to be"—a seemingly glib remark that hid a real concern: Industrialization would produce considerable hardship before a healthy modern economy took root.[61] Without measures to alleviate suffering—a security that investors would not provide—development might be derailed by political upheaval.

Indeed, nineteenth-century laissez-faire was inadequate due to a crucial market failure: the divergence between private and social utility. There was no incentive, to invoke Arthur Pigou's classic formulation, for an investor to train workers just to see them take their skills elsewhere, even though the societal benefits of a skilled workforce were innumerable. A business gained more by poaching workers from other firms, at the expense of the overall economy. This gulf between private and social interests meant that governments had to take on valuable economic functions—from workforce development to highway construction—that no individual or firm would find profitable. Regional development fell under this category: Without industrialization across many sectors at once, no single industry could thrive, since factories depend for profitability on a large market of buyers, available industrial products, and skilled labor. But since no entrepreneur could remunerate enough workers or invest in the range of industries needed to establish a vibrant economy, businessmen lacked the incentive to start the development process; better to wait—alas, indefinitely—for a willing fool to do so and then free-ride on his investment. The result was stasis. Only a public consortium with international financial backing could fuel the big push needed to cultivate cross-sectoral industry. What the region wanted, then, was an institutional framework for planning, financing, and oversight—an Eastern European

Industrial Trust or "planning board"—comprising both local and foreign representatives. Creditor governments could "guarantee [private] loans" or "lend the funds themselves," thus launching the aid-driven development of Eastern Europe.[62]

Rosenstein-Rodan renewed his call for aid-assisted industrialization a year later, now in a more monitory tone. Despite gradual gains in absolute living standards, he warned, inequality among states was rising.

> It is no wonder that many nations, many peoples, have become impatient. . . . [T]he degree of inequality of distribution of income as between different nations is considerably greater today than it was a hundred years or even a hundred and fifty years ago. That is not only a moral, but even more a political and economic problem, because we can assume that people will always prefer to die fighting rather than to see no prospect of a better life. . . . The development of economically backward areas of the world is, therefore, the most important task facing us in the making of the peace.[63]

He identified five such areas: the Far East, the colonial areas (notably Africa), the Caribbean, the Middle East, and Eastern Europe. Once again, Eastern Europe was the vanguard, the only one in which the solution "can be envisaged within the lifetime of one generation." It was therefore the "most fruitful and interesting field of action."[64] The region had important distinctions: It did not suffer from the Far East's population excess. And its infrastructure and industrial base stood far ahead of Africa or the Caribbean. Nor did its growth depend primarily on mineral extraction and land irrigation, as in the Middle East.[65] Nonetheless, Eastern Europe shared a number of traits with these less fortunate regions. All were primarily agrarian and faced a rural population excess that led to wasted labor and unemployment. All lacked the industry needed to accommodate additional workers. And none had adequate training facilities, not to mention the technology required for modern growth. These conditions necessitated "State" and even "international action." Southeastern Europe's cultural and linguistic variety was at once a challenge and a virtue. The region's successful development would signal that the Tennessee Valley Authority (TVA) model, first employed in the relatively homogeneous American South, might also apply in the globe's more patchwork geographies. Furthermore, Eastern Europe's "standard of living is higher than in other international depressed areas," and international effort "is therefore very much easier and could achieve the result required within twenty or twenty-five years." The region, in other words, "provides a model presenting all the problems which are relevant to the reconstruction and development of backward areas," along with the promise of timely success. It could thus demonstrate the wider possibilities of aid-assisted modernization, unburdened by particular regional histories.[66]

Others were more circumspect. Economic development, warned the Czech economist Antonín Basch in 1943, was an enormous challenge in an area as complex as Eastern Europe. "Leaving aside all political, racial, cultural, and historical differences—which are by no means unimportant—the plain fact remains that this part of Europe is far from being homogeneous either socially or economically," with economies ranging from industrial Bohemia to the agricultural Balkans.[67] And yet it was this type of region—what Basch called the "Danubian countries"—that was most in need of growth. Basch, who served in various public and private capacities in interwar Czechoslovakia before fleeing his country for posts in U.S. academia and the World Bank, took it for granted that industrialization and international aid offered the only cures for agricultural "overpopulation"—the only means for full employment and political stability in the poor countries. "With no large-scale emigration possibilities in sight, such as existed in the decades before 1914, the only alternative is *industrialization.*"[68]

The 1945 report *Economic Development in S. E. Europe,* drafted by the think tank Political and Economic Planning (PEP) using Chatham House data, reached similar conclusions. Rural overpopulation, its authors agreed, was both a symptom of backwardness and a resource for industrialization.[69] They did, however, add a political twist, arguing that economic development could induce East Europeans to subordinate conflict to partnership, fostering a habit of cooperation among peoples with a history of strife. The same benefit might accrue to other "undeveloped" multiethnic zones. Again, the problems that contemporary Eastern Europe faced either existed or impended elsewhere, and an economic uplift program honed in that region—with the aid of foreign investment and government planning—could prepare the way for the non-Western world.

From his wartime base at the Oxford Institute of Statistics, the former Frankfurt School economist Kurt Mandelbaum also modeled a global development plan on East European data.[70] His background differed from that of his East European counterparts. After economic studies in Munich and Berlin, Mandelbaum (who would later change his name to Kurt Martin) joined the young Institute for Social Research.[71] There, under the guidance of economist and sociologist Friedrich Pollock, he developed an interest in agrarianism, industrialization, planning, and Russian populism (which, as we saw, influenced interwar Polish economists). In *The Industrialisation of Backward Areas* (1945), Mandelbaum, like Rosenstein-Rodan, proposed to harness Eastern Europe's surplus farm labor for industrial growth through "the progressive transfer of working population from agriculture to light industry and services."[72] He estimated that 6–8 million workers in a rural labor force of almost 30 million could leave the land without reducing productivity, and he called for external financing to facilitate the shift. Like other regional templates, Mandelbaum's Eastern Europe had significant advantages as a test case. It offered accessible statistics; it was more advanced than other, non-European areas; and an industrialization program designed to re-direct "disguised rural unemployment" could make an immediate impact. Yet ultimately these differences were matters of degree, not of kind. All of the globe's impoverished regions were

> vast and densely crowded areas . . . where almost the whole active population has remained in agriculture, although the land offers productive and remunerative work only to part of this labour force. Industrial progress has bypassed these territories which between them contain over half the world's population. Large numbers in these areas eke out a precarious existence on submarginal land; others work better land with out-of-date tools, but even where yields per acre are not unduly low, yields per head invariably are, because too many people share in this output.[73]

Because of these similarities, successful East European industrialization could demonstrate the global validity of a development template, with "South-eastern Europe" standing in for vaster and poorer regions as a prototypical "backward society."[74]

Similarly, the Estonian-born, Vienna-trained Ragnar Nurkse, who made his interwar home at the League of Nations, argued that regional development had both local and global benefits.[75] During the economic collapse of the 1930s and the war that followed, Nurkse's primary concern was international monetary stabilization. His wartime essays examined the role of savings and currency reserves in offsetting foreign profit losses during an economic crisis.[76] Yet as Patricia Clavin notes, impoverishment was central to his agenda because of the economic disruption caused when "individual states, often without warning, abandoned the agreed rules."[77] Faced with such threats, Nurkse reiterated Rosenstein-Rodan's concern about the dangers of regional destitution, and he worried about a peripheral "Central and South-Eastern Europe" that supplied "foodstuffs and raw materials" to a booming Germany.[78] Unless the needs of these regions were met, they would deplete their currency reserves, increasing both domestic and systemic instability. "It is the unequal distribution of wealth and the unequal economic requirements of different nations," he fretted, "that largely account for the maldistribution of international currency reserves in the past."[79]

Like his confreres, Nurkse directed his postwar concern initially toward the "war-ravaged" economies and "agricultural countries" of his home region, extending it only later to the decolonizing lands.[80] But when he did so, it was with explicit East European references. "The problem of rural overpopulation," Nurkse stated in his influential 1953 treatise *Problems of Capital Formation in Underdeveloped Countries,* "is a characteristic feature of the densely populated peasant economies that stretch all the way from south-eastern Europe to south-eastern Asia. Chronic and large-scale underemployment is what countries of this type have in common."[81] The solution to this malady lay in Nurkse's famous proposal for balanced growth—synchronized investment and expansion across many industries at once, designed to create complementary markets for resources, labor, training, and buyers, thereby jump-starting industrial expansion. In poor peasant societies, "[a]n increase in the production of shoes alone does not create its own demand," explained Nurkse, since investors will have to search abroad for raw materials and consumer markets, raising the price of doing business to prohibitive levels. On the other hand, "an increase in production over a wide range of consumables, so proportioned as to correspond to the pattern of consumers' preferences, does create its own demand."[82] Balanced growth would fire Rosenstein-Rodan's big push.

Several years later, in 1958, another Central European émigré, Albert Hirschman, scion of an affluent Jewish family in Berlin, launched one of the first great disputes in development economics by challenging Nurkse's balanced growth postulate, arguing in favor of "unbalanced growth" that took advantage of leading industries to blaze a path for the rest of the economy. These pioneering firms created what Hirschman termed "forward- and backward-linkages" that spurred development in related sectors. A burgeoning shipbuilding industry, for example, could prompt local steel-making (a backward linkage) or naval investment (a forward linkage).[83] But what Nurkse and Hirschman agreed upon was also important, namely, the fundamental equation of development with industrialization.

Wartime economists planned intensely for the recuperation of their homelands. But their plans were not to be. By the time Alfred Sauvy minted the term *Third World* in the 1950s, Eastern Europe was lodged solidly in the Second, subject to Stalin's own modernization program and off limits to Western developers. Nonetheless, the region shadowed industrialization templates across the globe. As the Polish-born economist Ignacy Sachs remarked in 1971:

> We can fix the beginnings of the economics of underdevelopment, at least in the Anglo-Saxon world, at the time of the Second World War, and in the studies, in England, of Rosenstein Rodan, K. Mandelbaum, and a handful of others who were interested mainly in South-eastern Europe, and not the Third World proper. In their work, they took advantage of the discussions of the economists from Eastern Europe following the Great Crisis.[84]

Many of these figures, Sachs observed, later "established themselves in the West" to such an extent that their ideas informed standard "economic thinking about underdevelopment." Thus, Central and Eastern Europe owed its economic afterlife not only to its role as the first Third World, but also to the growing demand for regional émigrés in the multilateral institutions and decolonizing states of the postwar era. Mandelbaum's advice was tapped by state leaders in Asia and Africa, who saw his East European industrialization program as a way to strengthen their own economies.[85] After his 1940 move to the United States, Nurkse secured professorships at Columbia, Princeton, and Oxford, where he continued his work on international development, often in concert with compatriot economists.

Rosenstein-Rodan joined the World Bank in 1947, becoming assistant director of the Economics Department and head of the Economic Advisory Staff, whence he managed programs in India and Chile that distilled insights honed in Europe.[86] At the Bank, he joined a group of global experts who, as

Amy Staples put it, saw themselves as an apolitical technocracy and whose "international economic worldview" sometimes put them at odds with local and national authorities.[87] In 1953, he entered MIT's Center for International Studies (CIS), one of the cradles of modernization theory, which came to dominate U.S. aid policy from the late 1950s (see Chapter 4). In his second life as a member of an interdisciplinary modernization team, he penned the 1961 article "International Aid for Underdeveloped Countries," which laid out appropriate country aid levels based on their "absorptive capacity" (the amount of external aid that a country can put to fruitful use) and their "capacity to repay" loans—calculations that remain central to aid financing today.[88] Yet his most lasting contribution remains his earliest. In the generalized transfer of a regional model—twice abstracted: once into a composite regional model, and then onto other continents—to a global aid program, he inaugurated a practice that still shapes aid planning: the displacement of development templates from one region to another with only modest accounting for local history and circumstance.

By constructing their economic program for a target region, wartime and postwar economists gained a geographic anchor for their imaginations, a source to supply data and frame problems, strategies, and solutions. By then delinking it from its original geography, they turned their models into movable templates, widely applicable across the developing world. Thus, regional models had a paradoxical effect: their specificity lent scientific credence to an otherwise abstract economic program that could, in turn, be replicated elsewhere. Even as original geographic references fell away, the mobility of the template depended on the clarity won through regional grounding.

"Not by chance," concluded historian Michele Alacevich, "the late 1940s and the 1950s witnessed a proliferation of 'laboratories' for development policies," specific regions whose experience could be "generalized and replicated" around the world. Eastern Europe, Colombia, Italy, India, Indonesia, post–World War II Japan—each served in this capacity during the postwar era.[89] Decades later, one could add the East Asian Tigers and other exemplars. Overshadowing all these references was the steady allure of Western—European and American—industrialization. And it was not only that donor agencies peddled development templates; poor countries sought them. Many impoverished societies, wrote historian Corinna Unger, "looked for ideas and models of development tried out elsewhere, hoping that this would help them save time and resources and allow their countries to benefit from the practical experience of others."[90] Though Eastern Europe bore scant resemblance to Asia and Africa, its superficial similarity to agrarian societies everywhere made wartime models appealing.

The first migration of the East European development model was not beyond Europe but 1,000 miles south, to the impoverished Italian Mezzogiorno. Aid experiments in Italy under Marshall Plan and World Bank auspices reinforced the view that East European models were applicable to other agricultural zones. Indeed, Rosenstein-Rodan was involved in southern Italy, first as a World Bank functionary and then through the CIS.[91] While working in the region, he crafted a method for calculating disguised unemployment, a formula, he insisted, that could be widely applied.[92] "In this formational period," writes Alacevich, "the development plan for the Italian Mezzogiorno had a fundamental role, not because it succeeded—in fact, especially from the mid-1960s, the Italian South became an exemplary case of underdevelopment—but because in the early post-war period and for a decade or so it was considered one of the few observable laboratories of development policies."[93] As elsewhere, the power of a dehistoricized economic model rested on a concrete experimentation site, where effective 'proof of concept' gave it sanction to travel.

W. Arthur Lewis and the Caribbean Model

As the 1979 Nobel Award committee affirmed, the essay "Economic Development with Unlimited Supplies of Labour" secured St. Lucian economist W. Arthur Lewis's legacy—and it did so almost immediately upon publication. The 1954 article crystallized the basic mechanism behind Rosenstein-Rodan's industrialization program—the strategy of moving surplus labor from agriculture to the "capitalist sector" to foster industrial growth.[94] Despite its resounding impact, however, "Unlimited Supplies" is a misleading guide to the range of Lewis's thought. Indeed, its renown obscured the more qualified development judgments he expressed elsewhere, leading to a simplified version of the Lewis model that has enjoyed wide influence. Lewis himself was more circumspect, with an awareness of local economic variations and of the importance of agricultural improvement that belied his famous model.

"Unlimited Supplies" analyzed a topic that preoccupied agrarian economists: developing societies with rural overpopulation. As we have seen, Rosenstein-Rodan, whom Lewis knew at the London School of Economics (LSE), based his big push on the availability of potentially boundless labor pools that could be marshaled for industrial gain—a presumption that circulated widely among postwar economists. But if Rosenstein-Rodan took this feature of East European economies as representative of the general condition of 'backwardness,' Lewis acknowledged that it did not appertain everywhere. Western Europe did not suffer agrarian overcrowding during stretches of its industrialization, and parts of Africa and Latin America had "an acute shortage of male labour."[95] These caveats were significant, but they are often ignored by interpreters.

Lewis's pathbreaking essay advanced one primary argument: that the dualism characteristic of many developing economies—a capitalist (or modern) sector adjacent to a subsistence (or agricultural) sector—was not simply a problem to overcome but an opportunity to exploit. When one considers all surplus labor—"the farmers, the casuals, the petty traders, the retainers (domestic and commercial), women in the household, and population growth"—then it is "clear enough," Lewis wrote,

> that there can be in an over-populated economy an enormous expansion of new industries or new employment opportunities without any shortage of unskilled labour becoming apparent in the labour market. From the point of view of the effect of economic development on wages, the supply of labour is practically unlimited.

The mechanism for promoting development was the redeployment of this excess from agriculture and other traditional sectors to the industrial services that fuel modern growth. The process continues "until the labour surplus disappears." In fact, the most tenuous factor in the industrialization process, Lewis insisted, was not labor, but "the use which is made of the capitalist surplus," that is, the investors whose savings were needed to launch modern growth. For whereas labor was plentiful, capital was scarce, and industrialization depended on constant reinvestment through which "the capitalist sector expands."[96]

Inequality was an inherent feature of the cycle. "The central fact of economic development," Lewis stated, "is that the distribution of incomes is altered in favour of the saving class"—an unequal but generative capital-labor split.[97] Workers and the middle classes contribute little to "productive investment." It is capitalists who pump the bellows; their profits and savings boost growth and fuel development. What the poor provide is labor at market clearing rates, and if its cost is raised above subsistence levels, the "capitalist sector may be stopped." Indeed, mass poverty itself, per Lewis, does not prevent development. Quite the reverse: "The reason why savings are low in an undeveloped economy relatively to national income is not that the people are poor, but that capitalist profits are low relatively to national income." Echoing the Harrod-Domar model, he contended that

> [t]he central problem in the theory of economic development is to understand the process by which a community which was previously saving and investing 4 or 5 per cent of its national income or less, converts itself into an economy where voluntary saving is running at about 12 to 15 per cent of national income or more. This is the central problem because the central fact of economic development is rapid capital accumulation (including knowledge and skills with capital).[98]

One can hardly find a better encapsulation of mainline development thinking in the 1950s than this two-sentence summary.

The Lewis model articulated a straightforward strategy for marshaling surplus labor and capitalist savings to supercharge the industrialization of agrarian lands, relying on an inexpensive and widely available workforce.[99] And yet, as a wider review of Lewis's writing demonstrates, it represents only one facet of the economist's thinking.[100] Indeed, the core model, based on a closed-economy framework (one without external trade) and laid out in the first two-thirds of the article, is a distillation even of that essay, notably avoiding the complications introduced in an open economy. In the former, industrialization could be hindered if "the price of subsistence goods rises" or if "workers raise their standard of what they need for subsistence."[101] The latter, by contrast, offered opportunities for delaying this eventuality, since capitalists could either import unskilled immigrants or leave the country to take advantage of labor surpluses elsewhere.

Despite its advantages, Lewis at times seemed to regret the social inequity that fueled industrialization. "However vastly productive the sugar industry may become," he wrote of his native Antilles,

> the benefit accrues chiefly to industrial purchasers in the form of lower prices for sugar. . . . The prices of tropical commercial crops will always permit only subsistence wages until, for a change, capital and knowledge are put at the disposal of the subsistence producers to increase the productivity of tropical food production for home consumption.

The tendency of capitalist exporters to hold wages flat is offset only "if the capital is applied to cheapening the things which the workers import, or to raising wage costs in countries which compete in third markets (by raising productivity in their subsistence sectors)."[102] Indeed, Lewis suggested—but did not explain in this essay—that only improved agricultural production (a 'subsistence sector') or increased skills training for workers could alleviate poverty and put upward pressure on wages. One has to turn to other essays to see that Lewis's thinking cannot be reduced to a brief for industrialization. His wider oeuvre sometimes supports and sometimes opposes large-scale industrial projects, but it consistently advocates for agricultural innovation, mass education, and skills training.[103]

While the Caribbean roots of Lewis's landmark essay are not so obvious as the Central European lineage of Rosenstein-Rodan's, it is nonetheless noteworthy that, as the Barbadian economist Andrew Downes noticed, Lewis worked out his model through engagement with the question of industrialization in his home region.[104] Indeed, his hopes for industrialization as a pathway to development are clearest in his early essays on the West Indies. In 1933, Lewis left his native St. Lucia to study at the LSE. After receiving his Ph.D. in 1940, he remained at the same institution until 1948, when he moved to the University of Manchester as Britain's first black lecturer. His early forays into what would become development economics were drawn up for the moderate socialist Fabian Society, which he had joined in the 1930s. The Fabians, as Cowen and Shenton pointed out, had enormous influence on British colonial policy, encouraging the promotion of natural and human improvement—in a word, development—as a justification for foreign rule.[105] Lewis's essays concerned his home islands at a particularly tumultuous time. In the wake of labor strikes and protests across the British West Indies that culminated in the bloody 1938 Jamaica dockworkers' strike, the Colonial Office established a West Indies Royal Commission—known as the Moyne Commission after its head, Walter Guinness, the First Baron Moyne—to recommend reforms. Disappointingly for Lewis, the commission's report placed little faith in industrialization, advising instead a relatively modest package of agricultural improvements. "Some small increase of industrial employment may be afforded by the development of secondary industries," the commissioners wrote, "but these will at best be of relatively unimportant proportions, and would be dependent for their prosperity (on) agriculture."[106]

The Moyne Commission was not alone in focusing on agriculture as the key to Antillean stabilization. The Oxford graduate and Howard University professor Eric Williams, two years from his scholarly breakout with the book *Capitalism and Slavery* and two decades from the prime ministry of independent Trinidad and Tobago, did not even mention industry in his analysis of Afro-Caribbean peasants, calling instead for cash crop exports, agricultural extension, and rural cooperatives to relieve the poverty of the *colonos*.[107]

Lewis, who would later advise Williams in an official capacity, wanted none of it. The proper remedy for West Indian poverty and unemployment, he announced baldly, was industry, since the agricultural sector was already "relatively efficient."[108] In a 1939 pamphlet, Lewis prodded officials to subsidize "factories for refining sugar, making chocolate, utilizing copra, making dairy products, etc." and then let them "stand on their own two legs." No other policy, he felt, "offer[ed] such permanent prospects."[109] He expounded this program in three further essays written between 1945 and 1950, outlining in the process a nascent Lewis model of industrialization in poor, populous societies. The famous 1954 essay reflected a "formalization," per the Tobagonian sociologist and activist Susan Craig, of earlier "prescriptions . . . for the English-speaking Caribbean."[110]

The 1945 Report of Britain's Jamaica Economic Policy Committee, known as the Benham Report, marked another occasion for Lewis's ire. Its meager provisos on land reclamation, tourism, social services, and public works, he scoffed, constituted a "nightmare of nonsense" that would do little to reverse Jamaica's fortunes. They reflected "a strong prejudice against the development of local industries," and Lewis repudiated them strenuously. "It is clear as daylight," he insisted,

> that only a great increase in secondary industry can solve the island's employment problem. Her agricultural resources will not support a population of 1,200,000 increasing by 2 per cent per annum; there is not enough cultiva-

> ble land; indeed the land is already carrying more people than it can provide for economically. Mining, the tourist trade, nothing that anyone can suggest will make any substantial contribution to the 70,000 to 120,000 more jobs that the economic system must provide. Only industrialization can do that.[111]

Here we find the Lewis model in a nutshell.

The Second World War lent urgency to Lewis's position. Impoverished imperial holdings constituted a drag on the British economy, and in the postwar world, the U.S. and Soviet superpowers frowned on the perpetuation of empire.[112] Whether in Rosenstein-Rodan's Eastern Europe or the British Antilles, industrialization now seemed a way to allay these concerns, creating productive appendage economies that might contribute to postwar reconstruction and demonstrate the British hegemon's colonial beneficence. In this context, Lewis's interwar call took on heightened significance.

By the late 1940s, Williams, then deputy chairman of the Caribbean Commission, a joint U.S.-British effort to promote West Indian development, began to heed Lewis's warnings.[113] At his urging, the St. Lucian economist was engaged as a consultant to consider possibilities for Caribbean industry. In a 1950 essay that emerged from this partnership, Lewis explained why agriculture alone could not support needed development. In the West Indies,

> even when they are employing in agriculture the maximum number that agriculture will absorb at a reasonable standard of living, there will still be a large surplus of labour, and even the greatest expansion of industry which is conceivable within the next twenty years will not create a labour shortage in agriculture. . . . [A]griculture cannot be put on a basis where it will yield a reasonable standard of living unless new jobs are created off the land.[114]

Here we have, in short, a situation that meets the criteria for applying the later Lewis model. Yet even so, Lewis's proposal was not one-sided. "If agriculture is to give a higher standard of living, then industry must be developed," he declared. But equally, "if industry is to be developed, then agriculture must give a higher standard of living, in order to provide a demand for manufactures. The agricultural and the industrial revolutions thus reinforce each other, and neither can go very far unless the other is occurring at the same time."[115] This balance more aptly summarizes Lewis's long-term view than the industrialization-first model for which he became famous.

In the same years, Lewis found a Caribbean model of export-led modernization in Operation Bootstrap, the industrialization program for U.S.-owned Puerto Rico. After the Depression-era collapse of its sugar industry, the island experienced rapid growth under governors Rex Tugwell and Luis Muñoz Marin, using a plan drawn up by businessman Teodoro Moscoso. Through a state-organized holding company, Puerto Rico enticed U.S. manufacturing industries with tax exemptions and tariff-free reexport to the mainland, effectively turning the island into an export processing zone.[116] In the 1940s, as part of its international diplomacy, the United States touted the program as a model for Caribbean industrialization.[117] Lewis, a rising star in the economics profession, lent his name to this publicity effort. "In view of the smallness of the aid given, the programme has achieved remarkable success," he beamed after observing operations in the late 1940s. "Apart from 18 factories which the Development Company [a parastatal created by the government in 1942] has built for private manufacturers, another 32 factories have been established during the past two years." In total, the program had created or was creating 55 new factories employing 7,428 workers.[118] While this barely dented the island's unemployment, Lewis praised it as a strong beginning. In "an over-populated country like Puerto Rico," the program is attracting "an inflow of new industries."[119]

Lewis acknowledged that Puerto Rico differed from its British-colonial counterparts. Lodged within the U.S. free-trade zone, it did not require the kinds of subsidies needed by other islands. Nonetheless, Operation Bootstrap's combination of government support and private foreign capital had lessons for the wider archipelago. "Industries are like sheep," he quipped, "they like to move together"—and none would come until an industrial center was built. Since only governments could stimulate the big push needed to industrialize, Lewis decried the gradual, business-led, laissez-faire approach encouraged by the Colonial Office and pushed instead for a Puerto Rican–style Industrial Development Corporation for the British West Indies.[120] In 1956, when Eric Williams's People's National Movement assumed legislative power in Trinidad and Tobago, Lewis drew up an official industrialization plan for the islands. Coauthored with Moscoso, the "industrialization-by-invitation" program—with the government inviting foreign firms—soon became formal policy in Port of Spain.[121]

By then, Lewis's industrial advocacy had escaped its Caribbean origins. In 1951, he headed a United Nations panel that included the economist Theodore Schultz, later an intellectual nemesis. The panel's proposals reflected Lewis's leadership. "Rapid economic development," wrote the five-person team, is "the only fundamental remedy for disguised unemployment," since it would quickly create necessary jobs.

> [I]n most countries where under-employment is acute, nearly all the cultivable land is already cultivated. Effort has then to be concentrated upon creating new industries off the land, of which manufacturing industries comprise the largest and usually the most promising category. Thus, the most urgent problem of these countries is industrialization.[122]

This would seem an unequivocal expression of Lewis's forthcoming industrialization formula. But the panel softened its recommendation by agreeing that there was "no need to choose between developing agriculture and developing industry; both must be pursued," their ultimate weighting determined by the land and population.[123] This, too, reflected Lewis's conviction.

In the following years, sectoral balance became a more regular feature of Lewis's message, as shown in lectures delivered during a 1953 visit to Egypt. While industry was crucial in dense population areas, including "China, India, Japan, Java, some countries in the Middle East, Kenya, and some small islands, such as the West Indies or Mauritius," agriculture was "equal in status." But millions lived in countries with land to spare: much of Africa and Latin America, as well as parts of Asia. These had to *prioritize* (not simply equalize) agriculture.[124] Exports were moneymakers in both types of region, but whether they were manufactures or agriculture depended upon circumstances. Thus, a year from his famous 1954 essay, Lewis had qualified its argument. Even in populous India, he wrote after a 1952 tour, industrialization, though "urgent," belonged together with agricultural improvement, which "makes the farmers better off, and thus supplies a market for industry."[125] Lewis the industrializer was in fact an advocate of balanced agro-industrial growth.

Agriculture grew more pronounced in Lewis's writings on Africa, a continent that suffered mostly, in his view, from under- rather than overpopulation. In 1952, he was asked to advise the nationalist Convention People's Party

(CPP) in the British Gold Coast, beginning a long courtship with its leader, Kwame Nkrumah. By then, Lewis had already laid out an economic policy for colonial Africa that called for investment in farmer education; technical and marketing skills; infrastructure such as roads, railways, and water supplies; and farm-based implements, livestock, and fertilizers. The focus, in other words, was modern agriculture, and Lewis offered Jamaican farms as an advance model, citing peasant extension and village credit programs.[126] In a misnamed 1953 report, he again argued that manufacturing for the home market was not the top priority. Instead, the Gold Coast, where the CPP now shared power with the British, needed "a concentrated attack on the system of growing food . . . so as to set in motion an ever increasing productivity. This is the way to provide the market, the capital, and the labour for industrialisation."[127] One year before his career-making essay, in other words, Lewis warned against a headlong rush to industrialize without an appropriate agrarian base. "The truth is that industrialisation for a home market can make little progress unless agriculture is progressing vigorously at the same time, to provide both the market for industry, and industry's labour supply. If agriculture is stagnant, industry cannot grow."[128] Outside (perhaps) the cocoa industry, Lewis worried that Gold Coast cultivation was largely static, and thus the industry to which Nkrumah's nationalists aspired had to wait until food production increased—a caution that surprised colonial officials familiar with Lewis's earlier stances.[129] He would urge similar restraint a decade later when President Nkrumah asked him to serve as an economic advisor to newly independent Ghana (see Chapter 3).

The point, of course, should not be overstated. Industrialization remained integral to Lewis's economic vision throughout his career, as indicated by his defense of the "Unlimited Supplies" argument in two subsequent papers.[130] But even in these sequels, he affirmed the interdependence of industry and agriculture:

> If the capitalist sector trades with the peasant sector . . . its continued expansion would be menaced if the peasant sector were stagnant, since this would move the terms of trade against the capitalist sector. In practice, failure of peasant agriculture to increase its productivity has probably been the chief reason holding down the expansion of the industrial sector in most of the under-developed countries of the world.[131]

Over time, however, the program was pared back by proponents and critics alike, who focused on Lewis's call to industrialize while ignoring his more balanced pronouncements. In the 1960s, Theodore Schultz, Lewis's erstwhile copanelist on the 1951 United Nations report, disputed the rural overpopulation thesis, arguing that poor agrarian communities do not squander labor as the Lewis model proposed. (This is discussed below.) Similarly, the Hungarian-born British economist Peter Bauer, a forerunner of the 1970s free market revolt against development economics, characterized Lewis's dualism, with a "capitalist sector" growing "at the expense of the subsistence sector," as "too sharp" and neglectful of valuable interdependencies.[132] And proponents John Fei and Gustav Ranis, whose own widely read theories of economic development carried the Lewis torch, overwhelmingly emphasized the need for industry to abet growth.[133] Thus, Lewis became associated with an industrialization-above-all model that oversimplified his economic thought. The model eclipsed the maker.

Criticism of the Model

An intellectual line ran from Rosenstein-Rodan's big push to Lewis's industrialization with unlimited labor, the latter building on the former in an emerging postwar consensus. Even as it was coalescing, however, the model generated pushback. The strongest and most contextual criticism came from market advocates who objected to the priority placed on planning and state intervention. Peter Bauer, one such figure, became the most dogged and inveterate of development antagonists. Although it was not until the 1970s that he achieved renown, his early work displayed an opposition to mainstream development that stamped his career. Bauer's 1957 book, *The Economics of Under-developed Countries,* written with South African economist Basil Yamey, emphasized the diversity of almost all variables in developing economies, a kaleidoscope witnessed only by attending to local characteristics as he had in his early research in Malaya, Nigeria, and the Gold Coast. Despite some consistencies—poverty, dearth of capital, the family economic unit—one had to resist the tendency toward unjustified abstraction that shaped the development consensus. Only markets, Bauer believed, had the suppleness to coordinate wide-ranging social preferences and the sundry activities of small-scale producers.[134] By the 1970s, this critique took on new and, alas, parodic dimensions, as we will see in Chapter 6.

In disputing mainstream development doctrines, Bauer and Yamey drew on an influential study by the American anthropologist Sol Tax entitled *Penny Capitalism,* which depicted economic life in the indigenous lakeside community of Panajachel, Guatemala.[135] Tax, who was a student of the pathbreaking University of Chicago anthropologist Robert Redfield (Chapter 3), lived in Panajachel on and off between 1935 and 1941. The book based on his research finally appeared in 1953, amid surging interest in economic development and just prior to the CIA-sponsored coup that ended Guatemala's ten years of revolution. For development dissenters, Tax offered an empirically detailed (albeit static) ethnography of an apparently typical developing community in which the rural poor were entrepreneurial and efficient in their resource use, but lacked the tools and technical knowledge to advance their economic fortunes. Tax's peasants were, in short, rational actors who responded astutely to price signals and engaged in competitive behavior, "'capitalist' on a microscopic scale"—a stark contrast to the prevailing image of rural underemployment and lethargy. "There are no machines, no factories, no co-ops or corporations" in Panajachel. But there was also no wasted labor. "Every man is his own firm and works ruggedly for himself."[136]

Tax's Panajachel served as a set piece for Theodore Schultz's 1964 critique of the rural overpopulation thesis in *Transforming Traditional Agriculture,* a founding work in the field of human capital. Schultz, as we noted earlier, regretted joining Lewis as cosignatory of the 1951 United Nations report that highlighted rural unemployment.[137] Perhaps recoiling from that earlier episode, he devoted the remainder of the 1950s to elaborating an influential rejoinder to the Lewis model and its illicit in-smuggling of a demographic thesis drawn (in his assessment) from the Depression-era experience of unemployment in the West.[138] Disputing the doctrine of zero-value agricultural labor, Schultz found that villages such as Panajachel or Senapur (in India)—which, he argued, resembled many poor agricultural communities—demonstrated active commerce and effective use of scarce resources.[139] Although poor and illiterate, rural farmers were "competent entrepreneurs"; what they missed was modern skills and technology, for the lack of which no work ethic could compensate.[140] Bound to methods that had been used for generations, they suffered a stagnant production horizon that reflected their limited knowledge and outmoded equipment. There was, in sum, very little "opportunity for growth" in a penny economy because "farmers have exhausted the profitable production possibilities of the state of the arts at their disposal."[141] Instead, growth required technological change or, as Schultz advocated in his book's conclusion, new human capital, a term designating the skills and capacities (such as education or growth) that contributed to economic modernization.[142]

Also instructive is the work of the Burmese economist Hla Myint, who argued that the emphasis on a savings rate of over 10 percent as a precondition for growth—here he cited Lewis, Walt Rostow, and the Harrod-Domar model—drew a problematic "historical analogy" to the West's own industrial take-off.[143] Non-Western countries were "at very different stages of economic development," frustrating any effort at theoretical generalization.[144] Furthermore, one must avoid applying policies "appropriate for the overpopulated countries" to those that did not suffer from such density. "Instead of a monolithic theory to cover all the underdeveloped countries it will be more fruitful to look for alternative theoretical models to suit different types of underdeveloped country."[145] Like Lewis, Myint studied at the LSE, later taking posts at the University of Rangoon and then, exiled by a 1962 military takeover, back in England. He, too, took issue with the thesis of an inefficient subsistence sector, proposing instead an Adam Smith–inspired "vent for surplus" doctrine based on export-led growth.[146] Myint contended that peasant labor surpluses and agricultural overproduction could boost rural incomes if export markets were open. Labor did not need to move from the rural to the modern sector, and agricultural production could expand without radical technical improvements if "the peasants took to 'specializing' in export crops." By exercising this option, they "took full advantage of the *market opportunities* available to them."[147]

In 1965, Myint added another indictment of mainstream development: the tendency of planners to impose templates distilled from other developing countries. If some Western economists generalized from "the 'special case' of the advanced countries," others—Myint cited Rostow—abstracted "from the 'special case' of a particular type of underdeveloped country," usually India, which by the 1960s came to dominate conventional models of aid-driven growth.[148] Yet India was unique: Its population growth was high, in contrast to much of Latin America, Africa, and Southeast Asia, where the "concept of 'disguised unemployment' ha[d] limited application" and policymakers had to make efficient use of underemployed resources. The sheer size of India also gave its example limited purchase; even populous countries could rarely mimic the subcontinent's development through domestic markets. Furthermore, New Delhi had a more advanced "institutional framework" than most poor countries. Ill-advised imitation thwarted real development.[149]

In strict terms, Myint's theory did not contradict the economic development mainstream represented by Rosenstein-Rodan or the Lewis model. If the latter two devised programs for overpopulated societies, Myint focused on less congested areas with land available for export cropping. But Myint clearly opposed dominant development doctrines; his advocacy of export-driven growth prefigured a movement toward market-led development that would transform the field in the 1970s and 1980s.[150] More generally, the Burmese Myint disputed the tendency to think in terms of a standardized "developing economy," a windy generalization that shrank Asian, African, and Latin American societies into a few manageable rubrics, encouraging simplistic prescriptions that ignored local prospects and distinctions.

The concern for inapplicable models was not restricted to free-market devotees. Economist John Kenneth Galbraith, whose 1958 bestseller *The Affluent Society* called for greater public investment and made him a bête noir of free marketers, also questioned the tendency "to identify development as a whole with the experience of India." The subcontinent, Galbraith warned while serving as Kennedy's ambassador to New Delhi, had far more administrative infrastructure and capacity than many developing countries. "We can no longer have one diagnosis of the causes of underdevelopment," he concluded. "Rather we must have the particular diagnosis which fits the particular country. And in few cases will the causes of backwardness or the requirements of progress be quite the same."[151] Similarly, in lectures given in 1958, the Harvard economist Edward S. Mason, who would later consult for the World Bank and write its fortieth-anniversary history, disputed the relevance of nineteenth-century models for contemporary aspiring nations. Earlier industrialization, he insisted, provided little guidance since Western societies had advanced further by the time of their take-off than had contemporary poor societies, who had to develop in a world where they were catching up from behind. The conditions were simply too different for comparison.[152]

Nonetheless, among early development critics, the frequent combination of market allegiance and methodological localism was noteworthy, yielding a picture of developing-country diversity that escaped the more standardized models of mainstream development economists. To be sure, market proponents made their own generalizations: Bauer, Schultz, and Myint described rational if constrained rural entrepreneurs who exhibited a transcultural Smithian sensibility—a universal desire to truck, barter, and exchange. The market, these critics maintained, was a global mechanism, capable of registering, regulating, and fostering economic diversity. If this insistence was hardly without ideological freight—Bauer became a staunch defender of colonialism—the methodological tools of localism and empiricism at least allowed critics to challenge dominant templates. But they too were largely presentist, relying on recent data to depict a picturesque Third World peasantry, vibrant and colorful, economically resourceful, but ill equipped to change on its own. It would fall to several contemporary schools of thought—modernization in the United States, structuralism and dependency in Latin America—to introduce a deeper historical dimension into development theory.

Model-building was an essential strategy of postwar development economics, necessary to establish the social scientific credentials of the subfield and facilitate global programming. Nonetheless, it focused aid planning around an abstract and technical knowledge base that largely disregarded the particular experiences of developing societies. There is no denying the managerial power gained by employing more or less fixed models of development to address poverty in multiple regions. But the cost of such capsule narratives is a homogenizing program, promulgated by economists and donor institutions alike, that sees modernity as a blueprint and development as mechanics, stripped of local histories and cultural context.

3

A Thousand Valleys: The Enthusiasms of Postwar Development Practice

THERE WAS NO ZERO HOUR WHEN development simply burst into existence, and starting its history in the war years, as I did in the last chapter, omits important predecessors. This chapter begins, accordingly, by considering earlier sources of development programming in European empires and the American New Deal. From there, we examine postwar development practice from the late 1940s to the early 1960s, including America's Point Four program, Arthur Lewis's advisory stint in Nkrumah's Ghana, and community development programming in India. Along the way, I show that enthusiasm for the new development enterprise contributed to presentist tendencies, an emotive ahistoricism that still imbues the profession today.

Before going backward, however, it is worth noting the prominence of another postwar program in accounts of development's origins. The Marshall Plan is often called America's first aid program, the model to which others aspire. But the European Recovery Program (ERP), as it was officially titled, occupies an ambiguous position in development history. On the one hand, it is commonly seen as America's most successful foreign aid effort, a 'New Deal for Europe' that transferred $13 billion (about $140 billion in 2017 dollars) in money, capital, and expertise to the ravaged continent between 1948 and 1952.[1] Since then, it has been routinely cited as a template for the kind of massive, cross-sectoral investment that other regions need and deserve in the wake of colonialism (Africa), political transition (Eastern Europe), or war (Afghanistan).

On the other hand, the Marshall Plan plays a relatively minor role in many histories of foreign aid—and for good reason.[2] Fundamentally, the reconstruction of an industrial continent is different from the development of agrarian societies. So, too, is collaboration with longstanding allies who share cultural presuppositions—as opposed to postcolonial partners forced to reengage with their erstwhile masters. Europe had a skilled population and technological resources lacking elsewhere, as well as longstanding ties to its American benefactor.

All the same, the ERP elevated financial and technical assistance into a major plank of U.S. foreign policy and pioneered tactics that are now widespread in aid programs. Replacing the piecemeal assistance given before and immediately after the war, the new program, as its most significant recent historian has shown, became an overseas testing ground for New Deal ideas of public-private partnership; capital-intensive growth; economic integration; regional self-help; and collaboration among government, business, and trade unions. Marshall Planners "tried to transform political problems into technical ones that were solvable, they said, when old European ways of conducting business and old habits of class conflict gave way to American methods of scientific management and corporative collaboration."[3] Reconstruction assistance was designed to fuel economic recovery *and* supplant ingrained patterns of social and political strife. As another historian put it, the Marshall Plan was "[f]ar more than a humanitarian gesture, a response to the threat of Communism in Europe, or an effort to strengthen the economic climate upon which American capitalism to a large extent relied." It was also "a teleological vision: what the United States is today, the world will be tomorrow."[4] Exchanging Mars for Apollo, the ERP cultivated a practice of scientific and administrative collaboration involving heavy doses of technical assistance, indicative planning, and market regulation. All of this conformed well with America's commitment to what Charles Maier has termed the "politics of productivity"—the replacement of struggles over class and nation with growth for all (even if not in equal measure).[5]

In its day, the Marshall Plan had great rhetorical appeal. When it was proposed in 1947, exponents claimed that it distinguished American leadership from exploitative European colonial regimes, marking the start of a new and more enlightened internationalism. This image was crucial in the emerging Cold War as the United States had to demonstrate its anti-imperial credentials to newly independent Asian and African societies, a challenge complicated by its alliance with colonial powers such as Britain and France. Since then, the ERP has been repeatedly summoned as an example of American munificence. Kennedy cited it as a key predecessor in launching his Decade of Development.[6] The British economist Barbara Ward called for a revival of "the Marshall spirit" in 1962 to fulfill "our obligations to the underdeveloped world."[7] And to this day, the ERP is conjured, typically in the breach, to demand large aid investments in poor regions.[8] Critics also invoked the program. Indeed, beyond the Western world, the Marshall Plan was cited not only for its generosity but also for its prejudice: Why, Latin Americans asked, did the United States prioritize Europe even as it ignored its southern neighbors, whose need was just as great and whose wartime support was more steadfast?[9] Whether for or against, commentators turned the ERP into a puissant symbol.

A further effect of the Marshall Plan, one with implications for our story, was to push the World Bank away from its original mandate for European reconstruction and toward its now more recognized role as the globe's pivotal multilateral development institution. The Bank's $497 million for Europe paled in comparison to the $4 billion annually coming from the United States. In 1947, the second Bank president John McCloy surmised that "we are going to be driven into a very different field sooner than I thought, into the field of development."[10] As his prescience indicates, U.S. investments had enormous clout in the postwar period.

Colonial Development: "Knowing the Natives"

But the United States was not the only country shaping global development practice. If the Marshall Plan promoted technical approaches to reconstruction, colonial development programs, which ran from the late nineteenth century through the first postwar decades, deployed cultural knowledge alongside scientific expertise. As historians Joseph Morgan Hodge and Monica van Beusekom have shown, colonial ministers starting with Joseph Chamberlain in 1895 and Albert Sarraut in 1921 revised overseas mandates by calling for the development of their colonies (Britain's improvement of the "imperial estates" and France's *mise en valeur*) for the 'mutual' benefit of their populations and the empire overall—a nod, if only slightly, to the welfare of non-

European subjects.[11] This agenda was supposed to replace the exploitation and neglect of earlier imperialism with a beneficent and scientific version: the development of peoples as well as the development of land and resources. The dual mandate—the idea that empires are responsible for improving both the metropole and their colonial subjects—included considerable increases in funding, even as it furnished a new developmental justification for foreign rule.[12]

Colonial development was an important precursor of postwar aid practices, despite the embarrassment this ancestry may cause for today's development practitioners. Indeed, with the onset of decolonization, many old colonial hands shifted to new bilateral and multilateral organizations, carrying with them methods forged in earlier times.[13] It does not follow, of course, that colonial influence discredits later development as neo-imperial. There were crucial differences, most obviously the fact of non-Western sovereignty (however compromised by neocolonial influence). In recent decades, scholars have shown that, even as colonial technicians employed scientific development approaches that anticipated later trends, they also drew on indigenous knowledge and, starting in the 1930s, encouraged local participation in development programs, going well beyond the patronizing nineteenth-century call for colonial administrators to "know their natives."[14] Thus, even if the overall program of empire is unsalvageable, one might draw insights from certain colonial development strategies. Both divorcing aid from and equating it to its imperial predecessor are untenable positions for such a complex and contradictory enterprise.

Late colonial development exhibited its share of technological prometheanism. The spectacular failure of the Tanganyika Groundnut Scheme, which lived and died between 1947 and 1951, is a case in point. Embracing the recommendations of metropolitan agronomists and relying on mechanized production, project officials oversaw a vast mono-cropping effort covering more than 3 million acres. It ultimately ran afoul of both environmental conditions and local agricultural practices, not only failing to produce the expected bumpers but alienating farmers in the process.[15] It has stood ever since as an object lesson in development disaster. The Gambia Poultry Scheme, launched with little consultation in the 1940s, proved similarly ineffective, with typhoid killing much of the stock.[16] And as Grace Carswell shows, cash cropping sometimes failed even while local harvests flourished. In southwestern Kigezi province, British Uganda, European agricultural science was superimposed onto local practices, with mixed results for imperial modernization plans.[17]

But another approach also became widespread. Starting in the 1930s, as depression raised the specter of colonial rebellion, imperial technicians started compiling local knowledge and incorporating participatory elements in program design and implementation. This localization reflected both the accumulated awareness of decades of European experience in Africa as well as a growing appreciation for the continent's heterogeneity and the value of insights held by African communities, especially in the areas of ecology, agriculture, and anthropology.[18] In French Soudan, an irrigation and cotton cultivation project launched along the Niger River (in present-day Mali) faced production failures and peasant flight until the early 1950s, when managers began outreach efforts to settler-farmers who had previously rebuffed project stipulations (including forced labor). While conflicts persisted in the vast Office du Niger—and European officials never abandoned their racial outlook—a ground-level view of operations suggests a project that was more open to local input than is typically assumed of colonial endeavors.[19] Similarly, in the wake of Lugard's promotion of the dual mandate, British agents also turned to local knowledge, particularly in the 1930s, when an interest in ecology and overpopulation encouraged the careful study of regional agricultural systems.[20]

The most monumental in-gathering of local knowledge took place as part of the British Africa Survey from 1929 to 1939, headquartered at the Royal Institute of International Affairs (Chatham House—see Chapter 2). Its teams of natural and social scientists gathered information not just about geography and environment, but also about indigenous methods of cultivation, cropping, and husbandry. Furthermore, they undertook an anthropology of African peoples, a commitment institutionalized in Africa's first anthropological research center, the Rhodes-Livingstone Institute, founded in Lusaka in 1937.[21] While the impetus for examining the 'human side' of development came primarily from agents in the field, it did not remain there, but rose upward to inform imperial policy, including the Colonial Development and Welfare Act of 1940, with its expanded development mandate. Similarly, colonial officials in Dutch Java drew on empirical knowledge of local agriculture to argue for a revision of policies promulgated in The Hague. These regional experts urged "small-scale, locally sensitive technological development" under the colonial policy of Ethical Idealism, which encouraged collaboration with farmers.[22] Local participation was also used to beneficial effect in southern Rhodesia, where settlers in the remote Gokwe region increased their cotton production and cash intake as part of an agricultural resettlement project. In this case, the settlers adopted European technical and cultural procedures to employ in their new environs.[23]

To be sure, the gains of colonialism were meager and uneven. A 1987 encapsulation by the Ghanaian historian A. Adu Boahen remains apt:

> [T]he social services provided by colonialism were grossly inadequate and unevenly distributed. For instance, while in Nigeria by the 1930s, twelve modern hospitals had been built for Europeans, who numbered only 4,000, there were only fifty-two for Africans, numbering 40 million. In Dar es Salaam the ratio of beds to population by 1920 was approximately 1 to 10 for the European hospital and 1 to 400–500 for the African hospital.[24]

And whatever the sympathies of individual researchers, the compilation and deployment of local knowledge took place within a framework designed to uphold imperial dominion. For all the benefits of its desultory willingness to accommodate local practice, colonial development was never able to make colonialism palatable. Insofar as it was expected to do so—and clearly one of the goals of Britain's post-1945 policy was to burnish the reputation of empire—it failed: there was no vindicating foreign rule. Yet as van Beusekom and Dorothy Hodgson argue, Africans themselves, in resisting and modifying colonial development, drew on their knowledge of both local traditions and colonial practices.[25] If localism and cultural awareness can be used for exploitative purposes, they can also provide leverage for opposition and reform.

Enthusiasm

If 1950s colonialism elicited little international sympathy, the New Deal legacy—particularly its most attractive component, the Tennessee Valley Authority—inspired tons, allowing U.S. developers to go on the global offensive. Having escaped the war largely undamaged and newly committed to foreign involvement, the United States, liberal internationalists believed, could spearhead improvement on many fronts as a new and benevolent superpower. Aid's centrality to this mission can be seen in documents urging the export of the TVA model as part of an "American Century."[26] The emotional ballast for this belief ran deep in New Deal liberalism, growing especially out of President Franklin D. Roosevelt's apparent success in overcoming Depression-era economic woes.[27] What the United States brought to international development was a distinctive combination of technocratic expertise and New World exuberance, a can-doism born of an era in which the country had not only survived the war, but—in its telling—rescued the globe as well. To foreign policy elites, global leadership seemed the natural result.[28] The shift from European imperial to American postimperial helmsmanship also entailed a shift in the nature of development expertise. As part of its colonial legacy, Britain had built up a cadre of regional specialists. The United States lacked this cultural knowledge, but in its place offered technological prowess, abundant resources, and a working model of rural development success.[29]

And enthusiasm to spare. In its midcentury liberal dispensation, enthusiasm had perhaps no greater apostle than the American guru of can-doism, Norman Vincent Peale, whose 1967 volume *Enthusiasm Makes the Difference* built on his runaway bestseller, *The Power of Positive Thinking*. A Protestant minister and amateur psychiatrist, Peale did not write about development. But his media ubiquity helped to define the liberal optimism of the age. Along with religious faith, enthusiasm was a cornerstone of Peale's message, and he cast it as an explicitly ahistorical, or even antihistorical, emotion that individuals and societies would do well to cultivate. While history burdened Europe, the youth of the United States conferred a winning vigor and freedom from tradition that enabled not only mental expansiveness but worldly innovation as well. Enthusiasm, crowed Peale, was forward-facing, filled with "drive and vitality"—a "combustion" that propelled one goalward. Drawing on the philosopher William James, he maintained that true effort required the transcendence of mundane reality into an 'as if' realm where one "visualized" achievements and acted to realize them. Enthusiasm—not so much a philosophy as a temperament or disposition—powered this endeavor. It required, among other tactics, "mental ventilation," emptying one's mind "to prevent unhealthy thoughts from lodging in consciousness"—or, invoking Philippians, "[f]orgetting those things which are behind, and reaching forth unto those things which are before." The successful life practitioner "approaches each day on the principle that you get a new set of facts each morning. Then you convince yourself that you are going to take this new set of facts, be happy with it and do something constructive with it."[30] Retrospection was counterproductive. "Skip the post-mortems," he counseled. "Don't say, 'Why did I do that? Why didn't I do this?' Take the problem from where you now are." Or, in emotional terms: "Eliminate self-pity. Start thinking of what you have left instead of dwelling on what you have lost." This life approach had a political iconography: The Communist leadership is "tired, old and possibly all but passé." Ho Chi Minh is "a dried-up old man, dreaming the weary dreams of the aged."[31] Enthusiasm, by contrast, is youthful, dynamic, creative, hale—a quality of self-motivated individuals unbound by the past, quintessential American trailblazers. This had strong ties to the liberal ideal. As Beth Blum notes, "[b]oth self-help and liberalism depend on the construct of the autonomous, self-determining individual who is seen as the condition of possibility for democratic self-governance."[32]

Enthusiasm had its critics. In his 1950 bestseller, *The Lonely Crowd,* University of Chicago sociologist David Riesman pegged the enthusiast as a moralizer whose "political emotions frequently outweigh his political intelligence." Just as the religious enthusiast cultivates a fanatic faith based on a belief in divine inspiration, so the modern-day enthusiast, in thrall to one conviction or another, is apt to push beyond "the limits on change in human affairs," overriding "folkways" in the pursuit of "unattainable ends" and endorsing the "American penchant for activity as such" without concern for thought or context.[33] Riesman reminds us that the postwar American mood was characterized by much more than optimism. He worried about a society in which individuals increasingly drew their sense of worth from the approbation of others—yielding to conformism and docility. And his age saw plenty of anxiety: This was the high Cold War, when nuclear annihilation seemed plausible and McCarthy's red scare split the nation.[34] But development remains one of its sunnier products, casting rays of possibility over global growth endeavors. As a performative attitude, the enthusiasm that nourished it produced boldness and blindness at once.

Mr. TVA

Peale's enthusiasm book appeared in 1967, just as Great Society liberalism was unraveling in Vietnam War protests. David Lilienthal, by contrast, hailed the liberal sunrise two decades earlier, a dawn that he cast in bright modern hues. "I believe that through the practice of democracy," he wrote in the Preface to his 1944 book *TVA: Democracy on the March,* "the world of technology holds out the greatest opportunity in all history for the development of the individual, according to his own talents, aspirations, and willingness to carry the responsibilities of a free man. . . . I believe men can make themselves free."[35] Indiana-born and Harvard-educated, the thirty-three-year-old lawyer became one of the TVA's first directors in 1933, joining the three-member board with a particular brief in public utilities and power production.[36] A massive regional development project centered around the iconic Norris Dam on Tennessee's Clinch River, the TVA sought to lift up a region that, according to Roosevelt, was "the nation's No. 1 economic problem."[37] The agenda was long: "[a]griculture, industry, electric power, flood control, river navigation, public health, housing, malaria control, education, urban planning, and a host of smaller issues."[38] Combining top-down technocratic planning, massive technological works, and local community participation designed to nurture democratic involvement, the TVA became a national and international symbol of the potency of planned development. If, as David Ekbladh asserts, the TVA was the "grand synecdoche" of midcentury modernization, then Lilienthal was its enthusiast-in-chief.[39]

Known as a "wonder boy" with indefatigable marketing zeal, Lilienthal capitalized on the war's imminent conclusion to offer up the TVA as a template for "tomorrow." Eschewing speculative theories, he called for a practical utopia that stressed "real things and real people"—rivers, farms, factories. By his account, academic skepticism, not real-world enthusiasm, lacked pioneering vision; it led to either the socialist suppression of individual initiative or extreme laissez-faire that denied collective action—"overcentralized Big-government" or "domination by a few private monopolies." Instead, the world needed doers animated by a meliorist "faith" and employing "facts and reason" to build a "democracy" fit for the "machine age." A global makeover, he asserted, was already occurring. The Tennessee Valley is "one of the thousand valleys of the earth," but the TVA had revealed what planning, science, and energy could achieve. Despite different "tongues" and "racial strains," men everywhere live from the land and yearn to end hunger. And the TVA model could travel. "A river," after all, "has no nationality," and the technical problems associated with its development are the same everywhere.[40]

Lilienthal's rhetoric had a decidedly technological flair. "There is almost nothing, however fantastic," he gushed, "that (given competent organization) a team of engineers, scientists, and administrators cannot do today." Poverty, drudgery, disease, filth, famine, floods—none of these were inevitable, and the global yen for development—from the Ozarks to the Ganges—could be met by bootstrapping "inventors and engineers and chemists" who undertook "the Grand Job of This Century."[41] Others echoed his faith: The political scientist Herman Pritchett, who also began his career with the TVA, described the program as a "portent," a "symbol" of man's ability to "control . . . his environment" and "direct . . . his destiny." The TVA was, he wrote, the "New Deal's most exportable product."[42]

Lilienthal spent most of his volume laying out the elements of a "region building" program designed to combat rural Appalachian poverty. A former utility executive with a taste for public works, he found electricity production particularly urgent: "Plans for the industrialization of undeveloped countries"—here he cited the Soviet Union and China—"invariably begin with the production of electric power." (Kwame Nkrumah, as we will see later in this chapter, agreed.) Flood control and irrigation; mechanized demonstration farms; and other technological projects also received praise. But Lilienthal also celebrated the TVA's 'softer' cultivation of human resources—improved healthcare, education, and participatory social engagement—all of which gave rise to a "confident, sure, chesty feeling" among program beneficiaries, a powerful democratic potion.[43] His journal entries reveal that he understood these changes as part of a modernization agenda. "There seems to be a definite sequence in history in the change from primitive or non-industrial conditions to more highly developed modern industrial conditions," he wrote two years earlier. But he hoped that planning could accelerate progress. "Whether all those steps have to be taken and all the intervening mistakes made is open to question. . . . Don't we have enough control over our destinies to short-cut those wasted steps?"[44] In the ensuing decades, modernization theorists tried to do just that.

The TVA, Lilienthal concluded, launched a "new chapter in American public policy," one that brought together "the people and the experts."[45] Though planned by the latter, it made use of the energies and ingenuity of the former. Decentralization, in particular, housed management in local communities, combatting the "remote control" of past government programs. The resulting "citizen participation" would "invigorate" the "flabby muscles of community and individual responsibility," awakening people to "common moral purpose."[46] Indeed, the TVA represented, in Lilienthal's view, a "grassroots democracy" at work, with modern farms acting as "schoolrooms of the valley."[47] Of relevance for later development goals, it also transcended partisan politics: Technical decision-making and public-private partnership allowed "science and politics to live together."[48] It also betokened an administrative "revolution," creating a "single agency" to manage river development and ensure that "no one activity could be considered an end in itself."[49] All this marked a considerable historical departure.

Lilienthal closed his small conspectus by highlighting the TVA's relevance for "world reconstruction." A "world in microcosm," the program spoke in "a language of things close to the lives of the people," a vernacular understood by 11 million global visitors. This "steady stream," he marveled,

> reminds you of the way in which a farmer crosses the ridge to take a look at a neighbor's demonstration farm, to see 'how he does it,' so he can try it out in his own way on his own place—except that these neighbors may be from Auckland on the other side of the globe, or from Göteborg, Buenos Aires, or Tegucigalpa.[50]

An emblem of "man's creative genius," the TVA offered antidotes to rural stagnation everywhere.

This was high-flying praise, and Lilienthal clearly exuded the enthusiasm that Peale would later endorse. Both men championed a robust belief that men could flourish in the machine age and that optimism was a watchword of the day. Democracy, Lilienthal insisted, "is a literal impossibility without faith that on balance the good in men far outweighs the evil"; in this sense "[f]aith is the greatest power in the world of men, the most 'practical' force of all."[51] This was positive thinking *avant la lettre,* an emotive bedrock of midcentury liberalism. Indeed, for all of the themes in Lilienthal's book that found their echoes in later development practice—from apoliticism to technophilia—perhaps the most resonant was his sheer exuberance, the boyish confidence that development could rescue the world: "What American public opinion will support in world affairs," he wrote, "may well depend on whether at the hour of decision the dominant feeling at home is optimism and good will, or the fearful grasping of worried men intent on 'saving their own necks' by letting the world go hang." In contrast to Henry Luce three years earlier, Lilienthal believed Americans would rise to the occasion, embracing a "warm-hearted impulse to work with one's neighbor" and a munificence "upon which may rest the world's hopes for peace." Accordingly, the question was *how*, not *whether*, to implement global TVAs. "The pragmatic development specialist," as the historian Daniel Klingensmith summarized, "needn't worry too much about finding out exactly what the peasants want, because it is obvious: 'what they want is to become modern.'"[52] Context and history had little place in this agenda. While Lilienthal's "dreamers with shovels" have since embraced newer technology, his aid optimism, at once inspired and myopic, remains integral to current development practice.[53]

Though hyperbolic, Lilienthal's book captured America's postwar sense of mission, and it won a considerable readership, selling 200,000 copies and appearing in nineteen languages.[54] True to its message, Lilienthal went on to an active international career as a roving ambassador for development. Moving from the public to the private sector, he helped to establish Colombia's Cauca Valley Corporation, a decentralized regional development agency in the country's west.[55] His consulting firm supported the Shah's White Revolution in Iran, plying the TVA model on the Dez River.[56] And in the 1960s, he was called in to advise aid programs on the Mekong as part of America's Vietnam War effort.[57] Mr. TVA, as the press dubbed him, became a ubiquitous cheerleader for large programs centered around massive technological investments. And the TVA itself became a model of regional uplift, admired by leaders who aspired to rapid modernization. While Danube Valley dreams of a regional TVA fell prey to Cold War divisions, the Damodar Valley Corporation completed four dams in northeast India between 1948 and 1959; the Kariba Lake Committee, founded in 1955 in the Central African Federation (today's Zambia and Zimbabwe), credited the TVA's example; and the Helmand Valley Authority reflected, according to British historian and Chatham House director Arnold Toynbee, "a piece of America inserted into the Afghan landscape."[58] If these were not TVA copycats—Klingensmith calls Damodar a simulacrum, reimagined for the Indian context—they were inspired by its model. Lilienthal had many cosponsors in this "concrete revolution." As the geographer Christopher Sneddon shows, dams created particularly thick alliances of political and technical experts who envisioned river basins as coherent development units. The U.S. Bureau of Reclamation, a leading agency for fluvial projects, supported missions to over 100 countries.[59] Similarly, the TVA model of a public authority comanaging environmental resources with private experts spawned nonriverine spinoffs, including the Cassa per il Mezzogiorno, founded in 1950 to lead the industrialization of southern Italy.[60]

Lilienthal was not alone in his gusto. From the late 1930s, numerous authors looked to "God's Valley" as a model of development and democracy.[61] In 1944, the same year as Lilienthal's encomium, the newly established International Labour Organization published Herman Finer's *The T.V.A.: Lessons for International Application.* A Romanian-born political scientist and LSE lecturer, Finer is perhaps best known for a 1932 textbook praising government involvement in the economy and a 1945 broadside against Friedrich Hayek's *The Road to Serfdom.*[62] Affiliated with the Fabian socialists, he devoted much of his wartime writing to the defense of planning and the welfare state. In *The T.V.A.*, he praised what he saw as the novel use of capital investment, broad-based education, and technical knowledge to foster increases in living standard. Undertaken at a time of economic distress, the TVA underwrote "an economic policy of hope and expansion in which the Government would play a dynamic part."[63] The resulting success, he believed, had great implications for postwar development, not least due to the "democratic collaboration" and "local self-reliance" that constituted the program's moving spirit. Finer acknowledged that transplanting the TVA to foreign watersheds, especially those spanning international borders, would prove difficult, but he believed that with planning, collaboration, and foreign assistance it could succeed.[64]

The TVA also won political plaudits. Franklin Roosevelt and U.S. vice president Henry Wallace touted the paradigmatic value of what historian Henry Steele Commager dubbed "the greatest peacetime achievement of twentieth-century America."[65] So did President Harry S. Truman.[66] Across the Atlantic, British colonial officials praised it as an instantiation of the planning needed to develop their own colonies.[67] And British biologist and eugenicist Julian Huxley, who in 1946 became UNESCO's first director-general, endorsed it as "the symbol of a new possibility for the democratic countries—the possibility of obtaining the efficiency of a co-ordinated plan without totalitarian regimentation."[68]

A final legacy merits notice: If the TVA elevated a fascination for large industrial works, it also intrigued communitarians. "The South and West of the United States were the first industrially undeveloped areas to interest Northern industrialists," wrote James Dahir in *Region Building*, his 1955 primer on TVA community development lessons. These areas therefore offered potent examples for other impoverished regions around the world. For Dahir, the TVA's appeal lay not so much in its industrial feats as in its production of "healthy, happy, and free people" in "good communities."[69] Indeed, if 'big' is the common presumption about TVA efforts, 'small' could also generate excitement. Communitarians like Dahir found much to admire in the decentralization, democracy, and activism that the TVA fostered. For them, the program's icon was not Lilienthal, but the Authority's first chairman, Arthur E. Morgan, an engineer and administrator who pioneered town and community operations. He championed cooperatives, local currencies, and citizen participation—all of which Lilienthal dismissed as "basket-weaving."[70] Morgan's followers carried his vision to programs around the planet, urging officials to "'keep pace with people's enthusiasm'" through small-scale interactions aimed at village uplift. Whether large or small, in other words, the TVA inspired practical, "planned," and "reasoned" enthusiasm as development's emotive propulsion.[71]

Shirt-Sleeve Diplomacy

If the Marshall Plan for Europe is America's most famous foreign aid initiative, Harry Truman's Point Four program, introduced in his January 1949 inaugural address, was its counterpart for the rest of the world.[72] It, too, inspired enthusiasm. Point Four took its name from the fourth item of the president's foreign policy agenda, which called for a "bold new program for making the benefits of our scientific advances and industrial progress available for the improvement and growth of underdeveloped areas." It targeted the "more than half" of the world's population "living in conditions approaching misery." Not only did their poverty "handicap" them; the political and economic instability it engendered was also a global threat. Contrasting his vision to "the old imperialism," Truman cast Point Four as a "program of development based on the concepts of democratic fair-dealing" and designed to stimulate "capital investment in areas needing development."[73]

Point Four was both bigger and smaller than the Marshall Plan. Its geographic reach was far larger—indeed, englobing—as was its aspiration. "For the first time in history," Truman intoned, "humanity possesses the knowledge and the skills to relieve the suffering of [hungry, diseased, and impoverished] people," as capacious an endeavor as one might concoct. Like the TVA, Point Four emphasized the deployment of expert advice, the use of public-private partnerships, and the mobilization of citizens. Truman himself invoked the "immense undeveloped rivers and valleys all over the world" that might become future TVAs.[74] Yet Point Four's shoestring budget meant that it could not be so grandiose, instead supporting smaller community activities reliant on private initiative. Point Four projects typically offered advice and training—what is known as 'technical assistance'—so that locals could manage their own development.[75] And the ERP's continental programming scale found no parallel in Point Four's early years, though pressure to do so existed.[76] Truman had to moderate his funding request to win bipartisan support, and even so the Act for International Development took seventeen months to pass through Congress. It became policy in June 1950—with a tight three-year budget of just over $300 million, pennies compared to ERP allotments.[77]

The congressional gridlock revealed in the act's delayed passage reflected competing political agendas. In 1946, the first postwar election gave aid-skeptical Republicans control of the House and Senate. While they lost their majorities two years later, a chastened Truman felt he had to accommodate their disinclination to foreign expenditure. Technical assistance became a useful, low-cost expedient. It was not new in the postwar era. During the interwar years, Roosevelt's Institute of Inter-American Affairs had run programs in Latin America using a *servicio* model in which U.S. experts partnered with national agencies to cultivate an "ethos of 'self-help.'"[78] The Marshall Plan, too, offered considerable advice and training as part of its European recovery effort.[79] But Point Four consolidated this approach, merging initiatives under a single administrator that had previously been scattered across multiple agencies.

Yet if the program's individual activities were characteristically small, they contained grand ambitions. Overseen by the Technical Cooperation Administration (TCA), Point Four managed projects in thirty-five countries. According to the historian Tarun Bose, within six months of program launch

> some 350 Point Four technicians started operating in different countries scattered from India to Paraguay, setting up farm extension services and model health centres, spraying swamps with D.D.T., mapping mineral deposits, and advising governments on scores of technical matters, from small irrigation projects and improved seed grains to child welfare programmes and sanitary sewage systems. By the beginning of 1952, there were 216 Point Four projects in operation in 34 countries in Asia, Africa and Latin America. The number of American experts, teachers and technicians working in those countries rose significantly from 619 in the beginning of 1952 to 2445 by the middle of 1953.[80]

Point Four's community initiatives, as Stephen Macekura points out, bound economic development to U.S. foreign policy objectives, including the advancement of trade, access to resources, and resistance against communism. While the 1952 election of the ex-general Dwight Eisenhower steered U.S. policy away from development and toward security, advocates of the "bold new program" continued to promote it. Eisenhower himself dropped the name 'Point Four' but folded some of its activities into other TCA mandates. Although publicly favoring military aid and enacting cuts to economic programs, he recognized as early as the mid-1950s that development assistance could be an effective tool of Cold War diplomacy.[81]

Public debate over Point Four was vigorous, with criticism ranging from outright denunciation to qualms over strategy and impact.[82] The right-wing journalist and Austrian School publicist Henry Hazlitt assailed Point Four as quasi-communist.[83] On the left, some feared the opposite, warning that it was "an attempt to maintain and extend wherever possible the economic and military domination of the colonial areas."[84] If so, the business community was not readily on board: Despite program inducements, companies hesitated to invest in the impoverished or unstable lands where Point Four operated.[85]

But many were enthusiastic. The reporter and *Reader's Digest* executive Willard Espy adopted Truman's self-congratulatory tag—the "bold new program"—as the title of a 1950 book that lauded Point Four's reliance on private investment, contrasting it to both the Marshall Plan's "government grants" and the TVA's "mammoth" infrastructural approach. Instead, "the awe-inspiring potentialities of the Bold New Program stem precisely from the fact that it may enlist for peace and world prosperity . . . one of the most dynamic forces in the world—the self-interest of the American businessman."[86] To meet this goal, Point Four offered guarantees to private investors and in doing so, Espy felt, turned away from the communism of a "slave Europe."[87] The program seemed to him a remarkable break from the past, "an act of faith in the world—and in ourselves" that served as a harbinger of success.[88]

If Espy celebrated American entrepreneurial initiative, the TCA administrator and future congressman Jonathan Bingham extolled the ingenuity of individual citizens who traveled overseas to assist poor communities. Heroic and romantic, Bingham's "shirt-sleeve diplomats" sought to help villagers solve their problems—in the process advancing "the foreign policy of the United States." Bingham praised Point Four as "something new under the sun," for "[n]ever before in the history of world had a government launched a large-scale effort to help peoples to whom it was bound by no special ties other than a common interest in the world's peace and prosperity." His intrepid ambassadors furthered "the distribution of knowledge," training locals rather than doing things for them—an "infinitely appealing" and even "revolutionary" prospect, for history had progressed to the point where there was finally "enough knowledge to do the job."[89]

Much of Bingham's paean was devoted to tales—what today would be called 'success stories'—of development projects in "mud villages" around the globe. Some of these are composite fictions, such as an account of the country of Deserta, "somewhere in the Middle East," where a Point Four worker demonstrates Bingham's ideal operating procedure: identifying community problems; teaching residents at the grassroots level; promoting cooperation; acting on request; and collaborating with the United Nations. From Deserta, Bingham moves to India and Point Four's "classic story" of the Etawah pilot project (discussed below), in which extensionists boosted agricultural production in a traditional Uttar Pradesh village, promoting innovations in crop rotation, fertilizer, and farming technique. After India, we visit *inter alia* a "modern Johnny Appleseed" in Liberia, a water program in Jordan, fisheries in Indonesia, and credit programs in Paraguay.[90] His takeaway from this *tour d'horizon* was that, in foreign relations as in individual psychology, a healthy enthusiasm fuels our ability "to build a better world, little by little," using available ingenuity and effort.[91] "Nothing is more thrilling about the results of successful self-help measures," Bingham brimmed, "than the pride of accomplishment it gives to those who have cooperated, and the sense of confidence that yet better things can be done."[92] His celebration of Point Four's practical emissaries reiterated the trope, found in Marshall Plan and TVA reports, of confronting social problems with technical know-how and a readiness to dirty one's hands. Yet Bingham also warned against the temptation to "do-goodism"—what he calls "natural humanitarianism"—the desire to do things for others rather than train them in self-help. This "over-enthusiasm" can lead to mistakes, such as establishing institutions or introducing technology too advanced for a community—or, at a policy level, dumping U.S. dollars in foreign economies (he preferred local currencies) in the hope of a quick economic boost. All these bespoke an "arrogant" assumption that the American way of life was the only way. Bingham instead urged intercultural respect.[93]

As Lilienthal, Dahir, and Bingham illustrate, America's development mission conjured a new kind of enthusiast—a zealot for the practical, a believer in the ability of wit and grit to overcome poverty. Enthusiasm animated a moral and political commitment to global betterment, a mission that presumed not only willpower and technology, but also freedom from, as María Josefina Saldaña-Portillo puts it, "material and historical constraint."[94] These aspirations are not to be taken for granted. For much of history, people learned to live within natural and social barriers. The interventionist call for a kind of historical transcendence, encouraging societies to push through traditional barriers and embrace the struggle for self-overcoming, had a brash (if also cavalier) appeal. That early development practice coalesced around this forward-facing mindset—rejecting the past in favor of modern world-building—set it up for both potent achievement and regular disappointment.

"Partnership with a Lion":[95] Lewis, Nkrumah, and the Attraction of Large Dams

The TVA's technological gigantism, as we noted, mesmerized policymakers far beyond American shores. Enthusiasm for industrialization reached even greater heights when it joined with nationalist fervor in decolonizing lands. "Freedom time," after all, was never simply about achieving political independence.[96] Across Africa and Asia, it brought dreams of economic development as well, without which political sovereignty would prove impotent. While many economists were hired to advise new governments and multilateral organizations, few were more personally invested in the cause of decolonization than Arthur Lewis, whose "Unlimited Supplies" thesis we examined in Chapter 2. Lewis's globetrotting was driven not just by a desire to promote economic growth but by the thrill of supporting African and Asian independence, a movement of no small importance to an Afro-Caribbean scion of empire. Yet in his advisory role, he fell prey to his own caricature as an industrialization guru, a fate most evident in his work in Ghana.

In the late 1940s, the Gold Coast was a promising aspirant to independence, with an economy buoyed by cocoa profits, a restive population whose 1948 riot revealed impatience for self-government, and a charismatic leader, Kwame Nkrumah, who had met Lewis at the Fabian Colonial Bureau in London. In 1951 elections, Nkrumah's Convention People's Party (CPP) won a majority of Legislative Assembly seats open to African candidates, forcing the British to deal with a rabble-rousing nationalist who had spent time in colonial prison. A year later, Lewis was invited to draft an industrialization program for the colony. By then, his ideas were already drawing attention in the Caribbean, where Eric Williams, leader of Trinidad's People's National Movement, would soon incorporate the Puerto Rico model into his own plans.[97] On the strength of this work—and before the appearance of his 1954 "Unlimited Supplies" article—Lewis the industrializer was sought out by Nkrumah to advise on economic policy.

What Lewis's 1953 "Report on Industrialisation and the Gold Coast" recommended, however, was deflating for a headstrong nationalist.[98] Lewis did not view the Gold Coast as a promising candidate for rapid industrialization because it did not have labor surpluses to shift away from agriculture. Instead, the colony needed to privilege small-scale industries in primary export sectors such as cocoa, bauxite, and timber. An even greater need was agricultural improvement, especially food production, and Lewis advised directing resources toward research, education, and extension work. In the end, he urged a balanced agro-industrial portfolio, financed by a mix of domestic and international private-sector investment. Unsurprisingly, the reception of this advice among CPP stalwarts was "lukewarm."[99]

Lewis's wariness about Gold Coast industrialization did not (yet) tarnish his image with Nkrumah. In 1957, after an abortive effort to entice the economics professor to the University of Ghana, Nkrumah succeeded in bringing him to Accra as a UN-appointed economic advisor, a key voice in shaping the economic future of a new country dependent on its volatile cocoa proceeds.[100] Lewis's fifteen-month residency (October 1957–December 1958) required him to tack between the CPP's left and right wings; between the loosening ties of empire and the vital economic linkages it afforded; and, most tempestuously, between Nkrumah's ambitions and the requirements of sound economic policy. His tasks were myriad. At the start, Lewis worked to reinvest Ghana's financial reserves, held in once solid but now declining British securities that did not serve the country's liquidity needs. He also contributed to the 1958–59 budget, encouraging tax incentives to attract foreign investment. And, most personally significant, he helped to shape Ghana's Second Five Year Plan (1959–63), an effort dominated by his struggles to tame the fiscal ambition of Nkrumah and his ministers.

Lewis was not the first high-profile economic advisor to head to the Gold Coast. In 1952, as part of the colony's First Development Plan, the economist Dudley Seers, whose 1970s reformist thinking we will consider in Chapter 6, submitted an influential proposal to the Colonial Office. The Seers and Ross Report advised the monopsony state-run Cocoa Marketing Board to fix low product prices and then use the savings to build a development investment fund—effectively a tax on farmers that Nkrumah would later repurpose to generate monies for industry. At the time, the coauthors did not foresee immanent industrialization for the colony—they suggested small-scale import substitution and food-processing manufactures—but they did abide by standard growth models suggesting the necessity of savings to boost capitalization. Seers would later come to doubt these recommendations.[101]

Lewis agreed with Seers's restraint, but he favored private over state investment. The so-called Lewis Plan (he was only one of the Second Five Year Plan's authors) called for modest industrialization based on import substitution, substantial investment in infrastructure and services, and—surprisingly—very little support for agriculture. The direct production of goods, including agriculture, netted a mere 20 percent of the funding allocation.[102] The plan's centerpiece was an effort to attract private capital from abroad to finance development—a modified version of the Puerto Rican–inspired 'industrialization-by-invitation' model that Lewis was plying in the Caribbean. Though his proposal was criticized as overly cautious, even a continuation of colonial policies, it was implemented. But competing ambitions had already planted the seeds for its demise: a summer 1958 dispute with Nkrumah over the allocation of government expenses, followed by Nkrumah's refusal to grant Lewis greater influence, led to the economist's departure in December.[103] The plan was terminated in 1961. As Tony Killick points out, Lewis's stint illustrates the naiveté of assuming that economic planning can trump political imperatives.[104]

What were these imperatives? A chief bone of contention for Lewis was the Volta River Project (VRP), a centerpiece of Nkrumah's vision for the country. The VRP was in many ways a perfect emblem of big-push modernization: a TVA-style dam and regional makeover that would launch Ghana into the industrial age, supplying electricity for consumers and for an aluminum smelter to process local bauxite ore. Convinced that industry was the pathway to development, Nkrumah embraced a project that had begun, ironically enough, as a colonial effort to convert Gold Coast bauxite into low-cost aluminum for imperial use. Yet the Ghanaian leader saw it in terms of his own push for African economic sufficiency. "One thing is certain," he wrote in 1963's *Africa Must Unite,*

> unless we plan to lift Africa up out of her poverty, she will remain poor. For there is a vicious circle that keeps the poor in their rut of impoverishment, unless an energetic effort is made to interrupt the circular causation of poverty. Once this has been done, and the essential industrial machine has been set in motion, there is a snowballing effect which increases the momentum of change.[105]

Newer nations, he informed the National Assembly in 1961, must select a "large-scale industrial advance"; and since "[e]lectricity is the basis for industrialization," it provides a "justification for the Volta River Project." The VRP would enable Nkrumah to rear a modern state. Accordingly, it became his "baby," and an extensive public relations campaign cast it as the "dearest dream of Osagyefo" (Nkrumah's local honorific), bound up with independence and strength.[106]

Although the idea of constructing a dam at Akosombo on the Volta River was initially mooted in 1915, with planning intensified after World War II, negotiations stalled prior to Ghana's independence as Britain withdrew in the face of spiraling costs. In early 1957, Lewis himself urged CPP leaders to take the project out of "cold storage," and through the intervention of the Eisenhower administration, Nkrumah enlisted the American Henry J. Kaiser Company to update the engineering reports.[107] Yet even as the project raced ahead, Lewis came to regret his support, fearing that the VRP would suck resources from a more balanced agenda. "I considered the development of the country to be more important than the Volta River Project," he wrote in a private letter of February 1958, "which I consider to be of only marginal significance." Lewis was further disturbed by what he saw as the tendency for political demands to override economic wisdom. "It would be madness for us to use up all our resources in building this dam, and have to abandon all other development schemes," he told Nkrumah in December. "The benefits which this dam will bring are not great enough to justify such a sacrifice. We would be ruined financially, and become a laughing stock in the world's money markets, and such an example of financial mismanagement, that we would be unable to borrow for other purposes."[108] He advised building the dam only if investors covered most of the bill. Nkrumah ignored his plea.

Months after his departure from Accra, Lewis ventilated his grievances in an article questioning the ability of leaders in underdeveloped countries to manage development programs.

> The larger the program the less preparation is given to each project and the greater is the number of incompetent people appointed to public service. Programs fall into arrears, are overcostly and are badly executed. . . . The difficulty arises not in matching public supply to the needs of private commerce, but in deciding how much service to provide for domestic consumers, how high a priority should one accord to order supplies in the village, to rural electrification, to providing good road services even where road traffic is small, to hospital and medical services, to broadcast rediffusion, to decent prisons and to other consumer facilities.

These are "matters for political decision," but planners sometimes make unwise choices, favoring prestige projects that drain the treasury. Nkrumah was clearly the unnamed referent. "Perhaps someone is bitten with the bug of electricity, and puts in twice as much as is needed"; perhaps they are "hypnotized by the magic of large numbers." In the end, plans hashed out in the capital often ignored rural needs, even if "grassroots" participation offered a bit of compensatory insight.[109] In 1965, Lewis went further in a broadside against West Africa's one-party systems. "The single-party," he complained, drawing on a 1962 tour of Senegal, Nigeria, and Ivory Coast but recalling Nkrumah's "adolescent attitude to politics," could not "represent all the people; or maintain free discussion; or give stable government; or, above all, reconcile the differences between various regional groups." Partly a product of the "hysteria" of independence, when some men found it possible to seize the state and suppress their opponents," overpoliticization was a "sickness" from which, he hoped, West Africa would soon recover.[110]

Lewis's experience underscores the fiction that economic management can be sequestered from politics, surely one of the great illusions of twentieth-century development. His travails in Ghana—where his own reputation as an industrializer joined with Nkrumah's enthusiasm for modernization—illustrate how readily development proposals can harden into mantras that trap even their authors. In the same essay in which he warned of Third World administrative incompetence, Lewis attacked the template thinking to which his own writings contributed. Economics had few criteria for determining "whether a plan is good or not," he wrote; one decides "in light of common sense and experience, and not by applying any tests which economic science has devised."[111] This statement must have engendered some surprise among readers who knew Lewis as a leading purveyor of economic science. To be sure, he did not contend that planning was feckless. The planner, in his view, was something like "a doctor who is called upon to make a general medical examination. He has a list of things to look for, which experience suggests as the most vulnerable points." But the diagnostics change with time, and economists have to adjust. If templates offered managerial benefits, they also, he cautioned, blinded us to social and political realities.

While Lewis sorted through his West African sojourn, Nkrumah proceeded with his dam.[112] As opposed to other large barricades such as the Aswan, Sennar, Owens Falls, and Kariba, the Volta Dam, though conceived in colonial times, was built in an independent African state—indeed, as a symbol *for* independent Africa.[113] Groundbreaking coincided with Nkrumah's shift to a more aggressive, state-led industrialization program enshrined in the Seven Year Development Plan (1963/64–1969/70) championed by his advisor J. H. Mensah and the Hungarian economist Jószef Bognár.[114] Although socialist in leaning, it retained the VRP and its capitalist investors as an expensive set-aside. After a year and much negotiation, Nkrumah sewed up a deal with the Kaiser Corporation, which became the lead investor in the new Volta Aluminium Company (VALCO) consortium.[115] But as one analyst foresaw, "Ghana needs capital more than capital needs Ghana," and the terms were unfavorable, shifting risks to the government and ceding tax breaks that lasted for decades, including electricity purchased at cost and the tax-free export of aluminum.[116] Funding for other parts of the project—electricity plants, resettlement—was also passed to Accra.[117] In 1961, the new U.S. president, concerned to support modernization in a decolonizing Africa and prevent Nkrumah from turning to the Soviets, agreed to provide $133 million in loans.[118] Nonetheless, Ghana footed a bill of Ł70.5 million for the project, most of it financed through multilateral and bilateral institutions, especially a large loan from the World Bank.[119] In addition, Nkrumah relinquished demands that investors fund the development of Ghana's bauxite mines, abandoning hopes of an integrated domestic aluminum industry. These were striking concessions from a leader who, within four years, would describe multilateral aid as a "neo-colonialist trap."[120]

The Volta Dam has had a mixed developmental legacy. For the two decades following its 1965 completion, it supplied electricity to the smelter and to some Ghanaian and West African customers. To accommodate demand, capacity was expanded in the early 1980s by an adjacent dam at Kpong. Yet the massive hydroelectric works did not translate into overall national economic advancement (a tall order but certainly one of Nkrumah's goals), nor did it dramatically boost consumer electric supply.[121] In the 1960s and 1970s, Ghana's economy lagged behind those of other low-income countries, notably in areas such as capital formation and industrialization that the VRP might have been expected to support. The VALCO Agreement, whose benefits accrued disproportionately to Kaiser, sparked occasional protests that eventually prompted renegotiation in the 1980s.[122] Yet in the same years, irregular rainfall produced droughts and power cuts.[123] As a result, electricity surpluses shared with Togo, Benin, and Côte d'Ivoire in the early 1970s gave way to shortages in later decades, with Accra ultimately importing current from Abidjan.[124] Reliance on hydropower, in sum, made Ghana vulnerable to climate change.

Since the 1980s, studies have highlighted the dam's social effects, reinforcing complaints that the hydroelectric industry underestimated the negative consequences of its infrastructure.[125] "Massive technological development hurts," wrote the American anthropologist Elizabeth Colson in 1971, and social disruption is "largely ignored by economic planners, technicians and political leaders."[126] The resettlement experience in Ghana bore out this verdict. Despite earlier national examples to draw from, the size of the Volta resettlement was unprecedented: 80,000 people from 739 inundated villages were moved to 52 newly constructed homesites. The numbers alone suggest the challenges: communities of varied ethnicity, lifestyle, and tribal structure were relocated to modern towns, with compensation paid for lost homes and ancestral lands. Despite intensive planning and consultation, migrants arrived to find insufficient single-room houses for multigeneration families, inadequate land to support farming needs, competition with fellow settlers and prior residents, and paltry legal protection, including a lack of home and land titles. The result was steady out-migration.[127] Within the first year, more than half of new residents moved away.[128] Of course, the unanticipated results of the dam could be positive as well: While the downstream clam and fishing industry suffered, lakeside fisheries increased their yields, with some upstream migrants taking advantage of new harvesting opportunities. But these gains were not enough to compensate for the region's depletion.[129]

The VRP was part of a surge in large dam-building inspired in great part by the TVA—the "granddaddy of all regional development projects," to use James Scott's label.[130] During the midcentury, big dams became almost "synonymous with development and economic progress," supplying electricity as an industrial lifeblood. Their benefits were taken for granted, their costs tallied only financially—with social and environmental degradation largely ignored. Globally, dam-building "peaked in the 1970s," which saw "on average two to three large dams" commissioned every day, totaling 45,000 by the century's end—before pressure from environmental and rights organizations precipitated a decline in the 1980s.[131] While the 2000 World Commission on Dams Report identified dam contributions to development, it also highlighted the failure to meet water and energy targets; the inequitable apportionment of costs, with those displaced regularly missing out on benefits; and the damaging effects on wider riparian and regional environments.[132] If Lewis warned of the financial toll of unchecked technological enthusiasm, two generations later we have come to recognize its threat to natural and human ecologies as well.

Awakening the Village: Community Development in India

While there was plenty of enthusiasm for big thinking among postwar development planners, Daniel Immerwahr has reminded us of the prevalence of 'thinking small' as well. And if there is any place where the search for historical and contextual attunement might be expected in early development practice, it is in the wide-ranging community development efforts launched under Point Four in the 1950s. Yet even communitarians, as we will see, cultivated dam-sized ambitions for the grassroots level.[133]

The intellectual lodestar of American community development was the University of Chicago anthropologist Robert Redfield. A complex figure whose postwar oeuvre diverged sharply from his interwar thinking, Redfield became famous for an influential 1930 study of the village of Tepoztlán, which bordered a booming Mexico City.[134] In it, he scripted a romantic account of Mexican folk tradition threatened by metropolitan economic and cultural traffic, its primary focus the change wrought by modernization (a term the book helped to popularize) and the fear that, as his admirer Stuart Chase put it, "something precious" was vanishing, a "way of life" that the "western world" could not "regain."[135] Redfield described Tepoztlán as an "intermediate community" caught "between the primitive tribe and the modern city."[136] Unlike later modernizers, who saw tradition as an impediment to development, Redfield feared the extinction of lifeways and the disorientation of modern anomie. Indeed, his primary frontier did not divide town from metropolis; it split Tepoztlán from within, pitting "*los correctos,*" who admired city ways and traveled to and fro with ease, against "*los tontos,*" who held to their mores and ignored metropolitan temptations. The central Tepoztlán plaza became the radiating point of an expanding modernity, the locus of tradespeople "familiar with city ways."[137] The *barrios* on the town periphery, by contrast, insulated *los tontos,* though they engaged in regular market interaction with *los correctos,* leading to uncertainty and defensive pride.

Redfield craved a form of modernization that accommodated local tradition. In 1939 he articulated his quest as a search for "culture contact without conflict." This irenic social change required a specific type of culture, one that he found among Europeanized *ladinos* and Mayan Indians in the Lake Atítlan region of Guatemala (the site of Sol Tax's Panajachel discussed in Chapter 2). Their peaceful interactions, he believed, came about because of deep similarities between the more and the less modern groups, a result of centuries of exchange among "individualistic, commercial and moderately secular" lakeside communities.[138] This shared history prepared them to accept the considerable differences that remained, enabling a slow, gradual acculturation to modernity that preserved tradition rather than upending it. The need for prerequisite cultural traits, of course, limited the number of communities that could hope to pursue this benign modernization. And given the stormy decades in Guatemala that followed Redfield's pronouncement (see Chapter 5), one cannot help but wonder if he missed something vital.

Despite his concern for the historical changes wrought by modernization, however, Redfield also partook in modern anthropology's *a*historical tendencies. As enshrined most famously in Bronislaw Malinowski's classic account of the Trobriand Islanders, *Argonauts of the Western Pacific* (1922), the 'ethnographic present' that characterizes many anthropological classics suspends 'primitive' or 'traditional' societies in a largely timeless amber, the present tense of romanticized cultural purity, typically just before the onset of modernity.[139] Historical change—the shift to modernity—forms the interstice between two blocks: a largely homogeneous tradition and a relatively stable contemporaneity. This presentism was deliberate, adopted as a rejection of nineteenth-century evolutionary histories whose assumptions undergirded imperial rule. It also grounded a scientific anthropology in observable ethnographic data gathered in living communities. If some anthropologists banished history to terse references beyond the main ethnographic account, others, including Redfield, situated ethnography within a particular moment of historical change, even while maintaining a largely immobile conception of prior tradition. His early accounts of Central America make this clear. As anthropologist George Marcus points out, Redfield hoped to recover "authentic cultural remnants of some past purer period of cultural existence now decayed through contact with the West," a "static framing" for a superficial "temporal setting."[140] History irrupted at the juncture where tradition met modernity, but it was not wholly constitutive of either—a bracketing soon adopted by modernizers.

Redfield's ideas steered aid planners away from large industrial works and toward small communities. After the war, he turned his attentions to India, conducting a long-term investigation of the subcontinent's high and folk cultures, what he called its "great" and "little" traditions.[141] As opposed to Central America, where European conquest had largely suppressed traditional cultures, India, he wrote appreciatively, had kept its heritage intact. Thus it became a primary site for studying how cultures might modernize without Westernizing. Yet what Redfield understood as India's defining heritage was in fact just one of many bequests: high-caste Hindu Brahmanism, conveyed through the work of his interlocutor, the anthropologist M. N. Srinivas.[142] Based on fieldwork in the state of Mysore (now Karnataka), Srinivas argued that Indian villages were "little republics" characterized by relative "isolation and stability."[143] Against those who reported rural factionalization and caste hierarchy, Srinivas found "vertical unity" based on cross-caste complementarities, a graded harmony imperiled by modern social and economic forces.[144] This unity, he argued, arose through a process called "Sanscritization," whereby high-caste Sanskrit or Brahmanic traditions gradually absorbed lower-caste customs.[145] As Nicole Sackley notes, Redfield, following Srinivas, saw elites as keepers of this cohesive "great tradition," cultural stewards who tailored Indian life to modern changes while preserving its cultural core. Though Redfield had warned of losses in modernizing Tepoztlán, India safeguarded tradition by placing its management firmly in the hands of elites.[146]

Redfield was among many Americans academics and policymakers who saw India as the emblematic developing country, a land of villages in a decolonizing Third World populated by peasants. Although curiosity about Indian rurality dates back to colonial times, many analysts place the start of local community development in the district of Etawah, Uttar Pradesh, where in 1948 the urban designer Albert Mayer set up a sixty-four-village showcase project, supported by Point Four, that established a prototype—supplying seeds and training to increase crop yield, running inoculation and hygiene campaigns, strengthening schools and adult education, promoting local leadership through rejuvenated *panchayats* (or village councils), and encouraging "folk" development strategies. The goal was to "awaken" village India to its own needs and potential.[147] Mayer envisioned his program in explicit contradistinction to the "hydroelectric development" of the day. Based on sociological and anthropological studies, he incorporated staff positions such as the 'Rural Life Analyst,' who would investigate social structure and liaise with local activists.[148] Though not a direct influence, Redfield's interest in 'subjective' traits and 'the way a people feel' found an analogue in Mayer's quest for the "felt needs" of Indian villagers as revealed (if not always articulated) by villagers themselves.[149] "What we attempted at Etawah," he wrote, "was to understand the local culture fully, and employ it positively; to involve the villager not just on the mental plane and for economic reasons, but on the emotional plane as well"—an "inner administrative democratization" aimed at "reenergizing tradition," revitalizing institutions, brokering development.

Practically, this strategy required project workers to listen and observe, then stimulate activity and cultivate local leaders.[150] Citing the American funding that helped the project grow to 300 villages by the 1952, Bingham called it "Point 4's classic story."[151]

Etawah's joining of the old and new informed subsequent Indian community development. Its village-level workers—or *gram sevaks*—became fixtures of the official Indian plan.[152] So too did the organizational subdivision into blocks, subblocks, and districts for administrative purposes; and the commitment to strengthen (and at times reconstitute) village *panchayats,* making them hubs of community activity.[153] The Etawah model, in sum, was widely replicated, and the Ford Foundation, under its first president and former Marshall Plan administrator, Paul Hoffman, saw it as a key to overcoming the subcontinent's "poverty, disease, and illiteracy."[154] So did Jawaharlal Nehru, soon to be prime minister, who wrote to Mayer in 1946, on the eve of independence, that "[w]e want to raise living standards and . . . build up community life on a higher scale without breaking up the old foundations. We want to utilize modern technique and fit it into Indian resources and Indian conditions."[155] Yet this merger was tense. While agricultural improvement was only one facet of Mayer's vision, it was central to Indian officials, who saw wartime declines in food production (not to mention the disastrous 1943 Bengal famine) as a dangerous omen. This preoccupation set up a persistent contest between increased productivity and respect for local tradition.

Then there was the problem of village inequality. Mayer acknowledged that project designers "gravitate toward the wealthier, more adventurous people who can afford to take the chances involved" in battling routine and complacency. The program needed "natural leaders" who could stoke village confidence. This ability, he hastened to add, did not necessarily coincide with high-caste membership, which might reproduce traditional conservatism. Leaders need not be Brahmins. Furthermore, Mayer expected a leader to invite "the experience and advice of all those below him," so that the "lowest worker" feels free to share opinions "frankly and without fear."[156] But there is something tragic about his inability to imagine how his leadership preoccupation might hobble the village democracy he desired. Mayer wrote regularly about his hope that community elites and poor villagers would converse freely, "releas[ing] energies" of high and low alike.[157] Yet events suggested otherwise: Projects and meetings remained captive to preexisting hierarchies, which they even served to fortify. By the early 1950s, Mayer expressed frustration at what he perceived as a "slackness" in "village enthusiasm." He attributed it to incomplete democratization, and his pages filled with plans for generating new excitement, outlining everything from novel personnel qualifications to trial meeting formats to foreign consultancies.[158]

Etawah was only one source of Indian community development. The subcontinent was the first port of call for development cooperatives when the turn-of-the-century Raj introduced rural credit unions.[159] Under colonialism, several Indian states experimented with the use of community institutions, including *panchayats.* And as an administrator in Gurgaon district, Lord Lugard's nephew, Frank Lugard Brayne, devised a scheme for peasant uplift that he chronicled in several books.[160] American missionaries and philanthropic foundations also promoted rural development, setting up agricultural research centers, experimental villages, and assistance projects.[161] Village uplift was also crucial for those resisting British rule. Gandhi's call for independence began from the bottom—in 700,000 villages; he embraced cooperativism as a strategy for strengthening rural economies without eroding local culture. Similarly well known are Bengali poet and polymath Rabindranath Tagore's earlier experiments in rural reform at Santiniketan. More immediately, Surendra Kumar Dey, an advisor to the Ministry of Rehabilitation in the aftermath of India's bloody partition, worked on the Mazdoor Manzil scheme to settle and rehabilitate citizens driven from their homes in Pakistan, sometimes on land evacuated by Muslims. In the towns of Kurukshetra, Faridabad, and Nilokheri, he helped to launch development and extension projects for refugees using novel community development techniques.[162]

In 1952, these disparate threads came together in the vast Indian Community Development Programme (CDP), headed by Dey and funded in part through a $54 million Point Four package as well as large outlays from the Ford Foundation, whose India representative, the sociologist Douglas Ensminger, became a proponent.[163] Despite foreign monies, program advocates touted the local credentials of Indian community development. The objective, according Dey, who in 1957 became India's first minister of community development, was to awaken "slumbering" villages by breaking from a top-down "legacy inherited from the past."[164] The program's five-year pilot phase was already massive: 16,500 villages. By 1961, at the end of the Second Five Year Plan (commonly associated with the statistician Prasanta Mahalanobis's industrialization push), the CDP covered 70 percent of rural areas; by 1964, it reached the whole country. A program population of almost 17 million in 1952 leapt to over 253 million a decade later.[165] If this expansion was mind-boggling, so too was the range of activities. Anthropologist Shyama Charan Dube listed interventions in agriculture, husbandry, electrification, transportation, education, health care, housing, social welfare, and supplementary employment—nothing short of a complete makeover of rural India.[166] And the program was larger still. Complementing the government-sponsored *panchayats* was the private Sahakari Samaj, or cooperative movement, which provided credit, markets, stores, and other services, with local cooperatives as "the mother economic institution in the village."[167]

The program entailed numerous paradoxes. Even as it claimed to tap age-old communal impulses, developers acknowledged the need to modernize on a vast scale. Even as they hoped to cultivate village self-reliance, officials stressed the importance of government planning, initiative, and oversight. And as the range of tasks indicates, the tension between agricultural production and community development never dissipated.[168] These incongruities had practical effects: The Five Year Plans to which community development was bound employed targets and quotas that overrode communal priorities, but they were managerial tools that Brahmadeva Mukerji, a long-time administrator, defended on grounds of national interest and praised as instruments for channeling local ambition.[169] Unsurprisingly, coordination breakdowns multiplied.[170]

The first obvious indication of shortfall came via a 1957 evaluation led by Gujarati chief minister Balwantrai Mehta. Particularly concerning was the program's lack of community participation. Efforts to cultivate village involvement had not worked, and few local bodies showed "enthusiasm or interest . . . even the panchayats have not come into the field to any appreciable extent."[171] Evaluators saw two main reasons. First, the program, although conceived in apolitical and technocratic terms, had inflamed local factions, splitting communities along class and caste lines as groups sought to capture the institutions of local power. Second, as conflicts grew, many villagers simply withdrew out of apathy or disappointment, sensing that a program justified as democratization would instead entrench hierarchy. The imperative, according to the Mehta report, was to find a way to "evoke local interest and excite local initiative." To do so, programmers needed to address two misconceptions. First, community development was a long-term process requiring a lengthy commitment of resources—not, as officials had hoped, a brisk awakening to self-reliance. Second, administrators initially understood participation as popular contribution in kind to program activities; increasingly, however, it was imperative to incorporate villagers in determining objectives and priorities as well.[172] Accordingly, evaluators recommended much greater delegation of power and resources. "Community development can be real only when the community understands its problems, realizes its responsibilities, exercises the necessary powers through its chosen representatives and maintains a constant and intelligent vigilance on local administration."[173] They also encouraged set-asides for women and underrepresented castes, along with the promotion of local organizations such as cooperatives.

In response to the Mehta report, the CDP embraced 'democratic decentralization' through a policy known as the *panchayati raj*, rule of the village councils, whose desultory existence for centuries was now formalized as a central plank of Congress Party rule. For Dey, the expansion and institutionalization of the councils corrected the program's top-heavy bureaucracy and facilitated a shift from public management to democratic leadership.[174] In subsequent years, decentralization was expanded to include not simply "vertical devolution" to *panchayats*, which could increase local hierarchy, but also "horizontal dispersal" to authorities and subauthorities in NGOs and citizen groups.[175] These moves had some positive returns. "It is perhaps not entirely a matter of coincidence that the three best projects in the evaluation centres happen to be those where the project officers have made the largest use of the panchayat and the co-operative in the implementation of their development programmes," wrote new evaluators in 1959. "Organised and institutional participation by the public in development programmes is bound to give better, more consistent, and more lasting results."[176]

Yet the CDP continued to struggle in attracting participation. In journeys chronicled in her beautiful travelogue *Blossoms in the Dust,* the reporter Kusum Nair found disheartening conditions across rural India; although she witnessed some blossoms—successful activities that gave villagers hope—for the most part the program had left dust. In eastern Bihar state, for example, while peasants built infrastructure through voluntary labor, they wondered who would repair and maintain it. In another village, locals had helped to erect a community center, but were unsure why it was constructed. And in a third, the inaugural *panchayat* meeting drew only fifteen of 4,000 residents.[177] The numbers were similarly dispiriting elsewhere. Such profound ambivalence regarding India's modernization suggested to Nair that development planners had little understanding of the villages they served; the program lacked local roots. Predictably, Dey had a different take: He blamed shortcomings on overstretched official capacity and popular dependence on public assistance. Rural passivity, not planning inadequacy, explained program disappointments.[178] Yet official expectations for social change, it must be noted, were excessive even in community development terms. Changing mindsets, as Ensminger cautioned in the program's early years, is a very long process—three generations by his accounting, when the grandchildren of today's thirty-year-olds come of age.[179] Impatience was easy in the CDP's heady youth.

Part of the challenge was elite capture. Local planning was typically monopolized by those with local power.[180] Villagers often knew little about activities proposed in their name, and contributions of time and labor were consequently hard to muster (unless they were imposed). Another difficulty was conceptual. As far back as Mayer, community development emphasized the felt needs of villagers, discernible to those with proper training even if rarely articulated. Mukerji described the problem as follows:

> [O]ur villagers feel their wants usually in a general and not a specific way, e.g. they want more production from their lands, better animals, better health but are not able to relate these to wanting better seeds, fertilizers, better breeds of cattle and better feed for them, or safe drinking water and latrines. Their general wants have to be converted into such specific wants.[181]

Activities designed to meet these "specific wants" might in turn induce other needs about which villagers were unaware. But 'felt needs' are not static; nor can accurate translation be assumed. In practice, discerning needs entailed a hermeneutic problem: they could be expressed obliquely, gleaned through observation, or revealed in program activities, but they were rarely stated outright. Instead, they had to be interpreted by the village worker and conveyed back to the peasants themselves in lucid terms. It was easy, as Mukerji's quotation suggests, to impose official desires in the name of articulating peasant wants.

These tensions were felt keenly by the program's village-level workers, the most crucial nodes linking the national with the local. Recruited as "generalists" for "multipurpose" local tasks, *gram sevaks* nonetheless had to master relevant specializations, a high bar for the high school graduates recruited to fill the position. In practice, this typically meant expertise in agriculture, often learned on the fly. Despite the many sectors of program operation, a ten-day record of worker activities in Rajput village revealed an overwhelming, if not exclusive, focus on farming.[182] Furthermore, the *gram sevak*'s portfolio, which comprised thousands of villagers, meant that he was an outsider to most, and thus someone whose trust could not be assumed. Practically, the scope of activities necessitated a heavy reliance on local interlocutors—typically, village leaders—to channel desires from below. In a vast rurality riven by factions and ranks, this meant that *gram sevaks* could easily succumb to elite pressure, losing the confidence of a significant "fraction of the village population." Furthermore, village workers often felt subordinate to state or national officials, unable to venture ideas or contribute to plans, despite their mandate to do so. Instead, they understood their task as carrying out orders from above. "[T]he ideal would be for the VLW [village level worker] to discover local felt needs and for the Project to formulate plans accordingly," acknowledged Dube in 1958. "Yet out of concession to the realities of the day"—namely, the need for agricultural production—"it is felt necessary for the VLWs to achieve targets fixed from above."[183] As a result, villagers were unsure if the *gram sevak* was a local ally, a government functionary, or an appendage of the elite. The VLW himself was often similarly torn.

Particularly revealing of the tension between democratic rhetoric and top-down direction is the government-issued *Guide to Community Development*, written in 1957 by Douglas Ensminger and revised in 1962.[184] It lays out a detailed village improvement scheme, emphasizing both peasant aspirations and modern values. Program staff had to focus on "understanding the minds of the villagers," gleaning the ways they "think and feel about forces of change." Knowing past experience helped in this regard, as staff could recognize what communities had tried before. But the program also had to create "new values, new desires for improvement, new ways of living, and improved and new ways of making a living."[185] Sometimes the villagers were oblivious to these needs, and their awareness had to be stimulated from without. For this reason, extension—by which Ensminger meant the education of villagers—was a task of the first order. Its "purpose is to change attitudes and practices of the people with whom the work is done," making them more self-reliant, more responsive, more participatory.[186] Lest the need for change be doubted, the primer stressed the "deplorable living conditions" in India's countryside, the "cow-dung psychology" that induced residents to crowd together in "dirty villages" with little ambition or impetus.[187] And should anyone wonder whence reform ideas came, Ensminger himself listed improvements and "action steps" for village training—from agriculture and employment to schooling, health, cleanliness, and family planning.[188] To be sure, he wrote, though the "stimulus for change may be externally applied," the energy and "desire" came from "the minds of the people."[189] Yet he made clear—the language of felt needs notwithstanding—that community development was planned and prompted to a great degree from the outside. Coupling elite condescension with concern for village democracy, Ensminger insisted that it was essential to "create dissatisfaction with the way people currently live" before motivating them toward new things.[190]

By the early 1960s, another threat to community development loomed. Amid an industrial push, the Indian government was shifting its priorities from small to large, from community development to the as-yet-unnamed Green Revolution, with its promise of bountiful harvests generated by scientific advances. Motivating the shift was a crop shortfall of 1957–58, a drop of nearly 10 percent due to poor monsoons. Although India's grain yield had increased steadily up to that point, the dip caused alarm in New Delhi and abroad. When the 1961 census confirmed what policymakers already suspected—a meager 2 percent growth rate, with the population swelling from 361 million to 439 million in ten years—officials feared a Malthusian nightmare.[191] According to a 1959 Ford Foundation report, the country faced "the stark threat of a 28-million-ton shortfall in food-grain supplies by the end of the Third Five Year Plan (1966), unless rates of increase in food production are immediately accelerated to three times their present speed." Since community development stood at the forefront of grain production, it was subject to "emergency measures." Accordingly,

> Community Development and all technical agencies must be geared to mobilization and strengthening of village leaders and organizations, and effective channeling to village people of all information and help necessary to increase food output. The [Ford Foundation] team believes, therefore, that *all*

> *Ministries concerned with any aspect or programme relevant to food production must give top priority to food production now and for the period of the Third Plan.*[192]

By the time of the Integrated Agricultural Development Programme, launched in 1960, community development had narrowed its focus to agricultural yields, eclipsing earlier goals of democracy and social welfare. According to the activist and cooperative leader L. C. Jain, this shift enforced a top-down, "colonial pattern" of village administration.[193] As we have seen, community development's "agricultural bias" was there from the start. Easy to measure and essential for survival, food production supplied success stories from Etawah onward, and it invariably topped the list of CDP goals. In practice, however, productionist goals warred with aspirations to enhance democracy and transform village life. By the mid-1960s, the former won out. As if in acknowledgment, the name 'community development' was dropped in 1971 in favor of 'rural development.'

Tragically, the undermining of democratic participation enabled coercion as well. In the mid-1970s, rural development structures were marshaled in the Indian sterilization campaign, with the *panchayats* providing an institutional vehicle for the forced sterilization of millions. Globally, community development also sustained forced villagization campaigns, such as the U.S. Agency for International Development's (USAID) Strategic Hamlet program during the Vietnam War and, as we will see in Chapter 5, the Guatemalan government's razed-earth tactics in civil war. In this sense, even if community development embraced a more local and contextualized understanding of development than its industrial counterpart, it could be mobilized to serve troubling political ends. By overlooking the fraught realities of village life and propping up elites as the spokesmen of an idealized tradition, community developers cultivated their own ahistorical myths.

As the histories in this chapter reveal, development programs in the 1950s and 1960s generated enormous enthusiasm that they were rarely able to fulfill. What accounts for the gap between expectation and reality? In some sense, the fall was inevitable: The hopes for human betterment invested in technical and industrial development were liberal and even utopian, and they predictably struggled when encountering the friction of social reality in societies around the globe. Development planners and practitioners sought to leave the past behind in order to build a modern future, exhibiting little patience for the obstacles and ambivalences they found in local communities and traditions. In their exuberance, they often minimized longstanding local fault lines, embracing either a hubristic confidence that cultural sensibilities could be modernized or an idealistic belief in traditional communal harmony. Both were ahistorical, ignoring complex local experiences that shaped the success or failure of development programs. By the late 1960s, as we will see in Chapter 6, the gulf between aid enthusiasm and development disappointment had grown so wide that a new generation of developers felt the need to challenge the whole endeavor.

4
The History Wars: Modernization, Structuralism, Dependency

STARTING IN THE LATE 1950S, DEVELOPMENT began to coalesce around several expansive social-scientific frameworks—North American modernization theory and the Latin American schools of structuralism and dependency—that boosted its academic pedigree and installed it as a centerpiece of public policy. The emergence of these paradigms coincided with the independence of millions of people in former colonies, a timing that elevated these schools into widely regarded programs for national advancement. Much has been written about modernization and structuralism, and despite relentless criticism they remain frequent references today. If, as historian Nils Gilman remarked, modernization never seems to perish, structuralism and dependency have proved similarly durable.[1]

Although the Latin American schools arose in great part as refutations of modernization, all three share some common assumptions that allow them to be joined in this chapter. Most obviously, they understood development, above all, as industrialization. Additionally, they all incorporated history as a central methodological commitment, employing macroscopic historical analyses to explain modern economic trends; each was, in other words, a theory of development *and* a theory of history. While modernizers and structuralists, as we shall discuss, addressed history in radically different ways, both understood that a paradigm of development required a historical basis if it were to make any sense at all. Indeed, the fundamental disagreements among the schools can be boiled down to different understandings of that core premise. Modernizers presented Western industrialization as a template that all nations could follow. Structuralists and *dependentistas,* by contrast, embedded national trajectories in a global capitalist history that privileged some societies over others. But all three outlined structured processes of historical change. In so doing, they offered sweeping metanarratives that, to different degrees, suppressed local context and detail, illustrating what I call historical ahistoricism, the replacement of a varied historical landscape with an abstract model of history.

Modernization from Europe to the United States

Modernization theory is one of the most researched topics in development history.[2] Its tendrils extend deep into the canon of nineteenth-century European sociological thought, which sought to make sense of the dramatic changes facing an industrializing continent. One of the tendencies of this intellectual tradition was to distill from the ongoing European transformation a set of more or less consistent patterns said to characterize all modernizing societies, drawing from one continent a sociological template for wider application. With characteristic bluntness, Marx drew the ultimate conclusion: "The country that is more developed industrially only shows, to the less developed, the image of its own future." The non-Western past seemed nothing but stagnant tradition impeding the modern advance: India, Marx shrugged, had "no history at all."[3] Europe's past became *the* modernization template. Some social thinkers—Henri de Saint-Simon and Auguste Comte stand out—came to believe that the modernizing process could be managed, usually by a government, to accelerate change and minimize upheaval.[4] This conviction proved galvanizing in the subsequent century.

But while such themes pervaded nineteenth-century European thought, it was not until the mid-twentieth century and in the United States that modernization theory came together as a formal doctrine. Many factors account for the timing. Escaping the war with a buoyant sense of purpose, the United States, as we saw in the last chapter, embraced a new internationalism that encompassed not only the reconstruction of Europe, but also development in the Third World. Modernization became one of its central planks. Moreover, the country had resources to invest. U.S. universities and think tanks enjoyed public and private largesse as they drafted the intellectual blueprint for American globalism. Several institutions took the lead. The Harvard Department of Social Relations, where sociologist Talcott Parsons held court, devised an abstract and formal—read: scientific—theory of modernization. From the Committee on Comparative Politics at the Social Science Research Council (SSRC), an influential think tank founded in the 1920s, political scientists under the leadership of Gabriel Almond explained the threats engendered by the transition to modernity. And it fell to MIT's Center for International Studies (CIS), the outgrowth of a secret State Department psychological operations program, to carry the modernization framework to the halls of U.S. foreign policy. Philanthropic organizations, often in collaboration with official agencies, supported these endeavors. The Ford Foundation, for example, which we encountered in India in Chapter 3, helped to fund the establishment of area studies programs that built regional knowledge and applied modernization premises.[5]

Modernizers rewarded these ventures by offering theoretical props and academic pedigree to support American global engagement. Existing aid portfolios in the early 1950s seemed aimless and ill planned by comparison. While Point Four demonstrated America's aid commitment, actual outlays were modest, producing a hodgepodge of activities without either intellectual coherence or a systematic understanding of America's global role. Modernizers hoped to supply both. Furthermore, President Dwight Eisenhower's first term squandered American potential by focusing narrowly on military rather than development aid. Even earlier, President Truman's Mutual Security Act of 1951 had bound aid to political allegiance, leading some recipients to question U.S. commitment to Third World uplift.[6]

Modernizers expanded development theory in two obvious ways. First, they moved beyond the econocentrism that dominated earlier thinking, treating industrialization as the economic backbone of a more comprehensive transition encompassing social, cultural, political, and psychological change. Economists did, of course, join their ranks: Rosenstein-Rodan, employed at CIS, contributed to the program by further articulating his big-push model, which he likened to an airplane take-off (an analogy Walt Rostow made famous); and by elaborating the concept of 'absorption capacity,' a country's ability to receive and use foreign aid.[7] But even economic modernizers adopted a broad view. "[T]he economic decisions which determine the rate of growth and productivity of the working force and of capital," wrote Rostow, "should not be regarded as governed by the strictly economic motives of human beings. Economic action is judged the outcome of a complex process of balancing material advance against other human objectives."[8] Accordingly, internal debates among modernizers often concerned the relative priority of one or another dimension of change, with figures like David Apter attacking econocentrism from a political perspective, David McClelland and Alex Inkeles from psychology.[9] Modernization, in other words, was a societal, not just an economic, metamorphosis.

Second, modernizers broadened development thinking by introducing historical depth, envisioning modernization as a process extended over decades, sometimes centuries. Development economics itself had borne out the need for a dynamic model of change that broke with the static or stationary-state analyses of nineteenth-century marginalist economists. Yet history as a set of relevant past experiences tended to vanish from their models. Modernizers, by contrast, argued for the crucial importance not only of economic cycles and fluctuations—a preoccupation of Rostow—but also of longer secular transformations—the political, psychological, and social changes that gradually (or suddenly, as the case may be) introduced modernity.

Like any intellectual movement, modernization had internal variety. Nonetheless, most modernizers held some version of the following beliefs:

1. Societies were "coherently organized systems" with "interdependent" parts.
2. History revealed "two types of social systems, the traditional and the modern."
3. The modern was defined with reference to the West as "individualistic, democratic, capitalist, scientific, secular, and stable."
4. Modernization involved "non-revolutionary, incremental change."
5. Modernization had a strong likelihood of success, with "traditional societies" achieving "economic take-off to industrialization, democratization via law, and secularization and science via education."[10]

The inventory of changes varied somewhat by author, but modernization was generally thought to comprise many of the following:

Social Changes

A shift from kinship to national loyalty as the primary mode of social solidarity

Greater education, literacy, and media consumption
Social differentiation around work, with an emerging middle class
Greater urbanization
Increased social mobility
Increased roles for intellectuals in government and industry

<u>Economic Changes</u>
A shift from agriculture to industry
Increased mechanization of agriculture
Increased economic complexity and differentiation by sector
Increased entrepreneurship
Improving standard of living

<u>Political Changes</u>
Greater participation in society and government, with increased democracy and equality
Decline of hierarchical and sacral authority in favor of limited government with popular involvement
Appearance of political parties, parliaments, and bureaucracy
Increased suffrage
Growing media and institutions to gauge public opinion
Institutionalization of role authority over personal authority

<u>Psychological Changes</u>
Increased reliance on science and rationality over religion and traditional authority
Increased national and international awareness
Growing individualism
Increased sense of agency and efficacy, replacing fatalism and submissiveness
Stress on achievement over ascription as a source of authority

This list is fluid, of course, but it provides a sense of prevailing expectations.

Despite their range and variability, these characteristics were not considered a mere grab bag. Instead, tradition and modernity were coherent enough to be seen as packages. Economist and social scientist Daniel Lerner summed up this view by observing that "urbanization, industrialization, secularization, democratization, education, media participation do not occur in haphazard and unrelated fashion"; instead, they are "so highly associated as to raise the question whether they are genuinely independent factors at all—suggesting they went together so regularly because, in some historical sense, they *had* to go together."[11] The political scientist Robert Packenham described this conviction as the belief that "all good things go together."[12]

Furthermore, if modernity began in early modern Europe, its universal features meant that as societies advanced they came more and more to resemble the West. As sociologist Edward Shils put it, "[t]he model of modernity is a picture of the West detached in some way from its geographical origins and locus."[13] The Israeli sociologist S. N. Eisenstadt concurred:

> Historically, modernization is the process of change toward those types of social, economic, and political systems that have developed in Western Europe and North America from the seventeenth century to the nineteenth and have then spread to other European countries and in the nineteenth and twentieth centuries to the South American, Asian, and African continents.[14]

Gilman dubs this theory "diffusionism," with modernity radiating out from Europe to the world and converging on a Western mode of life.[15] The West was both exemplary and normative—a beacon for others to follow.

Historicizing Talcott Parsons

If modernization theory had an ur-text, it was Harvard sociologist Talcott Parsons's *The Structure of Social Action* (1937). Though it predated the movement by almost two decades, the book's presentation of modernity as a coherent social system with an underlying logic inspired younger scholars and furnished an optimistic assessment shorn of the darker tones of European social thought. Here was no Weberian iron cage, no Marxian revolution.[16] Expressly teleological, Parsons traced the "convergence" of social science around what he called the "action framework," a unified theory of modern society.[17] Drawing on Vilfredo Pareto, Émile Durkheim, and Max Weber, Parsons stressed the importance of both social structures and individual agency. At the individual level, this blend yielded the concept of the "unit act," a rational action structured by a range of choices, normative goals, and situational constraints.

With this abstract concept, Parsons hoped to supply a covering theory for various social sciences—economics, sociology, politics—that would allow them to converse in a grounded, scientific fashion about social life. In doing so, he presented modernity not as fractured or shifting, but as a rational system in which social structures channeled the competing interests of individual actors. While these induced conflict, modern institutions adjusted in predictable ways, widening the ambit of democratic activity and smoothing the course of social change. For all the difficulties entailed in this process, Parsons's message was optimistic: modernization was desirable in its promise of stability with flexibility, freedom with structure. If properly ministered, it could be relatively benign.

This vision helped to justify America's postwar modernizing mission, but it also bequeathed another tendency: The sociologist never fully acknowledged the importance of social or historical context. The German philosopher Jürgen Habermas criticized Parsons for presenting "too harmonious a picture" of social change, one that failed to acknowledge "pathological patterns of development."[18] This was in part, he argued, because Parsons did not succeed in explaining the gap between individual action and the social system. But it also derived from the level of abstraction at which Parsons's analysis transpired, preventing him from coming to grips with the role of cultural meaning and historical vicissitude. Unburdened by the peculiarities of any specific society, Parsonian structural functionalism, so called because it tried to analyze the structure and function of institutions within a social whole, claimed a theoretical purity that allowed it to comprehend modern life *tout court*—even while surrendering the ability to decipher individual societies and historical moments.

In 1951, with his University of Chicago colleague Edward Shils, Parsons added a new technique to the sociological armamentarium, outlining what he called "pattern variables"—dichotomous choices that people make (usually implicitly) to imbue their actions with meaning. In a feat of parsimony, the authors insisted that there were only five basic choices people make when navigating any social situation. These are:

1. Affectivity—Affective neutrality
2. Self-orientation—Collectivity orientation
3. Universalism—Particularism

4. Ascription—Achievement
5. Specificity—Diffuseness

When encountering a new circumstance, a person must decide whether to invest in it, or simply abide in relative neutrality, 'taking it as it comes' without strong emotional attachment. If the former, one must further decide whether to assess the situation with regard to how it affects you or, alternately, how it affects a wider collective such as family or nation. Next, one must determine whether to evaluate the situation through the universalizing lens of rationality or the particularizing lens of one's own self- or group interest. Regarding objects, one must choose whether to relate to them based on their fixed attributes (ascription) or to approach them instrumentally, asking what use they might be in reaching other goals (achievement). The implications of this choice are evident when the 'object' is another human being. Finally, one must choose which aspects of an object to relate to: the object as a whole, without restriction to function and attributes; or in a limited manner, specific to a particular need or context. Doubtless, these are not decisions taken consciously and sequentially. But Parsons insisted that they are implied in any scenario, and that they "constitute a system."[19] While pattern variables were presented as abstract antinomies, midcentury readers quickly recognized that they could be mapped onto the emerging distinction between traditional and modern, with the first term in each pair representing the desired modern trait. In this way, Parsonian variables could be historicized and embraced as a methodological tool for charting the conservatism or progressiveness of developing societies. That Parsons ultimately enlisted himself in his students' modernization program can be seen from his later books.[20]

Modernization Theory's Competing Models of History

Perhaps the clearest example of modernization's commitment to history is also the most renowned: Walt Rostow's *The Stages of Economic Growth* (1960), which presents, in its author's words, a "way of generalizing the sweep of modern history" as a "set of stages-of-growth." Given his reputation as an ideologue, it is worth noting that Rostow issued numerous provisos about the abstract and "partial" nature of his theory. "I cannot emphasize too strongly," said the Yale- and Oxford-trained economic historian, "that the stages-of-growth are an arbitrary and limited way of looking at the sequence of modern history; and they are, in no absolute sense, a correct way."[21]

Nonetheless, Rostow's stages were not merely heuristic. From the late 1930s, he and a team of economists examined the business cycles of an industrializing British economy, trying to reconcile its long-term growth trajectory with the briefer rounds of boom and bust.[22] By the late 1950s, as he moved beyond economics and beyond Britain, the concept of stages—which subdivided a lengthy and linear economic rise—allowed him to articulate his understanding of historical evolution. Thus, in seeming contradiction to the caveat issued pages earlier, Rostow now insisted that his historical account of the economy was "not merely descriptive . . . not merely a way of generalizing certain factual observations." Instead, it had "an inner logic and continuity . . . an analytic bone-structure, rooted in a dynamic theory of production" that gave the economy a sequential and empirical order.[23] In this economic prefiguration of the historical field, we see the remnants of his earlier studies: Growth cycles divided modernization into historical stages, which in turn offered a map for future modernizing societies. As commentators have long remarked, this account bears more than passing resemblance to the Marxist historiography that Rostow denounced in his subtitle.

Rostow's modernization stages are by now well known. Societies begin their developmental journey as agricultural, village-based, pre-Newtonian, religious, and fatalistic—in a word, traditional. Although critics have attacked 'tradition' as a static category, Rostow argued otherwise, contending that traditional societies experience constant churn as new industries develop, productivity fluctuates, and trade brings innovation. But there is a cap on productivity due to the lack of modern science, a ceiling that begins to crack in Stage 2, the Preconditions for Take-Off, when external pressure or intrusion brings new ideas and technology increases productive capacity. Initially, a small group of entrepreneurs arise to expand business horizons, but after perhaps a century, conditions ripen for the watershed stage of Take-Off, a period of several decades when economic growth becomes self-sustaining—"more or less automatic"—and social modernization accelerates. Rostow marked this phase with a familiar indicator: Take-Off occurs when savings and investment rise from around 5 percent to 10 percent or more of GDP, a figure drawn from Lewis.[24] The lengthy Drive to Maturity—Stage 4—sees increased agricultural commercialization and the spread of modern industry.

As efficiency grows, the economy settles into a global niche, while urbanization and rising incomes set the stage for participatory democracy and modern consumerism. With the fifth and final stage—the Age of Mass Consumption—consumer sectors come to dominate the economy, and a welfare state emerges. Henry Ford's United States, according to Rostow, was the first country to reach this niveau.[25]

Whatever one makes of this scheme, it is a kind of history. Indeed, Rostow's work enlarged the scope of historiography required to explain and justify development models, making explicit the social and economic conditions that must be in place for take-off to succeed. His version of the past, however, incurred criticism from fellow economists. Simon Kuznets, whose time-series accounts of economic growth buttressed midcentury development analyses, disputed the model on both empirical and conceptual grounds, arguing that growth stages for past industrializers were not clear-cut.[26] Similarly, the economic historian Alexander Gerschenkron worried that Rostow oversimplified the types and degrees of backwardness and that his stages were too starkly drawn.[27] Gerschenkron's widely read articles on "economic backwardness" in Central and Eastern Europe challenged Rostow in another way as well.[28] Unlike classic modernizers, Gerschenkron did not believe there was only one development path. Different degrees of backwardness necessitated different growth trajectories, and in some circumstances it conferred advantages on latecomers given the ability to copy technologies pioneered by those who went before. The history of industrialization was multilinear.

Political scientists also targeted Rostow's model. Karl Deutsch argued that modernizing states, in light of expanding social needs, might have to jump phases, leaping directly to state welfare provision rather than passing through the era of "near laissez faire" witnessed in the West. He suggested that each sector—social, political, economic—followed its own modernizing trajectory, a disarticulation that produced volatility and undercut Rostow's optimism.[29] Modernizers in general feared transitional instability. The "tragedy of the transitional society," remarked the political scientist and East Asianist Lucian Pye, is that it engendered "profound insecurities" and "individual isolation"; foreign aid could supply modern skills, but it did not necessarily foster peaceful acculturation.[30] Rostow too, of course, feared that incomplete transition increased the temptation of communism. But Pye took the further step of questioning whether Western political ideas were appropriate to Africa and Asia.

Though they had been a stimulus for Asian modernization, he worried that they sometimes provoked unnecessary upheaval. The overriding concern of political modernization should be to reconcile the universal dimensions of change with parochial concerns, since each community views itself as unique. "Without theories that reflect the realities of history," he cautioned, "we have no standards for judging performance in any particular situation."[31]

If Rostow was unique in distilling a universal model of history, he was not the only modernizer to employ historical analysis. Many of his compatriots instead focused on single regions. Of these, some adopted a thematic, theory-first approach in which regional history was judged against a set of global criteria of modernity. Here, Daniel Lerner's *The Passing of Traditional Society* (1958) is a characteristic case. Lerner laid out a typology of modernizing Middle Eastern countries, with Turkey the most advanced and Iran the least. He illustrated the two ends of the spectrum with individual types: the modernizing Grocer and the traditional Chief, both found in his exemplar village of Balgat, Turkey, eight kilometers from downtown Ankara. While Lerner invoked the dynamism of modernization, his six case studies are largely static and classificatory, concerned to rank countries along a scale from most to least developed. Similarly, Marion Levy's *The Family Revolution in China* (1949) assessed the traditional Chinese family according to structural criteria (e.g., role differentiation, solidarity, allocation of resources and power) taken from the modernization toolkit, and then, in the book's final third, considered forces of change in contemporary East Asian rurality.[32] The result in both cases was a stepwise picture of modernization. Societies were treated chiefly as sequential stills, with a largely timeless tradition giving way to a destabilizing period of change. Historical data could reveal tradition or modernity, but change itself appeared only in the shift from one to the other. This theory-first regional approach culminated in Gabriel Almond and James Coleman's *The Politics of Developing Areas* (1960), a *tour d'horizon* that compiled essays on modernization in five developing regions (Southeast Asia, South Asia, Africa, the Middle East, and Latin America) written by prominent sociologists and political scientists.[33]

These works cannot stand as histories in any strong sense, since their aim was to hone social-scientific categories. The same cannot be said for Levy's student David Apter, who crafted theoretically informed historical analyses of modernizing African societies. He provides the key example of our second approach to regional modernization studies. Rather than mining historical data for the purpose of clarifying sociological concepts (theory first), Apter drew on modernization categories to make sense of regional trends (history first). Apter's first two books chronicled the political transition from colonialism to independence in Ghana and Uganda. They did not fully escape the decontextualizing tendencies of the modernization credo—I will argue that Apter's theoretical goals pulled against his complex political narrative—but neither did that agenda entirely suppress the sensitivity to context. A student of Robert Redfield, Apter, unlike many modernizers, did not see tradition and modernity as opposed. Instead, they existed in dialectic interplay, sometimes bolstering and at other times challenging one another. The result was a historically and ethnographically richer version of modernization than many theorists offered, though one still beholden to its overarching frame of reference.

Apter's first book (1955) examined the potential for parliamentary governance in the decolonizing Gold Coast, the African colony, most agreed, that was best poised for independence. Its initial chapters offered boilerplate renditions of the colony's traditional systems—"tribal" structures with "a basic commitment to the past, to time immemorial," or, more pejoratively, "embalmed in custom"—that not only downplayed colonial spoliation, but saw Britain's empire as an agent for development and advancement.[34] The middle of Apter's book, however, presented a complex narrative of Gold Coast political history from the early twentieth century through the mid-1950s. Its chief aim was to describe the balance among three sources of political authority: the "traditional system of tribe, lineage, clan, and chief"; Marxist and socialist ideas, prevalent in Nkrumah's Convention People's Party (CPP); and the colonial inheritance, most specifically, the British parliamentary system.[35] Apter highlighted the ways that these competing sources, "so different in nature as to be directly contradictory," were nonetheless integrated into one system of indirect rule. The key antithesis, he wrote, was between a national politics that tilted toward secular and parliamentary forms of legitimacy (e.g., political parties, constitutional structures) and local leaders who enjoyed longstanding customary deference. Their interaction was often "dysfunctional" because they overlapped not only in jurisdiction but also in personnel.[36] Local leaders served in parliament and therefore had to switch between codes of political behavior; and the CPP, while overseeing the colony's modernization, had to engage with local authorities. At times, Nkrumah the modernizer adopted the mantle of tradition: In the Volta Dam debate, which otherwise exhibited the hallmarks of contemporary legislative practice, he stood as a charismatic "source of sanction," a kind of traditional leader with personal authority who acted through a modern parliament.[37] When the Volta River Development Bill came up for parliamentary debate in 1961, it passed after a mere hour's deliberation, signaling to Apter the success of Nkrumah's traditional-*cum*-modern domination.[38] But the debate also set up a "role conflict" that suggested incomplete modernization.[39] To "break the power of traditionalism and its residual hold upon the public," nationalist leaders were forced to adopt authoritarian tactics—even at times usurping traditional roles to use *against* customary authorities.[40]

In the book's second revised edition, printed six years after Nkrumah's 1966 ouster, Apter lamented the stalled modernization of Ghana's first president. "The nation replaced the ethnic community," he wrote, but without transcending its personal forms of allegiance.

> The Presidential-monarch replaced the chief. The authority of charisma ritualized into the special role of the warrior-priest. Ideology became a political religion increasingly intolerant of all other religions, monopolistic, expressed through the militant elect of the party. The writings and speeches of Nkrumah took on the quality of sacred texts.[41]

Partial modernization of this sort, he warned, could give rise to something worse: With Nkrumah's "socialist militants" gone, their successors might exploit the contradictions of an incomplete transition to promote factionalism or dictatorship. In 1955, Apter had feared transitional instability, even if he hoped that Nkrumah might overcome it. Twenty years later, his fears seemed prophetic.

If historical analysis helped Apter explain the interplay between tradition and modernity in Ghana, it served an even greater role in his sequel study of the kingdom of Buganda, the largest subunit in Britain's Uganda protectorate. But there he found a different pattern. As opposed to Ghana, where he (initially) foresaw a successful overcoming of tradition, Buganda demonstrated "a traditionalization of change itself," with the precolonial Baganda adapting instrumental modernizations without overturning ethnic custom or regional hierarchies.[42] As he put it in 1960, whereas Ghanaian modernization "require[d] a host of attitudes of mind and social organizations antithetical to traditional ways," in Buganda "the prerequisite to accepting any modern feature on the political level was that some real or mythical traditional counterpart had to be found for it."[43] The kingdom stood, in other words, as a challenge to simplified modernization tenets positing the stagnancy of tradition or its incompatibility with modern life. Instead, adaptive updates secured royal authority and customary land tenure within the structures of a modernizing, multi-ethnic colony.

Apter proposed Buganda's "modernizing autocracy" as a unique form of political transition that contrasted with Ghana's "mobilization" system (which suppressed tradition in favor of modern politics) and the consociational approach of Nigeria and the Mali Federation (which sought to unite diverse peoples while retaining subnational distinctions).[44] In Buganda's third way, the kingdom wrapped the practices of popular debate and political campaigning around a neotraditional core, retaining "the moral prescriptions of the past [but] apply[ing] them to modern conditions." This syncretism could function effectively until "the principle of kingship is itself challenged," at which point "either modernization and change are halted" or the system shifts to "a consociational or mobilization type."[45]

Perhaps the most striking methodological aspect of Apter's volume is the way that historical narrative—the bulk of the book runs from late nineteenth-century British occupation to the 1950s eve of independence—strains against the theoretical cladding introduced in the opening chapter. The modernization categories that frame the account could not clearly explain the patterns Apter discerned in Central Africa, and he was forced to concede that, while modernity and tradition were conceptually opposed, they could, in some cases, coexist. In this regard, Apter refused to allow his social-scientific impulses to override the "puzzling and difficult" historical pattern he identified.[46] What they did prevent him from seeing was the myriad possible social concatenations that fell outside or across the tradition-modernity dyad.

Apter's struggles are apparent in his discussion of the realignment of local politics after the Uganda Agreement of 1900, which formalized the British protectorate through a treaty with its largest unit. By his account, precolonial Buganda had two structures of political authority: one hierarchical, centered on the *kabaka* (king) and the *katikiro* (prime minister); the other pyramidal, built around the *bataka*, or clan chieftains. If the *bataka* technically owed their allegiance to the *kabaka,* in practice they used their authority to channel leverage to and from the peasants. The Uganda Agreement strengthened the *kabaka* at the expense of the clans, even as it reformed the traditional parliament and introduced freehold land tenure, fostering a growing inequality between elites and peasants at a time when Uganda was being drawn into colonial trade networks. Splits between Protestants and Catholics, whose numbers attested to the success of nineteenth-century missionaries, further intensified local conflict. And this is to say nothing of the inequality between Buganda and other peoples in the protectorate. As the largest and wealthiest of Uganda's subunits, Buganda became the focus of British development efforts. Its combination of imperial privilege and durable tradition nurtured a nationalism built around revised customary structures, placing a potentially separatist Buganda at the heart of Uganda and stoking grievance among other peoples.[47]

Whatever one makes of this history, the struggle between modernization and tradition is an unsatisfactory explanation of it. The problem is not that Apter's thesis is utterly implausible—one can of course read political struggles as intrinsic to a modernization prompted by colonial takeover—but that it is so general as to have little analytic purchase. How does one, for example, understand a figure such as Apolo Kagwa, Buganda's leading historian and head of the turn-of-the-century Protestant faction? He served as *katikiro* under King Mwanga (who first accepted and then declared war on the protectorate) and regent under his successor, using his access to gather and publish ethnographic accounts of Baganda kings, customs, and wars.[48] He was at once a Baganda nationalist and an agent of British power, a religious factionalist and a representative of traditional authority. To parse his actions according to a modernizing schizophrenia is to glean little about his motivations.

Moreover, Apter's account of adaptive tradition in a modernizing polity largely neuters the impact of politics. Indeed, as in the case of Ghana, it sidesteps the traumas of colonial occupation—the usurpation of resources, the loss of autonomy, external manipulation of domestic power—by either writing them off as growing pains or deflecting them onto Baganda culture itself, which could not accommodate full-on modernity. One need not read Ugandan scholar Mahmood Mamdani's 1996 account of how British authorities created "local despots" by undermining precolonial participatory mechanisms to recognize the process at work here, with authority and inequality an outgrowth of colonial intervention rather than residues of the past.[49]

Ultimately, we might ask whether the coexistence of tradition and modernity is really so puzzling after all. As Benedict Anderson has taught us, tradition is commonly mobilized—or invented—to bolster modern polities. Far from being opposed categories, they are frequently intertwined and mutually reinforcing—a possibility that Apter and other modernizers had difficulty conceiving. In the twenty-first century, we are fully aware that secular and religious, authoritarian and democratic, hierarchical and egalitarian outlooks commingle in societies around the globe. How useful is it to classify social components as either traditional or modern? It is a strength of Apter's history that he acknowledged such complexity—to the point that Apter the historian undermined Apter the modernizer. Perhaps for this reason, when he dispensed with historical analysis in a 1965 summary volume, the result was cleaner but less compelling than the case studies that informed it.[50] At a high enough level of abstraction, all history looks alike.

Though modernizers replaced particular histories with metahistorical models, their accounts were not without potency. In a development scholarship hitherto dominated by economics, they incorporated sociology, politics, culture, and psychology. And in a field shot through with presentism, they contended that development must be understood as change over time, stretching back centuries. Yet this breadth was both strength and handicap. Encompassing the vast range of modern history and society, modernization streamlined social reality, sifting facts and trends into fixed categories—tradition, modernity, preconditions, take-off—that substituted for the messiness of economic and political change. To its benefit, modernization theory proved 'truthy' enough to attract a substantial following.[51] Their accounts were also beguilingly 'history-ish,' presenting modernization as temporal and social transformation. Yet while modernizers proclaimed the importance of history, its variety eluded them. The past became a grab bag of examples used to mark the contours and stages of a universal model, deflecting the contingencies and ambiguities that careful examination reveals. Their historicism is, in this sense, ahistorical. For if everything reduces to a move from tradition to modernity, then history itself loses meaning. The only movement that matters is the tectonic shift of stages.

Rostow spent his academic career seeking the rhythm of economic history, the phases of modernization. Yet as Robert Nisbet pointed out in his trenchant 1969 critique, it remains extraordinarily difficult to apply an abstract model of social change to particular historical circumstances.[52] The unexplained remainder generally matters as much as the *explicandum,* even if it is obscured by methodological fiat. In addition, modernizers typically mapped a Western template onto non-Western lands. This process entailed a double elision: the distillation of a development model from a *longue-durée* history of the West; and then the application of that model in contemporary non-Western societies—the extraction, in other words, of a general framework from specific circumstances for use in new times and places. To modernizers, practicing historians must have seemed like so many Apolo Kagwas, fetishizing their facts and customs; social scientists, by contrast, assayed history to establish objective programs of uplift. In doing so, however, their model became, to use Michael Latham's label, an article of faith, an ideology—a parable for the United States as global missionary.

Modernization became foreign policy in the 1960s when Rostow joined President John F. Kennedy's administration and other modernizers took regular advisory posts. Over time, Rostow earned the nickname "America's Rasputin" for his staunch advocacy of military campaigns in Vietnam to prevent the spread of communism and support rural modernization.[53] While this conflict-mongering is partly attributable to his own personality, it emerged from modernization premises as well: The longer the Vietnamese resist, a modernizer might reluctantly argue, the firmer we must be in combatting traditionalism and eradicating the Communist temptation. Not only was war a potentially necessary jolt to a stagnant society, but the army could be an exemplary modern institution—a disciplined national force that embraced technology and public order. Lucian Pye understood armies as modernizing agents that spurred administrative advancement, even if they threatened democracy.[54] And Karl Deutsch described military mobilization as a metaphor for the modernization process itself.[55] Rostow, in other words, was not unique in his militarist inclinations. Faith in the armed forces, as we will see in the next chapter, blinded modernizers to the violent potential of their program.

Structuralism

Some of modernization's sternest critics came from the Latin American schools of structuralism and dependency. The disputes were partly familial, since the paradigms shared common roots in wartime and postwar development economics. The Argentine Raul Prebisch and the German-Jewish Hans Singer, generally recognized as the founders of structuralism, agreed with Rosenstein-Rodan and Lewis regarding the uniqueness of underdeveloped economies and the need for state involvement in markets. Both structuralism and modernization assumed a loose two-sector model of the national economy (a large agricultural sector encircling smaller modern enclaves), and both understood development to depend heavily (though not exclusively) on a capital-driven expansion of the industrial sector. As late as the early 1960s, Prebisch not only hoped that North and South could cooperate on development policy, but he joined in the early design of Kennedy's Alliance for Progress, a modernization omnibus.[56] Yet the Latin American perspective of the early structuralists—so called because they emphasized the way that international trade structures influenced development patterns—led them to doubt key tenets of the modernization agenda, especially regarding the importance of regional context and the nature of historical analysis.

Unlike other developing regions, Latin America in the late 1940s had enjoyed over a century of independence, but this fact came with a psychological toll: Why, observers wondered, had such a rich continent-and-a-half failed to develop under self-rule, despite initial promise and plentiful resources? Just as the Central European and American contexts infused the economic development mainstream, so the Latin American experience shaped the structuralists' answer to this question. Particularly crucial was the experience of war and depression. Whereas World War II in Europe brought slaughter and destruction, in Latin America it afforded a degree of economic self-sufficiency.

In the decades straddling the century's turn, Latin American economies were export-driven, and, in accordance with the theory of comparative advantage, they produced agriculture and raw materials for sale in northern industrial nations, amassing considerable profits for an economic elite. There was some industrialization in the early twentieth century, tied either to light consumer goods or export industries, but the 1929 economic collapse and ensuing Depression undercut these gains by cleaving the continent from its chief U.S. and European markets. Yet there was an upside to this divorce: local entrepreneurs gradually increased the production of goods for domestic consumption, especially in large markets such as Brazil, Argentina, Mexico, and Chile. This strategy of replacing imports with local manufactures, soon known as import substitution industrialization (ISI), not only helped to meet consumer demand but also contributed to domestically driven industrialization that lasted into the 1950s. This surprising turnaround led Raúl Prebisch to reconsider the tenets of neoclassical trade theory. ISI in Latin America, as Joseph Love put it, "was fact before it was policy, and policy before it was theory."[57] And while a devastated Europe looked westward for economic assistance, Latin America turned away from its northern benefactors, whose economic prowess throttled diversification initiatives.

Prebisch arrived at his influential thesis of the deteriorating terms of trade for primary product exporters by grappling with this recent legacy. By the time he accepted a temporary contract at the newly established UN Economic Commission for Latin America (ECLA—or CEPAL in Spanish) in Santiago de Chile, the Argentine economist had almost three decades of experience in government, academics, and the private sector, culminating in a 1935 appointment as director-general of Argentina's new central bank.[58] When he was dismissed from the post in 1943 by a military junta—which included an ambitious young officer named Juan Perón—he returned to teaching and consulting. Though often unwelcome in Perón's Argentina because of his association with the former elite, Prebisch enjoyed a fecund intellectual life during the subsequent decade, capped by his 1949 ECLA recruitment to pull together the final report of the *Economic Survey of Latin America*.[59] He would head the organization within a year.

Prebisch was not the only economist to moot the idea of deteriorating terms of trade for agricultural exports. In the same year as Rosenstein-Rodan's call to industrialize agrarian societies, the American economist Charles Kindleberger argued that the organization of production and differential demand elasticities worked against agricultural producers in the long run.[60] More famously, there is an unresolved dispute about whether Hans Singer, then working for the United Nation's Department of Economic Affairs, deserves authorial primacy. In honor of this dual origin, the Prebisch-Singer thesis has retained its hyphenated title.[61]

Regardless, Prebisch's thesis gained authority in postwar Latin America, where resurgent imports from newly opened Western markets undercut fragile local industries. Its most famous articulation came in a 1949 paper, entitled "The Economic Development of Latin America and its Principal Problems," prepared for ECLA's second meeting in Havana, Cuba, and known ever since as the ECLA or Havana Manifesto. Prebisch took particular aim at the classical trade pillars of comparative advantage and international specialization. "In Latin America," he told his audience, "reality is undermining the out-dated schema of the international division of labour," which assigned the "periphery of the world economic system" to roles as food and raw materials producers for industrial "centres." Not everyone gained from these allotments.[62] For poorer countries, modern trade set up long-term disequilibria—a comparative *dis*advantage that eroded economic prospects.

The postwar international order accelerated this decline. The United States, having inherited the role of global economic engine, did not import enough goods to sustain growth elsewhere. With its size, technology, and productive capacity, the United States was less dependent on import items than the former British hegemon, producing "conditions incompatible with the functioning of the international economy."[63] Other factors inhered in the structures of unequal trade. The drive to industrialize was quite costly: Latin America's reliance on outside investment, debt servicing, and capital imports forced the region to spend down its foreign exchange reserves, causing dollar shortages that placed a ceiling on growth.[64] Consumption patterns were another problem. As developing-country elites tried to emulate the lifestyles of their industrialized peers, savings dwindled and foreign currency drained away, enriching prosperous foreign economies at the expense of local industry. The finances of technological advancement also conspired against peripheral countries: Prebisch calculated that, even as new technology reduced manufacturing and agricultural costs, "the centres kept the whole benefit of the technical development of their industries, [while] the peripheral countries transferred to them a share of their own technical progress."[65] Primary producers were engaged in a losing race: The more they produced, the less they could purchase per unit of exchange. The division of labor, in sum, penalized the poor.

Prebisch also confronted an epistemological conundrum similar to that faced by Rostow. He had to explain how the cyclical volatility of free trade, which produced various positive and negative effects, yielded a consistently inegalitarian long-term pattern. What is the relationship, in short, between economic cycles and long-term secular trends? Rostow's answer was to divide the secular development process into stages, each with its own cyclical equilibrium, yet each advancing toward modernity. Prebisch, however, noticed that even if primary product prices tended to rise faster than manufactures in upswings, in downturns they fell more precipitously. Industrial prices, in other words, were 'stickier'—more steady, less volatile—than those for raw materials. In theory, this pattern should produce long-term equilibrium. Yet the economic history of the previous century showed the opposite: The fall of primary product prices in a downswing was consistently steeper than its earlier upswing, "so that in the course of cycles the gap between prices of the two is progressively widened."[66] Over the long run, raw materials exporters had to ship ever more product to purchase the same amount of manufactures. Prebisch attributed this secular decline to a political factor: labor organization in the industrial countries. Mobilized workers in developed countries won higher wages in boom times and resisted salary cuts in bear markets, passing on losses to poorly organized laborers in underdeveloped economies in the form of reduced profits and incomes. The geographic separation of producers from consumers in foreign trade ensured a widening gap by limiting occasions for empathy and solidarity. Prebisch also complained about free trade violations: the classical model presumed factor mobility, including labor, but the United States restricted migration and protected markets to preserve its living standard.[67]

In response, Prebisch recommended targeted import reductions—an ISI policy—for developing economies. He did not, it should be underlined, view this proposal as an alternative to export growth; instead, he saw the two as complementary, with growing export profits from ISI industries eventually yielding a new import composition geared toward capital products that would sustain further local industrialization.[68] Nonetheless, his attack on a core premise of the classical tradition—that trade is beneficial to all parties—marked a clear battle line.

Prebisch's structuralism also challenged the historical bases of modernization. European industrialization, he insisted, misled today's periphery. Whereas nineteenth-century growth had been spontaneous and gradual, today's developing countries faced an economic field tilted against them. They could not simply replicate, nation by nation, the experience of Great Britain or the United States, as modernizers hoped. Latin America's history was a better midwife for theory and policy than the European past. It showed that only a determination to compensate for structural constraints and avoid foreign "nostrums" could remedy economic disadvantage.[69]

All the same, structuralism contained generalizations that limited its ability to incite. To be sure, programmatic statements had a regional focus that reflected the methodological priority Prebisch assigned to recent history. Nonetheless, his application of history was limited and instrumental, used to generate questions and data that in turn gave rise to economic theses. Indeed, it is hard to imagine concepts more ready for sloganeering than center-periphery or declining terms of trade. Prebisch's work heralded the widespread entry of non-Western economists into the global development mainstream, and in the age of decolonization, he was well positioned to become a Third World spokesperson. His ECLA thesis, published first in Spanish and disseminated through Portuguese and English translations, wove its way into global demands for economic justice. Nonetheless, it fell to later *dependentistas* to further historicize the field of economic understanding.[70]

Celso Furtado and the Transition to Dependency

The 1950s were flush times in Latin America, but the boom economy hid dark omens. The ISI strategy did not so much reduce imports as shift their content away from consumer manufactures and toward capital goods needed by local industries, producing continued financial shortfalls.[71] In Brazil, an overvalued cruzeiro, inflated to prop up coffee prices, increased imports and lowered tax revenues, draining currency reserves. Structuralist prescriptions lost their purchase as the onset of recession prepared the way for Brazil's 1964 military takeover. Even Prebisch entertained more radical policies, such as restraining consumption among the wealthy, intensifying government planning, or instituting some kind of socialism.[72]

Where structuralism faltered, dependency theory proposed more drastic solutions. *Dependentistas* took over key structuralist premises, including the core-periphery model and the thesis of uneven trade terms, but they sought more radical policies to suit more desperate times, an urgency heightened by the Cuban Revolution and the Vietnam War. Under the influence of South and North American Marxists, they also expanded structuralism's historical reach: If Prebisch focused on the recent past, dependency theorists argued for the vital importance of a longer perspective on capitalist underdevelopment, tapping not only Marx's historical model (filtered through local interpreters such as the Peruvian José Carlos Mariátegui) but also regional debates over revolutionary strategy and the continental transition to socialism.[73] These debates encompassed two primary positions: dualists threw their support behind the native bourgeoisie, seeing their capitalist endeavors as a necessary prerequisite to socialist transition; anti-dualists argued that Latin America had been integrated into a global capitalist system for centuries and was ready for socialist policies. *Dependentistas* typically espoused the latter.

If Prebisch is the acknowledged founder of Latin American structuralism, his ECLA colleague Celso Furtado, the Portuguese translator of the Havana Manifesto, built the clearest bridge to dependency.[74] An early user of the term *dependency*, which he preferred to Prebisch's *periphery*, Furtado employed *longue durée* history to push a structuralist idiom rooted in the recent past toward a dependency analysis that reached back 500 years. This marked a methodological inversion as well: If modernizers and structuralists gathered historical data to support economic analysis, Furtado acted more as an economic historian, using economic tools to generate questions for the historical record to answer—or, as he put it, to "bring history near to economic analysis."[75]

Furtado incorporated history in two ways. First, the socioeconomic history of particular societies—in his case, Brazil—became a field for forensic investigation. This was most evident in his 1959 classic *The Economic Growth of Brazil*, a pivotal work in the shift from structuralism to dependency. Second, he employed history as a tool for the critical analysis of inherited economic doctrines, tracking their conceptual filaments to uncover hidden assumptions and constraints. This historico-critical approach is apparent in Furtado's other masterwork, *Development and Underdevelopment* (1961). What the former volume revealed by example, the latter argued directly: "It is not enough to construct an abstract model and provide an explanation of how it operates," Furtado asserted.

> [I]t is just as important to demonstrate the explanatory effectiveness of such a model as applied to historical realities. Only the latter procedure can reveal the limitations inherent in the level of abstraction at which the model is drawn up and suggest what changes must be introduced in order to make it valid from the point of view of a given reality.

While the economic discipline crafted essential analytic tools and concepts, overgeneralization distanced it from "concrete historical situations," limiting the capacity to explain. As a result, "we pass surreptitiously from the field of scientific speculation into that of dogma," generally by dint of "sheer repetition."[76] Historically informed criticism was a "prerequisite" for epistemological advancement.[77] Not only must economists set up a continuous dialogue with the past, but they had to constantly de- and reconstruct models to eliminate "simplifying assumptions incompatible with the historic reality."[78] Even classical formulations, Furtado observed, were overly abstract. The Ricardian theory of rent, based on a scarcity of arable land, transcribed English circumstances into universal science; yet it had limited applicability in land-abundant Latin America. Growth and development, in sum, had "clear-cut historical aspects," and only by descending to the "historical plane" could economics accommodate reality.[79]

The expansion of history as an economic field led Furtado away from Prebisch's recent focus and toward a *longue durée* account of Latin America from colonial times. *The Economic Growth of Brazil* charted the evolution of the colonial economy from its early boom as a sugar exporter to its subsequent decline in the late mercantile era.[80] Processing cane required plentiful land, a congenial climate, metropolitan investment, a colonial monopoly, and abundant slave labor. As the Iberian powers declined, however, and as sugar cultivation spread to the Caribbean, Brazil relinquished its market niche, shifting gradually and inadequately to gold mining and stock-breeding. Neither made up for lost revenue. Cattle ranchers in particular relied chiefly on local markets, with increased herd numbers reducing the price per head and contributing to the marginalization of Furtado's native Northeast, a dependent region within a dependent state.

By the eighteenth century, Portugal's colonial economy had become an affiliate of the British, yet separation from the center set up perverse incentives. In Britain, buyers and sellers fed the same national market and enjoyed collateral benefits, however unequally. As textile manufacturers competed to outdo one another, their investments, purchases, and technical innovations spurred domestic growth and social transformation. These gains were lost to Latin America, where capital and technology (and slave labor) came from abroad without the virtuous spillover effects of paying into a local supply chain.[81] Only the export enclaves saw gains from trade. Ultimately, Furtado concluded, there was little Brazil could have done to stave off decline, let alone replicate the rise of the United States, since the latter existed as an extension of the British economy, not an external appendage like South America.[82]

The dual nature of the home consumer market—a small export sector within an impoverished majority—also inhibited growth by segregating elites from the rest of the economy. Their luxury consumption sent money abroad for imports, while majority peasants lacked purchasing power. Whereas Prebisch felt that ISI policies could mitigate some of these effects, Furtado argued that dependency was too great for domestic restitution alone. Colonial bureaucratic and economic systems, as he put it during his post-coup years in Yale exile, gave rise to "patterns of income distribution responsible for behavior incompatible with the most rational utilization of available resources."[83] Even renewed growth during the nineteenth-century coffee boom did little to change Brazil's dependency. Markets remained overseas, profits flowed to an elite, and surpluses fled the country. Furtado did, however, note one promising glimmer: the wage-earning sector, remunerated by plantation jobs, expanded during these years. If the vast labor supply weakened incentives for entrepreneurial innovation, it did at least boost local demand. When exports collapsed in 1929, it was this popular market that sustained the ISI strategy.

Furtado broadened structuralism in several ways. First, he emphasized the need for a detailed understanding of each country to supplement the generalizations of center and periphery. The additional move from country to subregion—from Brazil to the impoverished Northeast—suggested further refinements. Furtado also demonstrated that economics alone could not provide a thorough picture of country fortunes. Political and social factors—decisions by kings and entrepreneurs, economies of taste—played crucial roles in fostering dependency. Because development was "a process of social change by which a growing number of human needs . . . are satisfied by means of differentiation in the productive system," it required a multidisciplinary understanding that drew on economics, sociology, psychology, and political science, pushing structuralism toward a political economy reminiscent of Marx and other classical thinkers.[84] It required, in sum, "a new reading of history."[85]

In addition, Furtado reinforced the structuralist thesis about the nature of underdevelopment. In contradistinction to modernizers, his work presented the global economy, not the colony or nation, as the proper unit of analysis. Examining the development of capitalism over centuries showed that most nations could not recapitulate the path of Great Britain. The earliest modernizing states (Britain, the United States) were never underdeveloped because they were never dependent. Instead, development in some regions came at the cost of underdevelopment in others.[86] Because Brazil was "unable to integrate herself into the expanding currents of world trade," it experienced sharp economic disparities both internally and vis-à-vis Europe—a historical fact that set up its twentieth-century "backwardness."[87] As Furtado put it in 1987, underdevelopment was not due to "destiny" but "to the action of identifiable social forces."[88]

Though more radical than Prebisch, Furtado was no revolutionary. A Keynes disciple, he accepted aspects of the modernization creed, including the view that growth and development, once launched, became "an almost automatic process."[89] But "the backward community tends to remain stagnant," he insisted, "because it is unable to set the process of development in motion by its own means."[90] In the hope of overcoming this hurdle, Furtado served in Brazil's government during the postwar years, first coordinating a development agency for the Northeast and then as minister of planning under the center-left president João Goulart. In a passage that Andre Gunder Frank would later pillory, he argued that timing rather than policy undid Brazil's 1950s growth:

> A good deal of evidence exists to indicate that industrialization has brought Brazil very close to the position where development becomes a cumulative circular process creating its own expansionary momentum. For Brazil, this point would have been reached when the barrier of the import capacity had been overcome. The economy would then have achieved the degree of differentiation in which planning of investments becomes a matter of economic options, without the physical limitations of a restricted import capacity. It can even be conceded that, had it not been for the worsening of the terms of trade after 1955, Brazil would have reached this decisive point somewhere in the sixties.[91]

Yet even sound ISI policy needed an economic upswing, and Brazil's recession undid its midcentury hopes. In 1987, Furtado summarized the policy implications of his theories as follows: the abandonment of comparative advantage as state policy; the introduction of planning; the strengthening of civil society, especially labor unions.[92] More radical *dependentistas* doubted that such an agenda would correct a system built on external domination.

Dependency: The Moderates

Among *dependentistas,* Osvaldo Sunkel hewed closest to ECLA's structuralist roots. He was an active participant in debates about the persistent inflation that, starting in the mid-1950s, tarnished the gains of ISI.[93] His disappointment at Latin America's economic record produced a growing suspicion that underdevelopment might not be surmountable. The prospects for wage employment in particular, he wrote in 1969, were truly "frightening," with even Puerto Rico, a Caribbean standout, stalled and sputtering.[94] In *Latin American Underdevelopment and the Theory of Development* (1970), Sunkel and his Mexican coauthor Pedro Paz described underdevelopment as a global "system" of privilege and dependency. The book's largest section criticized neoclassical economics for making historical assumptions with limited applicability in Latin America. The authors preferred a "historic-structural" method that revealed the constraints faced by a "dependent export economy."[95]

Arguably the most renowned dependency theorist, especially in his home continent, is Fernando Henrique Cardoso, who rose to prominence as a sociologist before launching a political career that led him to the Palácio de Alvorado—Brazil's presidency. Ousted from the University of Sao Paulo by the 1964 coup and partnering in Santiago with Enzo Faletto, Cardoso drafted what has been called the "seminal" dependency work, though the decade-long wait for an English translation delayed its wider influence.[96] *Dependency and Development in Latin America,* released in 1969, presented the continent's history in terms of the relation between "external and internal forces," which form (according to the English-edition Preface)

> a complex whole whose structural links are not based on mere external forms of exploitation and coercion, but are rooted in coincidences of interests between local dominant classes and international ones, and, on the other side, are challenged by local dominated groups and classes.

As with Furtado, Cardoso and Faletto emphasized "historical-structural contexts" and "concrete analysis of situations of dependency," for the lack of which he castigated modernizers.[97] But the book's most distinctive logic was the embedding of Latin America's economic downturn in a more fundamental analysis of the values, interests, and alliances of competing domestic groups who sought to channel international forces to their benefit. Politics was the determinant field.

Brazil's 'years of lead' (*anos de chumbo*)—the period of repression running from 1968 to 1974—coincided with Cardoso's return from exile to take up a post at the University of Sao Paulo, where he joined the leftist opposition. For all of its violence, the dictatorship also witnessed the reversal of Brazil's recession and the reemergence of a growth economy. As a result, some critics present the era as a classic case of elite willingness to trade democratic independence for authoritarian development.[98] The disjuncture between politics and economics impressed Cardoso and suggested to him openings within the international system for efficacious activism. *Dependency and Development* reflects this thinking.

The book's chief argument is that external dependency was *internalized* within each society in the form of changing class relations, or "structures of domination." Dependency, the authors wrote, "entails a link with the outside in such a way that what happens 'internally' in a dependent country cannot be fully explained without taking in consideration the links that internal social groups have with external ones."[99] This "internal expression" of dependency, in other words, reflected relations of domination and resistance that bound domestic and foreign players. It followed that domestic social and political structures were the primary levers of dependent subordination, supplanting even economic relations in priority. While industrialization and capital accumulation played into the authors' analysis, the lengthy economic discussions of Prebisch and Furtado gave way to reflections on class and social movements in individual countries, with each society evolving its own pattern of stratification and international economic insertion. By the end of the nineteenth century, the authors reported, a rising urban middle class had diversified demand and social power in Latin America. In places, this petit bourgeoisie blended with existing elites; elsewhere, it pushed them aside. Early twentieth-century industrialization, initially a byproduct of middle-class demand, produced still newer social hierarchies, with the nouveaux riches forming their own domestic and foreign alliances. The authors identified three types of "industrial bourgeois" engagement during this period: a "liberal" form in which private entrepreneurs and agro-exporters entered the international market; a "national-populist" form, in which industrialists, middle sectors, and trade unions shared the direction of development; and a "developmentalist state," in which a tax-funded government stood in for a weak local capitalist class, fostering the bases for growth.[100] By the late twentieth century, dependency grew more multinational still, involving webs of private linkages that escaped state control. Development and dependency, in sum, evolved together, and loss of control for some groups accompanied increasing wealth for others.[101] The most recent "internationalization of the internal market," with multinational firms embedded domestically and influencing national politics, came to approximate, in more extreme form, the experience of advanced industrial states, whose governments also struggled to manage global capital.[102]

Despite their incorporation of Marxian insights, Cardoso and Faletto took no clear stand in Latin America's polarized political debates, splayed between populism and authoritarianism. While the dependency school overwhelmingly identified with the left, Cardoso's analysis of domestic strategic alignments accommodated a wide range of political programs, from socialism to liberalism and beyond, in its quest for greater national autonomy. This became a source of contention when Cardoso moved from the lectern to the hustings. With the *abertura,* the gradual democratization launched in 1974, he entered formal politics, first as a senator in 1983, and then, a decade later, as finance minister, where he successfully tamed Brazil's hyperinflation. The malleability of his dependency subschool contributed to public controversy after he became president in 1995 and faced accusations (from, among others, his successor Luiz Inácio Lula da Silva) of betraying his roots by embracing neoliberalism.[103] Cardoso acknowledged this surprising flexibility in his postpresidential memoirs: While his prominent thesis was often "interpreted as leftist," he wrote, its "conclusions were not very leftist at all."[104]

Dependency: The Radicals

For all the provocation of their work, Furtado, Sunkel, and (to a lesser degree) Cardoso remained devoted to the left-Keynesianism they imbibed at ECLA. Another branch of dependency drew instead on U.S. and Latin American Marxism—notably the works of Paul Sweezy and Paul Baran—to advocate a more revolutionary attack.[105] This group included careful theorists such as Ruy Mauro Marini and Theotonio dos Santos, whose writings were well known across Latin America. But radical dependency also embraced less systematic thinkers who wrote more as dissidents than as system-builders.

Internationally, radical dependency is most associated with the peripatetic Berlin-born Andre Gunder Frank. Notwithstanding his own ambivalence about "the new fashion" of dependency, Frank indelibly shaped the school's reception—a surprising fate for someone who first arrived in Latin America in his thirties after earning a Ph.D. in the archliberal University of Chicago Economics Department.[106] But Frank threw himself into the political and intellectual life of his adopted continent, pouring forth books that offered variations on the theme of underdevelopment.[107] Perhaps in part because of his prolific record, he is both respected and dismissed in academic circles, and by the late 1960s, his sweeping polemics were attracting many barbs. As one scholar remarked, he was "a dazzling, fleeting comet . . . whose success was both resounding and comparatively short-lived."[108] Younger *dependentistas* such as Gary Gereffi, while sympathetic to Frank's aim of Third World promotion, regretted his tendency to overlook historical contingencies.[109] All the same, Frank remains the most prominent *dependentista* in Anglophone circles, and *Latin America: Underdevelopment or Revolution,* his 1969 essay collection, is a monument of activist scholarship.[110]

Frank was at his most incisive—and pugilistic—when dissecting other lines of thought. Perhaps most startling was the vitriol aimed at his own University of Chicago mentor, the sociologist Bert Hoselitz, who represented a "bourgeois" modernization theory that Frank found "empirically invalid," "theoretically inadequate," and "ineffective for pursuing its supposed intentions of promoting the development of the underdeveloped countries."[111] He presented Hoselitz and Rostow as two variants of what he called the "gap approach" to development, which he mocked in the following terms: "you subtract the ideal typical features or indices of underdevelopment from those of development, and the remainder is your development program." Hoselitz (variant 1) employed Parsons' pattern variables, which Frank dubbed "liberalism recast into technical sounding jargon."[112] Rostow (variant 2) introduced historical stages.

Frank targeted a 1953 essay in which Hoselitz outlined a three-part typology of development.[113] Where developed societies were universalistic in outlook, Hoselitz wrote, traditional societies remained particularist. Where modern individuals prized achievement, traditional persons held ascriptive forms of identity. And where modern societies were functionally specialized, with individuals holding clear social and professional roles, members of traditional societies took on diffuse duties—farmer, market salesman, repairman—that prevented gains from specialization. This is standard modernization fare, and Frank dismantled it ruthlessly. Where Hoselitz saw modern universalism, Frank cited the particularistic interests that drove much U.S. economic behavior, with profits accruing to individuals at the expense of society. Where Hoselitz lauded the American culture of achievement, Frank noted that recruitment to the mandarin professions was often based on family connections and class membership. And where Hoselitz presented the gains of modern specialization, Frank pointed to the many hats—father, CEO, coach, husband—that Westerners wore. Indeed, the press, social movements, and public opinion in developing societies, he remarked, were often far more globally aware than their Western counterparts since their fortunes depended on knowledge of the outside world. Additionally, in poor countries, it was often top businessmen, not chiefs or community leaders, who held economic and political power—thwarting development by cultivating Western ties.[114] Lower levels were staffed with similarly opportunistic achievers. And while the poor did indeed have to undertake disparate tasks to survive, many intermediate positions were quite specifically defined. Finally, Hoselitz failed to prioritize his variables, explain how they shifted over time, or examine the broader structures of underdevelopment. His pattern variables were, in sum, too vacuous to elucidate economic distinctions, let alone provide policy guidance. They made sense only in the "castle of American social science."[115]

Rostow concocted a similar fantasy. His stages did not reflect "the past or present reality of the under-developed countries whose development they are supposed to guide."[116] Ultimately, what Frank declared about the anthropologist Manning Nash held for Rostow and modernization *tout court:* it denied the poor any history by declaring that they had always been "underdeveloped."[117] Yet the opposite was true. Over centuries, capitalism had created underdevelopment as one of its chief products; poor countries today were not sloughs of tradition, but capitalist outposts. Rostow's stages were therefore chimerical. The early ones were "fictional," the later "utopian," and the theory as a whole lacked historical dynamism: it offered a "comparative statics" without explaining how one stage led to the next.[118] Brushing aside the claim that England developed from its own resources—what of the colonies? the slave trade? mercantilist monopolies?—Frank issued what became a widespread charge against modernization: that it lodged development within the nation alone, ignoring international economic structures. Like Parsons's variables, Rostow's modernization matched no known reality.

Relentless in criticism, Frank did not advance dependency's systemic analysis to the same degree as his fellow *dependentistas*. His popularization of the genre involved considerable repetition, simplification, and heat. Nonetheless, he was, like other dependency theorists, committed to a historical understanding of regional economies. Only "historical context," he insisted, could reveal "the development of imperialism in the world"; adequate policy was impossible without a knowledge of "past economic and social history."[119] Yet unlike the structuralists, who argued that Latin America suffered from an economic dualism of recent vintage, Frank insisted that the duopoly of center-periphery, which he renamed metropolis-satellite, formed part of a "single historical process" dating back centuries.[120]

> Underdevelopment in Latin America (and elsewhere) developed as the result of the colonial structure of world capitalist development. This structure has penetrated all of Latin America, thereby forming and transforming the colonial and class structure of underdevelopment throughout the continent on the national and local levels.[121]

Equally products of modern capitalism, the developed metropolis relied on the underdeveloped satellite for markets and resources—though only the former enjoyed the benefits. The poverty, exploitation, and dependency suffered by the latter was as much a feature of the modern economy as cars and factories.[122] Hence Frank's signature coinage: the "development of underdevelopment."

While Frank eventually acknowledged a limited role for domestic politics in dependent relations, there is little doubt that he placed priority on the dynamics of global capitalist exploitation.[123] Contra Cardoso, contra Furtado, he did not believe that "industrial development [could] break Brazil out of the cycle of satellite development and underdevelopment." For in the end, underdevelopment was due to the "same historical process" that elevated the metropolis in the first place.[124] While exit, or nonparticipation, could provide temporary relief, the only real choice was announced in his famous subtitle: underdevelopment or revolution.

Latin American School Influence

Dependency theory's policy impact was more diffuse than that of modernization. In part, this discrepancy reflected their opposed understandings of foreign aid. Modernizers incorporated aid as a development tool, and their assumptions shaped project design, as we will see in Chapter 5. For structuralists and *dependentistas,* by contrast, aid was mostly inconsequential in the face of larger economic forces. Accordingly, it did not become an essential item in their agenda, which called instead for systemic change or various types of protection and autonomy—strategies that are harder to translate into practice. Some authors even argue that, unlike the Marxist and ECLA program, dependency was primarily a "heuristic device" rather than a set of policy prescriptions.[125]

Yet the broad and penetrating influence of the Latin American schools can be discerned in many activist programs. Most obviously, in 1964, Prebisch was chosen to helm the new UN Conference on Trade and Development (UNCTAD), laying the groundwork for the G-77 push to establish a New International Economic Order (NIEO) in the 1970s and supplying the economic scaffolding of Third World self-assertion.[126] Structuralism and dependency, center and periphery, became a lingua franca for non-Western economic nationalists. Starting in the 1960s with analyses of several West African economies, the Egyptian Samir Amin, for example, mobilized dependency theory in his calls for "delinking" developing economies from capitalist networks.[127] Demands for autonomy and self-reliance rang from Kingston to Dar es Salaam.[128]

In its home hemisphere of Latin America, one finds traces of structuralism and dependency in many political programs. Prebisch's advocacy of regional economic association bore fruit in the Central American Common Market (1960), the Latin American Free Trade Association (1960), and the Andean Pact (1969). If these unions embraced free trade internally, they were established partly along ISI lines to cultivate a regional market shielded by external barriers. With the waning of ISI, dependency became common economic currency, entering the lexicon of even center-right officials. Under Eduardo Frei's Christian Democratic administration (1964–1970), Chilean foreign minister Juan Gabriel Valdés spearheaded the 1969 Consensus of Viña del Mar, promulgated by regional ministers; it placed the struggle against dependency at the heart of Latin American affairs, even as it requested continued foreign assistance.[129] Dependency's influence was even stronger under Frei's successor, Salvador Allende, whose *Vía Chilena* drew its economic program partly from ECLA. From his inaugural declaration that Chile's "backwardness" was rooted in the "dependent capitalist system," Allende tapped regional economic theories in his calls for socialism and independence.[130] The admiration was mutual, as Frank became a staunch supporter. In 1972, Allende hosted the third UNCTAD Conference, where he pitched new strategies to escape underdevelopment. His overthrow the following year ended Chile's turn as a stage of Third World solidarity.[131] A particularly flexible adaptation of dependency strategy appeared in Nicaragua in the late 1970s and early 1980s as the Sandinistas sought to overthrow the Somoza regime and establish a new revolutionary government. To expand their political latitude, they cultivated plural dependencies, fostering domestic and international alliances across the political spectrum to avoid dominance by any single partner.[132]

Arguably the most impactful legatee can be found in Liberation Theology, which embraced dependency analysis in its call for a just society. The 1968 Medellín Conference of Latin American Bishops oriented the regional church toward social and political activism, and declared that Latin American underdevelopment was "an unjust situation which promotes tensions that conspire against peace."

> We refer here, particularly, to the implications for all countries of dependence on a center of economic power, around which they gravitate. For this reason, our nations frequently do not own their goods, or have a say in economic decisions affecting them. . . . Because of the relative depreciation of the terms of exchange, the value of raw materials is increasingly less in relation to the cost of manufactured products. This means that the countries which produce raw materials—especially if they are dependent upon one major export—always remain poor, while the industrialized countries enrich themselves.[133]

In his touchstone 1971 book *A Theology of Liberation*, the Peruvian priest Gustavo Gutierrez wove together the ideas of Cardoso, dos Santos, and other *dependentistas* with those of Mariátegui and Catholic social thought, proffering a local understanding of Latin American reality that fueled regional social movements, guerilla and otherwise, in the 1970s and 1980s.[134]

Structuralism and dependency stand as momentous chapters in the history of development, perhaps the most impactful collective contribution of developing-country economists to the stock of development ideas. If modernizers could claim to have broadened the domain of development beyond economics and introduced history as a methodological commitment, Latin American economists showed the importance of regional particulars for an understanding of development prospects. Yet in crucial ways, modernizers, structuralists, and *dependentistas* shared a set of convictions that opened them to later attack: an overweening concern for industrialization; the embrace of state-led growth and planning; a high-level focus on the nation or globe; and an abstractness and generality brought on by the sheer scope of their enterprises. It was not without reason that David Apter called dependency "Modernization II"—a theory that highlighted many contradictions of the original model but held to some of its core beliefs.[135] For all the calls to regional historical analysis, the vastness of the structuralist and dependency programs discouraged concern for local distinctions. In this sense, Robert Packenham's argument that dependency politicized development knowledge is exactly backwards: because of its vast scope and global emphasis, dependency could have a *de*politicizing effect. Part of the problem was the nature of the arguments: If Frank's polemics made it difficult to engage in politics outside of revolution, Cardoso's malleability allowed him to forsake dependency for a millennial neoliberalism. Ultimately, the sheer size of the agenda made it hard to devise a practical politics for specific times and places. Squeezed between Kennedy's development revolution from the top and Frank's popular revolution from below, what influence could local experiments and regional campaigns have? As the 1970s dawned, a new generation of activists found it increasingly important to engage communities in decisions about their own uplift. Responsibility for mapping 'their future' devolved from grand theorists to program designers, evaluators, econometricians, and practitioners of various sorts, a story we track in Chapter 6.

5

Playing Both Sides of the War: The Contradictions of U.S. Modernization in Cold War Guatemala

JUST AFTER 3 A.M. ON FEBRUARY 4, 1976, a 7.5-magnitude earthquake struck highland Guatemala, toppling walls and ceilings onto sleeping families in a bloody gash that ran east to west across the Cuchumatanes Mountains. In the following days, hundreds of aftershocks raised the toll: over twenty thousand dead, a million homeless. Though merciless, the temblor was not indiscriminate. It devastated highland communities far more than wealthy enclaves on the Pacific piedmont or towns nearer the epicenter. Within Guatemala City, shanties collapsed while nicer buildings held. Poverty and exclusion intensified the quake's ferocity, extracting greater levies from the poor. The recovery was similarly unequal: Remote villages lacked the resources for triage and reconstruction, and rural clinics, if they existed, had insufficient supplies to stop disease. The "earthquake of the indio," as people dubbed it, tracked not only Guatemala's treacherous geology but its precipitous social and economic fault lines as well, with the indigenous poor, who had suffered centuries of exploitation, paying the premium for catastrophe.[1]

Nature's aftershocks foreshadowed even greater convulsion. The earthquake accelerated guerilla mobilization and government reprisal, tipping Guatemala's two-decade-long civil war toward genocide in the early 1980s.[2] Centrally implicated, for good and ill, was a set of institutions promoted by U.S. foreign assistance. Rural cooperatives, established to boost the incomes and well-being of impoverished peasants (*campesinos*), had a substantial history in Guatemala before USAID embraced them in the 1960s. But U.S. sponsorship enhanced their involvement in the country's rural development over the subsequent decade. The earthquake marked a turning point for the cooperative movement. From a USAID-reported peak of 510 rural cooperatives and a combined membership of more than 132,000 in 1976, highland cooperatives suffered a frontal assault in the next half-decade, experiencing what Harvard anthropologist Shelton Davis summarized as "the suppression of a rural development movement." Davis described the shuttering of cooperative training schools, the assassination of community leaders, the murder of bread-bakers and shirtmakers bound in cooperative alliance. "[T]he National Institute of Cooperatives (INACOOP), a government agency created with U.S. funds," became a "front for collecting names of the most active (and dedicated) people in the community—people who would later be eliminated."[3]

Davis was not the only commentator to notice that U.S. support set up recipients for execution. A report written by the USAID contractor Creative Associates in 1987 cited the riskiness of enrolling in cooperatives. Graduates of two USAID-funded cooperative training institutes—the Loyola University Leadership Training Course in New Orleans and the Center for the Training of Social Promoters (CAPS) in Guatemala City—were disproportionately represented among the country's *asesinados:* 750 according to the authors. "Though a direct link between these programs and the assassinations cannot be drawn, a number of participants expressed concern that the visibility of the programs may have helped identify individuals who would stand in opposition to the extreme factions in the country." USAID, the assessors warned, "does not want to implement a training program that may become a participant's 'death warrant.'"[4]

Ironically, even as the United States established cooperatives, it also funded the counter-insurgency that killed their members. That the United States played both sides of the conflict remains little known today. In 2006, the historian Stephen Streeter expressed surprise at the promiscuity of U.S. assistance, which went to both persecuted Mayans and their government hunters.[5] If this tragedy, as we will see, was rooted in competing visions of cooperatives, it also reveals the wider contradictions of midcentury modernization programming, a history that brings together two of the most insightful recent analyses of Guatemalan modernity. In *The Mayan in the Mall* (2012), J. T. Way argues that development projects were structured primarily to integrate the country into a modern capitalist economy. While these efforts were typically imposed from above—either by Guatemala City or its U.S. sponsors—they also tapped local aspirations for social and material improvement. "To this day people clamor for development," Way observes, "even though state-led and global development projects have done little but increase poverty and cloak violence from above."[6] Part of this clamor grew from the fact that, as Greg Grandin suggests in *The Last Colonial Massacre* (2004), development, like liberalism or communism, channeled powerful existential yearnings. Involvement in local uplift efforts, while often disappointing in the end, required a personal and communal labor that allowed *campesinos* to broaden their sense of self-worth and efficacy by committing to the improvement their communities. Ultimately, development entailed individual self-actualization *and* collective activism, hegemonic control *and* emancipatory practice. The battle over development, in other words, is *the* story of Guatemala's twentieth century.[7] And cooperatives were a particularly dense chapter in it.

Cooperativism: Third Way or Ideological Battleground?

According to the Brussels-based International Cooperative Alliance, a cooperative is "an autonomous association of persons united voluntarily to meet their common economic, social and cultural needs and aspirations through a jointly-owned and democratically-controlled enterprise."[8] Historically, the term encompassed a range of organizations, from production and sales collectives to credit unions and savings banks. Ideologically, these groups were as disparate as their services. While many were formed to boost worker competition in the marketplace and thus remained compatible with free enterprise, their promotion of worker-owners, not to mention the allegiances of founders such as Robert Owen, displayed a collectivist leaning. From birth, they have been labeled both capitalist and socialist, and they have comported with both ends of the political spectrum.

In her 1948 book *The World Co-operative Movement,* the English cooperativist Margaret Digby acknowledged this ambiguity.

> It has been said that co-operation is only a specialized part of the system of private enterprise and private capitalism. It has also, and more often, been claimed as a form of Socialism, a partial anticipation of the full Socialist society, 'a fragment of a better order embedded in an imperfect world.' It has been described, less ambitiously, as the defence of the community against

> the unchecked power of the individual capitalist or, by an inversion of the same idea, as the defence of the individual against the omnipotence of the State in economic affairs.[9]

Digby's book, which passed through multiple editions before USAID disseminated a 1965 translation in Latin America, traced the history of cooperativism from its nineteenth-century European origins. The movement was politically androgynous from the start. Its most renowned early instantiation was the Rochdale Society, which founded a famous shop near Manchester, England, in 1844. While Rochdale's seven principles could be seen as pointing toward a noncapitalist mode of production—the society's historian George Holyoake stressed its debt to Robert Owen and the Christian Socialists—there was nothing in the program that forbade market participation. On the contrary, its pioneers emphasized profit-sharing, and they sought to carve out a niche for small producers who, by pooling their efforts, could vie in the modern marketplace.[10] In this regard, cooperatives were less a means of challenging capitalism than of competing within it—a new form of leverage that turned workers into small businessmen. The charge of accommodationism, leveled by revolutionary Marxists against revisionist trade unions, could apply to cooperatives as well. Indeed, they were sometimes seen as a way to *improve* capitalism by training up entrepreneurs—schools for cultivating self-interest and individual gain, rather than subaltern mobilization and solidarity.[11]

Rochdale was only one form of early cooperativism. An alternative credit union model emerged in mid-nineteenth-century Germany, its target membership not urban producers but rural peasants and smallholders. Pioneered by the Rhinelander Friedrich Raiffeisen, credit unions were more centralized and state-controlled than Rochdale shops; Raiffeisen envisioned them as springboards for a federation of agricultural cooperatives. His model traveled widely. The Quebec-based Desjardins movement helped to seed cooperative banks in North America, where they convinced Boston department-store owner Edward Filene of the value of credit for the poor.[12] By the turn of the century, cooperative efforts also arose among Kansas farmers, who allied to purchase equipment and boost profits; and in California, where the Pacific Coast Cooperative Union entered the wholesale market. The Antigonish movement of Nova Scotia drew on Catholic social teaching to launch agricultural cooperatives during the Depression. Credit unions also spread to India, where the British adapted the Raiffeisen model for use "in undeveloped countries, among people generally illiterate and without business experience."[13] Although it is no accident that British colonizers tapped a top-down structure rather than their own native Rochdale, cooperatives were also understood—by the British and later by Gandhi—as training institutions for peasants clawing their way to self-reliance. They taught not only economic skills but democratic practice as well.[14]

Cooperativism also played a role in the socialist world. Although Marx only occasionally referred to cooperatives, they appealed to other early socialists, notably Owen, the putative "founder of the cooperative movement.[15] In the twentieth century, cooperatives were folded into Russian and East European communism, serving as agents of rural collectivization.[16] As Moshe Lewin put it, in the Soviet view "co-operation (the co-operative movement), together with industrialization, was the road which would lead the peasantry to socialism, the way to an improved standard of living for the masses and an increase in agricultural production."[17] Federations such as Centrosoyus and the Moscow Cooperative Society became arms of socialist outreach, with postwar East European states establishing similar institutions.

Another strand of cooperativism emerged from the Russian economist Alexander Chayanov, who argued that peasant economies were neither capitalist nor socialist, but operated according to the needs of family consumption. In lean times, peasants might toil more than market calculations dictated; in plenty, they could forgo easy but unneeded profit.[18] Cooperatives allowed them to carve out a space for their unique economy within a global capitalism that prized different incentives. Chayanov was executed in 1937 (five-year planners wanted collective farms, not peasant economies), but his ideas emigrated. In German translation, they influenced debates about economic agrarianism in Central Europe, notably Romania and Poland.[19] And the 1966 English translation of *The Theory of Peasant Economy* gave them new purchase at a time when Asian and Latin American peasant economies preoccupied development planners.[20]

In the years after World War II, cooperatives became part of the American development industry. TVA administrator Arthur Morgan and Etawah program founder Albert Mayer employed them in community programs, and Point Four proponents argued that cooperatives could support the foreign assistance effort. "The underdeveloped countries are, by definition, rural, poor, and illiterate," wrote one pair of advocates.

> It is all too clear that setting down a few factories in their midst would create the discords of industrialism without its benefits. Industrialism with an uneducated working class can only mean feudalism and revolution. For peaceful progress, the industrialization of the under-developed countries must be accompanied by widespread education, growing democracy and a maximum responsibility for all who will take it. No agency can implement this better than the cooperative movement.[21]

Cooperatives also assumed central importance in 1960s and 1970s Latin America, where local activists and international donors saw them as a way to overcome rural development bottlenecks. The economist Albert Hirschman noted this with some surprise during a 1983 tour of the region:

> For many groups, the fact of joining forces, be it even for a modest purpose, such as the setting up of a cooperative consumer store, has a great deal of symbolic value. It is an act of self-affirmation that fills people with pride and may even be felt as a beginning of liberation, particularly by long-suffering and long-oppressed groups. . . . In many ways, the setting up of a cooperative is the equivalent of achieving land reform and *is felt to be so* by the peasants.[22]

This was a cooperativism wholly in accord with both modernization and peasant uplift.

Guatemalan Cooperativism in the First Half of the Twentieth Century

As in much of Latin America, cooperativism came to Guatemala around the turn of the century with European migrants. The country enacted its first cooperative law in 1903. By the 1920s, cooperatives in the peri-urban fringes followed a playbook drawn from labor unions, organizing collectively to assert demands for land, housing, and other goods. Part of a nascent lower-class movement following the abolition of debt peonage, they once again faced repression under dictator Jorge Ubico (1931–44).[23]

The breakout period for Guatemalan cooperatives was the revolutionary decade beginning in 1944, when they became mechanisms for extending land use and collective property to peasants. After writing cooperatives into the revolutionary constitution, Juan José Arévalo's government established the Department of Cooperative Promotion to provide credit, training, and other support, hoping that collective production could shield *campesinos* from exploitation and provide a "school for popular education."[24] These impulses came to fruition in the Agrarian Reform Law of 1952 (Decree 900), which Piero Gleijeses called "the first comprehensive development plan in the history of Guatemala."[25] President Jacobo Arbenz's signature legislation, the law sought to modernize agriculture by abolishing servitude, boosting agricultural credit, introducing modern farming techniques, and encouraging rural growth and empowerment. It was explicitly capitalist. Its stated aim was to replace "the feudalist modes and relations of production with capitalist ones."[26] Cooperatives were only one strategy for doing so. More important, Decree 900 sought to redistribute land to impoverished peasants and agricultural workers through expropriations of uncultivated tracts on large private estates. Promulgated to redress Guatemala's horribly skewed land ownership pattern, in which, according to the 1950 census, over 75 percent of farms were under four hectares (a paltry 9 percent of total landholdings), the decree placed five-person local agrarian committees (CALs) in charge of implementing and adjudicating confiscations, which were turned over to peasants through either private ownership or lifetime usufruct.[27] By most accounts, the reform effected needed redistribution with little disruption: by mid-1954, almost a quarter of Guatemala's land—17 percent of the country's private property—had been or was in the process of being expropriated, without the predicted declines in output.[28] It was perhaps this initial success that proved most threatening to American Cold Warriors.

The Arbenz government (1951–54) ultimately narrowed the writ of the Cooperative Department, reflecting the preference of many *campesinos* for direct ownership of land rather than collective control. Indeed, the nine cooperatives founded on national *fincas* (plantations) prompted regular complaint and conflict. Nonetheless, cooperativism experienced considerable growth, and the combination of collective production and bumper harvests helped to boost peasant incomes. According to social scientist José Luis Paredes Moreira's tally, by the end of 1953—nineteen months into the reform—6,634 cooperativists had been awarded land from forty-four national *fincas*.[29] Grandin counts "395 cooperatives, free peasant leagues, and plantation labor unions . . . the vast majority in the western highlands and on the southern coast."[30] They had the potential, according to Guatemalan Workers Party (PGT) leader José Manuel Fortuny, to sow "the seeds of a more collective society."[31]

While Fortuny's communist PGT was a government partner, the agrarian reform was hardly the leftist menace that domestic and international opponents claimed. In disrupting feudal inequities, it shared with subsequent counter-revolutionary regimes the aim of creating a modern capitalist agriculture. Nonetheless, elites did have reason to fear revolutionary cooperativism: As one cooperative director remarked, referring to the 1949 General Law of Cooperatives, "against this capitalism, the cooperative has reacted, trying to make work the basis of profits by eliminating commercial capital."[32] When in March 1953 Arbenz decided to appropriate 234,000 acres of uncultivated land from the American United Fruit Company, Washington had seen enough.[33] In June 1954, a CIA-funded coup ended the ten years of spring.

The Catholic Rebirth of Cooperativism

Like the rest of the revolutionary program, cooperatives seemed doomed after the coup. That they took root again on inhospitable terrain is testimony to their ideological malleability: If they were associated with communism during Guatemala's ten years of spring, Catholicism gave them new life in the 1950s. Modern Catholic activism grew out of Pope Leo XIII's nineteenth-century revival of Church social doctrine, one of whose products was the Catholic Action movement, which introduced lay activism. Institutionalized by Pius X (1903–19), Catholic Action spread across Europe and beyond in the first half of the twentieth century, increasing its outreach among workers who might otherwise be tempted by socialism and experimenting with new organizational forms, including cooperatives.[34] Papal endorsement of cooperatives came a half-century later, as the Church prepared to launch its epochal Vatican II conference.[35]

In the 1950s and 1960s, Guatemalan rural society passed through its own Catholic revival.[36] In the late nineteenth century, the governing Liberal Party had "disestablished the church," exiling or retiring much of its personnel and leaving "just a handful of priests and no nuns in rural areas."[37] Left to their own devices, indigenous communities improvised a religious syncretism by combining Catholic rituals with traditional Mayan practices. Sacred functions were typically administered by brotherhoods (*cofradías*) made up of local notables, often Ladino rather than Mayan. Communal administration, in Grandin's summary, also

> centered around a complex organizational hierarchy of civil and religious *cargos* (offices). Village leaders who ascended through the highest ranks of this hierarchy were known as *principales* (elders). The cost of holding office was substantial, involving financial sponsorship of fiestas and other events tied to the yearly village cycle. From these *principales* came the *costumbristas,* those who defended customs and beliefs regulating such economic and social practices as land inheritance, uses of communal property, and life-cycle rituals. These hierarchies were linked to *cofradias* . . . that were often charged with carrying out specific village duties and rituals.[38]

Geographic remoteness helped to protect these practices well into the twentieth century.

Fearful of highland independence, however, Guatemalan leaders starting with Ubico sought to reclaim control by once again welcoming foreign priests to serve in rural districts, hoping that a conservative Church would help to reconsolidate official authority. Arriving first in the 1930s and then in greater numbers during and after the revolution, foreign missionaries sought not only to bolster orthodoxy, but also to combat the threat of communism, a cause dear to the heart of Archbishop Mariano Rossell y Arellano.[39] "By 1966," Bruce Calder writes,

> foreign religious workers had come to constitute 85 percent of the clerical population of Guatemala, with the percentage even greater in many rural Mayan areas than elsewhere. . . . The increasing clerical population was paralleled by institutional growth, with the number of dioceses (or dioceses in formation) expanding from three in 1950 to twelve in 1969. Since nearly half of these new jurisdictions were in the western highlands (and a number of others had significant indigenous populations), the Maya and their localities received even greater amounts of attention.[40]

Priests and nuns from the New York–based Maryknoll Mission, founded in 1911 and recently driven out of Communist China, formed a particularly significant cohort. From twenty-two priests in 1953, Maryknoll's Guatemala mission jumped to forty-one in 1960, along with nineteen sisters.[41] In rural areas, they often relied for outreach on catechists from the local Catholic Action network, founded in Totonicapán in the 1930s.[42] As the historian Betsy Konefal reports, although some Maryknolls became associated with leftist guerillas—Thomas and Marjorie Melville are the preeminent examples—the mission's social justice commitment was born chiefly of the desire to attract Mayans away from communism.[43] In remote northwestern Huehuetenango, this was done by downplaying the leftist strategy of cross-racial mobilization and focusing instead on activities aimed at socioeconomic uplift. To "save souls," many Maryknolls came to believe, they needed to "save men."[44]

The Guatemala mission participated in a larger Maryknoll turn to social activism in the 1950s and 1960s. At their 1954 Lima Conference, Maryknoll fathers from Guatemala and Chile prioritized economic uplift even over spiritual succor. "The principal need is more economic," asserted Father Arthur Allie of the Guatemala mission, "to bring up the level of the people, to counteract poverty and ignorance, immorality, and so on. I think the Church in many instances has been faulty in that regard."[45] Participants touted cooperatives as vehicles for both social and devotional advancement:

> Many of us think of co-operatives from a purely materialistic point of view, as a tool to overcome inertia and misery under the capitalistic regime, and perhaps we overlook one of the greatest aims of the Co-operative Movement—to teach the individual to take his place in society to co-operate with others for his own good and so bring about a solid community spirit which is an invaluable aid for the promotion of religion.[46]

Meeting less than two months after the coup that toppled Arbenz, Maryknolls worried that Latin American communism presented a major threat and that poverty and violence enhanced its appeal. Cooperatives seemed promising because they could alleviate the economic misfortune and further "a sense of belonging, of social participation."[47] By the early 1960s, these virtues encouraged the spread of missionary-directed credit unions.

Soon, this "second evangelization," as it has been called—the first followed the Spanish conquest—embraced development as a social and spiritual mission. Heartened by John XXIII's 1960 call for priests to serve in Latin America, missionaries and lay catechists promoted development as much as religious orthodoxy. Poverty, after all, "makes one forget God," remarked one bishop.[48] "What was necessary," recalled another, was not just "the Bible" but "a vision of development. In the beginning, we spoke less of Christianity than we did of cooperatives and how to approach development agencies. We spoke to the villagers about health care, digging wells for drinking water, and mutual aid within the community."[49] Indeed, for some catechists, development alone evoked an evangelical zeal: "We have the obligation to be like apostles," observed an activist in Sololá. "We have to be the propagators of cooperativism and teach the people who are still ignorant." And in development as in faith, conversion was a goal. As the anthropologist Kay Warren remarked, "the ideology of the cooperative is 'one for all and all for one,' a material version of orthodox Catholic beliefs."[50] Cooperativism was, according to anthropologist Karen Ponciano, "the Christian response to the social problem, because it succeeds in placing capital in the hands of the people."[51]

Along with schools, political parties, and peasant leagues, cooperatives featured in a new institutional landscape that upended traditional hierarchies. According to anthropologist Arturo Arias, they provided *campesinos* with "avenues for credit and savings and the consumption of new products, especially chemical fertilizers," sold at prices that undercut elite suppliers. They also served a social function, "sponsor[ing] political, social, religious, and even sports activities and develop[ing] into autonomous local entities."[52] Politics was not far behind: one of the most radical transformations effected by cooperatives was to challenge local elites—many of whom were Ladinos—by asserting Mayan autonomy. Douglas Brintnall calls this a "revolt against the dead." Of course, even as they empowered community members, cooperatives created divisions. Only comparatively wealthy residents could utilize their services, since most lacked the money to purchase fertilizer. In this way, cooperatives contributed to rural inequality, with more indigent *campesinos* drawn into peasant leagues.[53] They also stoked personal animosities, with some resenting the prominence of local cooperative heads. And as predominantly Catholic organizations, they deepened the rift between Catholics and Protestants, whose numbers burgeoned in the 1960s. Cooperativism, in sum, had prompted significant rural changes even before USAID embraced it.

Thus, by 1968, when the Conference of Latin American Bishops (CELAM) elevated cooperativism into a strategy for promoting "rural transformation," the official Church was playing catch up to the grassroots. Extrapolating from Vatican calls to attend to the poor, the 1968 Medellín Declaration, soon synonymous with Liberation Theology, emphasized the need of "peasants and Indians" for "effective intermediate structures, principally in the form of cooperatives."[54] Did Catholic advocacy legitimize cooperatives in the eyes of cultural and political elites? Or did it indicate a radicalization that made the Church suspect? The ambiguity of the new position invited multiple interpretations.

U.S. Aid in the Post-Coup Years

After the 1954 coup, Guatemala's anti-communist regime confronted the same skewed land pattern that had impelled Arbenz's reform, with population growth increasing rural density.[55] In place of land redistribution, however, President Carlos Castillo-Armas encouraged marketization and the colonization of underpopulated regions. By the early 1960s—with expropriation dropped and confiscated lands returned to original owners—the phrase 'agrarian reform' largely disappeared from official parlance. In this counterrevolutionary atmosphere, cooperatives suffered from leftist associations.[56] Despite acknowledgment in the 1956 Constitution, they were mostly ignored in practice.

U.S. assistance followed suit. In the mid-1950s, Guatemala was the exception to a general U.S. neglect of Central and South America. It was not until the end of the decade, in the wake of a disastrous regional tour by Vice President Richard Nixon and an even more frightful revolution in Cuba, that U.S. policymakers turned their attention squarely to their southern neighbors. By this time, however, Guatemala had already become a testing ground for later interventions. Prior to 1954, the United States' tiny country aid portfolio reflected the general continental disregard: nine technicians, $200,000 in funding, a technical assistance unit in the health ministry, and a small project aimed at launching noncommunist farm cooperatives.[57] But after the coup, President Dwight Eisenhower invested heavily, at first through military support and then with economic aid. By Streeter's accounting, the ICA funneled $63.7 million to Guatemala between 1955 and 1959, fully 15% of the sum given to all of Latin America.[58] Much of this money passed through *servicios*, bureaus set up to offer technical assistance to various government ministries. The impoverished countryside, where inequalities stoked popular anger, was an obvious area of concern.

In 1955, the State Department and the International Cooperation Administration (ICA)—the precursor to USAID—launched the Rural Development Program, managed by the nonprofit International Development Services (IDS). Its stated aim was to transform Guatemala from a "semi-feudal" nation of "subsistence farming" into a country of "independent, middle-class farmers"—not so different, it bears noting, from the previous revolutionary agenda.[59] IDS moved away from the "poorly, if not dishonestly, managed" Arbenz reform (a policy dismissed as "communist-oriented") toward "evolutionary rather than revolutionary processes" in which "any plan for redistributing the land would have to be part of the larger process of the development of agriculture in general." Accordingly, it too dropped the term 'agrarian reform' in favor of 'rural development.'[60] The program employed two main strategies for addressing rural poverty: land resettlement and technical assistance. The first was legally enshrined in 1956, when Castillo-Armas passed a new agrarian law to replace its revolutionary predecessor. In lieu of the confiscation of privately held lands, the government identified idle tracts for peasant resettlement on government-owned *fincas,* in new "development zones" along the Pacific Coast, and on land donated by the United Fruit Company. Once families moved, IDS provided "agricultural credit, adequate roads, instruction in improved farming methods, water, housing, health services and education facilities."[61]

Cooperatives played only a small role in this itinerary, with settlers on newly opened land encouraged to organize themselves for community and development activities.[62] Instead, the program prioritized credit for privately owned homesteads.[63] With a loan agent, families worked out a "five-year farm development plan," and by 1960 the project issued an estimated "4,000 titles." IDS community developers tried to create "an awareness within the families that they themselves possess the capacities and resources to solve their personal, home, and community problems," nurturing "a new class of citizens" who "by their own efforts can advance their personal circumstances and satisfactions as well as the quality of national life."[64]

By the late 1950s, Guatemala looked very different from the years immediately after the coup. The assassination of Castillo-Armas in 1957; the election of an erratic Ydígoras Fuentes as president; the regrouping of a leftist opposition; and the victory of rebels in Cuba—all these events raised U.S. concern about backsliding. Worried that "'primitive' Mayan Indians, who comprised half the population, needed to be 'integrated' into the national fabric lest they fall prey to communism," North American officials sought stronger medicine to heal the poverty and marginalization of the *altiplano*.[65] In this context, cooperatives had some advantages. Unlike unions, they did not have to be political organizations. They could concentrate solely on economic uplift, boosting entrepreneurship and marketization rather than challenging the social order. Yet despite the establishment of a cooperative section at the Ministry of Agriculture, Guatemalan officials were slow to embrace them, and it took John F. Kennedy's urging to push Guatemala City into grudging acceptance of their wider role.[66]

The U.S. rehabilitation of cooperatives began under Eisenhower. As part of a late-1950s shift from military back to economic aid, the administration introduced the Development Loan Fund at the ICA and a series of soft loans through the newly created Inter-American Development Bank.[67] Peruvian cooperatives were early beneficiaries when the Maryknoll father John Considine, building on a credit union movement launched near Lake Titicaca by a fellow priest, received loans for a network of credit and housing cooperatives.[68] His effort kindled regional interest. In 1960, the Organization of American States (OAS) recognized cooperatives as a tool for economic and social improvement and directed its officers to "(1) train leaders of the cooperative movement, (2) carry out pilot projects, (3) hold seminars and technical meetings, and (4) foster rural-credit, producer, consumer, low-cost-housing, and multiple-service cooperatives."[69]

The United States, of course, brought its own cooperative history to bear on the programs it funded. Its key contribution to the global movement was to amplify an individual self-help message that treated cooperativism as a school for entrepreneurship and a channel for marketization. According to the historian Judy Hilkey, the self-help mantra cast "the world as an arena in which—despite fast-paced change, intense competition, and the growth of large-scale industrial enterprise—the individual still had the ultimate power to determine his place," reflecting a faith that "upward mobility could eradicate the strife between haves and have nots and foster an ethos of class harmony."[70] In this sense, cooperativism had depoliticizing and deradicalizing aims, and Gilded Age writers pitted self-help against socialist notions of class contestation. Between 1920 and 1945, American cooperatives enjoyed countrywide growth and solidified their influence through the establishment of national guilds. In the process, the cooperative 'Middle Way' became a viable capitalist model, featuring prominently in Franklin Roosevelt's New Deal and serving in programmatic roles for the Agricultural Adjustment Administration, the Farm Credit Administration, and the Rural Electrification Administration.[71] The TVA, as we noted, established a string of cooperatives to assist poor farmers and laborers, placing them firmly on the agenda of midcentury American liberals and aid planners.

In the conservative retrenchment following World War II, many American cooperatives were forced into a defensive crouch similar to that of unions.[72] But in one area they achieved further success: U.S. cooperativism took on an international role, first in the reconstruction of Europe, and then in America's burgeoning foreign aid industry. Here, the self-help mantra had considerable appeal. According to President Harry Truman, cooperatives were "a positive plan of self-help for any country that wanted it," and Point Four employed them liberally in overseas activities.[73] American cooperative networks took note. The Wisconsin-based Credit Union National Association (CUNA) started working with U.S. officials to spread the credit union model to developing countries—with Peru and then the wider region among its earliest programming sites.

The Decade of Cooperatives

The years 1961–64 saw the initiation of an official U.S. cooperative program in Guatemala.[74] President Kennedy's election helped to lead the charge, and from this point Guatemalan cooperatives stood at the epicenter of rural development and conflict for twenty years. In 1959, then-Senator Kennedy called for government support of U.S. farm cooperatives in order to "place the farmer in the same position as his counterpart in industry when bargaining for a fair market price."[75] Two years later, the new president slotted cooperativism into his fight against Latin American poverty. In 1961, he inaugurated the first Decade of Development by passing the Foreign Assistance Act, which consolidated aid offices under the United States Agency for International Development; and by launching the Alliance for Progress as USAID's flagship program. Proposed as a not-quite-Marshall Plan for Latin America, the alliance is commonly seen as the representative modernization program, designed to develop the hemisphere by growing its GNP and integrating it into the global economy through a "revolution from above."[76]

As part of this effort, Minnesota senator Hubert Humphrey introduced an amendment that officially endorsed cooperativism. To support "free enterprise in achieving rising levels of production and standards of living," the United States would "encourage the development and use of cooperatives, credit unions, and savings and loans organizations."[77] Cooperatives were "democratic, self-help institutions," wrote an ICA administrator, that could channel external assistance and boost civic and community engagement.[78] A 1962 Senate report went further, describing their main advantage as social and political, not economic. Cooperatives "stimulate the sense of pride and stability that stems from the knowledge of ownership. . . . The word 'mine,'" rhapsodized the authors, "works magic. It causes houses to be painted, streets to be paved, fields to become more productive, children to be educated, and battles to be won." For the peasant and laborer, "the feeling of ownership and belonging which evolves from their cooperative can be a strong stabilizing ballast to citizenship. . . . A country covered with local cooperatives and their members—understanding owners—does not fear revolutions and military coups." Cooperatives served, in short, as "laboratories of democracy."[79]

Legislation favorable to cooperatives appeared throughout the decade. Soon after the passage of the Foreign Assistance Act, a Special Advisory Committee gave American cooperatives a champion at the highest levels of the foreign aid administration. Not only could cooperatives "increase productivity, income, and standards of living," the committee enthused, but they could also "provide an essential instrument for the implementation of sound agrarian reform programs, capital formation and an expanded ownership of capital, and an effective training ground in social and political democracy."[80] In the same year, the ICA launched a review of its cooperative assistance programs with the goal of expanding "the self-help objectives" of foreign aid.[81] Funding grew, and in 1966 Congress passed the Title IX amendment, enjoining "maximum participation in the task of economic development on the part of the people of the developing countries, through the encouragement of democratic private and local governmental institutions."[82] The bill's sponsor, Minnesota congressman Donald Fraser, feared that USAID was not doing enough to reform hierarchical institutions in poor societies. While aid officials balked at compromising neutrality, Title IX spurred them to seek out self-help organizations that engaged citizens in social activities. Participation, as Thomas Carothers put it, became a proxy for democracy, and it could be tallied in numbers. Three years later, the Moss Amendment sought to foster private-sector development by calling for loan guarantees to provide concessional funds for "small groups" that were "less creditworthy than [a] normal business enterprise."[83] USAID responded to both directives by boosting support for cooperatives.[84]

Latin America became a staging ground for this endeavor. In January 1962, Kennedy's first USAID administrator recommended a formal aid program for the region's cooperatives. In the same year, at Punta del Este, Uruguay, the charter inaugurating the Alliance for Progress seconded the call by requiring signatories to commit to an agrarian reform that included agricultural cooperatives.[85] Guatemala responded with 1962's Law of Agrarian Transformation, which enshrined the emergent strategy of resettlement and colonization, initially in Agrarian Development Zones along the Pacific piedmont and then more intensively in the underpopulated Petén and Franja Transversal del Norte (FTN) in the country's north.[86] Seeking to create a country of property owners, the law altered the dominant conception of land tenure from usufruct on communal lands to private ownership, and it parceled available tracts into *patrimonios familiares,* small plots meant to support a family.[87] Rural communities would be modernized through technical assistance, credit, market connections, and social services. Cooperatives were one such growth technology. To facilitate their role, Article 77 created an additional type of collective property, the *patrimonio agrario colectivo,* that could be held by groups in common; a 1966 emendation arranged for nationally owned land to be granted to them.[88] A new government agency, the National Institute for Agrarian Transformation (INTA), oversaw the changes, and by 1963, the minister of the economy had registered twenty-four cooperatives, of which fourteen were credit unions. In doing so, it established a framework for the aid-driven development of remote regions, a process aimed at opening channels for top-down control as well as boosting the national economy.

How did the Guatemalan government, ever fearful of peasant militancy, come to accept cooperatives as a vehicle for development? Economic factors were part of the reason. In the early 1960s, falling coffee prices induced a push for agricultural diversification and modernization. A spate of land occupations also contributed, underscoring the destabilizing effects of rural misery.[89] Cooperatives also had national advocates. In 1962, *El Informador Agricola,* the house journal of the National Agricultural Institute, promoted their value as marketing tools.[90] And cooperatives fit into the wider Green Revolution, enticing foreign and domestic officials.[91] For the elite, fear of a Cuban-style revolution was also a motivating concern. As Fidel Castro had demonstrated, the countryside could become a hotbed of resentment—and Guatemala stood on the Cold War front lines. Its use as a training base for the 1961 Bay of Pigs invasion stoked popular anger and fueled a new rebel group—the Fuerzas Armadas Rebeldes (FAR)—forged from remnants of a 1960 army rebellion. To an extent, of course, Guatemala City also had to accept what its northern patron offered—and in the 1960s the United States was backing cooperatives. But Guatemalan attitudes differed from those of their U.S. counterparts. While U.S. officials hoped cooperatives would promote independent citizen-entrepreneurs, the Guatemalan elite preferred subservient *campesinos.* The problem with cooperatives was that they reflected an unavoidably collective notion of small-scale empowerment, of citizen organization separate from the government. While the aspiration to collaborative self-help might appeal to a U.S. sensibility, it made Guatemalan officials nervous.

In response to official directives, Guatemala's new USAID Mission, headed by former CIA agent Keith Himebaugh, investigated the possibility of funding cooperatives. Citing Catholic efforts in Peru and the western department of Huehuetenango, a 1961 Mission memo praised Guatemala's recent cooperativism in anti-revolutionary terms. "Prior to 1957, the cooperative movement was dominated by political motives and was oriented strongly towards the 'Syndicate' system rather than in the democratic, non-political, Rochdale movement." New cooperatives, however, favored "[s]elf-help programs in housing, school construction, potable water supply systems, and certain activities in the rural development program," demonstrating the "feasibility of a group approach" to local problems.[92] In January 1962, a Bureau of Intelligence and Research memorandum noted that support for Latin American cooperatives might help to counter-balance unions, providing improved living standards through organizations that were less politically oriented.[93] They could, in other words, both modernize peasants and moderate leftists, expanding the network of 'safe' associations that broke with the revolutionary legacy.

In early 1962, USAID conducted a feasibility study on launching cooperative projects in Latin America, focusing especially on agricultural credit and cooperative banks. The Guatemalan mission responded with guarded interest, noting that "the number of cooperatives in country" and "the political problems involved in the early years of their formation" made them an intriguing case for support and a "potential value" for rural development. The memo warned, however, that "a lack of widespread interest in cooperatives" was an impediment.[94] Yet six months later, an embassy report identified Maryknoll "economic development" efforts in western Guatemala as a useful inroad. "Although the principle objective of the Maryknollers is spiritual," wrote Foreign Service officer Gerald Lamberty,

> in recent years they have devoted an increasing amount of their time and resources to helping the Indians of the Department of Huehuetenango in the fields of health, education and economic development. Moreover, quite recently two of the Maryknollers have been ordered to devote full time to spurring economic development of the Indians, thus establishing a sort of private AID program.[95]

By identifying "very closely with the interests of the Indians," Lamberty sensed, the Maryknolls were succeeding in altering communal patterns where previous U.S. and Guatemalan government efforts had not. Neither the Maryknolls nor their Mayan parishioners placed much hope in the Alliance for Progress. Yet their highland achievements may have contributed to USAID's decision to finance cooperative initiatives and the Maryknolls who sustained them, especially as the Catholic Church seemed like it "could be counted on more and more to push social action favoring political stability."[96]

In 1964, USAID opened its Rural Community Leadership and Modernization Program, made up of four components: a Credit Union Development Program led by CUNA, an Agricultural Cooperative School in Chimaltenango, a Training Center for social workers in Guatemala City, and a Rural Organization Development initiative run by the International Development Foundation (IDF).[97] Cooperatives were central to all four parts. Drawing on its work in Peru, CUNA tried to build a credit union network by extending loans to the country's existing community cooperatives, establishing new cooperatives, and providing assistance on organizational management. The numbers indicate some success. From an initial 29 credit unions in 1964, the project reported 114 by 1969.[98] Membership also rose—from 9,942 in 1965 to 20,289 at the end of 1969.[99] In addition, CUNA collaborated with a nascent coalition—The National Federation of Savings and Loan Cooperatives (FENACOAC)—to join remote and isolated credit unions into a national federation.[100] Founded in 1963 and officially sanctioned two years later, FENACOAC provided leverage for the cooperative movement.

Other components of USAID's rural program also relied on cooperatives. At the Chimaltenango-based Training School for Agricultural Cooperatives (EACA), founded in 1968, USAID mentored the staff members of agricultural cooperatives in technical and management skills, using government technicians as instructors.[101] As opposed to credit unions, which specialized in loans, agricultural cooperatives offered multiple services: fertilizer, equipment, literacy courses, organizational skills, administrative support, health provisions, and increased market share. A second training component—the CAPS, based at the Catholic Rafael Landívar University in Guatemala City—cast a wider net: it trained "social promoters [*promotores sociales*]" who went back to their communities to join various "self-help groups." In almost three years of funding, USAID reported 787 CAPS graduates, with an additional 1,511 taking satellite courses in their localities.[102] USAID also funded extension services in rural areas.

Yet the cooperatives developed more slowly than officials hoped, with a languor that one assessment blamed on community divisions, stubborn customs, unregistered migration, land inequality, and lack of training.[103] The paucity of rural NGOs made project management difficult, forcing USAID to rely on local interlocutors—expatriate priests, Catholic Action members—as liaisons. A thin Mission staff further limited oversight. Thus, while the partnerships benefited from mutual familiarity—expatriate aid workers 'recognized' expatriate priests, many of whom were American co-nationals—priests sometimes used the funds for empowerment activities unintended by the donor and undesired by elites. If U.S. officials hoped cooperatives would spark rural marketization, local activists could employ them for other goals.

Perhaps for this reason, appraisers found residual "antipathy" toward cooperatives among domestic officials.[104] Ultimately, neither the Catholic Church's anti-communist credentials nor USAID funding could shield cooperatives in the counter-insurgency war. Father Luis Gurriarán of the Spanish Sacred Heart order, for example, was vilified in the press when he sought official recognition for cooperatives, accused of trying to "introduce Arbenz's Communist system and imported models of organization foreign to the indigenas."[105] In the years following his 1965 expulsion, hundreds of cooperativists were imprisoned and assassinated. The grim irony is that just as USAID was funding cooperatives, the U.S.-allied government was attacking them. Modernization justified both policies: while cooperatives could help to prepare the countryside for economic take-off, they could also become agents for militancy. This Janus-faced quality made them regular sites of conflict.

A New Approach

The late 1960s brought a sea change in American development programming as faith in the modernization paradigm, which had dominated aid thinking since the late 1950s, dissolved in favor of a new focus on poverty and equity. Among the many reasons for this shift, discussed in Chapter 6, perhaps most concerning was the evident failure of economic growth to alleviate poverty. As economists and policymakers drew attention to ways that modernizers abandoned the earth's poorest, planners and practitioners turned to 'growth with equity' and the 'basic needs' of the impoverished (both names of broad schools of thought). In 1973, the U.S. Congress passed the New Directions legislation, which reoriented foreign aid toward poverty reduction.

Cooperatives, too, came in for criticism—indeed, they were fairly easy targets. It was clear in the 1960s that cooperatives disproportionately benefited well-to-do peasants; fertilizer, for example, which was heavily marketed by highland cooperatives, required up-front investments that were beyond the means of many *campesinos,* even at reduced pricing.[106] Cooperatives, nonetheless, proved durable. While they were celebrated by modernizers as tools for promoting growth, they could also be incorporated into a strategy for combating poverty through collective action. If they often left the poorest behind, the solution might not be to close them down but to deepen their reach. Thus, cooperativism not only survived into the new decade, but grew into a centerpiece of Guatemala's rural development strategy.

One would hardly guess from the political upheavals of the late 1960s that such a change was in the offing. In 1966, President Méndez Montenegro, claiming to be the third leader of the October Revolution, raised hope among the poor that their economic grievances might be met; his tenure saw some of the last national *fincas* handed to employee production cooperatives.[107] But his rhetoric scared the elite, and he proved incapable of controlling either the FAR rebellion or the military's crackdown. The United States contributed to the latter, supplying police trainers and overseeing assassination campaigns.[108] Echoing modernization theory, which, as we saw, took the military as a valuable ally, counter-insurgency funding rested partly on development premises. "Armies can play a constructive role in defending the aims of the Alliance for Progress," Kennedy declared, "by striking at the roots of economic and social distress"—and, he left unsaid, by combating seductive leftists.[109] Accordingly, starting in the early 1960s with a $5 million grant, USAID trained the Guatemalan military to carry out "civic action" programs that engaged soldiers in social works such as school building or cooperative assistance and facilitated government insertion in the Mayan highlands, helping to set up policies of surveillance and repression.

Amid escalating violence, fraudulent 1970 elections delivered the presidency to General Carlos Manuel Arana Osorio, known as the "butcher of Zacapa" for his counter-revolutionary brutality.[110] While Arana, like earlier leaders, doubted the loyalty of "socialist" cooperatives, his administration oversaw their increased use as agents of rural development, and he set about remaking the country's development infrastructure by establishing supervisory agencies.[111] Aid planners hoped to take advantage of this opening.

The economic face of rural Guatemala was changing as well. In the mid-1970s, the sociologist and revolutionary Gustavo Porras Castejón expressed surprise at the transformation he witnessed after a decade's exile.

> The *campesinos* were already immersed—the majority—in an increasingly commercial agriculture, since the use of chemical fertilizers had been generalized and this meant having available money and subjecting themselves to a money economy. After a short time, the peasants who used to be self-sufficient, who only bought a few candles, some batteries and perhaps a machete, now paid for most of their consumption with money, and for this they sold the fundamental part of their production. The *campesino* economy had been monetized, in the entire country the monetary relations had widened.[112]

The steady, if uneven, incorporation of the *altiplano* into the national economy did not reduce the precarity of life—quite the contrary, given the brewing civil war—but it did present new opportunities for enterprising peasants.

In the late 1960s, USAID revised its cooperative strategy based on several evaluations of the agency's half-decade investment.[113] Community cooperatives had mushroomed in the western highlands, with credit union numbers quadrupling from twenty or thirty at the mid-decade to over 100 by the end. But most of these were fragile and lacking in funds, leaders, market access, and government support.[114] According to a 1976 summary, the CUNA-financed FENACOAC "remained largely ineffective and did not provide many services to its affiliates. . . . It was not, in short, becoming a viable, self-sustaining, effective institution."[115] Another review questioned "the basic philosophy of establishing small cooperatives with weak support" and "doubtful potential for survival."[116] And land inequity had not fundamentally altered. According to an ECLA report from the late 1960s, 88.4 percent of Guatemala's farm units—comprising a mere 14.4 percent of its land—were too small to feed a family with two adult workers. By contrast, 0.01 percent of elite farms (*latifundia*) held 40.8 percent of agricultural land.[117] What good had cooperatives done?

These assessments, it should be stressed, simplified both the original purposes of USAID cooperative funding and its impact in the highlands. Evaluators focused mostly on cooperatives' institutional and financial viability, rather than on the wider democratic payoff foreseen by advocates. And they certainly did not attend to the social transformations that cooperatives effected—their ability to nurture new modes of individual and social identity and to challenge longstanding communal hierarchies. The failure to consider these changes helped clear the way for greater top-down control in the 1970s by prioritizing rural marketization above other goals.

The Rural Credit and Cooperative Development Project, launched in 1970, brought many changes to USAID's earlier cooperativism. For starters, USAID switched implementing partners, terminating its contract with CUNA and hiring Agricultural Cooperative Development International (ACDI), a U.S. cooperative collective.[118] ACDI, in turn, expanded its support from credit unions to multifaceted agricultural cooperatives.[119] The program strategy changed as well. In the 1960s, wrote David Fledderjohn, ACDI's new project director and a veteran of cooperative programs in neighboring Honduras,

> more than 100 cooperatives were organized and chartered in the Highlands. The experience of these small, informally run and feeble cooperatives gave

> ACDI plenty of evidence that, even with the advantage of resources from AID to 'patch up' the ailments of existing cooperatives, this sort of assistance would only have a short-run effect. The cooperatives were ill-conceived to deal with problems of administration, complex service demands of members and the requirements of institutional survival such as capital formation, growth, economies of scale and ability to deal with competition.

Instead, ACDI concentrated on establishing regional cooperatives encompassing "3,000 to 5,000 farmers" who joined as individual members. Increased size would enable greater services, economies of scale, and marketing clout; it would also require "professional hired management" and "strict standards of control." Project directors felt "that the general objective of regional cooperatives, managed by professionals and oriented and served by a national office, is virtually the only course cooperation can take with any hope of institutional survival."[120] Communal associations were not entirely discarded—farmers were combined into local groups of thirty or forty—but these were looser affiliations than the "little cooperatives" they replaced, and they avoided the "costly, time-consuming, and difficult process" of legal chartering. In this way, it was hoped, "economically viable, full-service, democratically representative agricultural and credit cooperatives [would] help 'effect a fundamental reordering of the essential economic relationships in rural Guatemala.'"[121] For Fledderjohn, the new approach balanced two competing imperatives—the need for a complex menu of services and the desire for organizational transparency.[122]

Part of the incentive for changing strategy was to bypass existing local cooperatives (and their FENACOAC federation), which were seen as weak and tainted.[123] For its first regional experiment, ACDI had adopted an older organization—a wheat-growers cooperative on the shore of Lake Atitlán—but after discovering bookkeeping problems and financial malfeasance, it came to regret the decision.[124] A partner federation ("Flor Chimalteca") in the cooperative center of Chimaltenango also proved difficult, so much so that ACDI came to doubt the effectiveness of working in traditional cooperative areas.[125] One casualty of this shift was EACA, the Chimaltenango-based training institute that USAID had financed since 1968. Its staff, wrote one evaluator, "strongly resented the appearance of the ACDI organizers, since they felt that the ACDI organizing activities threatened their own potential growth."[126] Their worries proved justified: In 1971, USAID terminated its funding for the school.[127]

Project managers also aspired to an explicit apoliticism that reflected USAID's preference for technical improvement over social confrontation. ACDI, wrote evaluator J. R. Davidson, "believed in non-political, economically viable cooperatives and consciously tried to instill a non-partisan, non-political ethic."[128] This effort demanded restraint. "Avoid, in early stages, speaking out on larger issues of public policy or legislation or even taking sides in minor community controversy," advised Fledderjohn in his 1990 manual on how to build cooperatives, "lest the cooperative appear primarily a pressure group."[129] Such reticence alienated more activist groups. The Campesino Federation of Guatemala, one of the leading peasant organizations of the 1960s, dismissed cooperatives due to their neutrality and econocentrism. "[I]t was potentially difficult to inspire national labour solidarity in a cooperative," writes Rachel May, because it was "concerned primarily with making economic gains for its particular community, and therefore was not necessarily interested in collective political strength."[130] Yet what was a demerit for peasant leagues was an asset for USAID: cooperatives were a safer bet than other popular organizations.

Apoliticism was accompanied by an explicit break with the past. Donors, of course, can and must adjust their programs in the face of assessment findings, and new contractors typically imprint their own stamp on a project, replacing previous strategies with new ones. Given the low capacity of Guatemalan cooperatives, Fledderjohn was hired to make changes, and ACDI, like any implementer, had to distinguish its approach from competitors since successful branding could benefit future bids. Inherited practices hold little interest for project managers—even if local partners and beneficiaries experience administrative whiplash.

ACDI consolidated its approach in 1974 with the creation of a new national federation—the Federation of Regional Agricultural Cooperatives, or FECOAR—to rival the CUNA-sponsored FENACOAC. At its largest, FECOAR comprised six regional cooperatives—five in the highlands and one in the east—with a membership of over 13,000 farmers.[131] Institutionalization helped to make cooperatives more palatable to Guatemalan elites, their activities "less political and more 'safe' than the activities of other popular organizations."[132]

Their depoliticization, however, was never complete. The problem with cooperatives, as J. T. Way reminds us, is that they are "inherently a form of popular organization."[133]

Turning Point

In 1974, Guatemalan cooperativism gained an ally in the presidential palace. After a March election, once again marred by fraud, General Kjell Laugerud García ascended to the Palacio Nacional on a platform that called for rural development. Taking a cue from the opposition Christian Democrats, he made cooperatives the cornerstone of his agrarian program, the channels through which training, marketing, and assistance would flow. Declaring that the *campesino* had "the right to live better," Laugerud praised cooperatives in terms previously employed by U.S. advocates, arguing that they retained "the principle of private property" and demonstrated "the benefits of individual work."[134] A cooperative, he expounded, "does not appropriate anything belonging to others, nor does it need to appropriate a neighbor's land or goods, or displace the farmer or agricultural company." Instead, it "allows small owners to join their efforts to achieve better production and higher profits." Laugerud set about further institutionalizing cooperativism by legally recognizing regional federations and publicizing their achievements.[135] He was, per press reports, a true believer. "[D]ue to the personal effort of President Laugerud," wrote one editorialist, "the faith in cooperativism is being revived as a norm of political action, an imperative—almost—in the emerging circumstances of our popular economy."[136] Cooperatives, opined another, aspire "to be the main partner of the government."[137]

Whatever his personal affinities, Laugerud's cooperativism also reflected the need to gain control of the countryside and win over peasants from a new insurgency. In the early 1970s, the Guerrilla Army for the Poor (EGP) formed in Mexico City from remnants of the FAR before moving its base to the western highlands.[138] Laugerud responded by invigorating the counter-revolutionary civic action program supported by USAID, with regional cooperatives as nodes of intervention. In the end, the combination of development and counterrevolution proved lethal, with cooperatives employed as staging sites by all players.

Cooperativism, as we have seen, was contested terrain—a socialist incubator for some, a government stooge for others—and Laugerud's example did not lead to its unanimous embrace. Important factions of the government and military—notably former President Arana, who entered the Defense Ministry—continued to denounce it as a brand of communism, a view that gained influence after the 1976 earthquake.[139] In light of this dissension and the continued targeting of cooperativists by death squads, some aid professionals began to question their support for the movement.[140] Some recalled that people were afraid of holding cooperative meetings even though Laugerud encouraged them. "Many leaders became known and very visible," they remarked, "and many of them are dead today."[141] The link between economic development and military reprisal would become explicit in the mid-1980s, when the army adopted a "beans and bullets" strategy in which 70 percent of the pacification effort was earmarked for aid projects—including the displacement of rural populations into model villages ("poles of development")—and 30 percent for repressive measures. In 1986, Air Force colonel Herman Grotewald Cerezo drew the blunt conclusion: "development is war carried on by economic means."[142]

These tensions were particularly high in settlement zones. Although colonization had been an official poverty-reduction scheme since the 1950s, migration was often locally initiated, not government-driven. The FTN was first opened to migrant *campesinos* in the late 1960s by Maryknoll priests based in neighboring Huehuetenango. Spurred by INTA promises of land, Father Edward Doheny established a colony in the remote Ixcán jungle along the Mexican border.[143] Its five subdivisions, or land parcels, were each organized around a cooperative that administered land, labor, production, and consumption. Unlike in the highlands, where cooperatives competed with other social networks, in Ixcán they became the primary hub of community life. By the 1970s, these colonies were legally incorporated as settlement zones, even as *campesinos* sometimes exceeded the "confines of the state's development plan" in ways that would later incur state wrath.[144]

Cooperatives were a social and psychological anchor for many migrants. According to the Jesuit priest and anthropologist Ricardo Falla, who worked extensively in rebel zones, settlers took "pride in belonging to the cooperative, because it structured a new society for the land owners." The Ixcán cooperative, he reported, "was more than an economic organization." It gave

> social reference to all the inhabitants of the project, in the style of the 'commune' of traditional indigenous peoples or in the style of religious organizations (Catholic Action) strongly linked to the political sphere (mayor's office, or *alcaldía*) of modernized municipalities. The cooperative was the matrix that registered all the efforts of the population, and it was the structure that represented it to the outside world.[145]

Beatrice Manz noted the same in neighboring Santa María Tzejá, where the cooperative "laid the basis for a community and became the soul of its success," breeding "a new, spirited confidence that in turn fueled social transformations."[146] Similarly, in La Esperanza "[l]ife revolved around the cooperatives," which ran classes and meetings to spread knowledge of rights and encourage independence. Indeed, the decision to colonize had emerged from cooperative discussions in the settlers' home municipality of Santa Cruz del Quiché.[147]

Yet cooperatives also bred resentment. While many migrants were lured by the promise of land, INTA allotted group "parcels" rather than individual deeds. As Falla put it, "conflicts over land prompted the inhabitants of Ixcán to seek forms of power on their own, without going through the mediation of project management," thus inflaming government suspicions.[148] A central controversy of USAID's later Ixcán project was anticipated when Bill Woods, Gurriarán's successor, shifted land organization from individual to cooperative ownership: "The colonizers were told, explicitly, by Padre Guillermo, that the purpose of the cooperative was to help them get their individual land titles," wrote James Morrissey. "Nothing was said to the colonizers, at any time, about working for a cooperative land title in place of individual titles."[149]

These debates were interrupted by the 1976 earthquake, which triggered popular outrage and turned cooperatives into channels for mobilization. Among the most influential organizations to emerge from the recovery was the Committee for Campesino Unity, which linked Mayan and Ladino activists in a national opposition movement. The group was, as Konefal points out, "a product of years of organizing within the cooperative movement and Catholic Action."[150] Yet even as cooperatives provided havens for peasant activism, they also became bases of government insertion. After touring the devastated highlands, Laugerud sent out military reconstruction teams, expanding civic action efforts to include rebuilding ruined communities. Often coordinating with local cooperatives, these teams enabled increased surveillance and control, setting a collision course with local activists.

This confrontation became manifest in Operación Ixcán, a military relief and pacification effort launched in Ixcán's colonization zone. By the late 1970s, Ixcán was an epicenter of the EGP insurgency. To thwart rebel appeals, Operación Ixcán sought to bolster "the cooperative movement and provid[e] assistance to different communities." Combining development and counterinsurgency, it "entrusted the Guatemalan Air Force with the mission of helping the Cooperatives" so that they could "solve problems of education, health, and agriculture, encouraging the construction of small schools, dispensaries, warehouses, as well as the substantial improvement of the existing airstrips and those that could be built in the future." According to a military spokesperson, peasants would receive this assistance at no cost to cooperative members.[151]

Yet local residents had reason to be skeptical. Improved airstrips and more troops not only brought in goods and services; they also allowed military penetration. The goal of army intervention, according to one informant, was not "service to the population but 'fixing the landing strips and transporting soldiers'"[152] Local cooperatives, initially established to meet peasant needs, became channels of military insertion.

Laugerud's successor, Romeo Lucas García, continued this cooptation. In December 1978, he established the National Institute of Cooperatives (INACOP) as a supervisory agency.[153] Over the next decade, INACOP oversaw Guatemala's officially sanctioned cooperative movement, providing credit, infrastructure, training, and other services. The condition for this support was that affiliated cooperatives remain "distant from all political activity," as INACOP's president remarked in 1981, "far from subversion."[154] Accordingly, the agency established new cooperatives in conflict areas and dropped those suspected of guerilla activity, hoping to show that cooperatives were "capable of acting in an entrepreneurial fashion and generating profitability in the production of goods and services."[155] The effort to convert them from social into market institutions entailed historical revision: In 1983, INACOP cited the original 1903 cooperative law to claim that cooperativism in Guatemala derived from government concern for citizen well-being, not popular initiative. Revolutionary cooperativism betrayed this legacy.[156] Apolitical, econocentric, cost-efficient, development-focused—cooperatives remained official institutions in Lucas García's National Development Plan even as he intensified violence against their members.[157]

Unsurprisingly, cooperativists in exile told another story, one in which the government usurped cooperatives in order to lock down the population and target members for assassination. One escapee reported a particularly gruesome episode:

> At 9 in the morning on March 14 [1982], Sunday, a helicopter flew very low over the cooperative [La Union in Selva Reina, Ixcán]. It turned three circles and people were terrified because it was Sunday and the day for going out—the market and the church were full of people. Nobody did anything about the helicopter. Twenty minutes later it appeared at the top of the runway along with a group of soldiers, over in the old barracks behind the market. People got scared. Then the army shot at them. . . . Then the soldiers herded everyone together, separating men and women. The children shut themselves in houses and storage facilities. On Monday they hanged the men from the houses and storage facilities and tortured them. They drove the women to the river, where they raped them. The children screamed in the storehouses. On Tuesday around 10 a.m., they started in with the murders. The men were almost all already dead and many were unconscious. The soldiers killed everyone, men and women, not with gunfire but with machetes and knives. At noon everything was completely quiet.[158]

More than 300 people died in this incident, according to testimony given to a German rights organization. Similarly, a 1991 report found that "approximately 250 cooperatives (80% of those in the rural areas in the west of Guatemala) were destroyed."[159] As Rachel May remarks, "INACOP became the headquarters for collecting the names of community leaders so that they could be eliminated."[160]

By the 1980s, some former cooperative members questioned whether cooperativism itself suited their needs.[161] In Mexican exile, refugees lamented the "political neutrality" forced on government-sanctioned cooperatives, complaining that

> they prevent their members from having contact with the country's political problems and are witting or unwitting accomplices of government policy.

> Their methods favor individualism, and they limit themselves to 'education' in professional competencies, without addressing the fundamental problems of Guatemalan society, without promoting objective judgment.[162]

Earlier migrants had tried to recreate peasant cooperatives in their new colonies; by the late 1980s, cooperativism itself was called into doubt.

Playa Grande

In the late 1970s, Ixcán stood in the crosshairs of national trends. With lands in the Petén increasingly claimed by elites, the FTN attracted not only poor migrants but also wealthy prospectors who bought up soil for cash crops, mining, and drilling. The late 1970s was also a tipping point in Guatemala's civil war, with Ixcán serving as a guerilla redoubt until the scorched earth campaign of 1982–83.[163] Almost inevitably, these two trends—incoming wealth and roiling insurrection—drew military and development attention. In the context of aid-industry doubts over the ability of modernization to combat poverty, Guatemala's longstanding strategy of colonizing underpopulated lands came in for renewed interest as a way to "accommodate the poorest of Guatemala's farmers, those who owned no land and lacked resources to acquire it."[164]

In 1975, USAID launched its own colonization effort in the FTN, laying claim to a thin substrip of territory along the Mexican border. The Small Farmers Project—also known as the Playa Grande or Ixcán Grande Project, after the administrative center where it operated—sought to resettle 5,000 families on land parcels of approximately ten hectares each.[165] As in the neighboring Maryknoll settlements, families were organized around community nuclei and assigned to cooperatives that assisted with health care, schools, and local administration. Roads were planned to connect the region with outside markets. Yet under this new colonization strategy, the project carried on with familiar practices. Intending to serve "landless residents of the densely populated highland regions," the implementer—once again ACDI—adopted the prior tactic of relying on cooperatives as managerial agents.[166] Cooperative federations were to lead the recruitment of *campesino* families for resettlement; and local cooperatives were to organize economic and social life in each community, handling trade, marketing, and (controversially) land-titling. Cooperatives not only retained their centrality in rural development plans, but expanded their reach by moving to new locations.

Many settlers appreciated cooperatives. Not only did they provide social and institutional centers for people trying to make a new life, but they channeled goods and services in the remote jungle. Indeed, USAID managers found that, despite their "hardy independence," *campesinos* did not aspire to be self-reliant frontiersmen; they expected government services such as schools and health clinics.[167] Thus, USAID tapped cooperatives as local venues for government provision and settler–state interaction. Fledderjohn, again ACDI's project chief, hoped the government would shift away from "the present cumbersome, paternalistic and closely guided approach" and toward "a more open, spontaneous settlement program carried out by organized cooperatives" with official support.[168] The regional cooperatives built in the early 1970s, he believed, could accommodate this task by serving as "the 'people department' of the project."[169]

Yet cooperatives were operational headquarters not only for aid planners and *campesino* settlers, but for other parties as well: insurgents hoping to win sympathizers and organize resistance; military counter-insurgents trying to root out suspected rebels; and government officials trying to gain a foothold in virgin territory. Ultimately, this proved too much for such modest institutions to bear. Rebel advances were hard to fend off. Both spontaneous colonizers and USAID-sponsored settlers interacted with the EGP, which—capitalizing on widespread sympathy for rebel grievances, if not for their tactics—looked to cooperatives as useful venues for infiltration. While support varied both among and within cooperatives, they became favored rebel-organizing mechanisms because their existence alone indicated a readiness by historically oppressed Mayans to exercise local control and engage in community activism. They were, in this sense, the social and institutional expression of a heightened political consciousness.

The government was also impossible to turn back, although here the Ixcán project played a facilitating role. In 1978, USAID provided the government with a $5.6 million loan to launch project activities, a partnership that stood at some odds with the donor's initial aim to support 'spontaneous settlement' and self-help by "holding government intervention to a minimum."[170] The collaboration also marked a departure from past practice: In the 1960s, USAID had to receive official licensing, but projects had minimal government involvement other than technical support in the form of assessors and trainers. With the accession of Laugerud, however, government openness to cooperativism encouraged USAID to start making loans directly to official agencies and rely on them for managerial input. For the Playa Grande Project, USAID turned to INTA—despite its oft-remarked inefficiency—to establish an "implementing unit" and prepare land titles.[171]

This partnership helped both the government and USAID overcome regional unfamiliarity. Through exploratory visits, the implementation team gained "insight on subjects ranging from weather, topography, and health conditions to crops, housing, travel conditions and problems present in the area." Some of the discoveries came as a surprise, revealing how little officials knew of the area. "For example, on one trip made in August 1977 [project manager] Thompson discovered that the land blocks (Polygons #12, #13, and #20) supposedly designated by INTA for this project, had actually been settled or committed to be distributed and therefore were not available."[172] Project reports also acknowledge heavy reliance on the military: "Through a strong civic action program, the military was the main route of contact with the outside world for pioneer families. Health services were also provided for the population and often project staff found excellent logistical support from military sources."[173]

Yet collaboration with the government was not easy. USAID reports are filled with complaints of administrative inefficiency. Problems began almost immediately. Despite over $5 million in loans in the first half of 1976, the project stalled due to interminable interagency planning.[174] It took a 1978 presidential decree to finally get it underway—several years later than intended. The recruitment of cooperative federations also proved nettlesome, so much so that exasperated managers likened it to "a mating ritual of exotic birds."[175] Of the four federations initially envisioned for the project, only two—the USAID scions FECOAR and FENACOAC—were contracted.[176] Yet INTA chafed at FECOAR's oversight of settler recruitment; and FENACOAC proved so reluctant to take advice that its subcontract was terminated in 1980.[177] Land rights also generated confusion, and conflicting INTA petitions for public land in the settlement area revealed an agency unprepared for the project.[178]

FECOAR and FENACOAC also had difficulty recruiting settlers. At the outset, ACDI expected to draw its greatest numbers from the western highlands, but when recruitment efforts met with peasant reluctance, it turned instead to central Alta and Baja Verapaz and to migrant workers along the coast.[179] Evaluation reports attributed the disinterest to communal attachments, distance from home, fears about the life in the FTN, and the "political situation" in the highlands. Managers blamed "rumors and doubts."[180] Yet decades of peasant experience raised a more obvious question: Why would *campesinos* want to come in the first place, given that the colonies were initiated from above? In the event, these fears proved prescient. Despite the sluggish pace of settler recruitment, the establishment of support services was slower still: most were not available when migrants first arrived in 1981. Worse, in 1982, oil exploration led the military to remove some settlers "as part of a security measure," and then to destroy three communities based on accusations of rebel sympathy. The project administration plainly had "counterinsurgency goals."[181]

Settlers also complained about the cooperatives at the heart of the project. Some resented being obliged to join them; others recalled "bitter experiences" in their home regions; still others said that cooperatives "had a history of outright fraud by their elected officials." Indeed, managers recalled several "ugly shouting matches" at their mention.[182] Although orientation trips and careful negotiation won over some migrants, subsequent policies, especially around land ownership, often undercut this faith. While some settlers believed they would receive individual titles, the project ultimately granted only use rights (usufruct) for land owned *collectively* by cooperatives. Settlers "commonly" called this a "'rip-off,'" acknowledged Fledderjohn and Thompson, "and wanted nothing to do with the idea." The policy, set by INTA, reflected valid concerns about equity: Guatemalan history is replete with examples of desperate peasants selling their plots for quick cash. Since the Playa Grande Project was designed to address land hunger, collective titles prevented sales without community approval. But it was nonetheless unpopular. In every case, reported the managers, "settlers requested their individual domain."[183] Evaluators noted the same: "Guatemalan peasants want their own piece of land, to which they can devote their own efforts."[184]

In the end, what frustration started, exhaustion finished. By 1982, with the project underfulfilled and over budget, ACDI ceased work. Although the "future is not clear," wrote the outgoing managers, they warned against discontinuation as an option "if the credibility of institutions committed to improving the lot of landless peasants is to survive."[185] Yet two years later, with only one project cooperative still operating, supplies confiscated or stolen by the military, and hundreds killed or exiled, project extinction seemed a fait accompli.[186] Fear, as evaluators noted, led people to avoid any community organizing that might draw government suspicion.[187]

Posthumous evaluations cite implementation failures such as drastic undersettlement, insufficient services, bureaucratic logjams, budgetary overages, and land title controversies. These were significant concerns, but they ignore the wider context that rendered the project dubious from the outset. What is strangely muted in reports is what evaluators euphemistically called the "security" or the "political situation." Indeed, the project's most effective year of operation—1982—came as Operación Ixil, the military onslaught led by Ríos-Montt—got underway, with the project area square in its sights. Yet while a 1984 assessment acknowledged "serious problems caused by armed conflict and military activities in the project area," it said little else, adding only that INACOP efforts "have been somewhat curtailed by adverse pressure from the military" and "[c]ooperatives are apparently regarded with some suspicion as potentially 'subversive.'"[188] According to another report,

> The level of political military violence within the project area in the period December 1981—March 1982, made it much more difficult for contractors and government agent workers to operate effectively. Work was stopped in the project area by military authorities in February 1982 for several weeks. During this period perhaps as many as 400 families left the project site, with two villages being evacuated. One other, Trinitaria, was burned to the ground. Since the change of government [to Ríos-Montt, later convicted of genocide!] in March, the military authorities in the project area have [been] considerably more cooperative and helpful, though difficult on the distribution of food for food-for-work activities. Farmers in the FTN reported that the military had confiscated stockpiles of corn 'to keep it from the guerrillas.'[189]

This is one of the more detailed USAID references to the violence, but it is mild language for a project with a front row seat to a massacre.[190]

Strikingly, four years later and freed from official constraints, the same evaluators whose bland language appeared in an earlier report offered more a forthcoming assessment to an independent journal.[191] While recalling positive collaboration with the Guatemalan government during the project's early years, the evaluators now acknowledged that projects "take place in a national political context, and in the case of Guatemala the context has been violent." If the EGP engaged in targeted assassinations, the military government's response "has been widespread repression, including the slaughter of whole communities." This violence was part of a historical pattern evident since the 1960s and rooted in the country's long chronicle of Mayan exploitation; but it was intensified in a regional quadrant of jungle that officials ominously dubbed "little Cuba."[192] What the authors could not acknowledge in their official evaluation, they did here: "between 1,000 and 5,000 Playa Grande residents were killed by the army," including cooperative members, who were "prime targets." Not only had the project done little to improve the situation, but the infrastructure it provided—roads, hospitals, settler registration—served the military campaign as much as *campesinos*, who were "both the beneficiaries of rural development programs and the objects of repression and violence."[193] Perhaps most disheartening, these conditions were not isolated to Guatemala. Citing similar circumstances in Vietnam and El Salvador, the authors recognized a core dilemma of foreign aid: the price of development is often government insertion, and the price of that may be repression. In Guatemala, the insistence on apolitical development, stripped of social and historical context, helped ease the way.

It is tempting, of course, to charge the project with gross negligence, if not complicity. But this is an oversimplification. Instead, we must understand how aid projects can operate in ways that muzzle staff concerns or enforce neutrality. In the fog of war, with rumors and accusations competing against government reassurances, local staff, even expatriates, rarely have much control. Decisions are taken far away by officials who are inadequately informed and who face political and funding pressures. Project managers must respond to these demands, even when they seem to nullify events on the ground. In this way, management structures can divorce project operations from local context, privileging political imperatives from above and contributing to practitioner (and beneficiary) disempowerment. In addition, the anodyne phraseology of official USAID reports, as Beatriz Manz has shown, makes political neutrality easier by sanitizing accounts coming from the field. To take one example, a statement in a draft Ixcán project report read, "Three of these 18 settlements (Trinitaria, Santa Clara, and El Quetzel) were exterminated by the military"; in the final USAID report, it was rendered as "Three of the uninhabited 18 settlements (Trinitaria, Santa Clara, El Quetzal) no longer have settlers."[194] Predictably, Washington policymakers who read this "odiously euphemistic language" had little sense of urgency.[195] Frustrated local staff, faced with a gulf between their official directives and their local context but reliant on government permissions and approvals, may resort to fulfilling tasks and offering what protection they can.

Despite the incentives to silence, however, it is doubtful that practitioners were unaware of the ongoing butchery. Aid workers routinely share their views on local politics over private meals or drinks. But on the job, projects can become black boxes, with high walls built of policy mandates and diplomatic norms that limit what can be said or done without cost. In the best of situations, these pressures impose subtle technical blinders, encouraging practitioners to focus on immediate activities with scant concern for the ways that broader political trends affect project results. In conflict zones, they make projects susceptible to government (or other belligerent) misuse in ways that may contribute to harm.

The history of U.S. cooperative programs in Guatemala is a story in two halves. From the early 1960s until 1970, USAID funded cooperatives in the hope of stimulating rural marketization and integrating highland areas into the national economy. But it did so without really controlling its experiments. Lacking knowledge of Mayan Guatemala and without emissaries in indigenous communities, USAID passed funds through expatriate priests and Catholic activists who established or expanded cooperatives in the highlands. Starting in 1970, however, USAID revised its agenda by incorporating cooperatives into a managerial framework that facilitated greater hierarchical control. This revision culminated in ACDI's Playa Grande Project.[196]

The concurrent support for cooperativism and counterinsurgency set the United States' Guatemala policy at odds with itself. Both were planks in a rural modernization program, with cooperatives an inducement to economic modernity based on market entrepreneurship, and counter-insurgency justified as prevention against what Walt Rostow called the disease of communism. To modernizers in the early 1960s, it was not inherently paradoxical to believe that counter-insurgency could clear the way for cooperative-led development—even if it displayed naiveté regarding Guatemala's long history of strife—or that cooperatives might help to replace revolutionary hopes with new market gains. By the 1980s, however, this faith should have been harder to sustain. Cooperatives were no longer simply tools for *campesino* uplift, as Catholic activists envisioned them in the 1950s. Instead, their use as government access points made them seem more like agents of counterinsurgency. To join a cooperative on a government-managed, U.S.-funded settlement—in a rebel infiltrated lowland—meant something very different to besieged *campesinos* in 1980 than it had to their impoverished parents in 1960, when cooperatives were small and local. Indeed, the gradual loss of peasant control—to development programs, to rebels, to the government, to the military—was both a cause and consequence of violence, and cooperatives grew ever more schizophrenic—ally and enemy—in their effect: institutions of peasant uplift *and* targets of official suspicion; channels for government services *and* staging grounds for military reprisal. Settlers on the Playa Grande Project were caught in the middle.

It did not end well. The well-proven fear that cooperativism singled out individuals and communities for reprisal led to a turn away from cooperatives in the Ixil region, though national and international donors continued to fund them.[197] By the mid-1980s, cooperatives began to shift away from the social and political activism of preceding decades, some turning toward income generation and traditional crafts programs, others to nontraditional agro-exports. As one respondent put it, a "business [*empresarial*]" model gradually came to replace a "social" model.[198] Where the indigenous activism of the war years frequently combined demands for cultural recognition with revolutionary solidarity across ethnic lines, public discourse after the genocide privileged a cultural agenda of protecting and preserving Mayan communities over political calls for autonomy and justice, with cooperatives helping to market traditional crafts for income.[199]

Although evaluators in the late 1960s complained about the limited impact of USAID's cooperative investments, a more local perspective suggests that this judgment might have been too severe. When USAID lacked administrative control, its funding had some effect—though not always as intended. In the 1950s and 1960s, cooperatives did indeed become bases of peasant empowerment that helped to transform communities—often without but sometimes with U.S. funding. They were used to challenge local hierarchies and promote peasant mobilization and self-reliance. They contributed, in other words, to a growing rural assertiveness that reached its acme in the 1970s. But thereafter, as USAID and the Guatemalan government achieved greater leverage over cooperatives, their influence as organs of peasant empowerment waned, veering away from social transformation and toward economic growth, expanding the provision of seeds, fertilizers, and market opportunities but narrowing the scope of *campesino* activism. Predictably, some communities began to doubt their value, seeing them as arms of government repression rather than tools of reform. Ironically, then, USAID's positive influence was greater when it had less control, leaving decisions to local leaders. That influence darkened when USAID and its government partners assumed greater authority over the parameters of cooperative action.

This administrative takeover artificially divided USAID's trajectory, drawing a bright line across 1970 as a past not worth revisiting. The long arc of awareness was not a concern of new project implementers at the dawn of the decade. Instead, they dismissed the past, avoiding traditional cooperative centers and former methods in pursuit of a top-down cooperativism designed to uplift peasants and assuage government partners. Also unnoticed was the history of official repression that might have suggested the dangers of such an alliance. The imperative to act and the need for managerial control deflected consideration of the wider social and historical dynamics at work in rural Guatemala.

6

The Presentist Bias: Ahistoricism and International Development in the 1970s

IN THE 1970S, THE FOREIGN AID community abandoned the Eurocentric histories that girded modernization and embraced the giddy freedom of amnesia. Robert Chambers, a pioneer of the evaluation method known as Participatory Rural Appraisal, recalled the sunny mood of young aid workers cut loose from professional enclosures and freed to experiment with new techniques.

> There I was, in Sri Lanka first, and later in Tamil Nadu, with months and months for fieldwork and no fixed agenda. Far from having a straitjacket of formal hypotheses and a research design, or being tramlined by a logframe, I was free to be flexible, to wander, to explore, to choose what leads to follow. No one breathed down my neck. Benny Farmer, our benign project director, was busy thousands of miles away in Cambridge [England]. My colleagues were far more competent than me in their own fields and got on with what they wanted and needed to do. I was in no way a supervisor. . . . My freedom was an extraordinary privilege.[1]

Chambers's experience captures the effervescence of a generation of developers-errant. The excitement was not the sole preserve of rookies. His veteran colleague Hans Singer, whose signature contribution to the Prebisch-Singer thesis (Chapter 4) had already set him apart from the development establishment, enjoyed a renaissance in this decade. At its end, he offered a sympathetic account of its development heresies: Emerging in the late 1960s amid doubts about modernization's growth mandate, a new concern for poverty alleviation grew into a focus on wealth redistribution and a call for addressing the basic needs of the poor.[2] Poverty itself, with its attendant miseries, burst into view as a condition that had to be relieved here and now, rather than waiting for the delayed manna of GDP growth to trickle down from above.

Situated chronologically between the bulwarks of modernization (1960s) and structural adjustment (1980s), the Second Development Decade has only recently drawn scholarly attention.[3] Its commitments were of a different ilk from the paradigms that bracketed it, not least because the decade's brisk logos—Redistribution with Growth, Growth with Equity, Basic Needs—did not denominate fully elaborated programs. The profuse fields and practices associated with the 1970s anti-poverty agenda—a short list would include participatory assessment, integrated rural development, appropriate technology, development ethics, development anthropology, microfinance, Women in Development, and education for development—were often mix-and-match strategies that ill suited disciplinary straitjackets. In the words of one proponent, equity approaches and their basic-needs siblings lacked "an authoritative, comprehensive, and definitive work," enabling "people with divergent views and ideologies to advance a wide variety of policies, institutions and strategies" under their names.[4]

Perhaps this fluidity arose partly because 1970s development innovations were driven by practitioners more than theoreticians. The thrust of new strategies was normative and practical, aimed more at problem-solving than theoretical integrity. As a result, new programs had a nuts-and-bolts quality foreign to modernization and a normative pique born of face-to-face encounter with the poor. To be sure, equity and anti-poverty commitments passed upward into the halls of power: the World Bank's Robert McNamara became a leading spokesman. But the decade remains the era in development history when the common characterization of foreign aid as an extension of foreign policy holds the least. It is also the period when many of today's baby-boomer aid managers first entered the field, and thus its assumptions remain remarkably current in the development industry. Despite several decades of neoliberal dominance, practitioners still fix on poverty alleviation, primary education, women in development, community-building, and participatory programming, all of which took shape during the 1970s as part of the call to reorient efforts toward "the poor of the earth."[5]

Yet despite (or perhaps because of) this reorientation, development grew more ahistorical than it had been under modernization. We have already seen that ahistoricism took several forms in development's first three decades. The 1970s introduced still newer types. Most particularly, anti-poverty advocates jettisoned the historical ahistoricism of modernization theory in favor of an immediate moral imperative to uplift the downtrodden. The 1970s was a time, wrote aid ethicist Denis Goulet, to "thrust debates over economic and social development into the arena of ethical values," a task that past experience was ill suited to assist.[6]

The decade's debates, I hasten to add, were not uniform in their focus on equity and poverty relief. Most obviously, these emphases only characterized the decade's mainstream thinking, not its market-oriented dissidents (discussed in the second half of the chapter). Furthermore, the modernization program, though weakened, never vanished: Seminal works, such as Alex Inkeles and David Smith's *Becoming Modern,* about social and psychological change in developing countries, appeared during the decade.[7] And even in the mainstream, the initial concern for *both* poverty *and* equity gave way in the second half of the decade to a primary fixation on poverty alone, a shift, as we will see, that prepared the way for the subsequent neoliberal ascendancy.

Development against History

During the modernization era, as we saw, development theories took Western industrialization as prototypical. This entailed severe reductivism—what I have called historical ahistoricism —but the incorporation of history was nonetheless significant. By the late 1960s, however, the modernization consensus was fraying.[8] In the West, student rebellions and urban unrest undercut the modernizers' assumption that prosperity begot stability. In Latin America, the site of the sprawling Alliance for Progress, modernizing societies witnessed coups and repression, starting with Brazil in 1964. Reports of famine in Bihar and Uttar Pradesh raised doubts about the efficacy of foreign aid in a country that had received large outlays.[9] The development industry also suffered from association with the Vietnam War, whose Strategic Hamlet program was built on modernization premises. No one knew, of course, when Robert McNamara, an architect of that war, resigned from the Defense Department to head the World Bank, that he would launch an anti-poverty crusade; but in retrospect the 1968 job transfer was an important marker. Quantitative studies took a bit longer to emerge, but by the early 1970s there was mounting evidence that industrial expansion did not necessarily elevate the lot of the poor; inequality, not improved welfare, seemed the rule in modernizing societies. In the face of new generational concerns about the environment, gender, poverty, and equity, modernization seemed not just outdated but antithetical to the global uplift it claimed to foster. Criticism of 'growthmanship' had haunted development economics for years, but it was only in the late 1960s that accumulating doubts finally loosened its grip on policy.[10]

For the intellectual tenor of development thought on the eve of the 1970s, Gunnar Myrdal's *Asian Drama* (1968) remains a bellwether, not because it offered novel development solutions but because it testified to the exhaustion of the modernization framework.[11] A Swedish economist and former government minister, Myrdal rose to fame with an analysis of "the Negro problem" in the United States; he then spent the 1950s outlining a vision of global welfare.[12] From there, he devoted the following decade to his sprawling account of South Asia: the final product—a three-volume tome spanning 2,200 pages—was as much an institution as a book, with numerous researcher-alumnae becoming leading figures in later reform movements.[13] The book itself, a vast regional analysis with India at its center, combined history, theory, and policy advice. But it was ultimately the pessimism that stood out: Myrdal advocated a wholesale but unlikely reform of Indian institutions, since no amount of growth or industrialization, in his view, could yield a modern subcontinent without a dramatic revision of basic structures. As opposed to Myrdal's United States, where the gulf between egalitarian ideals and slaveholding traditions might be overcome through ongoing modernizations, the inegalitarian traditions of India were so deeply embedded that he found it hard to imagine the realization of Nehru's ideals. Two thousand pages did not bring Myrdal closer to a solution.

What they did do, however—and quite emphatically—was demonstrate that inequality, not development or stability, had been the chief product of Indian modernization. The year after *Asian Drama*'s appearance, class-based rebellions convulsed areas that stood at the epicenter of the Green Revolution.[14] "The plight of the masses of people in the underdeveloped economies of South Asia would be serious enough if income were evenly distributed," Myrdal admonished, but "[t]he high degree of inequality means that the vast majority in each nation is forced to eke out an existence on annual incomes well below the already quite inadequate national average."[15] A particular culprit here, and one of the chief concerns of Myrdal's trilogy, was the inadequate development models forged on the basis of Western experience. The assumption of a large labor reservoir available for industry simply did not characterize an Indian peasantry bound by seasonal and traditional rhythms; they could not be expected to abandon longstanding customs and move to modern-sector jobs. Nor could one assume, as modernizers did, that growth-producing savings could be generated in a poor society, or that profits accrued by agriculture or industry would be reinvested rather than shoring up consumption. The Western examples that lured Indian modernizers were inappropriate. Only a thoroughgoing rationalization of institutions—a painstaking and lengthy process—could launch the country toward modernity. Indeed, Myrdal coopted the term *modernization* to characterize the goals and values of his study, though he distinguished it from what he called the "modern approach" that tried and failed to transplant Western stock to Indian soil.[16]

Myrdal's themes reverberated across the next decade. Among the champions of new development thinking was Dudley Seers, the founder and first director of the influential Institute for Development Studies (IDS) at the University of Sussex.[17] His oft-cited 1971 article "What Are We Trying to Measure?" articulated a sea change in development aims: "[R]educing poverty, unemployment, and inequality," not promoting growth, should become the primary mandate and the chief measure of success.[18] By the time of the 1969 talk that preceded his article, Seers was already a well-regarded economist who had worked for Britain's Colonial Office, ECLA, and the UN Economic Commission for Africa. The ECLA years (1957–61) in particular, when he collaborated with Raúl Prebisch, Osvaldo Sunkel, and others, turned Seers, according to his colleague Richard Jolly, from a Keynesian into a structuralist and made him a conduit for the Anglophone reception of dependency theory.[19] An Oxford statistician in his early career, Seers enjoyed regular stints as a foreign advisor: In Chapter 3, we encountered his work in the Gold Coast, where he coauthored a 1952 economic development plan for the colony. In the 1960s, he produced a similar plan for independent Zambia, the so-called Seers Report, which called for directing copper revenues to rural development and light industry, cultivating human capital, and attracting foreign investment in the local mines.[20] When Harold Wilson's Labour government came to power in 1964, he joined the new Ministry of Overseas Development, which, like Kennedy's USAID, consolidated Britain's aid architecture—a significant venture in the wake of decolonization.[21]

By the mid-1960s, these experiences had led Seers to question conventional development wisdom, and he was well positioned in 1966 to open Britain's first academic development institute, which soon became a fountainhead for new thinking.[22] IDS members—including Singer, Chambers, Michael Lipton, and Richard Jolly—collaborated extensively with multinational organizations, notably the International Labour Organization (ILO), whose World Employment Programme released path-breaking reports on growth-resistant poverty. Seers himself led five ILO missions, including the influential Colombia mission of 1970.[23] He stood, in sum, at the cusp of numerous development innovations.

Seers was, above all, a "practical visionary," to cite Singer's tribute, someone who wanted to reorient economics away from abstruse modeling and toward pragmatic development needs.[24] The modern economic discipline, he warned, offered poor guidance for developing countries. Its analytic categories reflected a Western understanding, and they had grown too abstract, embracing a tendency—particularly acute in macro-economics—to turn away from practical problems toward a realm of pure theory. While essential for economic computation, mathematics exercised an "unhealthy influence," since the quantification obsession hid failures of worldly practice, including a disregard of contextual factors that resisted tabulation.[25] Especially in developing countries, "there is a degree of fantasy about most published national accounts," even though they "mould our perception of reality."[26] Moreover, models "often rest on basic, but probably unstated, assumptions like a closed economy, perfect competition, constant tastes, constant income distribution and mobile factors of production, assumptions which are quite artificial even for industrial societies." The result is an economist who was adept on paper, but could not weigh in on "whether a steel industry should be established in Guatemala," one who could "manipulate" data but not "interpret" them.[27]

Seers gave history a largely deconstructive role in development planning—that of puncturing myths or cultural biases masquerading as neutral advice. When it came to program design, however, he found little use for historical analysis. In part, this was due to its prior misapplication. Modernizers had bequeathed a legacy of overgeneralized, inappropriate historical modeling that revealed the many problems inherent in trying "to copy the development paths of other countries." Their "theoretical equipment" was "twice removed from reality," reflecting "doctrines developed for *other* countries in response to *earlier* events."[28] In addition, recent social unrest had made Western societies dubious exemplars. In the wake of 1960s racial tension and war protests, few "rich countries now appear to the outside world as desirable models." Anyway, it was doubtful that "that the rest of the world could trace the history of industrial countries."[29]

An obvious way to avoid the "common mistake of transference" was by focusing on developing-country history. But already in 1962, Seers had warned that this, too, was not promising. Not only would "historical evidence" be "difficult to evaluate due to institutional changes," but data as old as "a decade or more may have little meaning" since "a developing economy alters beyond recognition in a few years." Alas, conclusions derived from "less than a decade's experience" were also suspect, since they were affected by "irrelevant" short-term contingencies.[30] Instead, development planning had to direct its gaze from past to future.

> Formerly the basic [planning] technique consisted in extrapolating past trends and choosing investment patterns that would produce an acceptable increase in national income in a five-year period, tacitly assuming many constraints as given—thus consumption patterns were projected in a way that assumed little or no change in income distribution or in tastes or attitudes. Now we must try to envisage what might be a satisfactory pattern at some time in the future, in terms not only of production and employment structures, but of the patterns of income distribution, consumer demand and jobs, and then work backwards, to see if there is any plausible path for getting there.[31]

This reorientation entailed not simply a repudiation of received ideas, but also a methodological turn away from historical extrapolation and toward the projection of future trends based on the observation of current affairs. The present and future, not the past, was the planner's field. Yet this change came with limitations: While Seers understood the need for practitioners to embed themselves in local contexts, he had few resources for analyzing how that context evolved over time or envisioning alternate possibilities. History was dismissed in favor of projections from current circumstance, without the longer perspective that informed the *dependentistas* he admired.

Seers's preference for the present was characteristic of the decade's development thinking. For many, the revolt against modernization began by disavowing the past. The 1974 Coyococ Declaration, issued by delegates of the new United Nations Environment Programme (UNEP) and the United Nations Conference on Trade and Development (UNCTAD) at a symposium in Mexico, exemplified this impatience. "We believe that thirty years of experience with the hope that rapid economic growth benefiting the few will 'trickle down' to the mass of the people has proved illusory. We therefore reject the idea of 'growth first, justice in the distribution of benefits later.'" Insurgent delegates blasted the "unilinear view which sees development essentially and inevitably as the effort to initiate the historical model of the countries that for various reasons happen to be rich today." The goal, they intoned, "is not to 'catch up,' but to ensure the quality of life for all."[32] Postcolonial countries faced a new horizon; their problems were here and now, and reflection on development precedents was at best a distraction, and at worst, false comparison. Historical models, with their focus on long-term growth, wrote the economist Louis Lefeber, left no room "for the attainment of social justice without which growth cannot be turned into development."[33] The urgency of the now, the structures of poverty, aching global inequality—these were the mints of a new development currency. Epistemologically and ethically, history had little value.

The past, however, was not entirely a cabinet of relics. Historical review retained some utility as a clearing operation, and the accounting of earlier failures remained a salutary task. Echoing his mentor Myrdal, the economist and IDS faculty member Michael Lipton disputed the analogy between European industrialization and postcolonial development partly on historical grounds. Despite rampant inequality, he wrote, eighteenth- and nineteenth-century Europe contained the seeds of later growth, when workers finally saw welfare gains. Not so in today's Third World. In his influential volume *Why Poor People Stay Poor,* Lipton cited four preconditions for the gradual amelioration of European poverty, none of which applied outside the West. A prior revolution in agricultural productivity had moved a large share of Europe's labor force out of farming and into towns and cities, creating the conditions for worker organization to combat inequality. Western industrialists saw the need for generating demand among workers as a way to avert price collapses, and thus came to acknowledge the need for increased wages—what Lipton called a pre-Keynesian consensus. Governments agreed—Europe's third distinction—and understood that boosting welfare would promote stability in a democratic age. And finally, European countries exhibited a national cohesion that fostered labor mobility and generated political capital for welfare projects. Poor countries enjoyed none of these blessings. The indigent majority was dispersed in isolated farmsteads where they were unable to mobilize or organize. Alliances between a small urban bourgeoisie and a rural "labor aristocracy" blocked policies that would lower profits and threaten status. Poor governments maintained stability by catering to these elites, while ethnic and religious factionalism exacerbated fragmentation among the poor.[34]

Lipton's chief aim was to point out the urban bias of development programming, a concern he shared with other poverty and equity advocates.[35] The 1970s, of course, was not the first decade to discover the importance of rural areas. Community developers and agricultural modernizers—not to mention colonial technicians—had worried about impoverished peasants from the 1940s onward. But Lipton lent the issue renewed urgency by highlighting how postwar industrialization mandates led planners to concentrate their resources in urban agglomerations that had sufficient infrastructure to sustain manufacturing initiatives and attract migrant workers, a pattern that mimicked British industrialization. This approach, he felt, got contemporary development backwards. Instead of equitable growth, it cultivated privileged enclaves—islands girdled by crowded slums in a wide rural sea. Nationalist leaders in the Third World aggravated the problem by using marketing boards and other devices to cap income for farm produce and keep urban prices low, a process we will see in Zambia in Chapter 8. The threat of urban unrest and the international encouragement of modern growth furthered this anti-development strategy.

The economist Hans Singer, Lipton's IDS colleague, also inveighed against the misuse of history. Europe's late-developers—such as Germany, Italy, or Russia—modernized under conditions so different from those prevailing in contemporary Asia and Africa that they offered little heuristic value. Crucially, the link between economic growth and improved technology that held for European latecomers was broken in the postwar world, where "labour-saving rather than capital-saving" development better suited the population-heavy tropics.[36] The reference to past examples of capital-intensive industrialization could only mislead today's developing countries, whose natural, social, and political endowments were too different from their European predecessors for history to give much instruction. The same message came from donor representatives: Ted Owens of USAID and Robert Shaw of the Overseas Development Council (ODC) agreed that the Western example offered little for today's poor—as did McNamara's World Bank predecessor, George Woods, in 1967.[37] Soon after taking the helm, McNamara said the same.[38]

Another IDS member, Robert Chambers (whom we met in the opening of this chapter), carried the battle against urban bias to the micro-level. In a widely regarded 1983 volume tapping his decade-long practitioner experience, Chambers described six biases that blinker the aid planner who tries to understand rural poverty: a focus on urban or easily accessible interlocutors (spatial biases); an interest in preexisting project areas (project bias); a preference for elite, male informants, for the fit and the living, and for aid-service users (person bias); a preference for dry seasons, when travel is easier but need is less (seasonal bias); excessive courtesy that prevents frank analysis (diplomatic bias); and professional biases that direct planners toward areas of technical interest. These tendencies keep assessors in or near cities, where meetings occur, with only occasional forays to the countryside for 'ground truth.' They limit not only the way planners think but the way they see as well, blinding them to the scope and variety of developing-country poverty. Without naming it, Chambers also implicated another bias: a neglect of the temporal dimensions of impoverishment and a preference for static regional aggregates, leading to snapshot appraisals that overlook the dynamics of destitution.

> A nutritionist may see malnutrition but not the seasonal indebtedness, the high cost of medical treatment, the distress sales of land, and the local power structure which generate it. A doctor may see infant mortality but not the declining real wages which drive mothers to desperation, still less the causes of those declining real wages. Visibility and specialization combine to show simple surface symptoms rather than deeper combinations of causes.[39]

Each example describes a process that occurs over time—declining wages, seasonal income cycles, local power dynamics—but goes unnoticed in superficial 'development tourism' (Chambers's term for brief fact-finding visits). In these ways, detemporalization prevents the kinds of witness needed to fulfill an anti-poverty mandate.

The Numbered Past

The accounting of past development failure also took statistical form. The skepticism of the 1970s about trickle-down growth burgeoned to the drumbeat of regular surveys challenging cardinal tenets of economic modernization.[40] Rebutting those who argued that economic increase would ameliorate the lot of the poor, new longitudinal studies revealed worsening inequality and deepening poverty despite record expansion. As Brazil's president quipped, the country's growth was "good for the economy, but bad for the people."[41] These findings contributed to the opinion that poverty alleviation, not economic growth, ought to be the development focus. The economist David Morawetz, whose World Bank–funded study of aid's first quarter-century came out in the mid-1970s, saw this shift as a recovery of aid's original mandate.[42] Regnant inequities were particularly galling in Asian states recently taken with the fanfare of the Green Revolution, launched by agronomist Norman Borlaug in 1940s Mexico and spread to Asia in the 1960s. Exuberance ran high for the eradication of hunger through modified seeds and agronomic improvements, but as data gradually revealed, the Green Revolution also increased inequality, since only prosperous farmers could afford new inputs.[43]

The *grand homme* of development econometricians was Simon Kuznets, recently dubbed one of the most important economists of the twentieth century.[44] His 1955 essay "Economic Growth and Income Inequality" is best remembered for its contention that modernizing countries would experience "wider inequality" in the short run before a convergence of incomes during later stages of growth (his inverted U-curve), a message his tough-minded colleagues took as justifying transitional hardship in the name of long-term prosperity. Yet the Russian-born Kuznets was neither so hard-nosed nor so hopeful: Because of already miserable living standards in the tropics, he feared, the prospect of worsening penury could prompt instability that might derail the growth process. In this sense, development required an understanding of social, political, and demographic forces that fell outside of "economics proper." Unfortunately, Western industrialization, which also saw ballooning inequality in the eighteenth and nineteenth centuries, afforded little guidance, since "the real per capita income level of many underdeveloped societies today is lower than the per capita income level of the presently developed societies before *their* initial phases of industrialization." Furthermore, "consumption propensities of upper-income groups are far higher and savings propensities far lower than were those of the more puritanical upper-income groups of the presently developed countries."[45] It was, in other words, not clear to Kuznets that inequality in the Third World would shrink with modernization, as it had in the West. The Kuznets curve was historically accurate but not necessarily predictive, and Europe's past did not clinch the optimism of midcentury developers.

But that was 1955, and Kuznets's warning did not resonate with ambitious modernizers. In the early 1970s, fortified with new data, he expressed renewed alarm.[46] Today's poor faced unprecedented economic challenges and were ill inclined to wait through a lengthy growth process. The problem with the European analogy, he now worried, was not that it was wrong—development *was* a long process that yielded social dislocation—but that it portended calamity: such a protracted path might take well over a century, an unbearable delay for the impoverished. Others concurred. If the rich allowed only "a trickle to flow down to the poor, it will take 50 years before everyone is lifted above the poverty line," chided the Indian economists V. M. Dandekar and Nilakantha Rath in a Ford Foundation study of their home country. "But much before this happens, the gulf between the rich and the poor will widen intolerably and inevitably undermine the democratic foundations of the economy."[47] And if development went awry in India, after twenty years of programming, it augured poorly for efforts elsewhere. Like many colleagues, Dandekar and Rath were appalled not only by the consequences for growth of extreme inequity, but by its raw injustice. "How rich the rich must be," they remonstrated, "before the poor may get the minimum?" It would take well into the next millennium, thirty-five years from 1971, for the second lowest decile (10–20 percent) to achieve even the modest consumption standard of Rs. 324 per year—long enough, in their opinion, for "silent frustration" to "turn ugly."[48] In this telling, Western models actively peddled policies that postponed development, stirring anger and instability. Other statisticians followed this lead: Richard Weisskoff highlighted the divergence between growth and equity in Latin America "despite the efforts by the respective governments to modify and lessen the stresses generally associated with Western development."[49] And Albert Fishlow, in an influential study of Brazil, spoke for many when he doubted the "capacity of developing nations to expand at rates in excess of 2 percent per capita" and decried "the little progress and, quite possibly, retrogression in the distribution of income."[50]

But numbers were not always dispositive. Though most economists agreed that "a great increase in data" over the decade enabled "cross-country and time-series" estimates that could be usefully compared, the indicators did not yield firm consensus.[51] The Indian economist and World Bank staffer Montek Ahluwalia argued that a lack of historical evidence weakened the value of econometric findings. The "stylized facts" of theory and policy—a term for simplified economic truisms based on desultory empirical data—could not firmly identify the engine of economic change.

> The use of cross country data for what are essentially dynamic processes raises a number of familiar problems. Ideally, such processes should be examined in an explicitly historical context for particular countries. Unfortunately, time series data on the distribution of income, over any substantial period, are simply not available for most developing countries.[52]

Morawetz bemoaned the over-reliance on statistical proxies that failed to explain the microeconomics of growth. "The only way of knowing what has actually been happening to the share of the poorest people in developing countries over time," he stated, "is to examine directly the historical evidence for particular countries."[53] Most economists did not.

Opponents of this new growth pessimism harked back to an earlier consensus. W. A. Lewis, the doyen of growth theory and now a professor at Princeton, acknowledged the evidence of widening inequality but insisted, per past models, that all countries suffer a transitional gap. Far from prompting riots and demonstrations (bad instability), inequality could foster economic innovation (good instability) by encouraging people to compete in the market. Although it might be possible for governments to restrain the grossest inequities without hampering growth, the modernizing elite should be understood as agents of positive change, and they were necessarily enriched before the poor, for it was their savings that advanced the economy. For Lewis, equity advocates had not allowed enough time—and European countries took the better part of a century—for inequality to moderate.[54] Reformers, predictably, placed little stock in such views.[55]

Particularly interesting for their efforts to replace a European template with a more recent and usable past were the economists Irma Adelman and Cynthia Taft Morris. Their influential 1973 study measured a range of quantitative and qualitative variables to determine the effect on equity of economic modernization. In line with the times, they found that elites, not the poor, benefited from growth, leading them to repudiate "trickle down" and the "faulty" Western analogy in favor of more recent post–World War II successes: Israel and the East Asian Tigers.[56] Their 1978 study of old Europe presented the continent's history as a cautionary tale, not a model: It revealed the same social devastation wrought by contemporary growthmania. "[I]n the early part of the 19th century, both rapid commercialization and industrialization typically depressed the standard of living of the very poorest stratum of the population for periods from a few decades to much longer."[57] À la Engels or Dickens, the authors saw the industrial revolution as a negative example, a dark contrast to the more enlightened Asian Tigers. Rather than launching growth first and hoping that profits would descend to the poor, Pacific Rim societies privileged asset redistribution and human capital over—even at the initial expense of—economic expansion. These policies, Adelman and Morris contended, offered a practical and moral instantiation of development without the heavy social cost. The authors passed, in other words, from the demolition of antiquated growth templates to the advancement of new equity models that inverted past priorities.

Yet Adelman's work also reinforced new forms of presentism. By substituting the recent past for the distant as a validating model, and by narrowing historical analysis to quantitative measure, the history of the relevant present could easily shade into a present without a relevant past.[58] Her work, in fact, reflected new types of ahistoricism that increasingly informed development thinking: 1) a methodological presentism that abandoned the histories of modernizers in favor of empirical snapshots of the contemporary poor or longitudinal accounts built on decontextualized indicators; 2) a normative presentism that demanded development "of the people, by the people, and for the people" because of the "dismal" and "morally unacceptable" performance of economic growth strategies in promoting "social justice"; and 3) a practical presentism that concentrated on alleviating poverty *now* for the very poorest, privileging the short-term over the long and making the poorest the "explicit focus of development policy"—often without exploring the causes of their poverty in the first place. "[T]he minimum short-run goal that we consider acceptable from the point of view of social justice," she insisted, "is to increase the average income of the poorest 40 percent at least as fast as the average income of the nation as a whole."[59]

These were laudable aims, and they fit smoothly into what the World Bank's Mahbub ul Haq, in his stimulating memoir of a Pakistani growth economist-turned-egalitarian, called "the most formidable challenge of our time."[60] Though versed in the arts of quantification, Haq too feared that its overuse prevented planners from understanding the depth and dimensions of poverty. After taking degrees at Lahore, Cambridge, and Yale, Haq formulated his views while working in Pakistan's National Planning Commission. His 1963 debut, *The Strategy of Economic Planning,* acknowledged that inequality generated growth surpluses, but warned that an excessive gap, such as that faced by the country's poorer East Pakistan wing, could skew development toward a rich minority and sow political discord, a message that prompted skepticism in Karachi but praise from the likes of Julius Nyerere and Indira Gandhi.[61] After joining the Bank in 1970, he became one of the leading proponents of a basic needs approach (discussed below), shifting from his earlier concern for equity toward a more outspoken anti-poverty evangelism.

Haq's 1976 book *The Poverty Curtain* expressed his disillusionment with conventional foreign assistance. Its opening chapter listed "seven sins" that hampered aid's anti-poverty mission: in addition to a quantification fetish, aid policymakers demonstrated excessive concern for bureaucratic controls, over-reliance on investment, a susceptibility to fads, a tendency to divorce planning from practice, a neglect of human resources, and a fixation on growth as the measure of development. Like Seers, Haq was, according to his colleague Amartya Sen, a pragmatist who displayed "impatience with theory."[62] In the interest of reform, he advanced an anti-poverty agenda that, he hoped, would produce a new, more equitable order, urging strategic patience for the Third World and reform for wealthy societies as they moved toward "resource transfers from the rich to the poor countries."[63] While he recognized, Sen wrote, that "a poor country may take a very long time to become a rich country through GNP growth, the conditions of human living can be changed much more rapidly through intelligent policy making."[64] Accordingly, his call to lift the "poverty curtain" demanded retrenchment from the modernizing past to the exigent now.

The Future Is Now

"A sense of crisis," remarked USAID staffer-turned-ODC advisor James Grant in the pages of *Foreign Policy*, "is the determining factor in creating a climate for change that forces governments to act."[65] The early 1970s, when Grant wrote these words, had crises to spare: war in Vietnam; an oil shock; famines in Bangladesh, the Sahel, and Ethiopia. As headlines publicized the sufferings of the poor, anti-poverty messages passed from academic conferences to aid agency boardrooms. What Grant called "the end of trickle down" prompted urgent new policy statements from multilateral and bilateral donors. The U.S. Congress acknowledged what Hubert Humphrey called the "intellectual revolt among scholars of development" by passing 1973's landmark New Directions legislation to redirect foreign aid toward poverty alleviation.[66] As a result, funds shifted to sectoral and local programs, abandoning broader growth trajectories in favor of education and health initiatives that had more immediate impact on the poor. Agriculture and nutrition also saw their budgets increase, leaping from a quarter of agency outlays to over 60 percent within three years of the legislation.[67]

The World Bank, too, directed its burgeoning outlays away from the industrial sectors and toward the poorest 40 percent, a move begun by erstwhile chairman George Woods but undertaken with the zeal of an apostle—or perhaps a penitent warrior—by its new helmsman, Robert McNamara.[68] Coming off his unhappy stint as secretary of defense and Vietnam War champion, McNamara brought to the Bank a penchant for quantitative analysis and centralized management. A self-styled paladin of the poor—Léopold Sédar Senghor dubbed him a "poet of action"—McNamara began his tenure in 1968 as a proponent of population control, took up the call for agricultural and education assistance, and in 1971 complained bitterly about poverty and inequality.[69] His thirteen-year presidency shifted the Bank away from its conservative founding mission to fund projects promising a rapid return on investment—typically in energy, infrastructure, or other growth-oriented sectors—and toward sectors such as health, education, and rural development aimed at impacting the poor directly. In speeches before the World Bank Board and other audiences, McNamara threw his weight behind the emerging goal of poverty alleviation, calling in 1971 for a "Marshall Plan for the world."[70] He also enhanced the Bank's research capacity, turning it into a central forum for development debates and innovation. In the process, the Bank became the decade's most prolific development lender and its president arguably the most influential pro-poor voice.

As a first task in office, McNamara organized the "grand assize" called for by his predecessor: a commission chaired by former Canadian prime minister Lester Pearson to review the international assistance regime and make recommendations for reform.[71] The 1969 Pearson Report urged wealthy states to raise aid commitments to 0.7 percent of GNP, but did not advise a radical revision of growth-based mandates; indeed, it called for a heady 6 percent growth rate in developing countries throughout the ensuing decade. What made the report immediately contentious, however, was its mild language, which hewed closely to a modernization agenda that many reformers decried. The Pearson Report, complained angry delegates at 1970's Columbia Conference on International Economic Development, offered proposals that "will appear 'acceptable' and 'reasonable,'" whereas a "frank" assessment would have offered a "more pessimistic picture." Its hope for a development partnership among rich and poor countries was illusory.

> We leave this Conference with the conviction that nothing is more unrealistic than the apparent realism of those who argue that the Pearson Report is fully adequate or even overambitious in terms of the future prospects. Such realism can only lead to growing confrontation between the developing and developed countries of the world, and to growing misery and frustration for a majority of mankind.[72]

A glance at the titles of prominent 1970s development reports reveals the growing doubt: two 1971 rejoinders to the Pearson Commission, the Founex Report on Development and Environment and the Commission on International Development's inequality-focused *The Widening Gap;* the Club of Rome's 1972 "Limits to Growth," followed in 1975 by the Dag Hammarskjöld Foundation's "What Now? Another Development"; in 1976, the RIO Report ("Reshaping the International Order") and the Argentinean Fundación Bariloche's *Catastrophe or New Society? A Latin American New Model;* and, closing the decade, the Brandt Commission's "North-South: A Programme for Survival"—to name only the most renowned.

If the Bank's clout was unimpeachable, fewer know of the catalytic role played by the ILO. Starting with Dudley Seers's mission to Colombia, the ILO, through its World Employment Programme (launched in 1969), released a series of country action plans focused on the Keynesian problem of unemployment.[73] It quickly became apparent to the ILO's teams of luminaries—Seers, Singer, and Jolly among them—that un- and underemployment, those conditions which, according to earlier economists, assured an "unlimited" labor pool for the industrial sector, did not accurately characterize Third World conditions. Whether rural or urban, the poor could ill afford to go jobless; theirs was a tragedy of nonproductive, unremunerative, bone-grinding labor for pennies a day. The problem of unproductive labor could not be solved by an employment strategy alone because it implicated too many factors, from poor health and education to inefficient agriculture, weak markets, and population pressure—many of them beyond the economist's ken. The plight of the poor required a wholesale revision of superannuated policies and a concentration on immediate needs across a range of sectors.

The ILO's 1972 Kenya Report revealed the hallmarks of this emerging consensus in its focus on population growth, rural-urban imbalance, and agricultural need. Despite Kenya's success in stimulating growth and Africanizing the civil service, commissioners concluded that current policies were "unlikely to broaden the base of income-earning opportunities for the majority of people." Instead,

> a class of poor and disadvantaged persons, already prominent on the Kenyan social scene, may over time be enlarged and suffer further relative impoverishment, in the absence of a strong and coherent strategy for rapid economic growth accompanied by a more egalitarian distribution of the benefits of growth.[74]

As this passage indicates, the report did not reject growth per se, but it did call for augmenting expansionist policies with welfare measures designed to share economic gains. Though commissioners acknowledged "Kenya's past achievements," earlier efforts were largely antithetical to the needs of the day.[75] For it was not just the red herring of Western history that had to be scrapped; even the local past held few clues for development. If Kenya was to confront its growing inequality, the country needed a "broad sweep of re-orientation," a "radical change," and a "major re-structuring" of its policies and institutions—in sum, a "break with familiar traditions."

The Kenya report became a touchstone for the nascent strategy of redistribution from growth, a term coined in its pages.[76] The strategy initially called for directing marginal profits toward better services and minimum incomes for the poor without impinging on the assets that fostered growth in the first place. Two years later, redistribution *from* growth became redistribution *with* growth as the ILO embraced a less incremental approach that would redirect assets as well as profits, though not to such a degree that growth would stall.[77] The 1976 World Employment Conference report went further still, advancing a new basic-needs platform. Development was now called to meet the fundamental needs of the poorest—for health, education, water, nutrition—even at the price of restrained growth.[78] Equity, in this vision, was less important than assuring minimum standards for all. As Samuel Moyn pointed out, the gradual eclipse of equity concerns drew attention away from the distributional justice agenda of the decade's early years.[79] If equity was a puissant coinage of the 1970s' first quinquennium, basic needs and poverty alleviation became the currency of its second.[80]

The needs strategy found a leading spokesman in Paul Streeten, a Central European exile-economist—the German-Jewish Streeten was born Paul Hornig in 1917 in Vienna—who spent his educational years on the run after the Nazi Anschluß.[81] Trained in Austria, Scotland, and England (and informally in British internment camps in Canada), Streeten, like many in his generation of economists, was taken with Myrdal's ideas, working with the Swedish economist on the research for *Asian Drama*. With Dudley Seers, he helped to establish the IDS, and in the early 1970s he became a founding editor of the journal *World Development*, a leading venue for new thinking. In the first years of the decade, he lent his voice to the 'redistribution with growth' chorus and the censure of Western development models.[82] By the mid-1970s, he had largely abandoned growth and called for programs directly targeting the poor even if they reduced a country's overall economic advance. To use the slogans of the day, he moved from the classical "grow now, redistribute later" to "redistribute now and grow later," leapfrogging the indecisive middle position.[83]

In the mid-1970s, Mahbub ul Haq enlisted Streeten to plan the World Bank's basic needs strategy.[84] In that capacity, Streeten pushed for more vigorous public investment in anti-poverty initiatives than earlier reformers.[85] Of note was the normative pitch of his program, which treated basic needs as tantamount to rights. "If it is accepted that our common humanity and our membership in specific societies such as the state impose some obligations on us, the right to a fair share of the available resources would appear to be a human right, complementing the negative human rights."[86] Whatever the complexities of equating material needs with rights—and the declaration of the latter did not lessen the logistical problems entailed in fulfilling the former—the language of legalism and ethical imperative muted social and historical nuance. In the basic-needs conception, the developing poor remained tabulae rasae, undifferentiated peasants with urgent needs but few experiences to bear on them—and this despite Streeten's call for the poor to participate in project planning.[87] If modernizers understood development as a meta-historical template, basic-needs advocates cast poverty in the decontextualized space of pure injustice that demanded immediate redress.

This contextual vacuum was particularly stark in the work of Streeten's Oxford colleague and sometime coauthor Frances Stewart, who highlighted the importance, for planning purposes, of simplifying the needs strategy by excluding "material, social, cultural, and political" particulars and concentrating on a universal, scientific baseline for "health and to some degree education."[88] Stewart's "meta-production function" stressed physiological universals amenable to scientific treatment. While basic-needs theorists at times acknowledged the complex, socially determined nature of their core concept, Stewart exemplified the ineluctable gravity, in the name of streamlined planning, of a simple biological ground. Physiological basics became the implicit standard of needs-driven development, for "above a certain physiological minimum" it was impossible to rank needs objectively. In the name of urgency, she exchanged the modernizers' *longue durée* for the *court*—"a five- or at most ten-year period"—filled with the imperatives of life and death.[89] One can see why Dudley Seers dismissed basic needs as an appropriate policy only in a "well-run zoo."[90]

Elevated in 1976, demoted by the early 1980s, basic needs prevailed in development circles for a brief five years.[91] One cause of its hasty demise was the unfavorable attitude of developing-country leaders, who saw in the framework a patronizing effort to divert monies from modernization and into short-term crisis management that would perpetuate dependency. Streeten himself came to question some of its priorities. In a 1984 speech in South Africa, he asked "whether the basic needs approach mobilizes the power of the poor to improve radically their situation or whether it reinforces the oppressive existing order." After all, he remarked, "the freedom to define one's needs is itself a basic need"—a concern that cuts not only against paternalistic governments but also against experts who imagine that they know what is best.[92] In a subsequent elaboration of his talk, Streeten asked numerous pointed questions: Who determines basic needs? Are they merely physiological or do they include cultural and social goods as well? How do they relate to participation in political and social processes? What effect does a basic needs strategy have on production, on inequality, on human and financial resources? These remain pressing questions today.[93]

During their heyday, needs advocates employed a normative and technical vocabulary—including a rhetoric of moral urgency—that pervades aid discourse to the present, surviving subsequent ideological and policy shifts. In the words of a community development handbook published in 1984, relevant aid programs must prioritize "issues of importance NOW to participants."[94] Few would deny, then or today, the ethical urgency of addressing poverty and hunger. As a sustainable solution to poverty rooted in an understanding of its causes, however, the statement gives greater pause.

The Anti-Paradigm

Development reformers in the 1970s never fledged a full replacement for the growth and modernization theories they spurned—nor was it their intent to do so. Instead, their normative-*cum*-practical bent yielded numerous programs for action as maverick economists and exuberant fieldworkers shelved outworn models in favor of a new experimentalism. Indeed, 1970s development approaches might be dubbed anti-paradigmatic, since they often constituted heady clearing operations for on-the-ground exercises. And since the themes and tools introduced during the decade remain current in today's development practice, any review needs to consider some of its programmatic innovations.

Particularly stimulating was the Brazilian educator Paolo Freire, whose pioneering adult literacy program, launched near Recife in the late 1940s and expanded across Brazil in the early 1960s before its closure by the military regime, was publicized in the 1968 book *The Pedagogy of the Oppressed.* In its 1970 English translation, Freire's volume became a bible for education programmers worldwide. It described his efforts to set up literacy classes in impoverished communities and engage residents in the analysis of their own condition. The curriculum was designed for consciousness-raising (*conscientização*—or *conscientization* in its awkward English rendering)—that is, to inculcate among the poor an awareness of the social and historical roots of their poverty. Freire's maieutic or problem-posing approach used flip charts (*rotafolios*) covered with words, questions, and images as prompts to engage learners in the examination of their social circumstances—a strategy he contrasted with the "banking" approach to education in which students received and stored knowledge handed down by experts. If the latter was hierarchical and teacher-focused, the former emphasized student-centered participation. Freire's method became popular among 1970s aid practitioners—though often in a form that diluted its revolutionary message of social transformation. Shorn of his explicit political intent, Freire now appears largely as a far-seeing technician of student-centered pedagogy.[95] Regardless, the embrace of community education marked an important challenge to prevalent human capital models of schooling as an instrument of growth.[96]

Another defining figure was E. F. Schumacher, a German émigré economist whose iconoclastic volume *Small Is Beautiful* (1973) rethought the equation of development with industry by advocating 'appropriate' or 'intermediate' technology.[97] Schumacher had worked with Rosenstein-Rodan and William Beveridge in England before advising UN missions, including a fateful sojourn in Burma, where he likely encountered the Buddhism that preoccupied his later thought. By the mid-1950s, he began a break with mainstream economics that culminated in his bestselling book, with its roving chapters on alternatives to economic modernity. In development circles, intermediate technology became its most influential proposition. Rather than basing projects around cutting-edge equipment, for which impoverished users lacked both technical training and replacement parts, Schumacher urged planners to consider what level of technology would be appropriate to the needs of a host community—neither too technical or expensive to sustain, nor so basic that it discouraged new skills. Many Third World leaders disdained the appropriate technology movement, fearing that lesser tools would keep their countries backward and sensing a whiff of racism in the reservation of modern contrivances for the 'advanced.' Nonetheless, Schumacher's work prodded development planners to consider more carefully the contextual appropriateness of their technologies.[98]

Though his books would not appear until the next decade, Robert Chambers also developed new techniques during the 1970s.[99] To correct the biases of standard needs assessment, his Rapid Rural Appraisal (RRA) approach (later the Participatory Rural Appraisal [PRA] and other hybrid forms) enabled wide-ranging and reasonably concise needs assessments that incorporated the poor in the analysis of their own communities. Chambers's Freirian-inspired visual and group activities (e.g., community mapping, drawing relationship webs, focus-group discussions) have since entered the basic toolkit of program planners and evaluators, fueling a concern for beneficiary participation in development programming that continues today.[100]

In addition to novel tools, the 1970s ushered new populations into the development field. Particularly significant in this regard is the work of Danish economist Ester Boserup. Like Myrdal, whom she assisted in India, Boserup wielded an admirable interdisciplinary breadth, encompassing anthropology, archaeology, and history. While she is best known for launching the Women in Development movement—we will come to this below—her first book challenged the widely held belief that population excess could slow development.[101] Boserup argued that demographic growth in all but the poorest countries encouraged farmer innovation, particularly around land use. Citing historical and anthropological evidence, she noticed that local farmers left extended tracts uncultivated, a unique fallowing strategy that balanced the cost of labor, the potential for yield, and a population's food requirements. Their inventiveness, she felt, recommended a development strategy focused on agricultural innovation rather than urban growth—*pace* Myrdal and the widely held theory of rural surplus labor.[102] "Past experience," she averred, showed the ingenuity and adaptability of local practices, and it had "relevance for the planning of agricultural growth in the underdeveloped world."[103]

Boserup's work on agrarian economies brought her to the topic of women's roles in development. While investigating labor migration, she took interest in the economic activities of women left behind in their home villages when their husbands and sons took remunerative urban jobs. The power of her 1970 book *Woman's Role in Economic Development* lay primarily in its descriptive account of "sex roles" in the urban and rural sectors. Fundamentally a survey resting on basic statistical tabulations, Boserup's study showed how modernization disempowered women by advancing employment practices and agricultural techniques, including plough cultivation, that privileged men. In disrupting prior family economies, modern labor specialization imposed a gender hierarchy: salaried work went to men, with women increasingly excluded from formal markets. This division contrasted sharply with traditional farm systems in sparse population zones where men cleared fields and women did the planting and harvesting—also a hierarchy, but one that involved women as breadwinners. By contrast, extension services, vocational training, modern hiring strategies—all reinforced modern gender stratification. Boserup herself was no radical, and indeed held some modernization convictions. Family migration to the towns, she felt, allowed many of the world's poorest women to exchange "a life of toil for a life of leisure"—albeit, later feminists might note, one enforced by relegation to the home.[104] During British industrialization, she averred, such idleness was necessary to avoid competition with men for scarce jobs, although the continued availability of rural life in the contemporary non-West—many labor migrants travel between city and village—meant that foreign models provided little contemporary guidance.[105]

Boserup was pioneering in several ways. Without disclaiming the benefits of modernization, she highlighted the perverse effects of a development framework that promoted social and political equity in rhetoric but weakened it in fact. In doing so, she helped to inaugurate the Women in Development movement, which placed women, who were disproportionately represented in the most vulnerable demographics, at the heart of the aid agenda—a precursor to strategies such as microfinance that saw women not only as victims of poverty, but as potential entrepreneurs.[106] If her work furthered the practical and ethical bent of the decade's development thinking, it also employed a less presentist approach than that of many of her colleagues, using historical and anthropological data to sketch a dynamic picture of social changes wrought by economic advancement.

Two further trends warrant mention, though they extended beyond development. Emerging out of postwar preservation and conservation efforts, the sustainable development movement erupted at the 1972 United Nations Conference on the Human Environment in Stockholm. Advocates took aim at the damage wrought by growth and industrialization, embracing innovations such as Schumacher's appropriate technology as a more responsible development approach. Environmental sustainability became a core concern in the ensuing decades, even if developing countries balked at having to restrain their own modernization to compensate for damage wrought by earlier industrializers.[107] Similarly, the 1970s saw the emergence of human rights as a global campaign. As we saw in the case of Streeten's equation of needs with rights, advocates could be deeply ahistorical in their assertion of high-minded norms. In some cases, the tendency to elide past imperial depredations and concentrate instead on contemporary abuses committed by African or Asian leaders courted accusations of hypocrisy.[108] These tensions notwithstanding, the rights movement introduced a political component to the aid mandate, requiring planners to consider the behavior of the regimes with which they partnered. Both environmentalism and rights asserted global imperatives that threatened to trump the complicated tradeoffs entailed in growth and development.

The decade's innovations incorporated historical analysis to varying degrees. Yet the overall emphasis on the immediate, the practical, and the ethical afforded little room for questions about origin and causality. In this sense, although development ahistoricism was hardly born in the 1970s, it did receive a powerful impetus from an era when strategy and practice opened up in otherwise remarkable ways. The neglect of local history is particularly striking for a time in which aid reformers celebrated localism. But like their modernizing predecessors, equity programs failed to integrate "analysis and prescription with the underlying political, economic and social forces, both at the national and international levels. With all the emphasis on 'structural transformations' and awareness of the importance of political power, they remain largely technocratic exercises."[109] Modernizers, as we have seen, had long been ahistorical, albeit with a meta-historical veneer. But so too, in a different way, was the rhetoric of ethical imperative deployed in the 1970s, for it privileged the urgent now and dismissed the nuanced, time-consuming analysis of context and precedent.

The lessons drawn by 1970s reformers were important corrections to modernization precepts: Growth alone does *not* relieve inequality, and it can make it worse. Western industrialization, in distilled form or otherwise, is *not* an adequate model for development in non-Western lands. Poverty and inequality *do* need to be confronted directly, and both are urgent. Yet these messages—truisms by now—hide a complexity that was often ignored. The result was a set of slogans and techniques that could not fully grasp the rudiments of contemporary impoverishment. In their own way, of course, these mottos implicate certain historical positions. To argue that earlier industrialization templates are inapt; to deny Western history as irrelevant; to dismiss local development experiences as chronicles of bankruptcy—these claims take a historical stand, even as they discount history as a useful field of inquiry. Yet if the *intellectual* converse of the modernizers' Whig history is tragedy (we have failed the poor), its *practical* opposite is often no history at all. The point is not, as IDS commentators worried in 1969, that development economists make "bad historians." The problem, rather, is that ignoring the past hampers the ability to design sensible programs by overlooking local resources and valuable precedents. IDS editorialists were correct that developing countries are often dismissed as having "no history," despite their ample experiences of tradition and change.[110] Others, too, saw that this amnesia detracted from current programming. "[T]he major dilemma of development planners," warned Mahbub ul Haq, is that "they need a fairly long time horizon to plan structural changes, yet national governments and the international development community, for legitimate political compulsions, generally focus on the immediate problems and short-run solutions."[111] The problem persists today.

The Classical Revival

Intellectual upheaval came from the free-market right as well, and by the decade's end market proponents would claim policy victory. This is rather surprising, since free marketers did not exist at parity with anti-poverty advocates for most of the 1970s. The latter dominated public discourse and held positions of authority at aid agencies, while free-market dissidents remained a marginal insurgency until the late 1970s, when their proposals finally received official welcome.[112] Market criticism of development economics was, of course, coeval with the field itself. The most tenacious critic was the British economist Peter Bauer, who spent lonely years contesting almost every premise of the midcentury development consensus, including the very independence of development economics from the wider economic discipline. He was convinced, he told an audience at Duke University in the 1950s,

> of the very wide applicability to underdeveloped countries of the basic methods of approach of economics. . . . I am thinking especially of the elements of supply and demand analysis and its simpler conclusions, the tendency of people to seek activities and occupations which yield the highest net advantage within the opportunities open to them, the implications of the concept of complementary and competitive relationships between productive resources, and many others.

Bauer's conviction relegated social context and history to the economic margins: "Much mischief has been caused," he expostulated, "by the failure to see that reference to its psychological or political background does not affect the validity . . . of a generalization of positive economics."[113] This universalism would inform the broader classical revival in development economics.

Bauer commended free trade as a motor of growth, arguing that the price incentives unleashed by commerce would encourage productive activity and weed out traditions that impeded development. Indeed, success or failure, he maintained, was ultimately determined by "attitudes, beliefs, and cultural traditions" that either sustained or undermined productivity.[114] What was needed in Africa and Asia, therefore, was a "modernisation of the mind" that could be fostered through contacts brokered by trade and exchange. Bauer envisioned this process as a kind of Westernization: "The concept of material progress, of steadily increasing control of man over his environment, is Western, as are the modes of contact which derive from it. . . . [T]he idea of modernization without Westernization is self-contradictory." Accordingly, he discounted large swathes of human history. "Without expatriates," Bauer remarked, quoting the Trinidadian writer Shiva Naipaul, the country of Zambia "would fall apart. Zambia makes nothing. Zambia creates nothing."[115] It followed that colonialism proffered significant social and material benefits. "With relatively little coercion, or even interference in the lives of the great majority of the people," he wrote, in a shocking display of opacity, "the colonial governments established law and order, safeguarded private property and contractual relations, organized basic transport and health services, and introduced some modern financial and legal institutions"—all while fostering the external contacts needed to stimulate trade, innovation, growth.[116]

The 1970s opened with Bauer's *Dissent on Development* (1972), an essay collection-*cum*-manifesto for the classical revival that gave its author a prominence unlikely even five years earlier. The book usefully challenged some myths of development discourse, drawing attention to the abstraction of economic statistics, the prevalence of decontextualized models, and the tendency to overlook market activity in developing countries. But Bauer's dismissal of opponents was clumsy at best, and often downright crude. Consider his polemic against Nurkse's poverty trap, which maintained that poverty itself hindered development. This diagnosis, he sneered, was "demonstrably invalid" since individuals and communities *have* risen from poverty in the past: Q.E.D.—it is "refuted by the very existence of developed countries."[117] Whatever one makes of the poverty trap thesis (which Jeffrey Sachs would revive in the next millennium), the fact of past development hardly disproves the existence of contemporary barriers. At worst, Bauer employed insults and bluster. Development economics, he snorted, "conflict[s] with obvious evidence" and has "no intellectual substance"; it reflects "political or emotional" biases rooted in western "guilt" and "resentment."[118] He scorned planners as authoritarian—"more interested in controlling people's lives than in liberating their minds or augmenting their resources"—and likened development planning to Soviet economics. Marxism-Leninism, he announced laughably, was "current orthodoxy" in aid circles. And in a further reductio ad absurdum, he described planning as "the replacement of human society by a standardized mass, subject to rulers with unlimited power."[119] Even more troubling was his contempt for African and Asian traditions, and the attendant celebration of a beneficent colonial enterprise.[120]

If Bauer was the most inveterate critic of development, he was scarcely alone. In the 1950s, as we saw in Chapter 2, Sol Tax, Theodore Schultz, and Hla Myint defended the entrepreneurial sensibilities of non-Western peasants. Similarly, the second-generation Austrian Schooler Gottfried Haberler, in the United States since 1936, advocated for a Liberal International Economic Order (LIEO), which he pitted against the New International Economic Order (NIEO) espoused by Third World leaders in the 1960s and 1970s.[121] Milton Friedman too, dean of Chicago School economics, chided Indian planners for overemphasizing capital accumulation, relying on the public sector, and encroaching on private markets.[122] Soon after the publication of *Capitalism and Freedom* (1962), he warned that Indian planning, per the Soviet prototype, endangered democracy itself.[123] What underdeveloped countries need, Friedman wrote, was not the imposition of "political and economic controls" to supplant inherited "cultural and social restraints," but the "release of the energies of millions of able, active and vigorous people" through the provision of "maximum opportunity for individuals to experiment and of incentives for them to do so . . . in short, a vigorous free capitalistic market." This advice, he declared unabashedly, came from "our own experience" and "our own ideology." Accordingly, Friedman opposed aid because he felt it required a central state planner, a "basic premise of the Communist ideology."[124] Trade, not aid—and certainly not developmentalism—promised economic reward.

Alas, Bauer was not alone in casting cultural aspersions either. The Canadian economist Harry Johnson, a professor at the University of Chicago and the London School of Economics, was a partner in crime. While the burst of nationalism attending non-Western independence was understandable, Johnson conceded, it encouraged top-down planning as a misplaced modernization strategy. For Johnson, like Bauer a veteran of 1950s development battles, the mistrust of market capitalism revealed the pernicious influence of Keynes, reflected in the spurious doctrines of disguised unemployment and capital-driven growth, which contributed not just to poor economic policy but to authoritarian governance. Growth—or lack thereof—sprang from "cultural values and social structures," a thinly veiled swipe at non-Western traditions.[125] Had Bauer and Johnson not been rescued by more sophisticated free-market disciples, it is hard to see how they might have risen in the ranks of development pioneers.[126]

Costs and Benefits

Market-led development found its chief innovators in a newer generation of economists who turned from polemic to quantitative performance assessment. Chief among them was the Briton Ian Little, who pioneered a method of cost-benefit analysis that has, in updated formats, remained part of project analytics to this day.[127] Cost-benefit analysis does just what its name suggests: it evaluates the potential benefits of an intervention against the costs associated with it in order to determine not just whether an activity makes a positive change, but how expensive the change is and if that expense might be better applied elsewhere. This calculus enables decision-makers to weigh the cost-effectiveness of different development strategies. In its basic form, costs appear as financial expenditures, but according to Little and his coauthor James

Mirrlees in their influential *Manual of Industrial Project Analysis in Developing Countries,* Volume II (1968), the new social cost-benefit analysis could provide development programmers with a metric for assessing the value of a project even in the absence of exact prices. "The essence of cost-benefit analysis," they explained,

> is that it does *not* accept that actual receipts adequately measure social benefits, and actual expenditures social costs. But it does accept that actual receipts and expenditures can be suitably adjusted so that the difference between them, which is therefore very analogous to ordinary profit, will properly reflect the social gain.[128]

In a word, their formulas quantified "shadow prices"—costs and benefits beyond those captured by price indicators—that could be factored into programming deliberations. The process was necessarily inexact, and Little envisioned its approximations as defining an "optimum" or nth-best (as opposed to ideal) set of economic interventions for use in the 'real' world of imperfect information. In this way, his innovation enabled one to estimate projected costs and benefits even in countries with poor data—an approach that quickly became an industry standard.[129]

Yet the apparent neutrality of the metric hid policy commitments. As Malawian economist Thandika Mkandawire noted tartly, the "mathematical rigour" of the models could "bedazzle" opponents even as it dismissed or trivialized extra-economic influences that were not easily quantified.[130] In employing microeconomic tools, Little and Mirrlees posited the universality of cost-benefit incentives—the idea that economic agents everywhere made choices based on the best available price estimates—a view at odds with the midcentury consensus that developing countries faced considerable market failure. Although they acknowledged some market malfunction, cost-benefit analysts claimed their method corrected for much of this signaling confusion. Going beyond earlier workarounds for faulty information, they undertook an explicit economization of noneconomic factors. Yet even while trying to correct for inadequate data, the method left little room for other incentives—religious, political, cultural—that might affect developing-country entrepreneurs. Furthermore, what certified the method was a severe epistemological monism: Useful knowledge had to be quantified, and what could not be quantified could not be applied. This insistence had practical implications. As against the broad macro-economic markers favored by earlier planners, the new performance assessors adduced the benefits of gathering meticulous micro-economic data. In keeping with this focus, they questioned top-down planning and supported the decentralization of economic decision-making. Furthermore, they emphasized *project* rather than *program* aid. Programs were typically sprawling, nationally managed affairs that were, in effect, assessment-proof. Projects, by contrast, were local and self-contained, with bounded contractual mandates and specific targets; they could be managed and measured, their success or failure tallied against original goals.[131]

Ultimately, Little tied his arguments to market positions, contending that postwar free trade would not only "encourage semi-industrial countries to overcome the problems of transition," but also induce "smaller countries just embarking on industrialization to avoid the route of high protection, which is most unlikely to be in their long-run interest."[132] Though lacking Bauer's ire, Little too swept aside heady debates over political and economic choices with the calm certitude of calculation, asserting in his 1982 textbook that "there is no economic justification . . . for the highly restrictive trade regimes of most LDCs." The NIEO, the structuralists, development economics—these reflected a "politicization of trade" that "the strong are likely to win."[133] And if cost-benefit analysis offered a useful corrective to unwarranted aggregation, it was nonetheless, as Mkandawire alludes, deeply ahistorical, excerpting project operations and assessment data from wider context. In the name of optimality, it dressed up the messy world of development in the rarefied garb of mathematics.

Similarly, Bela Balassa, a veteran of socialist planning debates in Hungary, devoted his career-in-exile to devising metrics for studying the role of economic protection in a "liberal economic philosophy."[134] Like others in this economic counter-revolution, he dismissed "noneconomic factors" that were "not amenable to evaluation by economic tools and would bring a considerable degree of vagueness into the discussion." And he embraced the universality of classical economics, shifting his attention from industrial to developing countries without concession to their supposedly altered market conditions. In an early essay that laid out recurrent themes, Balassa disputed the distinction among developed, developing, and socialist economies, preferring the term "semi-industrial economies" to designate states such as Argentina and Czechoslovakia (he disregarded poorer and more agrarian Asia and Africa), where inward-looking growth strategies produced "prematurely old" economies.[135]

But Balassa was not opposed to all forms of protection. He distinguished between the nominal or official rate of protection applied to a commodity as a whole and the effective or value-added rate, which included charges added to component parts—the latter reflecting an acute danger of compounding expense. Although tariffs and other protective measures imposed costs, Balassa accepted the venerable doctrine of infant-industry protection—countries may need to protect their new industries until they became robust enough to compete internationally—while opposing longer-term ISI, whose popularity had surged in the 1950s.[136] He dubbed these strategies first- and second-stage import substitution. The former had a valid role in industrial development; the latter was an unfortunate extension of policies that should have ended sooner.[137] The evidence, he felt, was conclusive: "countries applying outward oriented development strategies"—mostly in East Asia and Scandinavia—"performed better in terms of exports, economic growth, and employment than countries with continued inward orientation"—mostly in Latin America—"which encountered increasing economic difficulties."[138] The Prebisch School was a particular target of reproof.[139]

According to Balassa, it was contemporary Pacific Rim economies—South Korea, Taiwan, Singapore—that best exemplified the benefits of export-driven development. Admiration for the East Asian Tigers (or Dragons) took hold among many free marketers, but their characterization of these economies has garnered significant skepticism.[140] South Korea, arguably the most representative case, received large sums of American aid and made heavy use of industrial planning and policy—hardly a free-market paragon.[141] The Asian Tigers remain a fraught example today: Free marketers credit their success to export-led growth; planners appreciate their active industrial policy; protectionists highlight their strategic import substitution; and equity advocates cite land reforms and education investments. Balassa singled out export expansion as the main factor behind their remarkable growth. Yet by the second half of the 1970s, he worried about a "new protectionism" driven by the oil embargo and based on disruptive forms of quantitative restriction.[142] He was, accordingly, sympathetic to the calls for structural adjustment that arose in the early 1980s.[143]

Quantitative economic analyses—on topics ranging from project cost-benefit to protectionism, currency devaluation, and exchange controls—proliferated throughout the decade.[144] If, as we noted, Little and Balassa discounted factors that eluded their quantitative methods, others tried to annex for economic calculation more of the 'residuals' that fell outside the disciplinary purview (e.g., politics, cultural norms). Anne Krueger's calculation of the costs of political "rent-seeking" is a case in point, as are public-choice economists who likened political incentives to economic.[145] They cast doubt on concepts such as the 'common good' or 'national interest' that had animated earlier policy discourse, arguing that all political actors, like all economic ones, were driven by self-interest. Societies were groups of utility-maximizing individuals; and collective concepts, such as 'national welfare,' were either nonsensical or could be dissolved into their individual atoms, subject to micro-economic analysis. The role of macro-economics in this agenda was subtractive: to *remove* the state wherever possible, to *rescind* collective notions of well-being—and in so doing to enable individuals to operate freely according to 'rational' market signals. If this amounted to a necessary critique of the sweeping modernization edifice, it also discounted contextual insights that were ill suited to quantification.

Planning for Markets

If Balassa's personal reference was the socialist planning experiment in Hungary, economist Deepak Lal's was the extensive state-led development plans of his native India. Given their prominence, Indian plans had long been a target of market evangelists: Friedman, Bauer, and Krueger all penned criticism.[146] But Lal's engagement was personal: He grew up "in the shadow of the Nehruvian settlement" and worked for the Indian Planning Commission before embracing classical liberalism.[147] Planning, he wrote in 1980's *Prices for Planning,* a study that applied cost-benefit analytics to the preparation of the fifth five-year plan, "cannot be uniquely identified with what is current in Soviet or Chinese practice." The latter, which entailed "suppression of the price mechanism," the use of "quantitative targets or commands," and a commitment to "public ownership" or "equality," Lal termed "directive planning." Yet the term *planning* also referred to other forms of government oversight designed to promote the market and tailor private activity to public goals, including those that took price data as indicators. To facilitate this "indicative planning," Lal called for the introduction of pricing information into the Indian planning process so as to expand marketization and establish an incentive structure for "individual actions."[148]

The distinction between indicative and directive planning underpinned Lal's more provocative likening, two years later, of mainstream development planning with the Soviet and Marxist approach. "[D]evelopment economics is closer to the neo-Marxists [roughly, dependency theorists] than to orthodox economics," he contended, particularly in its view that "mutual gains can be realized only after legitimate departures from the orthodox case for free trade which must be enforced by government action."[149] Lal labeled this the Dirigiste Dogma, and he dissected it in two volumes, published ten years apart.[150] Lumping development planners with Soviet central planning—an elision perhaps easiest to make in India, where fascination with Soviet industrialization ran high—Lal argued that both tended toward dictatorship, a slippery-slope argument that recalled Friedrich von Hayek's insistence that the similarities among central planners were more significant than their differences. Even if Lal's indicative planning preserved a place for official involvement in the economy, it marked a considerable recasting of the government's earlier economic role. Where midcentury planners used the state to hem in markets and promote public goods, Lal viewed government regulation as largely a matter of rules-keeping, designed to prevent disruption of free markets. Once clear price-signaling was established (no small task in India), the government's role would largely be relegated to oversight.

Like many trade advocates, Lal disputed development warhorses such as balanced growth, the Prebisch-Singer thesis, the two-gap model, and the foreign exchange bottleneck.[151] He lamented that techniques such as national income accounting and input-output analysis, as well as the country statistical offices that employed them, lent Keynesian "myths" an undeserved authority. A more neutral economics, he opined, would have a free-trade bent: "The obstacles to the growth of developing countries' exports are largely internal, not external," Lal asserted in the early 1980s. "[E]conomic agents in these countries have reacted to the distorting incentives created by protectionist regimes of trade control much in the way that standard economic theory predicts; planners have often shown a lack of foresight which would have swiftly bankrupted a private agent!" It was, again, the Asian Tigers that showed the way, bucking development wisdom by relying on trade to catapult growth. The case for liberalization, Lal concluded, was "incontrovertible," and the "demise of development economics is likely to be conducive to the health of both the economics and the economies of developing countries." Yet since bad ideas "never die," it could be necessary for a "courageous, ruthless and perhaps undemocratic government . . . to run roughshod over these newly-created special interest groups."[152] The irony is rich: Since Hayek's *The Road to Serfdom* (1944), market advocates had warned that central planning tended toward political authoritarianism. Lal showed that market economics could justify it as well. In the new millennium, he even entertained a return to empire in order to secure the benefits of globalization.[153]

If such warnings reveal Lal at his most Bauer-like, he also embraced a more accommodating rhetoric, notably toward the NIEO. Writing in 1978, at the height of debates over Third World solidarity, Lal seconded legitimate complaints against First World protectionism and aid "paternalism" rooted in the "bureaucratic colonial tradition." Yet he also condemned Third World remedies. Not only did demands for a global reordering misdiagnose the ills of Asia, Africa, and Latin America, but they stemmed from "misguided, historically conditioned attitudes to foreign trade" and specious claims of the "superiority of a State run by Platonic Guardians." What developing societies required instead was a "liberal international economic order"—recall Haberler—based on the "demonstrable merits" of classical economics.[154] In tone and substance, Lal echoed his counter-revolutionary generation when he declared market incentives not only an immemorial human motivator, but the supreme form of social regulation.

All programs, of course, tout their own effectiveness, but neoliberalism elevated this self-regard to a quasi-religious certainty. Basic needs asserted biological universals, but its framework enabled a range of policy experiments. Neoliberalism, by contrast, proclaimed a fixed psychology of incentives *and* a policy agenda viewed as absolute. The field of history, with its varied record of social and economic experiments, had little to offer other than curated examples of right and wrong.

The Chilean Laboratory

Many of the free market ideas canvased here remained in the relatively abstract form of economic theory and debate, more or less marginal to the decade's dominant development programs. But the 1970s classical revival—

soon to be subsumed under the sobriquet 'neoliberal'—did not entirely lack real-world laboratories. The most notable was Chile, where Theodore Schultz of the Chicago School of Economics, whom we met in Chapter 2, helped to launch an economics research and teaching hub at the Universidad Católica in Santiago, with funding from the U.S. International Cooperation Administration (ICA). The Chilean 'Chicago Boys' remained marginal for more than two decades, debating principles of market economics and placing themselves in opposition to the state-led planning approaches emanating from ECLA (Chapter 4). However, following Augusto Pinochet's 1973 overthrow of Salvador Allende's socialist administration, as well as the promulgation of a new *Programa de Desarollo Economíco* (known widely as The Brick [*El Ladrillo*] for its extraordinary print size) and Milton Friedman's 1975 visit to the country, Chile embarked on a rapid marketization and privatization that is now considered one of the most audacious examples of 'shock treatment'—the sudden liberalization of an economy—in recent history.[155] The sale of state assets, the liberalization of trade, the retrenchment of public services—these caused abysmal hardship among the poor and working classes. And the program was born bloody: The regime practiced widespread torture and extrajudicial killing, with over 2,200 murdered and nearly 40,000 victimized during its seventeen-year rule.

The connection between Pinochet's abuses and his market reforms, however, remains fraught. One of the best commentators on this history, Sebastian Edwards, doubts that a neoliberal economic revolution could have occurred without dictatorship.[156] Yet liberalization not only withstood Pinochet's removal and the 1990 return to democracy; but by the new millennium Chile had the highest per capita income in the region, with commentators hailing the economic 'miracle' as a new development model and severing it from the accompanying rights abuses. This appreciation became harder to sustain after growing inequality led to Covid-era protests and the 2021 election of leftist Gabriel Boric on a platform that harked back to midcentury social welfare policies.

For our purposes, it is important to note that the liberalization framework "excluded ethical, cultural, political, or social considerations," repudiating Chile's relatively egalitarian past. "The neo-liberal economist," writes the historian and former politician Juan Gabriel Valdés, "scorns the historical, social, and political complexity of developing nations. He regards differences between political systems, and the historical context of collective attitudes in a country, as irrelevant to the drawing up of a program to totally reform the way a society functions."[157] This clean-slate approach would prove resilient, appearing again in Eastern Europe (and, as we will see in Chapter 8, in Africa) after the 1989–91 collapse of state socialism.

The Convergence of Left and Right

If the 1970s marked one break in postwar development history, the 1980s saw another, as market economics swept the Western political establishment, including its aid institutions. The classical revival of the 1970s laid the groundwork for this change by dismantling arguments for state-led planning and a separate development economics. Free marketers took aim at both modernizers—too state-centered, too enticed by directive planning—and structuralists—whose *Marxisant* writings blamed global forces for domestic policy failures. The market shift, as economist Charles Gore observes, was accompanied by a refusal of the historical thinking associated with modernization and the rise of an "ahistorical performance assessment" based on decontextualized, quantifiable indicators.[158] Freedom from history seduced equity advocates as well (Gore cites David Lipton's work). On the pro-poor left, development analysis became rapid and situational—designed to facilitate immediate remedy, not to understand the long-term conditions of global poverty. Both left and right, in sum, dismissed history in favor of an empirical-*cum*-ethical presentism that employed micro-analytics to make categorical development claims.

An occasional contemporary noticed this decontextualization. In 1978, the British economist Keith Griffin and the Bangladeshi economist Azizur Rahman Khan argued that a quarter-century of growth and development had not reduced poverty in Asia. "The most outstanding facts" of recent Asian economies—they surveyed Bangladesh, India, Indonesia, Malaysia, Pakistan, the Philippines, and Sri Lanka—were "the worsening distribution of income and the declining real income of the poor." These problems were missed by economic models cast in terms of "atomistic households" or "decile rankings," which decontextualized want by disaggregating it into abstract units. Yet poverty, the authors insisted, "is associated with particular classes and groups," and it would be difficult to understand unless one accepted that it was "a product of a social system and reflects differences in access of various groups to sources of economic and political power." Only structural change, not "micro- and macro-economic tinkering," would relieve it by "changing the distribution of productive wealth" and "increasing the participation of the poor in decision-making."[159]

In other respects as well, basic needs and neoliberalism flowed together. Both invited donor involvement in the domestic economies of lendees. By disaggregating the nation into economic strata and urging policies aimed at redistribution, equity proponents demonstrated an interventionist impulse that set the stage for later free-market conditionality. In addition, by shifting from the development of poor nations to the relief of poor individuals, needs advocates unwittingly prepared the ground for their ideological opposites, who praised the individualism of choice and initiative offered by free markets. Both left and right, moreover, found a common enemy in the developmentalist state. The state-funded modernization programs of Asian and African governments, needs advocates argued, largely benefited an elite; free marketers agreed, though they added the claim that the market was a better social arbiter. In this regard, their disparate attacks made common cause. It is also worth recalling that, while early 1970s reformers saw inequity and poverty as interrelated concerns, the former gradually gave way to the latter, with mid-decade developers increasingly focused on providing a minimum for the poorest rather than rectifying the steep wealth gradient that characterized modernizing societies. For market advocates, of course, wealth and inequality were not problems; on the contrary, they encouraged competition that could unleash growth. On both sides of the political spectrum, then, concern for inequality waned. The irony is that if many of these debates—from aid interventionism to disputes over the developmental state—arose first among an energized left, the ultimate beneficiary was a renascent right that dismissed equity and poverty concerns in favor of renewed market orthodoxy.[160]

Yet poverty abolitionists (to use today's term) were not easily dispensed. Some, such as Robert Chambers, drafted influential strategies well into the subsequent decades. Others, such as James Grant and Richard Jolly, joined new institutions—in their case, UNICEF—and pushed for pro-poor modifications of structural adjustment.[161] Mahbub ul Haq worked with Amartya Sen, Paul Streeten, and Frances Stewart to promote the UNDP's Human Development Index, challenging the dominance of GDP with new indicators designed to measure a broad spectrum of well-being.[162] In other words, if pro-poor reformers no longer occupied the heights of development policy, they were deeply embedded in its managerial architecture, where they continued to advocate policies for ameliorating want. And below this level, many on-the-ground practitioners retained the anti-poverty convictions of their youth, employing the language of Freire and participatory appraisal, needs and equity, in projects around the globe. While market-led adjustment dominated aid policy in the 1980s, practitioners continued their efforts to uplift the poorest communities directly.

Post Mortem

As if in acknowledgment of this twin assault from left and right, the end of the decade christened a new genre: the post mortem for development theory. In the most widely read example, Albert Hirschman dilated on the field's rise and fall. Development economics, he reminisced, had always been hybrid, sharing with structuralists the view that developing economies worked differently from their industrial counterparts (Hirschman called this the rejection of mono-economics) and with classical economists the conviction that aid benefited both donor and recipient (the mutual-benefit claim). This hybridity accounted for the field's "old liveliness," but it also alienated both left and right, who preferred purer, cleaner propositions. For Hirschman, the source of development economics was the Keynesian revolution, which

> firmly established the view that there were two kinds of economics: one—the orthodox or classical tradition—which applied, as he was wont to put it, to the "special case" in which the economy was fully employed; and a very different system of analytical propositions and of policy prescriptions (newly worked out by Keynes) that took over when there was substantial unemployment of human and material resources. The Keynesian step from one to two economics was crucial: the ice of monoeconomics had been broken and the idea that there might be yet another economics had instant credibility.[163]

Starting in the 1940s, development took hold of this second economics, identifying two areas of poor-economy distinction: rural underemployment and late industrialization. Economists argued that investor countries could facilitate a big push toward modernization, prescribing planned, state-led initiatives that would not only foster growth but also open new and mutually advantageous trade opportunities. The unexpected failures of this program invited attack, even as development economists, Hirschman among them, modified their theories to account for changed circumstances. Ultimately, however, the inability to find a grand theory covering all developing economies, combined with Third World political disasters such as civil war, military intervention, famine, and inequality, signaled to many that modernization had failed. Development theory could not survive.

If Hirschman's eulogy was tinged with nostalgia, Dudley Seers, in a disciplinary obituary from the same year, expressed relief. His origin story differed from Hirschman's: development was born of colonial economics, not Keynesianism; its main focus was the promotion of dynamic growth rather than the maintenance of economic stability. If imperialism marked a suspect beginning for the subfield, Seers was equally concerned about planners' oversimplifications: the use of a single growth "yardstick" for development "eliminated" questions regarding the distribution of benefits, producing models "of very doubtful relevance" that served chiefly to keep programs "manageable and free of factors to which economists were unaccustomed." More disturbing, fast growth often exacerbated social distress, making midcentury prescriptions not simply feckless but positively damaging.[164] Instead, Seers highlighted structural challenges faced by poor countries; the need for autonomy, self-reliance, and equity; and the importance of a multidisciplinary development program. While acknowledging the diversity of non-Western societies, he echoed his 1970s colleagues by insisting on the global structures of inequality—a universalism that neoliberals also espoused by returning to a classical mono-economics that applied everywhere, with little accounting for context or experience. Unwittingly, the one prepared ground for the other.[165]

7

Touching Distance: The Emergence of Microfinance in 1970s Bangladesh

RECENTLY, THE HISTORIAN JOANNE MEYEROWITZ argued that calls for economic redistribution in the early 1970s gave way by the next decade to an embrace of microcredit as the preferred strategy for addressing global poverty.[1] This shift, in her view, reflected fading ambitions for restructuring the global economy, with egalitarian hopes supplanted by a market-friendly mechanism for drawing the poor into international value chains at the lowest level. A central figure in her story is Muhammad Yunus, the founder of Bangladesh's Grameen Bank and the most iconic representative of the microcredit movement. In her telling, Yunus appears as a charismatic businessman who excelled at social entrepreneurship, turning his Grameen Bank—in Bengali *grameen* means "village" or "rural"—into a global NGO. For the 1970s anti-poverty crusaders whom we discussed in the last chapter, microcredit offered an ingenious strategy for aiding the impoverished. For the free-market right, it integrated the poor into local economies, opening new markets and monetizing rural communities. Indigent men and women, Grameen seemed to demonstrate, were natural entrepreneurs, ready to build small businesses if only given the means. For those who mistrusted government programs—and these included many on both left and right—Yunus's barefoot bank showed the extraordinary potential of NGOs to promote development in economically and geographically remote regions. And for feminists and gender advocates, the attention to village women conveyed a special thrill. Wherever one stood on the political spectrum, the Grameen Bank offered something to like.

Yet even as Grameen became an international darling in the 1990s, its reception simplified both its own anti-poverty strategy and the context from which it emerged—namely, Bangladesh in the 1970s and 1980s, the decades just after independence. The acclaim of Grameen and other microfinance NGOs—BRAC, for example—obscured the broader range of Bangladeshi experiments in rural development and poverty alleviation that occurred in these years, and it has abridged our understanding of Grameen's own original purposes, which extended well beyond credit provision. Starting in the late 1980s and peaking in the following decades, global microcredit advocates promoted a decontextualized model of a culturally embedded program, an image that fed the over-hyping of microcredit as a development panacea. In many ways, the recent disappointment with microcredit as a poverty solution grows less from liabilities inherent in the strategy, which has done considerable good for many people, than it does from the "evangelism" or "hard selling" of its backers, who expected more miracles than credit provision could ever hope to deliver.[2]

By contrast, other rural development initiatives slipped into the shadows. Yet the decades surrounding Bangladesh's independence witnessed rich and sundry efforts at rural empowerment, cooperativism, multiservice microfinance, and state assistance. This ferment has been lost in the global retelling of the era, but its recovery can offer useful development alternatives for consideration today, in an age when market entrepreneurship as an engine for growth no longer commands the respect it once did. In the previous chapter, we saw that an early 1970s concern for inequality and poverty gradually morphed into a preponderant emphasis on basic needs to ensure the poorest a minimum standard. The response to inequality among Bangladeshi NGOs was somewhat different: Over the course of the 1970s some NGOs embraced a strategy of mobilizing poor communities, while others preferred a 'targeted' approach of providing credit to poor individuals. A third, aggregate approach—the community-wide cooperative model—continued as well, although it drew criticism for entrenching elite hold in rural areas. To understand how microcredit won out over its competitors, we have to examine the society from which it emerged.

The Independence Era

NGO activism in 1970s Bangladesh was part of a global "power shift" that transformed a development industry dominated by governmental agencies into a field rife with private actors and investors.[3] By the late 1960s, NGOs with nimble structures and extensive networks increasingly pressured donors regarding global policy, implementing programs both on their own dime and as contractors for public institutions. In the ensuing decades, they routinely took on project management duties, with official agencies relegated to contracting and oversight, a process accelerated by staff reductions in many Western ministries before and after the Cold War. As Bangladeshi anthropologist Manzurul Mannan explains, NGO involvement in development and poverty alleviation had unintended consequences: Even as they enhanced the range of technical capabilities, NGOs also employed a homogenizing language that denied local variety in the name of managerial convenience. Furthermore, while advocating modern meritocratic notions of expertise and equity, they often reproduced local hierarchies in their own staff structures.[4] This was more than just inconsistency: As private organizations, NGOs did not face the same accountability as government actors, despite their considerable leverage over development policy. In Bangladesh, which is characterized by what Gunnar Myrdal called a "soft state" with limited reach and capability, NGOs provide services that the government is unable or unwilling to maintain, thus carrying out duties typically assumed by the state.[5] While these efforts plug essential service gaps, they also raise concern about the cultivation of a "franchise state" in which important functions are contracted out with little public oversight.[6]

The history of Bangladesh's development NGOs is rooted in the trauma and triumph of the early 1970s: the Bhola cyclone, the independence war, the famine of 1974. BRAC, the seminal NGO in an impressive field, was born in the wake of the cyclone that hit the Bengal delta's coastal islands in November 1970, killing nearly half a million people, many of whom had been forced onto insecure lowlands by poverty and landlessness. For East Bengalis, the devastation attested not only to the terrors of nature, but also to the negligence of what was increasingly perceived as colonial rule from Islamabad. Achieving independence in 1947, Pakistan was one of the more untenable states born of the faltering British Empire, a bifurcated territory whose two wings—West and East Pakistan—were separated by over 1,000 miles of India. The poorer and more populous East struggled continuously against West Pakistani hegemony, starting with the 1952 language protests, when Bengalis decried the imposition of Urdu as the official state idiom. Economically, the delta saw its aid receipts and jute revenues siphoned toward development initiatives in the West.[7] Islamabad's sluggish response to catastrophe, therefore, was understood not simply as an indictment of official disaster preparation, but as a signal failure of longstanding Pakistani rule, including the top-down modernization policies of the country's post-1958 dictatorship. Witnesses at Dhaka airport cite one lone Pakistani jet amid fleets of foreign aid deliveries. This apathy inflamed Bengali resentment and affirmed what nationalists had long contended: that East Pakistan was an internal colony, not an equal partner in a joint state. And it occurred less than a month before the first free elections in over a decade.

Official indifference contrasted not only with foreign but also with local relief efforts. In response to the cyclone, many middle- and upper-class Bengalis—from journalists and artists to political leaders and businessmen—traveled to the coast to witness the destruction and assist as they could, a spontaneous activism that translated into social and political militancy in the months to come. Famously, the Awami League (AL) head and soon-to-be independence icon Sheikh Mujibur Rahman visited the stricken region, met local leaders, and walked the treacherous landscape to survey the damage. So did politician and pro-poor spokesman Maulana Bhashani, then eighty-five years old and in poor health, but still one of the country's most charismatic leftists.[8] Artists, too—soon to join the struggle for Bangladeshi independence—took to their feet and picked up their pens. Perhaps most significant, the painter Zainul Abedin, already renowned for his depictions of the 1943 Bengal famine, made a scroll composed of stark ink-and-watercolor drawings about the agony he witnessed along the coast.[9] Social and economic leaders also took the journey, among them the accountant Fazle Hasan Abed, son of a well-to-do family and recently returned from years in the United Kingdom. Shaken by the horrors he saw, Abed left a lucrative corporate career to spearhead relief efforts and went on to found, in 1972, the Bangladesh Rehabilitation Assistance Committee (later the Bangladesh Rural Advancement Committee, and later still, just BRAC), the first of a congeries of influential NGOs established in the 1970s to combat the country's chronic poverty.[10] Commentators on this "vernacular humanitarianism" have highlighted its character of witness and accompaniment, of walking with devastated locals and traversing the ground of disaster. The experience proved transformative for Abed and others, inspiring them to work directly with their impoverished fellow citizens.[11]

Elite solidarity with the country's poor was part of a global 1970s phenomenon of middle- and upper-class concern for victims of abuse in the Second and Third World.[12] What distinguished Bangladeshi activists was their physical and emotional proximity to the poor, including personal or family encounters with poverty and joint engagement in the liberation struggle. Though sheltered from intense suffering, well-to-do Bengalis could justly claim that their cross-class solidarity after Bhola grew from a shared destiny that bound together residents of Pakistan's riverine East. Such engagement hardly reduced inequality, but it did imbue local activism with an urgency that proved galvanizing.[13]

Rage over Islamabad's "criminal neglect" contributed to the overwhelming victory of the Bengali nationalist AL in December's election, held less than four weeks after the cyclone. Mujib's party swept 160 of 162 parliamentary seats allocated to the East, an absolute majority in the country overall. The victory, viewed with tremendous alarm in West Pakistan, capped a nationalist effort that had accelerated throughout the 1960s into calls for greater autonomy, representation, and budgetary allotments. In the process, a "vernacular elite," in Rounaq Jahan's term, came to privilege its Bengali identity over the Islamic ties that had swelled pro-Pakistani sentiment in the 1940s.[14] Military leader Yahya Khan's March 1970 announcement of elections kicked off a concerted AL campaign based on the party's longstanding Six-Point Program for political, economic, and cultural autonomy. When Mujib's party won in December, Pakistan's rulers refused to seat the new legislature and instead offered a 'compromise' power-sharing pact between the AL and the runner-up (West) Pakistan People's Party. This was manifestly intolerable to East Bengalis, and it led in early 1971 to popular unrest, the incarceration of Sheikh Mujib, a genocidal military crackdown, and a civil war that, with Indian Army assistance, birthed a sovereign Bangladesh by year's end.

The second major bloodletting of the new decade, the Liberation War increased the NGO activism initiated by Bhola.[15] Perhaps the most prominent organization to emerge from this field of battle was the health NGO Gonoshasthaya Kendra (GK) (which means 'For People's Health'), founded by the U.K.-trained surgeon Zafrullah Chowdhury to provide medical services for the freedom fighters (*mukhti bahini*). GK's wartime field hospital, established along the Indian border, relied on volunteer staffing, particularly untrained women from nearby refugee camps who served as nurses.[16] After four weeks of instruction, they administered basic medicines and assisted doctors, a valuable addition in a country that lacked skilled labor—and a strategy that would later influence Yunus. The recruitment process was arduous: in conservative rural communities where purdah was preferred, if not always feasible, for young women, families did not readily allow their daughters to work outside the home, especially in jobs that required social circulation. Chowdhury built his staff slowly, focusing on the village where activities were to occur, employing trial and error, and accommodating local social patterns.[17] With the war's end, he set up a seed clinic in the village of Savar, west of Dhaka, where he outfitted female staff with bicycles for home visits—a model eventually expanded to fifty communities. Like Abed, he describes "walking many miles" to conduct home visits, peregrinations that revealed to him the country's vast need. Without the war, he maintained, he would likely have become a Dhaka surgeon. Instead, he became a spokesman for self-reliance, a pioneer of locally manufactured drugs, and the overseer of a large cancer hospital in the capital—as well as a strident government critic.[18]

The Nixon administration greeted the new country truculently by disparaging it as an "international basket case."[19] But the raucous social and political activism in Dhaka and elsewhere belies this description. Bangladesh was anything but prostrate; instead, its independence-era population was boisterous, energized, politically engaged—despite (or rather because of) its traumas. Mujib embodied this fire, espousing socialism, nationalism, secularism, and democracy as principles of the dramatic makeover he planned for his country. As in the case of other Third World leaders, his socialism accorded with the pragmatics of liberation: While the Soviet Union and India supported Bangladesh in its independence war, the United States aligned with Pakistan, then serving the Nixon administration as a liaison to China. Socialism was primarily a nationalist and egalitarian doctrine for a traditionally hierarchical society, and Mujib insisted that he was no Communist despite his admiration for Mao's experiments.[20] Yet the long years of nationalist agitation, argues Talukder Maniruzzaman, had produced genuine radicalism among influential segments of the population, a hunger for social change that erupted into guerilla warfare and social missionary efforts.[21] The nascent NGO sector has to be understood as part of this activist spirit.

For Naomi Hossain, one of the most astute scholars of contemporary Bangladesh, the transformational quality of early 1970s activism arose from the decay of two tacit hierarchical "contracts" that had stabilized Bengali society for generations: the patron-client structure, whereby peasants traded service to a local power broker for security and protection; and the patriarchal bargain in which women were sheltered and provisioned by husbands and fathers. By the 1960s, these traditional systems had weakened under the pressure of land scarcity, political instability, and economic exploitation. The shocks of the early 1970s finally tipped sentiment in favor of radical social change.[22] The era's rebelliousness was reflected in a fervent student movement that filled the ranks of the independence struggle and suffered accordingly in the genocide. It is no accident that one of the first targets of the Pakistani counterinsurgency starting in March 1971 was Dhaka University, where professors and students were executed in a coordinated barrage. If middle-class students rallied first for national liberation, they soon embraced a leftism dedicated to combating poverty and inequality, embarking by train, bus, boat, and foot for rural areas to work with upstart organizations assisting the poor. Thus, the transformational journeys undertaken by elites after Bhola were reprised in the politicization narratives of young idealists. For our purposes, it is crucial to highlight that NGOs emerged as a particularly enduring legacy of this activism—even if, as we will see, they sometimes dissociated themselves from its more radical aspects.[23] The *de*politicization of NGOs that we will observe over the course of the 1970s stood in marked contrast to the original motives of the sector.

Another preoccupation of early 1970s activists was rural women, a kind of terra incognita for middle-class project workers who set out to understand women's lives and provide for their uplift. The concern was both social and economic: Village women, advocates pointed out, were doubly oppressed, by poverty and gender; moreover, the country could scarcely thrive if half its labor force were locked away. To be sure, the "patriarchal bargain" that sequestered rural women was never complete. In the countryside, purdah was a luxury that only wealthy peasants could afford: The more income a family had, the likelier their women were to retire from social life.[24] Poor women—and these were the majority—had to work, sometimes in the *bari* (home compound), sometimes beyond, though always in more circumscribed conditions than their male counterparts. Yet even as land shortage straitened household economies, the crises of the 1970s dramatized the failure of the agrarian social system to protect and provide for its members—and to protect women from wartime rapes—inducing gradual changes in gender norms. Thus, the lives of the rural women 'discovered' by 1970s activists were already in flux, with wives and daughters taking jobs, donning the veil as a mobile purdah, and entering leadership roles as part of the NGO workforce, where they were recruited for their unprecedented access to the poorest populations.[25]

Two leading proponents of this new public policy interest were Tahrunessa Abdullah, of the government-run Bangladesh Academy of Rural Development (BARD), and Rounaq Jahan, of the University of Dhaka. Both penned influential studies of village women. The fact that their books were published by the Ford Foundation and the ILO indicates their policy aspirations: they sought to facilitate women's development by identifying program entry points.[26] Jahan was more direct in labeling the lives she observed as oppressive. The scope of women's exclusion, she insisted, required more than just an effort at social integration; it demanded new NGO operating procedures and dramatic structural change in Bangladeshi society.[27] Abdullah, by contrast, called on programs to meet rural women where they were, to accept social segregation as the starting point for work aimed at improving their lives. All the same, both hoped to "modernize" women in the name of national development and social equity.[28] Given the lack of data on women's lives, programming had to be experimental and bottom-up, responsive to unfolding needs: a project was, in this sense, a research effort, and Abdullah treated her work on the BARD-run Integrated Rural Development Programme (IRDB) as continuous with her scholarship. For the local NGO community, the new appreciation of gender proved defining, and it remained central to programming even in the less politicized atmosphere of the late 1970s. The timing was fortuitous: With the rise of the Women in Development movement in the mid-1970s, strategies that targeted poor women were poised for funding and recognition. Indeed, Abdullah's 1982 book *Village Women of Bangladesh* was prefaced by none other than Ester Boserup.

So far, we have highlighted two traumas that shaped Bangladesh's NGO community in the early 1970s: the Bhola cyclone and the Liberation War. The third, the cataclysmic famine of 1974, slew approximately 1.5 million people and upended relations between the population and its new leadership. The disaster had multiple causes: Severe flooding in mid-1974 inundated fields and ruined crops, buffeting an already fragile economy. Hardly three years out from devastation of Bhola and the Liberation War, the government lacked the capacity to manage the crisis: Mujib, everyone agrees, was a better resistance leader than prime minister, and by 1974 his reputation had plummeted. International politics added to the country's travails. The dramatic increase in food prices following the 1973 oil crisis menaced a population that depended on imports. And when Bangladesh agreed to sell jute sacks to Cuba, Washington imposed sanctions (selectively, as it turned out, since it did not do so when Egypt sold cotton to Castro), barring food aid that helped fill government coffers and supplement caloric intake. Shortages were exacerbated by a food rationing system that favored 'priority groups' such as urban residents who exercised political influence.[29] As Amartya Sen points out, partly in reference to this episode, famines are rarely caused by absolute deprivation, but instead result from distributional failures, a lack of economic entitlements among the poor, and policies skewed toward political rather than economic needs.[30] Scenes of rural poor dying on the streets surely sped Mujib's demise. In January of the following year, he established a one-party state—the BAKSAL (Bangladesh Worker-Peasant People's League) regime—in the hope of stabilizing the society and quelling threats to his rule. That summer, mere months after his presidential takeover, he was assassinated in a bloody coup d'état.

The famine redirected NGO operations as well, undercutting the socialist aspirations of the independence years and prompting new strategies aimed at directly assisting the poor. With survival at stake, there was little patience for the time-consuming task of building communal solidarity; more imperative was promoting self-reliance and securing basic needs. In these circumstances, the strategic shift to microcredit and individual entrepreneurship among NGOs made sense, marking a disillusionment with the collective aspirations of prefamine times—a trend seen across Bangladeshi politics and society. Furthermore, the window for leftist experimentation closed considerably with Gen. Ziaur Rahman's 1975–77 military takeover.[31] In addition to ending elections, the new autocrat shifted the government firmly to the free-market right even as he reintegrated Islam into public discourse. These changes were accompanied by new economic opportunities: for men, a market in migrant labor opened in the Gulf States, as Zia repaired a relationship with the Arab world strained by the Liberation War, when Muslim leaders sided with Pakistan; and for women, a readymade garment industry inaugurated in 1977 with the Korean Daewoo–Desh Garments joint venture.[32] In the 1980s, factories and sweatshops mushroomed around Dhaka. Zia also tried to bolster his support by creating the first village-level governing bodies in Bangladeshi history, the *gram sarkar,* or village government, with members chosen at local meetings and overseen by state officials. Although this innovation fostered some enthusiasm around the self-reliance movement (discussed below), the general result of Zia's rule was a retreat from revolutionary sentiments. NGOs dedicated to popular mobilization continued to appear late in the decade, but the long turn away from political activism had begun. The rise of microfinance transpired against this backdrop.

For those who had been caught up in the heady aspirations of independence, the failure of radical social transformation and the advent of military rule prompted years of reckoning. The economists Nurul Islam and Rehman Sobhan had launched their careers by analyzing the internal colonization of East Pakistan before joining Mujib's government to author the country's first five-year plan.[33] In *Development Planning in Bangladesh* (1977), Islam, by then the *former* head of the Planning Commission, affirmed the centrality of socialism and development to the promise of the young state. But the regime, he regretted, faced extraordinary headwinds, and its efforts to modernize were hampered by a debilitating lack of local expertise after Pakistani administrators fled. Equally daunting, the AL coalition was too large and fractious to govern effectively. A vast umbrella party riven by factions, it relied on village elites for local support and patronage, an alliance that thwarted efforts to relieve inequality and poverty for the peasant majority. Politicized students, too, were gradually alienated from the party, sidelined in favor of technocrats and political appointees. As corruption proliferated, AL officials treated independence as an opportunity for spoils.

Six years later, Sobhan and his co-author Muzaffar Ahmad followed with a 600-page post mortem of their own, one focused on the AL's class and socioeconomic structure.[34] Adopting Polish economist Michał Kalecki's concept of an 'intermediate regime,' the authors argued that the party rested on a petty bourgeois and upper peasant social base, rather than a more developed bourgeoisie that might have spearheaded modernization. Barred from top political and economic positions in Pakistan, AL operatives lacked the administrative and technical training required to lead a state; instead, they took state capture as an occasion for personal enrichment. Without a native entrepreneurial class, Mujib had to use the public coffers to fund development investments, even while relying on costly national and local patronage to secure widespread support. But he was hobbled from the start: The task—to use robust state action to create a modern economy—lacked the socioeconomic basis—a productive middle class—needed for success. The collapse of Mujib's Bangladesh, in sum, capped a tragedy of state-society contradiction.

BRAC and Company

This political tumult proved fertile for local development NGOs, and BRAC was the pioneer. The story of its evolution can be told in three projects spanning the decade—the Sulla project launched in 1972 in the remote northeastern district of Sylhet; the Jamalpur Women's Program, based from 1975 in flood-affected north-central Bangladesh; and the Manikganj Integrated Programme, opened the following year near Dhaka to provide economic assistance, including small loans, to the poor. In Sulla, BRAC shifted from an early focus on the rehabilitation of war-ravaged communities to a wider integrated rural development strategy with activities across numerous sectors (health, literacy, agriculture, housing, vocational education). On the strength of this effort, UNICEF urged the organization to design activities for women in the Jamalpur region that would complement its own relief and development efforts. Initially limited to providing education for poor women, the project gradually introduced a 'targeted' programming approach that moved away from community-wide activities and toward those that singled out vulnerable populations for education and food-for-work opportunities. This shift progressed further in Manikganj and elsewhere in the second half of the decade.

BRAC programs had numerous features that influenced Bangladesh's broader NGO culture. Most innovative was the 'functional education' portfolio that Abed understood as the core of BRAC activities. Representative of the decade's wider leftist activism, functional education was rooted in Paolo Freire's concept of *conscientização,* which Abed and other NGO leaders encountered in the 1970 English translation of *Pedagogy of the Oppressed.*[35] We saw in Chapter 6 how Freire was domesticated in his North American reception, turned into a spokesman for student-centered pedagogy but stripped of his revolutionary credentials. The reception was quite different in Bangladesh, where activists embraced the call for *conscientization* as a way to build solidarity among the poor. Here is how one report put it:

> BRAC's functional education, with its problems and solution-posing methodology, is basic to all BRAC development activities. Briefly put, the methodology is based on learner's participation through dialogue facilitated by the teacher. The curriculum centres on real life problems and possible solutions. The aim of functional education is not only to make each learner critically conscious of her/his environment, but also to motivate the learners to take action to beneficially effect [*sic*] this environment.[36]

While BRAC was also committed to increasing food production, Abed viewed *conscientization* and solidarity, not aid and credit, as his early watchwords. Only a vigilant and active citizenry, he felt, in line with independence-era radicalism, could overcome the delta's endemic poverty and inequity. In the first half of the decade, this attitude was trendsetting.

In other ways, BRAC echoed the dominant practices of the day. The issuance of rural credit has a long history in the region, dating back to the introduction of credit unions at the century's advent. More recently, the Pakistan Academy of Rural Development (PARD), based in Comilla, introduced a two-tiered cooperative system as a framework for credit and training delivery—a model adopted by BRAC and other programs. Grameen microcredit, it is important to stress, was not the first credit initiative for the poor, although its approach had other distinctions. Furthermore, BRAC's effort to target poor rural women for education and economic support—part of the wider government and civil society interest in gender inequities—predated Grameen's famous experiments in women's entrepreneurship. If BRAC programs did not always succeed at raising the consciousness or income of local women—the 1978 Annual Report expressed disappointment at the inadequacy of program results—they nonetheless signaled an increasingly focused strategy of assisting the country's poorest demographics.[37] In none of these practices was BRAC the pioneer, but as a prominent early development NGO, it did help to standardize their use.

A further point bears highlighting: Throughout this book, I have underlined the tendency of top-down planners to ignore local circumstances in countries around the globe. BRAC and other Bangladeshi NGOs exemplify a very different process based around bottom-up research, trial and error, midstream correction, and long-term relationships with the poor. Advocates describe BRAC as a "learning institution," a designation that, to a greater or lesser extent, characterized other Bangladeshi organizations as well.[38] Indeed, one of the striking features of Bangladesh's early 1970s NGO field is the degree to which it engaged with local populations in face-to-face interaction, experimenting with new strategies in response to emerging needs. This contrasts sharply with programs planned in the West and exported to new countries with only minor accommodation to domestic conditions.

In retrospect, BRAC's most consequential programming shift began in the late 1970s as it reduced its emphasis on collective empowerment and prioritized targeted microfinance interventions. The shift occurred for multiple reasons. We have already noted the de-politicizing effect of the 1975 military coup, the foreclosure of opportunities for radical activism in Zia's Bangladesh. In this atmosphere, one had to consider the advisability of mobilization efforts that might endanger implementers and beneficiaries alike. Furthermore, by the decade's end, as we will see, a microfinance countermodel, employed by BRAC but popularized by Grameen, achieved success in reaching poor Bangladeshis. By the early 1980s, the lure of microcredit proved difficult to resist.

But BRAC's turn was also informed by its own research efforts, which cast doubt on the efficacy of its earlier community approaches. Most influential was a booklet called *The Net* (1980), which put in consumable form an image of the elite capture of relief and development goods that was already widely supposed.[39] If it was not utterly surprising to learn that local elites benefited disproportionately from assistance programs, what proved more shocking was their frequent and widespread collusion. The advantages of wealthier peasants did not derive simply from the tendency of modern inputs to favor advanced farmers; it also came about due to elite networking, with well-to-do residents using their power to commandeer goods for personal gain. Tubewells were a case in point: Installed across the country by the World Bank and other donors, they were commonly monopolized by large landowners who diverted water to irrigate their fields. Alas, solidarity efforts among the poor had not undercut these practices.[40] Drawing the logical conclusion, BRAC decided that a more targeted strategy of putting financial resources in the hands of the poor might yield better results. Accordingly, it bent increasingly toward microcredit—sometimes delivered individually and sometimes through cooperatives. The Manikganj Integrated Development Programme and the Dutch-funded multi-district Rural Credit and Training Program exhibited this new focus.[41]

BRAC's turn to microfinance, however, caused internal organizational tension, leading some of its staff to splinter off and form the new NGO Nijera Kori in 1980, dedicated to the continuation of collective empowerment strategies. Their disappointment was rooted in fond memories of BRAC's earlier commitments. In the mid-1970s, young fieldworkers used *conscientization* and mobilization techniques to help poor communities understand the political origins of their deprivation.[42] In keeping with the leftist tenor of the age, these efforts incorporated class analyses designed to highlight the need for popular pressure and solidarity in confronting clientelistic structures. While microcredit could provide temporary relief, it did not, this minority believed, promote the empowerment needed to secure long-term development.[43] By the late 1970s, the new strategy had altered not only BRAC's programming priorities, but also staff relations with poor beneficiaries. Now a fieldworker became, in the words of one Nijera Kori founder, "the person with the money, someone they had to pay." Instead of "accompaniment" designed to empower the poor, staff members implemented "top-down development."[44] For these schismatics, the professional hierarchies that microfinance entrenched betrayed the social values of the era. To this day, Nijera Kori remains unique among national NGOs for retaining *conscientization* as a fundamental strategy and refusing the turn to credit.[45]

Proshika, founded in 1976 by students Kazi Faruque Ahmed and Rahat Uddin Ahmed, also exhibited these tensions. Begun as a Canadian University Service Overseas (CUSO) project, the new organization blended service delivery with a Freirian commitment to organizing and mobilizing the landless—what early documents called "walking on two feet." Galvanized by relief work undertaken during the famine, when he witnessed landowners denying food to the poor, Kazi Faruque hoped to cultivate self-reliance by empowering the poor to break their dependency on patronage. Proshika's dual strategy, however, may have contributed to its 1981 split into two organizations, one adopting a credit approach, the other prioritizing empowerment.[46] By the mid-1990s, Kazi Faruque's Proshika had become one of the largest NGOs in

Bangladesh, providing microcredit but also mobilizing its members against religious fundamentalism.[47]

The Association for Social Advancement (ASA) followed a similar trajectory. Inspired by the recently deceased Maulana Bhashani, founder Shafiqual Haque Choudhury established ASA in 1978 to promote peasant mobilization and political activism. By the mid-1980s, under pressure from the military dictatorship and the growing popularity of microcredit, ASA shifted from revolutionary goals to a more integrated approach that included a significant credit component. In the early 1990s, facing still further demand for financial services, ASA transformed once again, dropping its commitment to education and empowerment altogether and stressing microcredit alone, designed to encourage self-reliance. "My heart still aches for those early days when we dreamed of a peasants' movement that would take political power," Choudhury recalled in 1994. "After the 1971 struggle most of us were primed for a socialist approach. I now find I am confused about these issues: am I a traitor? But I had no alternative. Financial services have proved to be easily the best way to help the poor."[48] His remark illustrates not only the distance traveled, but the loss entailed in abandoning the revolutionary past.[49]

As this discussion makes clear, Bangladesh in the 1970s was very much a laboratory of aid ideas, many of them generated by the NGO community.[50] But the fact that these ideas spread beyond Bangladesh had to do with a very different kind of aid lab that the country had also become. According to Rehman Sobhan, Bangladesh offered a case study in foreign aid dependence, with aid disbursements financing around 10 percent of GDP, over 60 percent of the development budget, and over 60 percent of imports in the early 1970s. Aid commitments from all sources between December 1971 and 1974/75 topped $3 billion.[51] In lieu of native investment, Sobhan regretted, Bangladesh relied on the "narcotic" of foreign assistance to stabilize its accounts and build its infrastructure, an addiction that led to increased food imports, declining savings, and loss of political control—as well as aid-fueled corruption and "malgovernance" that shapes politics to this day.[52] Years later, Nurul Islam also lamented the unequal partnership between Bangladesh and its donors, with Dhaka forced to endure World Bank disapproval of its early socialist policies and accept partial liability for Pakistan's outstanding debt.[53] Contributing to the international attention were the dramatic relief efforts that opened the decade, capped by George Harrison and Ravi Shankar's Concert for Bangladesh. In sum, the world watched Bangladesh more closely than it did most other developing nations, and its 1970s aid experiments were more broadly noticed. In a decade dedicated to uplifting the poor, the delta's suffering attracted a bright spotlight. It was, to cite the World Bank's country representative, a "test case of development."[54] In this regard, Czech novelist Milan Kundera got it wrong when he remarked that the groans of Bangladesh would soon be forgotten.[55]

The State Role in Development

Since the 1970s, it has become common to contrast government development efforts disfavorably to nimble NGO programs. Yet the Bangladesh experience testifies to a more complex reality. The celebration of microcredit as a supposedly nongovernmental—even *anti*-governmental—strategy for poverty alleviation ignores the ways in which both public and private agencies—the state and NGOs—worked in tandem to promote rural development during the decade.

Almost all Bangladeshi interlocutors credit the origins of the country's rural development achievements to Akhter Hamid Khan, the West Pakistani founder of the PARD (later, BARD) in Comilla, just over 100 kilometers from the capital. Although the program echoed prevalent international development trends of the 1960s, the intensity of its rural activities was new in East Bengal and represents one of the few bright memories of the Pakistan era: a commitment to rural uplift that stood in sharp contradistinction to the general picture of neglect. PARD incubated many of the country's subsequent development models.

As part of the British Raj, East Bengal had witnessed desultory community uplift efforts since the turn of the century. In Chapter 5, we noted F. L. Brayne's interest in rural India and the introduction of agricultural cooperatives. Indeed, credit as a tool for relief and development was decades old by the 1970s.[56] But the remoteness of the delta—webbed by jungles and rivers that only gradually yielded to an eastward-shifting settlement frontier—as well as its religious distinctiveness—a majority Muslim pocket far from the religion's geographic center—meant that East Bengal was not the focus of colonial development efforts.[57] When the 1905 administrative division of Bengal (later rescinded) sparked nationalist riots, leading to a shift of the Raj capital from Calcutta to New Delhi, East Bengal grew remoter still. A hinterland within British India, it gradually developed an identity that was separate from both West Bengal and the minority Hindus who lived in its midst, an identity reinforced by Muslim resistance to Indian nationalism. Yet despite this isolation, East Bengal remained dependent on West Bengal's mills and factories to process its chief export, jute. In this sense, the delta might be described as doubly colonized: by the British from across the ocean, and by the West Bengali gatekeepers of its primary industry.[58] Accordingly, the 1947 partition of the Raj into India and Pakistan, which finally sundered East and West Bengal, hurt the delta economically as it lost access to vital processing plants.

It soon became apparent that one form of colonial rule had replaced another. Troublingly for movements of Third World solidarity, Pakistan became a festering example of non-Western internal colonialism at a time when many Asians and Africans were still fighting the Western brand. (For this reason, Bangladeshi independence was not welcomed by the Muslim world.) Nonetheless, programs for rural development in East Bengal began in earnest during the Pakistan period as part of a push for modernization mounted partly to win over Bengali sympathies. The first of these was Village-AID (V-AID), inaugurated by the government in 1953 with funding from the American ICA, the Ford Foundation, and other international donors.[59] Though locally managed, V-AID's emphasis on community self-help projects reflected global development thinking. The Ford Foundation and Michigan State University, both deeply involved in India, provided training and advisory services to program leaders, including PARD founder Akhter Hamid Khan, perhaps V-AID's most important product. Khan joined the program early on but left after one year over strategic disagreements, particularly what he viewed as insufficient training for villagers and aid workers.[60] Yet as a program designed to tap rural initiative and organization, V-AID set a standard that would shape Bangladeshi efforts for years to come.[61]

The community focus was further entrenched in 1960, when Pakistani military ruler Ayub Khan introduced the Basic Democracies program, which set up a five-tiered system of local governing councils, including union and *thana* (or subdistrict) councils that became a staple of later development interventions.[62] The union council, one tier higher than the *thana,* comprised representatives from several villages, plus officials and citizen appointees. Government civil servants were assigned to provide agricultural expertise.[63]

As channels for modernization, the new councils had limited impact, in part because they were subject to elite capture—"Bourgeoise Democracy," in Sobhan's tag.[64] Yet as a framework for subsequent rural development efforts, these structures endured.

Khan rejoined V-AID in the late 1950s to establish the development academy that would make his name. Founded in 1959, PARD broadened the local self-help formula of V-AID by establishing training and research as program cornerstones. For ten years, PARD dominated East Pakistan's rural development landscape, organizing experiments in the 'laboratory' of Kotwali Thana, Comilla District, a jurisdiction that comprised around 150,000 residents. From these experiments emerged what has come to be known as the "Comilla Model" of rural development.[65] Some of PARD's basic premises tracked contemporary community development portfolios: the belief that programming must be rooted in villagers' "felt needs" and capabilities; that communities are capable of effecting change if properly guided; and that villages must be approached as a unit, not as separate individuals. Khan also accepted the need for increased food production, agro-technology, and family planning. Indeed, the international connections of the delta's development pioneers (including those, like Khan, who were from West Pakistan) means that we cannot view Bangladeshi experiments as wholly domestic in origin or insulated from global streams of thought.[66] This does not diminish the importance of local interaction with farmers and peasants in shaping Comilla programs. But it does suggest that 'homegrown' and 'international' are not mutually exclusive categories.

The Comilla model, however, differed in an important respect from community development programming in neighboring India. The latter relied on the village-level worker-animator, rather than training institutes, to spearhead local programs. In Khan's view, this approach did not properly mobilize peasant-farmers as agents of their own advancement. Instead, he argued, villagers had to be well organized and provided with the institutionalized coaching necessary to foster participatory modernization.[67] His PARD model, accordingly, had four chief components:

1. a two-tiered cooperative structure at the village and *thana* levels, designed to organize farmers for credit and technical inputs (this was its most lasting legacy);

2. a Thana Training and Development Center (TTDC) to educate village cooperative leaders in modern farming techniques;
3. an irrigation program that provided tubewells and pumps to village cooperatives; and
4. a rural works program focused on road drainage and other infrastructure, designed to make use of landless laborers.

These components ultimately produced an integrated rural development program of the sort carried forward by BRAC and other organizations in independent Bangladesh, blending the goals of increased food production and local peasant empowerment. The results in Comilla were deemed generally positive: loan repayment rates were manageable, and new tubewells, high-yield grains, and other inputs more than doubled crop production over the decade.[68]

Yet Comilla drew criticism as well as praise. Perhaps the most consistent complaint is that while it targeted small and midlevel farmers, the real beneficiaries were large farmers who reaped the most technological inputs and accrued leadership posts on cooperatives and councils. In this way, the program ended up reinforcing rural inequality.[69] Its agricultural focus also meant that East Pakistan's growing landless population, a key target of 1970s microcredit, benefited little from PARD experiments in the 1960s. A further complaint concerned the model's lack of replicability. Comilla's success depended on several features that could not easily be reproduced in other parts of Bangladesh: an active and engaged peasantry; an intensive set of inputs, including credit, training, research, extension, and agro-industrial products; and a strong, innovative leadership, embodied in the charismatic Khan. All of this required heavy investments of time, personnel, and materials, making the prospects for a country-wide scale-up unlikely. And it was arguable that the comparatively egalitarian Comilla District provided an adequate model for more remote and unequal areas to the north and west, let alone for the geographically precarious coast.[70] Some critics also worried that the model produced a kind of dependency that might make it difficult to wean even Comilla residents of continued care and support. It was, in effect, something of a hothouse flower.

Demerits notwithstanding, plans were made before the Liberation War to extend the Comilla Model to other districts through the Integrated Rural Development Programme (IRDP), inaugurated in 1970. Despite Khan's postwar departure for Pakistan, the program continued into the early 1980s, when it merged into the new Bangladesh Rural Development Board (BRDB).[71] Though based on the Comilla Model, IRDP marked a considerable diminution of its program, adopting mainly the two-tier cooperative structure, which by 1980 had spread to over 250 *thanas*.[72] Without Khan's leadership and the funds lavished on Kotwali, the program thinned as it spread, with leaner training, fewer technical inputs, and low farmer enrollment in cooperatives. Numbers tell the story: From roughly 11,000 village cooperative members in Kotwali *thana* in 1968, enrollment dropped under IRDP to an average of just over 4,000 per *thana* in 1971–72 and just over 2,800 in 1977–78, with middle- and upper-income farmers overrepresented.[73] On a return visit to Bangladesh in the late 1970s, Khan fretted that the IRDP was adrift—suffering from bureaucratic lethargy, a weakened training curriculum, and mechanical replication. It is not clear, of course, in the straitened circumstances of postwar Bangladesh, that it could have happened otherwise; the Comilla Model was perhaps always too resource-intensive to travel. But Khan felt the program had evolved in a paternalistic direction, undercutting the spirit of the original.[74] In the same years, Yunus was even more unsparing, denouncing the IRDP as inefficient and elitist.[75]

Nonetheless, it is important to emphasize that government agencies were partners in the development experimentation of the 1970s and 1980s, despite the tendency to see credit programs as an NGO initiative. Here, Grameen-centrism blocks a more comprehensive historical understanding. The Bangladesh government supported rural development by managing its own projects on cooperativism, credit provision, and the promotion of women (Tahrunessa Abdullah, it should be recalled, was an IRDP staff member); joining with NGOs (BRAC, for example) on credit and training projects; offering agricultural credit through domestic banks; holding conferences that convened development partners and implementers; and maintaining research centers such as BARD, the Bangladesh Institute of Development Studies (BIDS) in Dhaka, and the Rural Development Academy (RDA) in Bogra.[76] Among other functions, it fell to the government to run programs supporting populations and needs underserved by NGO providers. Based on the concern that sectoral and targeted approaches fragmented the development field, BARD launched the Total Village Development Programme—later, Comprehensive Village Development Programme (CVDP)—in 1975 to consolidate activities at the local level. The program tried to recapture the integrated Comilla approach through a "unified Co-operative structure with participation of all the targeted groups"—one village, one institution, as a BARD director put it. By the mid-1990s, the CVDP operated in the Comilla and Sylhet Districts.[77] In addition, the Small Farmers and Landless Labourers Development Project (SFDP) was designed in contraposition to IRDP: Rather than forming cooperatives, farmers and the landless were organized into disparate groups for the dispensation of short-term, collateral-free credit.[78] Launched in 1976 at the encouragement of the UN Food and Agriculture Organization, the SFDP proceeded haphazardly through the subsequent decade before BARD took over leadership in 1985, offering low-income loans to promote employment activities at a time when NGOs focused increasingly on the landless. In sum, rural credit was not an NGO monopoly; complementary government efforts contributed to new models.

Another movement, the Swanirvar (or Self-Reliance) Movement, also illustrates the complex interactions among government, NGO, and local initiatives. Swanirvar emerged out of disparate local self-reliance efforts that gained urgency during the 1974 flood and famine. Its most recognizable spokesperson was Mahbub Alam Chashi, a public official whose work in the Gumai Beel wetland of Chittagong helped to frame the movement's goal of making "each family, each village, each union, each thana, each sub-division, each district, and the nation self-sufficient," particularly with regard to food.[79] Like its NGO counterparts, the movement also offered microcredit, though advocates feared that the release of "individual self-seeking initiatives" might disrupt the "harmonious development" of self-reliant communities.[80] In keeping with the growing concern for foreign aid dependency, Swanirvar spokespersons tended to cast their approach as anti-Comilla, objecting to the latter's reliance on external aid and heavy technical inputs, as well as the hierarchical nature of its cooperatives. Despite its local orientation, Swanirvar never succeeded in galvanizing widespread popular involvement. Institutionalized as a national program after a well-publicized 1975 conference, its activities were generally initiated by officials, often through the *gram sarkar* (village government) that Zia, a Swanirvar patron, formalized.[81] Zia's 1981 assassination ended formal support, and Chashi's removal from his Ministry of Agriculture post, followed by his death in 1983, marked a further blow to the movement. By the mid-1980s, Swanirvar had become an NGO with voluntary government participants, a shadow of its initial aspiration. As Sajjad Zohir put it, Swanirvar could never balance the competing pulls of external "professionalism" and local "idealism," popular self-reliance and top-down direction.[82] These tensions, as we shall see, shaped the wider NGO sector as well.

Grameen and the Emergence of a Bangladesh Model

Poverty is a dynamic condition involving material and financial deprivation as well as vulnerability and lack of power. An effective anti-poverty program must confront these many dimensions, adjusting for geographic and seasonal variations, political winds, and economic cycles. In Bangladesh, natural disaster can dash hard-won gains; conversely, unexpected windfalls from a micro-enterprise or remittance can do the reverse. Poverty is not so much a state as a process, and this makes the effort to combat it a volatile, shifting affair.[83] One of the strengths of NGOs in Bangladesh was their preference, as we noted, for bottom-up, trial-and-error approaches that enabled considerable flexibility. Nonetheless, the range of experimentalism narrowed starting in the late 1970s, and in global circles Bangladesh's NGO sector is now associated with a microcredit and entrepreneurship model built largely on the success of the Grameen Bank, a model that obscures the wider experiments of a generation of anti-poverty crusaders. Ironically, it also flattens Grameen's own development ambitions.

When the Liberation War broke out, the young Yunus, a wealthy jeweler's son, was completing doctoral study at Vanderbilt University. While still in the United States, he founded the Bangladesh Information Center and co-edited a newsletter promoting his country's interests in the West.[84] Upon his return home in 1972, he joined the economics faculty at the University of Chittagong after a brief stint at the Planning Commission. He was, in sum, like others in his generation of activists, a well-educated, internationally connected, middle-class scion. From here, the story of Grameen Bank is well known.[85] Appalled by the famine and desperation he witnessed in his hometown, Yunus initiated several experiments to help the poor in the nearby village of Jobra, the site of Grameen's now-famous first project, established in 1976 with small grants from the Ford Foundation and the Bangladesh Bank. These efforts yielded the fundamental principles of Grameen microlending—launching, according to celebratory retellings, a "revolution that is helping the poor to change their lives."[86] Perhaps recoiling from his country's political turbulence, Yunus disputed the idea, widely accepted in international circles, that the state was essential to development. Instead, he argued, the poor themselves were entrepreneurs, and they did not require training, employment, or cooperatives to unleash their potential. What they needed was capital—in small amounts. The success of microloans in Jobra, where women used the funds to set up small businesses, led to a 1979 expansion in Tangail, north of Dhaka, the first step in Grameen's remarkable rise.

Grameen microcredit began as a reaction against prevalent banking and development practices. Yunus's condemnation of the normal bank policy of refusing small loans to the poor is recounted in his autobiography, though it is worth recalling that the Comilla program and government-funded banks had provided loans for years, often using group lending techniques to reduce the administrative overhead. Grameen's use of microloans for *nonagricultural* entrepreneurship, however, was distinctive; historically, most loans had gone to farmers to support new agro-technology. Yunus also criticized dominant international development strategies, particularly those embodied in the World Bank, with its predilection for consultants, trainings, and large integrated programs.[87] Structural adjustment, a policy whose rise coincided with Grameen's own, elicited his particular ire: "When we hear about how countries are made to pay these debts through their noses, surrendering the bulk of their export earnings," Yunus wrote, "we find it difficult to accept as banking."[88]

Structural adjustment was only one example of a broad tendency toward top-down planning. Most national and international aid agencies, Yunus wrote in 1974, produced unrealistic plans based on rigid growth models mapped over five-year calendars. Both their goals and timeframes were unworkable. Planners generally emphasized economic growth rather than true development, which required not so much increased production as structural and institutional change. Input-output models missed the real development story: "Between the bulk of inputs on the one side of the production process and the output on the other side, there is a fascinating human story where Time, Nature, bureaucracy, greed, ignorance, and many more elements come into play." Yet aid institutions skipped this tale, preferring instead an abstract calculus of targets and deadlines. "Economics is the study of people," Yunus insisted, but its "[z]ealous mathematization . . . tends to take it away from people," producing "canned formulas" and homogenizing models. Furthermore, a five-year planning horizon was impossibly long to predict. What was needed instead was *annual* planning, which allowed—indeed, necessitated—regular change and revision. Development should be "unique for each society," a fact that required "disaggregated, decentralized planning" to enable participation. Planning is, after all, a form of "dreaming," and it "must be within touching distance of the individual." In Bangladesh, alas, programs typically started "at the political level" and unfolded according to a "bureaucratic approach" that favored technical interventions over human engagement.[89] IRDP was a case in point: Low disbursement levels, poor coverage, ineffective training—the government's flagship program was a parody of development that relied, like other projects, on cooperatives: "closed clubs of kulaks."[90] Women and the landless were ignored, farmers privileged over the 'poor,' tubewells subject to elite takeover.[91] Paternalism reigned, with officials training peasants who supposedly lacked the knowledge to succeed. For Yunus, quite the opposite held: the village poor had skills and entrepreneurial drive; what they lacked was the means.

Much of Grameen's literature had promotional aims, so it makes sense that Yunus sharpened his brief against alternate development strategies as he molded his own organizational strategy. The provision of loans to the poor, as we have seen, was not a new idea in Bangladesh, but Yunus revised it by stripping away the inputs associated with integrated rural development and providing a credit-only (or mostly) program. Gone were earlier strategies of cooperativism, training, conscientization, and mobilization; instead, he adopted the targeted approach of reaching the poor through microloans designed to promote entrepreneurship. Gone, too, was the emphasis on farming. Instead, Grameen targeted women and the landless—the delta's poorest—by encouraging them to start income-earning micro-enterprises that might buoy their livelihood. The causal linkage—or 'theory of change,' in today's parlance—was straightforward: If what the poor lacked was the ability to invest in their own skills and ideas, then what was needed was money for the poor to use themselves—not training or new community organizations. Loans could underwrite small businesses, which would spur development. For this reason, Grameen's program is often referred to as a minimalist model: microcredit alone, not microcredit plus accompanying interventions. "Money can speak," Yunus told his early employees; it unleashed the energy and ideas of the poor; it reduced dependence and increased agency.[92] In a swipe at other strategies, he described his program as "anti-training"—true "rural development," with the *grameen*, or village, at its heart.[93]

Yunus the economist, of course, knew that loans to the poor were an investment risk because of the lack of collateral. Money did not come for free, and credit had to be repaid. Government programs had secured such operations in the past, partly by bundling tiny needs into larger, more manageable sums. But Grameen adopted a novel tactic: grouping poor lendees into five-person groups, or *samities*, that could encourage and monitor each other in a joint liability system. Default by one member jeopardized loans for all—thus forming a kind of social collateral or peer pressure as leverage. Early reviews showed positive returns on the model, both in terms of income stabilization and loan repayment. Also central to Grameen's success was its ability to distance poverty alleviation from the politics of the time, offering a financial mechanism for assisting the poor that sidestepped the turmoil rocking the country. By focusing on the technical dispensation of microcredit, Grameen created a de-politicized model that could operate largely undisturbed under the country's military dictatorship. Other organizations, as we have seen, explicitly embraced the political passions of the day, espousing conscientization and mobilization, aligning with the leftist ideals of the country's founders. Subsequent history has rewarded Grameen's strategy, enabling replication both within and beyond Bangladesh.

It is easy to see how such a model could appeal to both anti-poverty activists and market proponents in the 1970s. Like the cooperatives discussed in Chapter 5, microcredit was an ideological mirror, reflecting back the convictions of its admirers. The demise of modernization and the rise of poverty alleviation as a chief development aim encouraged a positive reception of Grameen's program among basic needs advocates. The Women in Development movement responded similarly: The fact that so many Grameen loans went to women suggested a promising new approach to female empowerment. Here was a program dedicated to the uplift of the poor directly, whose founders shared the general critique of growth-oriented economics. Free marketers could also embrace microcredit, seeing in it a market-based solution to poverty that opened vast entrepreneurial horizons. Against the backdrop of Third World calls for a New International Economic Order, here was a path toward non-Western development that did not threaten the global economy. Furthermore, in an age of rising anti-government sentiment, the fact that Grameen was a private bank operating (mostly at least) beyond state auspices was added allure.[94] In these ways, Yunus's bank appealed across an ideological divide, attracting both the pro-poor left and the free-market right. Yunus himself described Grameen as neither right nor left. Governments, he noted, should "encourage businesses to move in directions desired by society," and entrepreneurship should be understood not as a quality of the capitalist class, but as an inherent human propensity.[95]

An illustrative case of Grameen's ideological reach is the economist Atiur Rahman, the governor of Bangladesh's central bank from 2009 to 2016. Rahman began his career in the 1980s as a Leninist interpreter of his country's rural class structure *and* a proponent of Grameen's model. From his University of London dissertation through studies undertaken for BIDS, Rahman argued that modernization and the Green Revolution produced rural stratification that mirrored Lenin's theory of capitalism.[96] The Union Parishads, created under Ayub Khan's Basic Democracies program, had become "kulak clubs," a "fiction" of popular government organized "to make a false impression that it is the masses who actually run the state."[97] Yet Rahman was sympathetic to Grameen microlending, a market-friendly intervention that he understood as a way to address the Leninist problematic of how to reach the poor.[98] He doubted that loans alone could resolve rural inequity, given Grameen's inability to reach large numbers and the danger of local market saturation. But if it could not obviate the need for growth and structural change, microcredit was nonetheless an important tool for rural uplift within Rahman's leftist framework.

One of the quirks of microcredit's historical reception is that it produces a misunderstanding of Grameen's own ambitions, which were always greater than lending—indeed, not as far removed from 1970s mobilization strategies as its global brand suggests. Of most relevance for illuminating this breadth are the '16 Decisions,' a set of social development commitments required of each Grameen lendee. The 'Decisions' emerged gradually out of a series of public workshops in program communities. They range from building productive personal habits (cleanliness, exercise, good nutrition, clean water, sanitation) to family responsibility (family planning, shared work) to cultural change (prioritizing education, renouncing dowry so that a bride's family need not pay the groom's) to communal engagement (helping one's neighbors, participating in social activities).[99] In requiring lendee commitments, Grameen acted as more than a bank, using credit to leverage personal and communal changes that it saw as necessary for development. Here, then, was its real innovation: Grameen reversed the formula typical of Bangladeshi NGOs in the first half of the decade. Rather than prioritizing food production or community development as a framework for introducing credit, it used credit as a means for furthering development.[100] Rather than beginning with the community as the fundamental unit of social change, it addressed the individual as an agent of communal uplift.

The early success of microcredit inspired followers. Over the course of the 1980s and 1990s, NGOs that once subscribed to multisectoral mobilization or community development approaches turned to more minimalist microfinance strategies. Starting in the late 1970s, BRAC, as we have seen, shifted from communal mobilization and integrated development toward approaches targeting the poor for direct assistance, often using microfinance. ASA, once dedicated to empowerment, became by the 1990s a microfinance-only organization. These changes were in part politically induced. The space for radical activism, as we saw, shrank dramatically under military rule, making credit and service delivery a safer option for NGOs. But international trends contributed as well; as donors shifted toward free-market policies in the 1980s, funding for empowerment and mobilization strategies dwindled. Perhaps unexpectedly, the return of democratic politics in 1991 also furthered de-politicization. In the neoliberal atmosphere of the 1990s, politicized approaches and peasant mobilization smacked of yesterday's socialism. In Dhaka's cutthroat politics, outspoken NGOs became associated with one party or another, endangering organizational prospects if an opponent won. Thus, Proshika, one of the largest microfinance organizations of the 1990s, fell afoul of the Bangladesh National Party (BNP) in the 2000s because of its perceived alliance with the rival Awami League. Its fortunes swooned with the BNP's 2001 return to power, a decline capped by accusations that it had enlisted the police to harass microloan defaulters.[101] With politicization equated to party boosterism, there was little room for mobilization as a development strategy.[102] 'Mobilization for and against whom?' one had to ask. 'Who might feel menaced by our organizational activism, and what power do they have to disrupt our operations?' To this day, remaining apolitical is a safer option. The decade also saw Islamist threats against NGOs and the women's empowerment movement; in 1994 arsonists burned BRAC schools and uprooted project mulberry trees, sparking a multiyear conflict between Islamists (including the governing coalition party Jamaat-e-Islami) and secular NGOs.[103] A low profile, which Abed kept better than Yunus, had its benefits.

Financialization as Panacea?

The Grameen microfinance model enjoyed remarkable success starting in the mid-1980s, when international replications and early praise began to appear.[104] In the 1990s, political leaders such as Bill and Hillary Clinton embraced the model, and in 1995 the World Bank (once a target of Yunus attacks) established the Consultative Group to Assist the Poor (CGAP) as a clearinghouse for microfinance research and promotion.[105] The decade also brought positive evaluations, notably the quantitative studies of World Bank and former BIDS economist Shahidur Khandker, who found that microlending reduced poverty and raised consumption among poor borrowers and their wider communities.[106] To crown his achievements, Yunus won the Nobel Peace Prize in 2006. Microcredit was indeed having its time in the sun.

Yet this success came with subtle shifts in messaging, as an NGO built on close attention to locale and arrayed against imported models suddenly confronted the demands of global brand management. Like BRAC and other NGOs, Grameen's template evolved out of trials, stumbles, and successes. Central to this effort were participatory processes designed to maintain close contact with village borrowers and solicit feedback on programming.[107] In attempting to capture this experience in speeches and publications, Yunus developed a promotional style that has been central to its global success ever since: Grameen tells stories, the most important of which—Yunus's autobiography; tales of women who stabilized their lives through microfinance—are biographical and autobiographical narratives.[108] These stories are amplified in talks given around the world by the charismatic Yunus. Yet such repetition has a paradoxical effect: In Grameen's case, it led to the gradual distillation of the organization's story origins into a fixed model—group-based microlending for entrepreneurship focused on the landless poor, especially women. By the late 1980s, as replication efforts spread to Malaysia, the Philippines, and elsewhere, guidebooks and training materials called for close adherence to Grameen's example, a message that jarred with its own experience of trial and error, of interactive community experimentation. Manuals did encourage some local adjustment, but, in the name of quality control, they limited its scope.[109] This recipe rested on the mostly (but not always) implicit assumption that while cultures differ, people are largely the same; while poverty is multidimensional, its solution can be simple.[110] As a result, opined Ben Rogaly, "Experiences such as those of Grameen Bank are hailed . . . as solutions rather than dynamic processes of learning and institutional change"—frameworks to be tweaked, not processes to be discovered in concert with local participants.[111] And if Yunus was understandably bullish about his organization, others offered fulsome chronicles that largely ignored the complexities of its origin.[112]

Since Yunus's Nobel Prize, microfinance has come down to earth a bit, facing criticism across several fronts. Some complaints have been relatively mild, questioning loan mechanisms or repayment schedules, but not fundamental premises.[113] Others were public hit pieces that simplified Yunus's motives and the program's effect. Most threatening were attacks by the AL government after its 2009 return to power. These were politically motivated and factually suspect, and Yunus worked actively to parry them.[114]

Other concerns, however, were more substantial. Starting in the late 1990s, the randomized control trial (RCT) studies of economist Jonathan Morduch cast doubt on microfinance as a long-term poverty-reduction strategy. Morduch used new statistical techniques (see Chapter 9) to argue that, when similar households were compared in control and treatment groups, microcredit did not increase earnings or consumption—although it did smooth income variations, allowing the poor to bridge lean periods and seasonal revenue droughts.[115] Other RCTs confirmed this assessment, showing that microfinance offers security for the poor, but not a path out of poverty, let alone broad community growth.[116] Additionally, Morduch argued that Grameen's financial success rode on the considerable subsidies it received, making it difficult to replicate.[117] Another widely recognized demerit is that microfinance programs do not effectively reach the very poorest. In fact, the need for organizational profitability may induce MFIs and *samity* members to exclude the poorest and riskiest clientele for fear of jeopardizing the bottom line. Entrepreneurial credit itself is more valuable for "the better-off amongst the poor," who can use it to expand their small businesses; the poorest must spend their income on basic consumption.[118] Like other aid panaceas, the promise of microcredit seemed oversold.

That microcredit is no cure-all should not be a surprise—Yunus himself acknowledged this—and findings in the new millennium challenged the wider hype surrounding it. If, as urban scholar Ananya Roy concluded, microcredit is primarily a "coping mechanism," then the bold predictions of unleashing the entrepreneurial potential of the poor are overstated. Such a goal requires broader development infrastructure.[119] But the difficulties run deeper. Even if microcredit can augment the earnings of individual households, this does not necessarily lead to village, regional, or national advancement.[120] As Naomi Hossain put it, the "individual empowerment" of the "cash-earning consumer" has rarely "aggregated to institutionalized forms of collective power."[121] BRAC economist Hossain Zillur Rahman concurred: There is a difference, he insisted, between poverty resilience, which microfinance offers, and graduation to higher income levels, which is less common.[122] The former does not necessarily translate into the latter; indeed, microfinance could do the opposite by cultivating dependence.

The late aughts also brought damaging news about suicides among Indian micro-debtors that accentuated the tension between microcredit's banking function, which prioritized loan recovery, and the repayment capacity of poor lendees.[123] Borrowers, reported journalists, might take second or even third loans to repay the first—a practice known as loan recycling—even as they suffered increased anxiety and pressure from debt collectors. If this was a minority experience, findings in Bangladesh suggest that it was not isolated:

> Despite the success of the Grameen Bank in delivering loans to poor women and bringing socioeconomic change to many of these women's households . . . there are still many borrowers who become vulnerable and trapped by the system; they are unable to succeed. At the level of grassroots credit operation, bank workers encounter institutional pressure to increase loan investment and maintain high recovery rates on their invested loans. The bank workers and peer group borrowers inflict an intense pressure on borrowers for timely repayment, rather than work to raise collective responsibility and borrower empowerment as originally envisaged by the bank.[124]

Anthropologist Lamia Karim went further, examining the "everyday mediations" of large microfinance NGOs—their on-the-ground interactions with borrowers. She found increased indebtedness, loss of family and community solidarity, and the exploitation of local cultures of deference and shame to enforce repayment—lending a dark significance to Grameen's 98 percent repayment rate. The financial priorities, or "hidden transcript," of MFIs, she inferred from her interviews, frequently overrode the rhetoric—or "public transcript"—of rural uplift.[125] Predictably, reports of microfinance as a debt trap soured public attitudes and lent fuel to the exaggerated political attacks noted above.

Of particular import, given Grameen and other MFIs' longstanding claims, was the impact of microloans on women's empowerment. Here, appraisals varied. The Malaysian journalist Helen Todd found that female lendees became partners in family decision-making, even when they did not control household cash. Grameen microcredit, in her assessment, weakened gender hierarchies more effectively than mobilization approaches, allowing women to act as "termites, hollowing out structures quietly from within, rather than pushing them over" in an act of revolutionary zeal.[126] Other analysts were lukewarm, arguing that the receipt of funds could boost self-worth, but did not necessarily elevate women's status or autonomy.[127] Indeed, if the money went to husbands and fathers, the female lendee might be doubly exploited, for homekeeping and for cash income. In the end, argued demographer and BIDS Research Director Simeen Mahmud, much depended on prior wealth: better-off women gained more leverage than the truly indigent.[128]

An intriguing line of argument—and one with particular resonance for this discussion—concerns the development alternatives that microfinance superseded. For Joanne Meyerowitz, the success of microcredit displaced considerations of redistribution that influenced both international and Bangladeshi debates in the 1970s. For Dhaka sociologist M. Anwar Hossen, internationally accredited microfinance was yet another development solution propped up by external forces that overlooked locally and environmentally specific techniques for managing resources and sustaining communities.[129] Over time, Stuart Rutherford has shown, large, globally connected NGOs and formal credit providers overshadowed informal financial networks organized by the poor, though the poor, he insists, would prefer formal services with someone else doing the administration.[130] And Shakhawat Ali has recently drawn attention to the Ahsania Mission, founded by Khan Bahadur Ahsanullah in the 1950s as a domestic organization rooted in Sufi religious culture. In the 1990s, under the leadership of Ahsanullah disciple Kazi Rafiqul

Alam, Ahsania expanded into a large and active NGO, but its Sufi roots remain a distinctive feature in a development landscape dominated by Western-educated leaders.[131]

Other commentators worried that an institutionalized NGO network undercut government effectiveness and democratic accountability. For sociologist Shelley Feldman, the NGO-ization of otherwise public service functions can hamper effective development, allowing officials to dodge responsibility for public welfare by blaming problems on private providers. Furthermore, NGOs have restricted structures of accountability: While they may meet citizen needs, she writes, "they do not usually share collective ownership of resources for redistribution or encourage collective decision-making. Instead, participation consists of the voluntary, individual decision to join the organization, a decision that is often based on the need to access resources not previously or readily available elsewhere."[132] Not only does this provider–client relationship constrain institutional accountability, but it may also defer structural change in favor of short-term individual or community access.[133]

An institutionalized NGO culture of service delivery and advocacy can also displace a more active and engaged civil society, de-politicizing poverty relief by substituting clients for citizens and supplanting the language of activism and redistribution with that of entrepreneurship, individualism, and self-reliance. NGOs become, in Roy's terms, not "people's organizations or citizens' associations"—a typical understanding of civil society groups—but "managers and trustees of development."[134] Nor do they necessarily weaken the clientelism that suffuses Bangladeshi history. Not only are social hierarchies sometimes reproduced in NGO management structures, but the push for individual entrepreneurship, as Wood noted in 1994, can contribute to the fragmentation of the rural economy—loosening communal ties, rending the fabric of family and community, or imposing new hierarchies based on money and 'merit.'[135]

While defending itself against skeptics, Grameen implicitly acknowledged some of these charges in the early 2000s by rolling out program revisions that became known as Grameen II. The proximate catalyst of these changes was the floods of 1998, after which administrators noticed that nearly 20 percent of Grameen borrowers were having difficulty repaying loans.[136] Their livelihoods destroyed, lendees were now trapped in debt. In response, Grameen switched from group to individual lending, provided flexible loans for borrowers facing hardship, allowed repayment postponement, and offered new savings, insurance, and credit products.[137] BRAC, too, innovated in these years. Recognizing that microfinance often left the poorest behind, it launched a 2002 initiative to train indigent women for entry into its microcredit program.[138] While Grameen, BRAC, and ASA continued to dominate the national microfinance landscape, they also diversified into new ventures ranging from retail to phone and IT services, blurring the line between development NGO and business conglomerate.

In sum, the new millennium brought a more modest consensus on the value of microcredit. Kabeer's summary is characteristically judicious: "Financial services are important if [poor women and men] are to cope with crisis and respond to opportunities, but on their own, do not equip them with the capacity to translate these services into lasting economic progress or to engage with 'bad governance' at the local level."[139] Perhaps the only surprise in this statement is that people might have believed otherwise. One cannot suppose that market access translates readily into social and political empowerment. As Kabeer contends elsewhere, "part of the explanation for why Bangladesh has performed so poorly on the governance front is that a key force for social change within the country, its development NGOs, have been transformed over time from organizations willing to challenge socioeconomic injustice into organizations largely committed to the values of the market place."[140] The better questions to ask, then, are not *if* microcredit works, but *when* and *how*—in what cultural and political circumstances, and to what socioeconomic effect. In trying to answer these questions, Kabeer beckons toward the mobilization strategies of an earlier era.

Bangladesh's development relied heavily on foreign assistance. But to a degree rarely matched in other countries, it also devised local strategies that later traversed the globe. Whatever the strengths and limitations of these strategies, 1970s Bangladesh marks a unique episode in development history. Yet if microfinance still dominates the Western image of Bangladeshi development, it is not without costs for our understanding and practice. Few in Bangladesh today doubt that NGO services provide valuable assistance to the poor. Yet equally few would credit the country's extraordinary growth to their provisions. The former "basket case" has indeed experienced a remarkable rise, with a surging GDP, falling birth rates, and recent entry into middle-income-country status. Primary credit for such unanticipated success tends to go to the booming garment industry, which brought millions of young women from rural areas and sent their salaries back home; and to remittances from migrants working in the Middle East. The former grew a thousandfold from 1984 to 2019, from $32 million to $34 billion; the latter from $2 billion to $20 billion in twenty years.[141] In recent decades, the liberalization of trade with China has also brought cheaper machinery to the countryside, boosting local industry.

Yet if the country has seen remarkable developmental success, its continued climb remains fraught with peril. The growth of global industries has been accompanied by renewed concern over regional inequities, a rural-urban divide, a breakdown of social cohesion, and religious radicalization. And the country's bare-knuckled politics, which until 2006 saw the main parties trade five-year terms, yielded after 2009 to a stifling one-party dominance characterized by patronage and corruption. Sobhan recently dubbed this "the Bangladesh paradox": successful development and entrepreneurship coupled with flagrant clientelism and malgovernance.[142] If the country is to advance further, from a low-income labor supplier to a secure middle-income manufacturing hub, it will need to achieve a new "political settlement," as Ali Riaz puts it, one that microfinance is ill equipped to provide.[143] For it is hard to imagine that political change could occur without collective pressure. NGOs alone cannot do it. The 2024 ouster of the AL government in the face of popular protests made this need plain. But to note this need invites a return to the mobilization and solidarity strategies of the 1970s. While these were designed for another age, they provide a useful place to initiate conversation on political and development strategies rooted in the country's experience.

In this regard, microfinance-centrism not only blocks our view of Bangladesh's development history; it also thwarts our ability to imagine useful strategies in the present and future. Of course, the questions that dominate political discourse today in Bangladesh are different from those that prevailed five decades ago. While much of the population still confronts dire poverty, as well as a treacherous new vulnerability to climate change, one can no longer dismiss the country as irredeemable.[144] But revisiting the 1970s allows us to invigorate our understanding of the interrelationship between government accountability and NGO activity, between economic growth, poverty alleviation, and burgeoning inequality—all issues hotly debated at the time. As

Bangladesh's experience suggests, moving beyond income stabilization and toward a resolution of poverty requires a confrontation with the inequalities that increasingly divide the country. International anti-poverty advocates of the early 1970s recognized that the two were interwoven, though in the decade's second half they leaned toward addressing the basic needs of the poor rather than pushing an equity agenda. In Bangladesh, a similar dynamic can be witnessed in the move from empowerment strategies of the early 1970s to microfinance in the following decades. But the country's recent development underscores their continued entwinement: without redressing prevalent social, economic, and political exclusions, microcredit and other strategies for alleviating poverty will face a ceiling on their success.[145]

The Liberation War decade *was* a different era, but the political discourse of today—and here I am thinking not only of Bangladesh—may bear more resemblance to the 1970s than the 1990s. In the 1990s, we were sure that markets would solve economic and social problems—this was one of the lessons of communism's collapse and one of the promises of microcredit. Today we are less certain: We live in a time when faith in global markets no longer inspires people, when in-country inequality has exploded and technocratic remedies are challenged by activists from below—a world where individual entrepreneurship does not satisfy our aspirations, but we seek instead new notions of collective solidarity and empowerment. In this context, recuperating the history of the wide-ranging Bangladeshi initiatives of the 1970s, including microcredit and its many competitors, may offer valuable insights for future development programming.

8

"Until Lions Have Their Own Historians": Zambia's Missing Narrative of Structural Adjustment

IN 1997, JOSEPH STEPANEK, USAID'S former mission director in Zambia, deplored the tendency of even his own aid agency, "which talks about ownership, sustainability, and collegiality," to push assistance packages "without ever asking a government official." He recalled with particular chagrin receiving a USAID health-sector proposal that paralleled a Zambian initiative already underway.

> I went to the Permanent Secretary of the Ministry of Health and said: "We're working with you on this health reform program. We have this tangential effort. I am very interested in knowing what you think of it and whether we should change or modify it. What do you think?" The conversation came to an end, and the Permanent Secretary of the Ministry of Health just sat there, stony-faced. I thought to myself: "Oh, boy, I really misspoke this time." The Permanent Secretary then said: "Joe, you have to give me a minute to collect my thoughts. Nobody's ever asked me before for my views."[1]

Stepanek served in Lusaka from 1994 to 1996, during the run-up to the country's first presidential election since independence icon Kenneth Kaunda, Zambia's only leader for its first twenty-seven years, lost power. Although the 1991 electoral victory of the Movement for Multiparty Democracy (MMD) prompted widespread euphoria, the subsequent five years bated hopes that the country's new leader, Frederick Chiluba, might finally lift its economic fortunes. In Stepanek's tenure, reports of official corruption proliferated, and Chiluba's 1996 constitutional amendment barring candidates with non-

Zambian parentage from running for president—a swipe at Kaunda, his main rival, whose parents came from neighboring Malawi (then Nyasaland)—was deemed so offensive that international donors withheld foreign aid at the urging of government critics.[2]

Kaunda's resurgence was surprising given how soundly he was defeated in 1991. Yet by the mid-1990s it was clear to many Zambians that the MMD's tenure had not improved their economic straits. Judging from press reports, the Chiluba honeymoon lasted about a year and a half—from the October 1991 electoral sweep of Kaunda's United National Independence Party (UNIP) until mid-1993, when the increasing pain wrought by economic liberalization started dampening earlier hopes.[3] While these hardships were encountered across Africa in the 1980s and 1990s, they were particularly bitter in Zambia given the exuberance of the 1991 transition, the vigor of the subsequent liberalization, and the memory of the country's economic promise. Under Chiluba, Zambia implemented one of Africa's most orthodox structural adjustment programs (SAPs)—less than five years after aborting an earlier adjustment effort. It thus affords a valuable opportunity to compare divergent structural adjustment experiences within a short span of time and to consider the fate of alternative reform proposals that challenged neoliberal prescriptions.

Structural Adjustment

Structural adjustment was based on a free-market understanding of development that had been, as we saw in Chapters 2 and 6, a dissenting opinion among economists through the postwar era. Mainstream development economists commonly cited market dysfunction in agrarian economies to justify extensive planning and government regulation. There were, nonetheless, isolated examples of market-driven aid programs before the late 1970s. In Latin America, where neoliberal monetarism and left-leaning structuralism competed for political space, the 1950s saw short-term free-market experiments in Chile, Argentina, Peru, and elsewhere. The late 1960s and 1970s, in turn, witnessed concerted efforts at the market restructuring of Southern Cone economies by authoritarian regimes. After coups in 1973 and 1976, Uruguay and Argentina, respectively, introduced inflation stabilization efforts followed by adjustment policies comprising deregulation, privatization, and currency devaluation.[4] And as we saw in Chapter 6, no example of neoliberalism in action was as notorious as the economic program that University of Chicago–trained free-market acolytes unleashed on Chile after the 1973 coup.

These individual experiments were eventually enshrined in the international policy of structural adjustment that came to dominate Western thinking about indebted Third World economies after 1980. There are numerous ironies in this turn of events. First, the term *structural adjustment* and its associated policies originally targeted *industrial* countries, which were admonished to dismantle protectionist barriers in order to assist developing nations.[5] Further, as Patrick Sharma shows, structural adjustment lending was not initially counterposed to poverty alleviation (as would later be alleged); instead, it grew out of the 1970s pro-poor agenda as its continuation and expansion. Finally, as we discuss below, it was Robert McNamara's World Bank—once the institutional hub of the anti-poverty revolution in development planning—that led the structural adjustment charge.[6]

Structural adjustment loans were not given for individual projects—the typical Bank modality for decades—but to a nation's general budget or sectoral budgets (health, education, etc.) on the condition that the government enact long-term 'structural' changes (not short-term fixes) to its economy. The rudiments of this program date back decades, even to the origins of the Bretton Woods system. Program lending—or budget support, as it is sometimes called—involves funds provided directly to country coffers, not earmarked for specific projects; and loan conditionality—policy reform requirements attached to credit lines—was an instrument available to the World Bank's partner, the International Monetary Fund (IMF), from its beginnings, though it was rarely used before the late 1970s. As first conceived, the IMF focused on macro-economic issues, providing temporary infusions of foreign capital to stave off balance of payments deficits. The World Bank, by contrast, was a project-loan facility that funded discrete activities, usually in areas such as infrastructure, energy, or other vital investments that promised rapid economic return.[7] Until the 1970s, the two institutions rarely infringed on each other's domain, though there were exceptions, such as a World Bank experiment with budget support and policy conditionality in 1960s India. Although the India strategy was deemed ineffective at the time, some program administrators, notably Ernest Stern, the Bank's head of operations from 1978, later became advocates for a similar approach elsewhere.[8]

By the late 1970s, World Bank officials saw two advantages to structural adjustment loans. First, they could be made more quickly than project loans. From his appointment in the late 1960s, McNamara dramatically expanded disbursements, using quantitative targets to motivate greater lending and boost pro-poor initiatives. From commitments of $847 million in McNamara's first year of presidency, Bank outlays rose to $8.8 billion in 1981, his last.[9] This expansion not only created more staff work; it also necessitated a steady pipeline of projects to keep the money flowing. Since projects require extensive negotiation, research, design, and analysis before they can be approved for funding, McNamara's financial expansion encountered logistical bottlenecks. Program lending directed to a country's regular budget—without project specifications—shortened the preparation and helped to break the logjam. Furthermore, the budget support mechanism conferred greater donor leverage. Although project cancellation is disruptive to staff and beneficiaries, the disarray can generally be contained within the regions and sectors of operation. Program funding, by contrast, sustains many national priority areas, including debt repayment and currency stability. It thus grants donors considerable influence at the highest echelons of host-country power, since termination can devastate a range of basic functions. It is, in other words, easier to attach economy-wide reform conditions to program loans than to project aid. These concerns contributed to an internal Bank debate in the 1970s that was eventually won by the advocates of adjustment.

Political and economic trends also made program loans appealing. During the 1973 oil embargo, OPEC members invested much of their windfall profits in Western banks, which in turn lent 'petrodollars' to non-oil exporting countries (NoPEC, in the shortened lingo) to continue their modernization efforts. Easy credit and rising fuel costs ballooned the Third World debt. Worried about the increased need for aid and facing fundraising headwinds during an economic crisis, McNamara used his pulpit to encourage the dollar 'recycling' process. Not only did he accept petrodollars for his own organization, but he lobbied for private loans to poor countries to meet their development goals. Program loans helped to streamline this effort. African and Asian leaders also appreciated them, since—at least prior to the heavy enforcement of conditionality—they left economic governance largely in domestic hands. Donor projects, by contrast, usually stood outside national plans as independent islands. This flexibility, however, came at a cost: depending on the aid levels—and they were high in Africa in the 1970s and 1980s—budget support set the stage for increased donor leverage once easy credit dried up and debts came due. When OPEC failed to repeat its earlier success during the 1979 embargo, banks ceased lending to highly mortgaged countries, growth and modernization ground to halt, and international creditors scrambled to forestall collapse. Mounting debt, in turn, led to calls for drastic reform. Driven by the need to disburse monies and induce reforms that could make aid more effective, McNamara embraced adjustment lending officially in 1979, making the first loans to Kenya and Turkey in the following year.[10]

These policy shifts were consolidated in the early 1980s as the conservative ascendancy in the West brought free-market advocates to power, turning conditionality into a widespread mechanism for reforming economies and shrinking governments. In August 1982, Mexico's announcement that it could not pay its arrears sparked an international debt crisis and accelerated the rightward turn among donor agencies. From five structural adjustment loans in 1980, the Bank's annual issuance grew to fifty-two by 1989.[11] Over time, donors applied a relatively fixed set of stabilization and adjustment criteria around the globe, with limited accommodation for country circumstance. The most pronounced geographic transfer was the shift of packages honed in the Latin American debt crisis to post-socialist Eastern Europe in the early 1990s. The Latin American experience, recalled a group of influential economists in 1991, "led to a wide consensus on the essential ingredients for a successful package."

> [H]ow much of what we have learned is relevant for Eastern Europe? Clearly, the issue there is not to repair the damage to an existing market economy but instead to jump-start one. Aren't the initial conditions so different as to require a drastically different approach? We do not think so. Most of the logic behind the standard stabilization package applies to Eastern Europe as well.[12]

Sub-Saharan Africa received the same medicine. Indeed, with fully thirty-five countries implementing some kind of SAP between 1980 and 1993, Africa was the world's most adjusted continent.[13] Structural adjustment became the face of the neoliberal order in the developing world, applied globally to address the debt catastrophe. Its ascendancy is particularly striking because of the brief turn to localism that had characterized many mainstream development programs in the 1970s.

Debate about the efficacy of SAPs is still far from settled, though arguments by proponents and detractors tread well-worn paths.[14] Critics decried many aspects of the policy. With the net transfer of resources from the First to the Third World turning negative in the 1980s—that is, more money flowed from the poor to the rich countries—some charged the Bank with perpetuating a neocolonial agenda that harmed the poor to benefit investors.[15] Others observed that structural adjustment did not in fact change very much, but simply intensified the capitalist modernization of earlier development programs.[16] Many veterans of the 1970s anti-poverty movements accepted the need for functioning markets but charged that structural adjustment irreparably harmed the poor by dismantling subsidies, social services, and public sector employment. The classic statement of this position is the two-volume 1987 work *Adjustment with a Human Face*.[17] A related but analytically distinct complaint was that SAPs prioritized stabilization in order to restore equilibrium and clear arrears, even as they discounted the medium- and long-term goals of development.[18] Since the latter were favored by African leaders and the former by international financial institutions, this tendency yielded the further charge that SAPs marginalized African viewpoints. Finally, a growing international consensus in the late 1980s and early 1990s argued that first-generation SAPs, in focusing overwhelmingly on economic reforms, missed the centrality of governance problems; accordingly, 1990s aid packages typically attached political as well as economic conditions.[19]

There were also prominent structural adjustment defenders. Consider the 1993 article by economists Lawrence Summers and Lant Pritchett, who asserted, based upon longitudinal comparison of adjusted and non-adjusted countries, that "adjustment lending works" to lessen economic crises.[20] While they acknowledged that the poor were often "hurt in the stabilization phase when recession is unavoidable," in the long run they "fared better on average in adjusting nations."[21] Structural adjustment, they reminded readers, was not a singular policy framework, but a learning process in which a raft of free-market strategies were tested, revised, and reapplied. This trial-and-error produced some features that did not succeed, but the basic economic premises were sound, with the 'intensive-adjustment-lending' countries "enjoy[ing] faster growth, higher export and savings shares, and lower fiscal deficits in the second half of the 1980s, both compared with other countries and compared with their own earlier performance."[22] Despite difficulties in measuring precise impact, SAP countries, they maintained, excelled in rural poverty alleviation (if not always among urban constituencies).

If the liberalization agenda rarely paid more than lip service to African experiences, deferring instead to elite economic knowledge lodged chiefly at institutions abroad, this was not due to a lack of African assertiveness. The *Lagos Plan of Action,* drawn up in 1980 by the United Nations Economic Commission for Africa (UNECA) under the directorship of Nigerian economist Adebayo Adedeji (1975–91), called for less stringent solutions to the continent's mounting debt. To the degree that Western officials took note, they tended to dismiss UNECA's framework as unrealistic or redundant.[23] In 1985, the Organization of African Unity reiterated some of UNECA's positions in Africa's Priority Programme for Economic Recovery (APPER), which stressed the agricultural sector and food self-sufficiency. Yet the United Nations Programme of Action for the African Economic Recovery and Development (1986–90), designed to operationalize APPER, did little to deflect global attention from the SAP juggernaut.[24] Four years later, a similar disinterest met UNECA's African Alternative Framework to Structural Adjustment Programmes (1989). Efforts at regional integration to promote greater African self-reliance also had a marginal effect on international programs, even though external trade and regional marketization were pillars of the liberal economic order.[25]

Yet as with many talking points in the ideological minefield of structural adjustment, the common charge that the IMF and World Bank strong-armed economic liberalization requires some qualification. Another anecdote makes this plain. In 1987, four years before his rule ended, Kaunda withdrew from a SAP that had roiled the Zambian economy and provoked food riots in urban areas. At the behest of the international financial institutions (IFIs), donors cut budget support in retaliation, though some aid projects continued to operate. After a brief rally under the New Economic Recovery Programme (NERP), the economy continued its freefall. Faced with compounding debt (over $7 billion, or twice the country's GDP) and possible default, the IMF and World Bank sent agents to Lusaka to negotiate new terms of agreement.[26] Here, recounted an IMF representative, the dance of expectations began. At a poolside meeting in one of Lusaka's finer hotels, a Zambian permanent secretary asked for instructions on "what we have to do" to restore international confidence and restart the flow of aid. "No," explained the IMF official, "you have to come up with the program. What would you like to achieve?" It took a week of negotiation, according to the official, for Zambia's own reform itinerary to emerge.[27] If these memories must be taken with a grain of salt, they nonetheless suggest ambiguity as to the origins and ownership of financial reform.[28]

Structural adjustment in the 1980s and 1990s entailed complex lender–recipient bargaining. During initial negotiations, donors and lendees outlined a set of goals and conditions to accompany new loans. The ensuing implementation process was generally a mix of fulfillment, violation, and renegotiation of these early terms—with donors playing the role of monitors supervising the African recidivist.[29] Annual decisions to continue financing, tranche by tranche, marked further occasions for parley. While the power advantage clearly lay with donors—"the hand that receives," remarked one of my interviewees, "is lower than the one who gives"—the donor–recipient relation was a dynamic one, with give and take on both sides.[30]

We are left, then, with a paradox: extensive dialogue and solicitation regarding structural adjustment, yet persistent complaints about its imposition, severity, homogeneity, and inevitability. The political scientist John Ravenhill notes this discordance in the World Bank's adjustment policies throughout the 1980s. The most famous early articulation of structural adjustment was 1981's Berg Report, *Accelerated Development in Sub-Saharan Africa,* which Ravenhill describes as a "confrontational" insistence on market liberalization designed to "'get the prices right'" and "'get the government out of the economy'"—a "sharp, shock treatment for African economies" whose domestic policies were responsible for current woes.[31] The next eight years saw a gradual relaxing of this position—if not a pullback from its basic premises—led by Bank moderates. Yet at the end of the decade, two reports revealed continuing internal disunity. If *Africa's Adjustment and Growth* declared the success of structural adjustment policies—dismissing critics in ways that "not only damaged relations with African governments but also the credibility of the Bank's statistical analysis"—the report *Sub-Saharan Africa: From Crisis to Sustainable Growth* ceded some points to critics and invited revision by Africans themselves.[32] In sum, it is sometimes hard to tell whether SAPs tried to balance between international financial standards and African political systems—or simply superposed the former on the latter.[33]

One challenge to adjudicating these debates is the lack of quality data. Ironically enough, the trimming of state functions associated with structural adjustment also starved census bureaus. In 2007, neither the Zambian central statistical office nor the University Library Special Collection had economic reports from the relevant adjustment decades.[34] Perhaps as a result, the literature on structural adjustment tends toward either abstract econocentrism or high-minded moralism, neither of which leaves much room for contextual understanding.

Kaunda's Economy

At independence in 1964, Zambia's copper mines, which accounted for two-thirds of its GDP, over 90 percent of government revenue, and almost 14 percent of the world's copper output, made the country one of sub-Saharan Africa's wealthiest.[35] The collapse of copper prices ten years later initiated its slide to one of the continent's poorest. The fall was precipitous. By the mid-1980s, Zambia's share of world copper output had dropped to under 7 percent, slipping in absolute and relative terms even as imported fuel and machinery costs spiked.[36] By the late twentieth century, Zambia had the unhappy distinction of being the only country whose standing in the Human Development Index had fallen since 1975, with per capita GNP sinking by one-third in twenty years.[37]

It has become standard to indict Kaunda for this debacle. This is partly warranted. According to the economist Manenga Ndulo, Zambia's much delayed and ultimately aborted Third National Development Plan (1979–83) failed to achieve its growth and employment goals due to regime mishaps such as poor planning, bureaucratic disarticulation, and over-reliance on expatriate expertise.[38] Agriculture was particularly penalized. Although Kaunda promised to boost farmers in the name of equity and self-reliance, in practice he suppressed rural incomes to supply inexpensive food to the urban residents who mined the country's copper and generated its foreign exchange.[39] Privileged in rhetoric, farmers were constrained in fact.

Yet Kaunda's economic policies must also be seen as an effort to rectify colonial dislocations. At independence, Zambia's economy was extravagantly imbalanced, with wealth and productivity concentrated along the "line of rail" from Livingstone in the south through Lusaka to the northern Copperbelt. Deeply impoverished hinterlands stretched to the east and west.[40] Sectoral employment figures mirrored this skew: the copper industry that generated the bulk of the country's revenue did not employ the most people, who languished in rural smallholds. This core-periphery structure derived from colonial times, when copper-rich Northern Rhodesia served as a mineral reserve for the wealthier Southern Rhodesia (now Zimbabwe). And like many African countries, Zambia is ethnically and linguistically diverse. Kaunda was acutely aware that economic inequities could aggravate factionalism.

Kaunda's economic policies also had to balance among competing interests within his UNIP coalition. Though a professed nationalist and egalitarian, as embodied in his philosophy of Humanism, the Zambian president was flexible with regard to economic ideology, tacking from left (socialist and statist) to right (market-oriented and liberal) to appease factions in his administration. Robert Bates and Paul Collier described his process in the following terms:

> [W]hen he sought to change policies, he attempted to move the locus on decision making from one of the bureaucracies to the other. The movement to market orientated reforms privileged the technocrats from the Ministry of Finance and the Bank of Zambia; the switch to a control orientated regime was orchestrated through advisors with close links to the Central Committee of UNIP.[41]

These maneuvers generated considerable turnover, producing both allies and opponents and jolting the economy with destabilizing policy shifts.

Other policies showed a similar mix of political acumen and economic impropriety. Kaunda imposed uniform agricultural prices across the country, regardless of regional output and differential transportation costs. Enforced by a monopsony marketing board and state-owned cooperatives, the policy was meant to challenge grievous regional inequalities, but it also reduced rural income and encouraged cross-border smuggling as farmers sought better prices. Similarly, in using copper revenues to promote import substitution, Kaunda diverted profit from the mining sector, starving the money-maker of needed reinvestment. The result: the industry that generated the most profit (copper) and the sector that employed the most people (farming) were constrained to serve each other, and in the end, the country was neither diversified nor industrialized.

Kaunda's policies can also be understood in terms of the 1960s commitment to human capital (Chapter 2). He sought not only growth and industrial expansion, but also the cultivation of a trained and educated workforce. Faced with a largely white postcolonial managerial elite, Kaunda launched a Zambianization policy—one of many Africanization programs during the independence era—to build an educated African technical class. Revenue from Zambia's copper earnings sent promising students overseas for higher education; others received their schooling and apprenticeships through the Industrial Development Corporation (INDECO), the state-owned holding company formed to foster the country's modernization. After training, many young Zambians gained entrepreneurial experience in INDECO companies, built to replace imported manufactures with domestic-made goods. "Were it not for the state-run sector," explained one respondent in 2019, "I would not be trained."[42] Still others, in a country with under 100 university graduates at independence (in a population of about 3.5 million), benefited from the opening of the University of Zambia in 1966. Ironically, many members of this nascent entrepreneurial and intellectual class would later join the opposition.

It has become common to refer to Kaunda's policies as socialist or socialist-leaning.[43] This echoes his rhetoric, but it is misleading. As James Ferguson points out, Kaunda's Humanism—a version of African socialism—was more of an ethical framework elevating community and cooperation than it was an organized doctrine.[44] "The impetus toward socialism had nothing to do with Cold War alignment," wrote the Zambian politician Guy Scott. "Most of Kaunda's 'socialist' measures are more or less standard for any country regarding itself as being at war," as did frontline Zambia in its battles against Ian Smith's Rhodesia, Lusophone colonialism, and South African apartheid.[45] Economic policy was similarly hybridized. Nationalization, instituted in the early 1970s, did not result in a full takeover of most independent companies, but followed what became known as the 51 percent rule, in which the state held a controlling interest in large businesses but left as much as 49 percent of shares available for private ownership. This not only allowed private and foreign firms, such as the South African Anglo American Corporation, to retain a foothold in the economy. It also enabled Zambian managers and technicians to acquire entrepreneurial skills by treating their parastatals as competitive enterprises, as happened in the copper industry before 1982, when the Nchanga and the Roan mine companies merged to form Zambia Consolidated Copper Mines (ZCCM).[46] Although excessive competition was discouraged, it was not unknown for ambitious managers to engage in corporate jockeying within the nationalized market. Thus, in the 1970s, a native business class emerged that was at once indebted to Kaunda and angered by the restrictions of his developmentalism.[47]

International and regional politics also shaped Zambia's fortunes. Kaunda participated actively in Third World self-assertion projects, hosting the Non-Aligned Conference in 1970 and inviting aid from Eastern and Western countries. As Alastair Fraser recounts, these policies reflected both conviction and strategy.

> Recognizing that Zambia was a "price taker" in an unequal global economic bargain, [Kaunda] worked with other leaders of the Non-Aligned Movement to campaign in the UN for a New International Economic Order (NIEO). In 1967 Kaunda attempted to give the campaign some economic muscle, gathering leaders of four of the world's main copper exporting countries (Zambia, Chile, Peru, and the Congo/Zaire) in Lusaka, with the aim of establishing a price- and quota-fixing copper cartel along the lines of that recently announced by oil-producing countries when they formed the Organisation of the Petroleum Exporting Countries (OPEC) in 1960. The new body would be known as the Intergovernmental Council of Copper Exporting Countries (CIPEC).[48]

CIPEC never took hold, but it nonetheless expressed the multiple interests that Kaunda brought to Third World solidarity efforts. In the 1980s, he supported Adebayo Adedeji's alternative development strategies promulgated at UNECA and, more fatefully, provided assistance to liberation movements across southern Africa.[49] The latter cost him Western support, notably from the United States.

Yet in the face of an unabating copper slump, Kaunda ultimately bowed before Western creditors that he had resisted in other forums. Zambia took its first IMF Stand-by Loan in 1973, assuming it would be a temporary stopgap. An additional loan in 1976 failed to stem the recession, and in 1978, Zambia signed another Stand-by agreement that is sometimes seen as its first stabilization loan. Until then, loans had borne minimal conditionalities. The 1978 loan, however, increased the influence of the IFIs and required considerable fiscal restraint on the part of the government.[50] Alas, these measures did little. By 1983, with the second oil crisis driving up import prices, creditors curbed lending to the country, forcing Kaunda to agree to his first SAP: a ten-year rescheduling of Zambia's 1.3 billion kwacha indemnity (around one-third of its GDP) in exchange for an austerity pledge.[51] In 1985, the government introduced a foreign exchange auction, allowing the exchange rate to float according to "demand and supply" at weekly biddings.[52] Predictably, the artificially inflated kwacha (K) tumbled in value, from K2 = $1 to K21 = $1, theoretically boosting exports and discouraging imports, but also inflating prices on needed goods and delivering "havoc and ruin to a large number of enterprises."[53] After urban food riots in 1986, Kaunda pulled out of the SAP in May 1987 and launched the NERP, which promised "growth from own resources" (to cite its slogan) and capped debt repayments at 10 percent of GDP annually. Despite initial growth from increased copper prices and a good maize harvest, shortages mounted in the following year. By early 1989, as the ranks of the poor swelled, Kaunda returned to the IMF to negotiate a new adjustment loan. His efforts were too late: not only had donors lost trust in his leadership, but so had much of the citizenry.

The years leading up to 1991 brought extraordinary change to Zambia—a time when, according to the democracy activist Akashambatwa Mbikusita-Lewanika, it seemed possible to rekindle hopes that had moldered after independence, to launch a "re-decolonisation" of the country.[54] Zambia appears in the voluminous writings on structural adjustment, but much of the coverage features high-level political and economic maneuvers without the accompanying social and intellectual ferment.[55] As a result, we miss the wide-ranging debates over Zambia's socioeconomic future that Zambians themselves undertook in these heady years.

The Transition

Several constituencies made up the small but increasingly oppositional civil society in Zambia.[56] The most obvious was trade unions, organized through the Zambia Congress of Trade Unions (ZCTU), with Copperbelt mineworkers at the heart.[57] Although Kaunda established a one-party state in

1972, he did not concentrate as much power in his hands as other African leaders, seeking instead to balance among competing interest groups and political factions. Economically, he was forced to keep food costs low for urban workers through subsidies and price ceilings, a steady drain on the budget. Fatefully, as Zambia embraced IMF prescriptions in the mid-1980s, he lost mineworker support. Frederick Chiluba, head of the ZCTU, blasted structural adjustment and became one of Kaunda's most prominent critics. Miles Larmer describes a famous incident in Chiluba's rise:

> In 1986 Chiluba condemned the IMF for putting African governments on a collision course with their peoples and warned against the proposed removal of food subsidies. Nevertheless, in December 1986 the removal of subsidies led to a doubling of the price of mealie meal [the main staple, also known as maize meal], sparking widespread looting and rioting in the Copperbelt mining towns. In the wake of the riots, Chiluba claimed further concessions to the IMF would make the rich richer and poor poorer. Zambia, he declared, was the only "socialist" state implementing monetarist policies. The rioting, in which 15 people were killed, led to the immediate restoration of food subsidies, and played a significant part in the government's decision to break off cooperation with the IMF in May 1987.[58]

Although Chiluba cheered Kaunda's termination of structural adjustment, the previous events had demonstrated UNIP's vulnerability to popular protest.[59]

Churches also joined the opposition. With a churchgoing laity of over 80 percent of the Zambian population, Catholic and Protestant officials (operating through the Council of Churches in Zambia and the United Church of Zambia, respectively) exerted substantial influence, with the former particularly critical of the regime.[60] Individual church leaders attended opposition events, including the July 1990 meeting that founded the MMD. Poverty evoked their particular ire. Cardinal Joseph Mazombwe, for example, advocated debt cancellation during the 1980s, and in 1987 the Justice and Peace Commission, organized by the country's main Christian groups, issued a report deploring inequality and immiseration.[61] Church officials also served as political brokers. In mid-1991, after a student-organized convention, leaders of several denominations arranged a meeting between Kaunda and Chiluba at the Anglican Cathedral of the Holy Cross, hoping to dispel tensions over a proposed multiparty constitution.[62]

Businessmen, too—many trained in UNIP-funded programs—chafed at price controls and preferences given to state enterprises, forming what Bates and Collier called a "dissident political faction" that operated within and beyond government auspices and sometimes "backed the makers of coups."[63] The business community overlapped with another contingent of Kaunda opponents: former UNIP officials who had fallen out with the regime. Since Kaunda regularly maneuvered among blocs in his coalition, UNIP comprised, at any given time, officials who supported and rejected current policy. Committed planners and socialists, such as Leonard Chivuno, resisted structural adjustment and market reforms; others, such as Humphrey Mulemba, favored the free market and denounced Humanism while advocating liberal reforms.[64] These fractures eventually generated an enduring opposition. Arthur Wina, a market advocate, parliamentarian, and independence-era minister of finance and education, became a founding MMD member in the late 1980s. John Mwanakatwe, also a former finance minister, openly criticized government policies. Former foreign minister Vernon Mwaanga played a prominent role in the early MMD, leading electoral campaigns and joining Chiluba's administration. Indeed, "[n]o fewer than 20 MMD candidates in the 1991 elections were former or sitting UNIP MPs and 12 had been cabinet ministers or central committee members. Another six had been UNIP regional secretaries or district governors and four were former army officers."[65] Clearly it no longer 'paid to belong to UNIP,' as party banners once announced.

In the late 1980s, another small but active set of Lusaka-based organizations entered the fray, linking Zambia's intelligentsia with the halls of power. The Economic Association of Zambia (EAZ), the Zambia Research Foundation (ZRF), the Zambia Branch of the African Political Science Association, and other groups helped to generate ideas and organize meetings that fueled the multiparty platform. The EAZ was the hub of this network, partly because it enjoyed funding from the Friedrich Ebert Foundation (a German foundation affiliated with the Social Democrats) starting in 1985, which transformed the dormant talking club into a vibrant intellectual society that drew thirty to fifty participants to twice-monthly concourse at Lusaka's Pamodzi Hotel.[66] Under the presidency of Mbikusita-Lewanika, a U.S.-trained political scientist and economist who had spent his early career managing parastatals, the association brought together academics, businessmen, and disgruntled members of Kaunda's UNIP party.

The EAZ gathered diverse opinions ranging from staunch liberalizers to proponents of state planning. Mbikusita-Lewanika argued for a government-planned liberal economy to serve a nationalist purpose. Upset by the termination of the NERP in 1989, he contended that Zambia had never succeeded in de-colonizing its economy. As a result, it suffered from two distortions. First, it was grossly imbalanced, with a small and lucrative mining enclave sitting atop a vast reservoir of peasant farmers whose main function was to provide cheap food and labor for the extraction industry. Second, it remained disarticulated: its modern industry did not provide market and production opportunities for other sectors. The country, in other words, had never dismantled the bifurcated structure of a colonial economy. The "mission of the times," accordingly, must be "to deliver the long-deferred promise of independence: democracy and development to the legions of disenfranchised urbanites in shanties and the de facto-expropriated rural poor in scattered and dilapidating villages." Structural adjustment would not do so, since its "trickle-down theory" perpetuated "dependence and underdevelopment." While 'Aka,' like most Zambian opposition figures, endorsed liberalization as a necessary caustic after years of government misrule, he repudiated laissez-faire and pushed instead for "an independent, nationalistic and country-specific programme based on self-reliance," one that required an activist state and careful planning to promote growth and resist outside control.[67] A plan is "a nation's dreams," he remarked in 2019, and without one, ministries become subservient to donors, turning national aspirations into mere "compliance issues."[68]

Other EAZ members disagreed. There were outspoken structural adjustment champions in the association. According to one interviewee, attitudes toward the Bretton Woods organizations depended significantly on one's specialization. Those trained in macro-economics (balance of payments, currency, privatization) generally supported structural adjustment and bemoaned UNIP's partial and uncommitted implementation of it. Situmbeko Musokotwane, for example, currently in his second stint as Zambia's finance minister, argued in 1988 that the introduction of user fees in health posts was necessary to reduce service consumption, part of the wider task of confronting Zambia's yawning macro-economic imbalances through demand management. The reliance on expensive imports was a particular driver of debt.[69] Sectoral specialists in areas like agriculture and health, by contrast, tended to doubt structural adjustment, citing concerns over poverty, equity, service provision, and development financing.[70] Take the example of Katele Kalumba, a health researcher at the Institute for African Studies and later a minister of health and finance under the MMD. In a 1989 article co-written with the American anthropologist Paul Freund, Kalumba called for a new kind of health planning to promote equity. While he decried the longstanding urban bias of Zambian policy, he also challenged the World Bank's prejudice against government regulation. "Planning is needed," he and Freund wrote,

> precisely because structural deficiencies in setting priorities exist, and because the constituent political forces registered within the state policy planning system do not agree about the structures of authorization and allocation. . . . The range of planning discourses, the themes they address and the strategies they propose are there because consensus on the substantive issues is non-existent. What we want to stress is that 'bad planning'—like the 'bad organization' implicit in models of centralization and decentralization that are often prescribed for 'effective administration' in implementation literature—is a superficial diagnosis. The polarity between . . . centralization and decentralization—in which one masquerades as oppression and the other as freedom—is a myth.

While Kalumba did not oppose market mechanisms or the curtailment of free medical services, he felt that these changes should be matched with a "pragmatic" and "dialectical" planning whose "ultimate social function should remain that of redistribution."[71] Over the next decade, unsurprisingly, he became a critic of structural adjustment.[72]

Another prominent voice was that of the University of Zambia economist Gilbert Mudenda, who published regular newspaper columns in the years straddling the 1991 election. An advocate for privatization as an economic accelerant, Mudenda nonetheless worried about "ideological intrusion from the IMF and the World Bank, which glorif[ied] privatization as the universal panacea for all economic ills in all societies including Zambia."[73] While Mudenda abhorred the inefficiency of parastatals and warned against using foreign intervention as a bugbear for staving off reform, he affirmed the political motive that had led to nationalization in the 1970s—namely, the desire to end the "predominance of foreign ownership." This remained an essential item in 1991: After all, most Zambians did not have the money to purchase privatized assets, leaving the field vulnerable to foreign takeover. Indeed, through subsidiaries and minority shareholding, foreign firms had been able to disguise their ongoing influence throughout the Kaunda years.[74] Parastatals were, in effect, state capitalist institutions, lacking public accountability and unable to nurture individual initiative since they were often denied control over personnel. Markets offered a needed check on public power, but Mudenda feared a "violent swing" from left to right. "We should not apologise," he insisted, "for the fact that the state plays a role in any economy" by creating an "environment which encourages personal enterprise and minimizes individual excesses associated with the egoistical of [*sic*] profit."[75] While government outlays should encourage production, they should also promote employment, income, welfare, and de-pauperization—all goals that structural adjustment routinely undermined.[76]

As these summaries reveal, there were numerous areas of concurrence among EAZ members. All agreed that the Kaunda economy was in freefall, and they shared the view that some form of privatization and liberalization was mandatory to constrain the public sector. There was also a general consensus that subsidies—on food, fertilizer, and other goods—would have to shrink since they constituted an unsustainable budgetary burden. And everyone understood that the artificially inflated exchange rates would have to be abandoned in order to boost exports and reduce the black market. Furthermore, in a decade when many feared the impending exhaustion of Zambia's mines, there was widespread discussion of how to diversify the copper economy.[77] But these agreements on what was wrong masked considerable diversity of opinion about how to structure the post-Kaunda economy. It is probably true that broad alignment among elites on certain key principles helped to ease the way for rapid liberalization after 1991, suggesting an illusory accord and hiding important differences in economic vision. But the MMD consensus was always partial and superficial, which helps to explain why it dissolved in the years following victory.[78]

New ideas circulated in other organizations as well. The ZRF, under the chairmanship of economist and political scientist Derrick (Mbita) Chitala, and the Zambian chapter of the African Political Science Association led discussions on political change. The Institute for African Studies (IAS), especially after 1988 when it came under the directorship of economist Oliver Saasa, moderated symposia and held conferences related to socioeconomic reform.[79] In 1991, at the instigation of UNZA students, Saasa presided at talks in Lusaka's Mulungushi House that brought together UNIP, the MMD, and other civil society organizations. The IAS also housed Dieter Orlowski, a representative of the Friedrich Ebert Foundation, which, as we noted, funded the EAZ, ZRF, and other civil society organizations. The press as well publicized new political and economic proposals—particularly the *Weekly Post* newspaper, founded in 1991 by Fred M'membe; it became the preferred outlet for opposition voices. Within these organizations, one encountered various viewpoints, some backing structural adjustment as a necessary tonic, others deriding it for initiating "growth without development."[80] New economic initiatives found a sympathetic ear in more official circles as well, including the Bank of Zambia and the Foreign Ministry. Indeed, they gained traction within UNIP itself, with regime functionaries not only countenancing but tapping into these conversations as a source of new ideas. One interviewee recalled that officials sometimes attended economic debates and solicited advice from their participants. Particularly under the NERP, Kaunda sought innovative economic programs, and he brought together prominent intellectuals and businesspersons who were part of the EAZ, at times appointing officials who would later join the MMD. Thus, one should not paint too stark a divide between the regime and the opposition around economic policy: As one participant remarked, "on the political side, Kaunda was rigid; on the economic side, he was flexible."[81]

Ultimately, the late 1980s saw two intellectual shifts among the activist intelligentsia. Through the middle of the decade, some of those who later advocated staunch liberalization professed socialist viewpoints, publishing tracts in Zambian and foreign journals that promoted anti-capitalist and Afro-Marxist perspectives. Mbita Chitala, for example, worked with the South African Marxist Joe Slovo and edited the *Journal of African Marxists*. Donald Chanda, a future economic advisor and overseer of structural adjustment, published socialist essays through the Harare-based think tank Southern African Political Economy Series (SAPES) Trust. Chiluba himself, the trade union leader turned president, publicly upheld socialist positions.[82] In many ways, theirs was a pragmatic socialism, a product of the anti-Western sentiments common in the independence era. Nonetheless, the shift to market advocacy in the late 1980s was striking. After a ruinous economic decade, the implosion of East European communism tarnished the wider socialist project with which Kaunda identified, and liberalization seemed a way to wrest power from UNIP and win international support.

This set up the second shift: the turn from economics to politics. If intellectual opposition to Kaunda was stirred initially by the country's flagging economy, the goal that finally mobilized political action was ending UNIP's governing monopoly. Yet the desire for economic change long antedated the demand for Kaunda's removal, and one should not assume that the call for economic or even political reform in the late 1980s necessarily implied multiparty politics—for many activists, it did not. Thus, one reads the following sentence in MMD Finance Minister and former UNIP member Peter Magande's recent autobiography: "I hold a strong belief that, if President Kaunda allowed open debate on the state of the nation and presented a reform programme and leadership succession plan to his rule at the Fifth Convention of UNIP in March 1990, Zambia would have taken a different and perhaps a more progressive path towards the twenty-first century."[83]

But in the end, he did not, and as the 1990s opened, Kaunda's recalcitrance increasingly frustrated activists. When multipartyism finally appeared on the reform agenda at the turn of the decade, it became rallying cry.[84] And where the EAZ felt constrained to speak, other organizations entered the breach. Chitala recalls proposing discussions of democratic pluralism to the EAZ but detecting "elements of fear in the majority of the members who did not want the Association to be politicized," as well as worry about "arrest and detention."[85] His own organization, the ZRF, was already set up to discuss governance, and it agreed to organize a conference on multipartyism. Thus, at considerable risk and expense, activists convened a fateful two-day meeting on July 20–21, 1990, at the Garden House Hotel in Lusaka, where the MMD, which took power fifteen months later, was born.[86]

The papers delivered at the Garden House, compiled and published by the ZRF, testify to the power of a timely conviction. Arthur Wina's opening speech declared the one-party state a "colonial legacy" and tallied its failures, the greatest of which was the political stunting of the Zambian people. In place of UNIP, he advised a bounded multiparty system, ideally with no more than three parties. For Vernon Mwaanga, the one-time UNIP minister, the problem was not party monopoly but "the over-concentration of power in the hands of one man." Likewise, the lawyer and future foreign affairs minister Remy Mushota dismissed Humanism as a colonial residue of British utilitarianism, which justified unitary rule in the name of the "common good." As Donald Chanda put it later in the day: "This country has been a victim of several imported ideologies, ideas and policies which failed and are failing us. The answers lie in ourselves . . . not externally." Aka too offered a message of democracy and self-reliance, basing his condemnation of Kaunda partly on the recently reintroduced structural adjustment: "[W]hile structural adjustment is necessary, it is not sufficient. Structural Adjustment Programmes are concerned essentially and primarily with monetarist adjustment—not transformation." Democracy required true national self-determination, not "[e]conomic liberalization under a One Party State."

It is worth underscoring the paramountcy of economic concerns at the conference. "We see a situation," remarked Chiluba, "where political stability has been over-emphasised on [*sic*] the neglect of economic development"—and he ventriloquized an unnamed scholar in observing that "Zambians have enjoyed peace and stability, but for sure our stomachs have not known peace at all." Aka added his own quip, characterizing Zambia as "a very democratic country—in terms of the breadth of participation in poverty and other socio-economic ailments." It was Chiluba, however, a year away from the presidency, who cinched the point:

> The precise problem as I see it is that Humanism fails to distinguish between the rich and the poor. It assumes that the dignity of man derives from mere existence whether that man lives in squalor or high society does not matter. But we know that human dignity derives from ensuring the basic entitlements to man; man must have equal opportunities and access to good shelter, food, education, health and gainful employment.

UNIP, despite its promises, supplied none of these.[87] In this sense, the 1980s, for delegates, marked not just the disappointment of earlier hopes for prosperity, but the betrayal of a vision of African self-reliance that "KK" himself had nurtured.[88]

Meanwhile, political turmoil continued. Kaunda's new adjustment measures aggravated his difficulties, requiring "a freeze on capital projects and an increase in consumer prices on maize meal of up to 275%."[89] Inflation and shortages prompted further riots and, weeks before the Garden House conference, a coup attempt led by a disgruntled army lieutenant. Donors were ill inclined to sympathy: they rejected Kaunda's effort to lighten austerity measures. The MMD's summer call for multiparty elections thus sparked the popular imagination, forcing Kaunda to concede a referendum on the issue (which he ultimately canceled) and then a constitutional amendment to allow for multiple parties by year's end. Weeks after the December amendment, in January 1991, the MMD registered as a political party and launched an electoral campaign. In October 1991, it swept Kaunda from power. By this point, political scientist David Bartlett reminds us, business elites committed to liberalization had already outflanked more progressive and egalitarian forces to take control of MMD planning. Chiluba's sudden conversion to structural adjustment advocacy drew them behind his leadership, forging an unlikely business–trade union pairing that directed the MMD's future course. In this regard, the election of 1991 marked an elite transfer, despite the active energies and popular support of large segments of Zambia's population.

Structural Adjustment under the MMD

The MMD's electoral victory in 1991 ushered in a period of domestic euphoria that the new government used to introduce dramatic economic reform, including renewed structural adjustment in such an orthodox vein that it would likely have sparked riots under UNIP. In the first year, the MMD devalued the kwacha, freed the exchange rate, deregulated prices, removed food subsidies, introduced service-user fees, and initiated the privatization of parastatals. As one veteran of the administration remarked in 2019, "We implemented structural adjustment probably to the book."[90] The result was punishing—somersaulting inflation, slashed public services, and ballooning unemployment—but also hopeful—the rapid appearance of goods in stores and the launch of new infrastructure projects. By 1993–94, as privatization and job losses accelerated, the government imposed fiscal controls—including a cash budget requiring all expenses to be covered by existing resources—that gradually restrained inflation.[91] This was, in sum, a rapid and thoroughgoing adjustment, and the population bore it. While the years from 1995 onward saw burgeoning corruption and the erosion of SAP integrity, the first few years of adjustment did indeed make Zambia an IMF model.

How is it that Zambia came to embrace one of the most orthodox SAPs on the continent? Given the various postures espoused by activists during Kaunda's final years, why did this one prevail? There were a number of reasons. International circumstances contributed to the choice. The end of East European communism (watched closely by Zambian activists) coupled with the dominant Washington Consensus on market-led development (Chapter 9) seemed to confirm the fact that liberalization was the only game in town. This message was reinforced by the success of export-driven economies in East Asia and the concomitant failure of African socialist projects, notably in neighboring Tanzania, where Julius Nyerere had been Kaunda's ally and mentor. The tight coupling of democracy and marketization—political and economic liberalization—made the latter seem a necessary partner of the former, and international debates generally revolved around which came first—democracy or marketization—not whether they had to be joined.

Another factor was the influence of the donor community. International aid increased steadily after the 1960s, growing from 1.8 percent of GDP in 1971–74 to 18.2 percent in 1989–93.[92] It spiked after 1991, as donors sought to bolster Zambia's transition. "The importance of aid to Zambia cannot be overstated," write three Zambia scholars.

> At their peak in 1992 the disbursements from multilaterals and 22 bilaterals amounted to US$1,479 million, equal to 67 percent of export earnings and 77 percent of total public expenditure. More than 35 percent of the government's budget is financed by the donor community, and donor financing accounts for on average 80 percent of the budget for capital expenditure, according to the Zambian government's 1999 budget address.[93]

Given this dependence, and international willingness to withdraw assistance to combat economic backsliding (demonstrated in 1987 and again in 1991), donor commitment to structural adjustment provided a strong inducement to comply. Zambia was, after all, a "receiver of policy rather than an initiator," and by the time of the MMD's accession to power, it had a $7.3 billion debt—over 230 percent of its GDP—placing it among the most indebted countries on earth.[94] Mounting arrears left the new government scant negotiating power, prompting Chiluba booster Richard Sakala to assert that there was "no choice" and that structural adjustment was 'inevitable,' to cite a widely used word.[95]

Another reason for Zambia's adjustment orthodoxy was the nature of donor negotiations. As Matthew Martin has shown, decisions about IMF loans and debt rescheduling were taken in secretive meetings under conditions of limited debtor empowerment and knowledge. With Zambians ill informed of procedures and expectations, it is little surprise that creditor concerns about loan repayment took priority over long-term development and poverty alleviation.[96] In this regard, donor recollections of regular consultation with host-country officials, cited at the start of this chapter, downplayed the power imbalances that framed adjustment negotiations in the first place. Despite reforms in the late 1980s that brought greater transparency, the policies conveyed a sense of fait accompli: Recipient countries were lesser partners, and external priorities circumscribed domestic policy, contributing to what Larmer described as Lusaka's "limited capacity" to "reflect popular opinion when [it] conflict[ed] with donor priorities."[97]

In addition to external pressures, there were internal inducements to structural adjustment. The view that markets were essential to economic and political reform was broadly shared by the domestic intelligentsia. "The political change we wanted was tied to liberalism," recalled one official in 2019. "Initially we felt we needed political liberalism, but we then realized it was tied to economic liberalism since the only way to engage the economy was to engage private actors."[98] Although elite agreement was superficial, it no doubt facilitated adjustment: If everyone appears to support liberalization, it is hard to sustain a language of alternatives. The preference for rapid and thorough adjustment was also enforced by the negative example of Kaunda's inconsistent liberalization, a failure that MMD leaders were keen to avoid. One respondent maintained that Kaunda never "believed" in his earlier SAP program: his implementation was partial and halting, focused chiefly on foreign exchange, and he resisted multilateral calls for privatization and price liberalization.[99] The rise of businessmen within the MMD coalition gave market-friendly views an additional policy advantage. There were also darker motives. Amid falling life expectancy, increased user fees, dramatic cuts in education, and agricultural decline, liberalization had its winners: A privileged elite increased its wealth by purchasing company stock in "the opaque processes of the Zambia Privatisation Agency (ZPA)." Among the payees were former finance ministers, overseers of the process.[100] In this way, marketization enjoyed a powerful inside constituency.

The fate of the EAZ is instructive in revealing how alternative economic futures could be marginalized. The association threw itself behind the MMD in the election campaign, and many of its members took posts in the new government. But after the vote, club members decided not to align with Chiluba's administration, preferring to retain their independence by distancing themselves from a trade unionist turned president who had never been fully comfortable in their intellectual ranks. According to one respondent, the EAZ faced growing irrelevance as Chiluba turned to a new source: a group of advisors sent in 1990 by the Harvard Institute for International Development. Initially recruited by Kaunda's minister of finance, the foreign advisory team eventually became a World Bank requirement for the renewal of credit.[101] Stalwart advocates of structural adjustment—the "Harvard Boys," as many Zambians knew them (though not all of them were men)—soon won out in debates over economic reform, steering the country toward more rapid liberalization than many local advisors preferred.[102] Economist Caleb Fundanga may have had this team in mind when he wrote that "[t]he main players have become foreign experts and those local anchormen or 'creatures of the IMF and World Bank' as they are often called. This, to a large extent, has compromised the quality of SAP programmes that have emerged." While he acknowledged that local experts played a role in designing and popularizing SAPs, Fundanga worried that even they had become tools of foreign authority.[103] Outside encroachment occurred beyond the policy level as well. Despite a few government programs to support those who lacked purchasing power, most Zambians did not have the means to buy shares in privatized parastatals. As a result, foreign investors snapped up state assets, launched new construction, and sold goods once offered by shuttered industries. As a respondent in 2019 remarked, multiparty politics brought not only increased marketization but also growing "domination by international actors."[104]

The MMD itself contributed to the sense of disempowerment. Chiluba is a fascinating figure in this regard. He joined the MMD at the Garden House meeting despite little involvement in its prior discussions. Retrospectively, some commentators describe him as an interloper who jumped to the top of the movement and cut short the discussion of economic options. Yet while he is widely disparaged today because of the corruption associated with his second term, in 1991 he had a solid reputation as the head of the ZCTU, and his MMD leadership rested on strong credentials. He was one of the few widely known Zambians outside the UNIP governing party. He was untainted by compromise with UNIP, as opposed to the many senior MMD members who had once worked in the government. And he led the trade union congress, for years the leading voice of opposition to both Kaunda and structural adjustment.[105]

Yet the MMD, like UNIP, embraced a top-down leadership model. One respondent likened the pattern of presidential deference under Chiluba to that of his predecessor, with ministers anticipating presidential wishes and refraining from counter-argument.[106] Indeed, "the constitution did not change the balance between executive and legislative power," reported two analysts. As under Kaunda, a "'presidential court'" held sway.[107] Negotiations with donors abroad were restricted to a small cohort, usually led by the finance minister, and economic deliberation did not reflect the openness of 1991. Indeed, Chiluba's powerful finance ministers, Emmanuel Kasonde and, after 1993, Ronald Penza, defended structural adjustment so vigorously that the latter earned kudos from the IMF magazine *Euromoney* as one of the best ministers of finance in Africa.[108]

The choice for shock therapy also reflected the sense among MMD leaders that they had only a short "honeymoon period" during which the population, desperate for change, would tolerate further hardship.[109] "Free enterprise" and entrepreneurship stood at the heart of their campaign promises, and candidates in 1991 had warned of coming sacrifices, a message that citizens seemed to accept.[110] As one trade union leader recalled in 2003:

> I think the first few years of MMD in power, you know we had given them the benefit of the doubt. Most of the people in Government came from our [trade union] movement, including the President. They made an appeal in 1991. They wanted people to sacrifice, and we agreed, all of us. In most of the campaigns the question was asked 'Are you ready to sacrifice?,' and we said 'yes.'[111]

Liberalization was part of a wider commitment that Chiluba had made at the Garden House meeting. Yet when addressing the role of workers in the ongoing opposition, he also censured Kaunda's Humanism in the name of "social justice," calling for greater income equality, "equal opportunities" for all Zambians, and improved "access to good shelter, food, education, health, and gainful employment."[112] How jarring the shift when, a few years later, the newly elected Chiluba directed trade union leaders to convince their workers "to die a little so that prosperity is not overburdened with a crippling debt and an economy shattered beyond redemption."[113]

The Zambian economy slipped further in the mid-1990s. Although most economists acknowledge that structural adjustment leads to short-run dips in production and purchasing power, growth that was supposed to follow from new efficiencies never seemed to appear. Part of the problem was natural disaster. Adjustment began in 1992 as a severe drought struck southern Africa. Even as bilateral donors struggled to distribute food relief, price controls were lifted and subsidies removed on fertilizer and maize meal.[114] In agriculture, early and hasty market reforms, sometimes ill conceived or underprepared, led to confusion that cost farmers needed income.[115] By 1993, grim reports of impoverishment and official corruption signaled the waning of the MMD's honeymoon, and the second half of the 1990s saw macroeconomic backsliding that soured relations with the IFIs. Citizens evinced a growing cynicism toward Zambia's *nyu katcha* (new culture) of personal responsibility, holding out little hope that their circumstances would improve in the face of rampant inflation and unemployment.[116] Despite the appreciation of opportunities for free expression and initiative, many felt that MMD officials were capturing riches for themselves. Indeed, "the democratically elected MMD Government," wrote two aid scholars, seemed to "manifest less concern with social equity issues than its predecessor UNIP, although poverty reduction features as a national goal in policy documents." Fully 84 percent of the population was classified as poor or very poor by the World Bank and UNDP in 1997, with the percentage rising throughout the decade. The new government, it seemed, had "moved away from balanced regional and district budget allocations towards a system built on political favouritism."[117] How much of this can be laid at the feet of structural adjustment, as opposed to political cronyism and incompetence? What is at least clear is that SAPs did little to stop the descent. As one academic warned about Africa in general, "[p]olitical liberalization is not likely to guarantee the appearance of new political alignments that favor sustained neoclassical economic reform."[118]

Ultimately, the choice for shock therapy over gradualism, simultaneous reforms over stepwise change, proved destabilizing, with austerity strangling short-term growth. Agricultural services such as marketing boards and cooperatives were dismantled before the private sector could fill their niche; subsidies were removed during a time of privation and price hikes; and parastatals that might have survived with timely injections of cash simply collapsed, increasing unemployment and glutting the informal sector.[119] One rural respondent spoke for many when she recalled giving up her fishmongering business because competition for buyers became too fierce; the newly retrenched had all entered the informal market.[120] Such memories are backed by statistics. As Peter Dwyer and Leo Zeilig tell it,

> From 1992 to 1998, Zambian GDP fell by an average of 0.2 percent per annum. Formal-sector employment fell from 544,200 in 1991 to 436,066 in 2004. Social indicators drastically declined under the MMD. Education spending as a percentage of GNP fell from 4.5 percent in 1991 to 2.9 percent in 1994 (although it subsequently increased). In 2002, 33 percent of children were not attending primary school, while only 22 percent received secondary education. Health expenditure fell in proportion with overall cuts in government spending at a time when the impact of HIV/AIDS was devastating. Infant and child mortality increased with the introduction of user fees; access to clean water and sanitation services declined. . . . The percentage of Zambians living in poverty rose from 70 percent in 1991 to 73 percent in 1998.[121]

It is little wonder that some rural Zambians recall fondly—if also selectively—the days when NAMBoard, Kaunda's farm marketing parastatal, reliably purchased produce—albeit at below-market prices.

Workers faced particular disorientation under the MMD, in part because the party was led by one of their own and its policies came as a bitter fruit of victory.[122] In the mid-1990s, new laws stripped ZCTU of its "legal monopoly over union affiliation," capping a steady decline in trade union power.[123] Churches, too, were disappointed: While priests and bishops welcomed the end of Kaunda's rule, they were scandalized by growing poverty and corruption, and they criticized structural adjustment for its contribution to both—sometimes becoming political targets as a result.[124] Some MMD proponents disavowed their earlier support for liberalization. Mbikusita-Lewanika abandoned his post as minister of technical education and vocational training in 1992, the MMD the following year; he went on to form the opposition National Party and, later, the Agenda for Zambia.[125] Mbita Chitala, who stumped for privatization and attacked liberalization opponents when he was deputy minister of finance in the early 1990s, felt "ashamed" of "defend[ing] structural adjustment programmes with such zeal . . . I was just parroting bourgeois nonsense with attractive words."[126] Peter Magande, too—sent overseas, he surmises, because of poor relations with the MMD—lamented the suffering of ordinary Zambians.[127]

Compounding these worries was a growing rural-urban divide, with cities attracting migrants from the countryside and development from abroad, while rural residents languished. This gap is vividly illustrated in the experiences of Nasula, the heroine of Binwell Sinyangwe's 2000 novel *A Cowrie of Hope,* as she travels to Lusaka to vend her last bag of Mbala beans and earn money for her daughter's schooling. When the bag is pilfered by a disreputable businessman, a shattered Nasula determines to get justice. Her experience chimes with its era: Nasula is not only deprived of her goods but dismissed as irrelevant by a big man with no time for her needs. She desires not only remuneration but recognition, cathartically supplied in the penultimate scene when she finally gets payment through the intervention of an upstanding police officer. Alas, this was a fantasy for most. Because the Zambian economy was "unprepared" for shock, the 1990s became "a lost decade in GDP growth."[128] Sinyangwe put it baldly: "The years of the rule of money. The years of havelessness, bad rains and disease. The harsh years of madness and evil!"[129]

There were defenders of Zambia's structural adjustment and the bitter medicine it prescribed. Advocates acknowledge short-term dislocations, but argue that they were needed to promote macro-economic stability, with bilateral donors providing cushion for those most hurt. One senior Zambian advisor noted that although the IMF stood firm on core principles, it was open to requests for modification; it was, in other words, more flexible than critics allow.[130] Supporters of liberalization often argue that reform sequencing, not speed, caused the primary mischief. Privatization occurred too early, before fiscal balance and macro-economic stability could be achieved.[131] Furthermore, the delayed privatization of ZCCM deprived reformers of essential taxes, exports, and jobs that the rejuvenated copper mines might have generated.[132] There were also positive returns. Some respondents took advantage of new opportunities to start businesses.[133] Private transportation, such as Lusaka's ubiquitous minibuses, blossomed in the 1990s, providing a sorely needed service. Even Sinyangwe concluded his novel with his heroine boarding a "good new bus, a bus of the nineties," to return to her home village.[134] But these were glimmers in a general despair. In the extreme, the defense of structural adjustment takes the form of an acknowledgment of the decade's severe developmental losses as the lamentable but necessary price for establishing a macroeconomic "enabling environment" and allowing debt cancellation through the Highly Indebted Poor Country (HIPC) program launched by the IMF and World Bank in 1996.

Ultimately, Zambia's economy did grow in the first decade of the 2000s—according to the World Bank, over 5 percent annually between 2005 and 2013—although this was likely driven by rebounding copper prices more than SAP reforms. While Bank statistics indicate some decline in the poverty level, it remained stubbornly high, at 54.5 percent nationally in 2015, including over 75 percent in rural areas.[135] As the latter figure suggests, inequality persisted, with growth alleviating poverty at the upper margins, but barely touching the country's rural majority. Curiously, then, Zambia can be classified as both a lower-middle-income country (as it was in 2012 by international institutions) and a least-developed country, testifying to its intractable bifurcation.[136] Indeed, economic duality, argued University of Zambia economist Venkatesh Seshamani, is not just a result but a cause of poverty's self-perpetuation:

> High growth has led to slower poverty reduction in Zambia due to persistent high levels of inequality. . . . [T]he lack of a pro-poor stance in the distribution of the benefits of growth (seen from the shares of the bottom 10% and top 10%) and the persistent levels of high inequality (seen from the Gini coefficient values) have contributed to the unabated levels of poverty in Zambia.[137]

Even as Chiluba's successor Levy Mwanawasa directed new revenues to the social sectors, much of the country's poverty remained obdurately growth-resistant, with increases accruing disproportionately to the advantaged.

Multiparty politics, in sum, did not yield multiple economic choices. In the political and economic literature, structural adjustment is typically cast as either a morality tale of common-sense (if bracing) reforms, a necessary astringent on the way to economic recovery; or as a counter-morality tale of neocolonial cruelty, of industrial nations and neoliberal cons boosting their profits at the expense of the poor. Both narratives lack local voices, and both reflect the largely ahistorical quality of their subject: a structural adjustment template applied in universal and decontextualized fashion. "Until lions have their own historians," an African proverb has it, "tales of the hunt will always glorify the hunter."[138] Indeed, what is most striking about the local history outlined in this chapter is how little it is known. For the most part, the intellectual history of Zambia's transition is not formally written; clues to it are scattered in people's heads, in a few published memoirs, in newspaper back issues and unpublished reports. Recovering this "missing historical narrative" is not simply an exercise in historical reclamation; it also affords the chance to revive alternate economic possibilities, to recover forgotten Zambian visions of their own development.[139]

9

Conclusion: Development as History in the Making

THE END OF THE COLD WAR BROUGHT both excitement and uncertainty to international development circles. With the expiration of the mandate to combat communism, it suddenly seemed possible to focus aid around development rather than foreign policy. At the same time, aid's diminished political urgency meant that USAID faced budget cuts and skepticism about its mission. Its full-time staff thinned from 3,406 in 1992 to 2,346 in 1998, a 31 percent reduction in forces (RIF) that reshaped operating modalities.[1] Culminating a decades-long transformation, USAID became largely a contractor rather than an implementing agency—a "wholesaler to wholesalers," as deputy administrator Carol Lancaster put it—with many of its former experts relocating to non- or for-profit organizations and operating under the supervision of contracting officers who had less experience than the teams they managed.[2] By 2000, with aid portfolios proliferating in other agencies, USAID had to justify its continued relevance amid turf wars and funding competition.[3]

Amid these changes, the era witnessed both persistent and novel forms of ahistoricism. The outbreak of Western triumphalism following the collapse of communism in Eastern Europe and the Soviet Union illustrates the former, with Francis Fukuyama's end of history thesis giving voice to the feeling of post–Cold War vindication. Fukuyama has been widely pilloried for arguing that modern history, understood as a two-century debate over the best sociopolitical order, had finally come to end with the decisive victory of liberal democracy and market capitalism.[4] He saw the modern era as a bitter struggle among competing ideologies—before communism there was fascism; before fascism, nationalism—that concluded in 1989 with the liberal vanquishment of its final competitor. History was teleological, and it had reached its end. Fukuyama did not, however, think that the future—post-history—would be uniformly bright. Not only would stragglers resist the inevitable transition to liberalism, but man's need for recognition would sometimes take megalothymic form—the desire to dominate or supersede others—that liberal democracy, with its egalitarian ethos, could not satisfy.[5] But this was not the takeaway for most readers. Instead, pundits saw a victory lap: The West had won; its system would prevail. Fukuyama's thesis framed much of the democracy and governance programming undertaken by USAID in the 1990s. To bolster democratic and capitalist institutions, including active civil societies modeled on America's Tocquevillian self-image, aid practitioners spanned the globe, secure in their understanding of the liberal goals (if not always the means) of political transition.[6]

John Williamson's 'Washington Consensus' also described a U.S. capital besotted with liberal self-assurance and a post-historical conviction that ideological debates were over. An economist at the market-oriented Peterson Institute for International Economics, Williamson delivered his famous statement on the ten components of Washington's foreign policy agenda at a 1989 conference. Published the following year, his label stuck, becoming a byline for the free-market, export-oriented reforms that Bretton Woods institutions had advocated for a decade. Williamson's ten-point list summarized inside-the-Beltway principles for economic reform: fiscal discipline; reordered public expenditures; tax reform; liberalized interest rates; competitive exchange rates; free trade; foreign direct investment; privatization; deregulation; and property rights. Though Williamson professed agnosticism about the individual items, he endorsed their general thrust of "prudent macroeconomic policies, outward orientation, and free-market capitalism."[7] The program was hardly neutral. It excluded anything that was "primarily redistributive," since Washington of the 1980s was "contemptuous of equity concerns."[8] Gone were the Marxist, dependency, and basic needs paradigms that had once riveted development planners. Similarly, it abjured midcentury statist and Keynesian approaches. Ultimately, the Washington Consensus label was employed by advocates and critics alike, though Williamson spent the subsequent decade defending his coinage from the charge of neoliberal boosterism.[9]

The Washington Consensus did not go unchallenged. The loudest objections emanated from Keynesian economists such as Joseph Stiglitz, who called for a post–Washington Consensus that embraced sustainable development, egalitarian growth, and democratic governance.[10] Others, such as economist Nancy Birdsall, then at the Carnegie Endowment for International Peace but soon to found the Center for Global Development, which helped to shape U.S. development policy in the new millennium, raised alarm about persistent poverty and widening inequality.[11] Harvard's Dani Rodrik complained that Washington Consensus policies were too broad and undifferentiated. Standardized blueprints did not travel well because they took little account of local histories and institutional configurations; development required sensitivity to "context and needs."[12] As these critics averred, contemporary policies marked the return of a kind of modernization theory (Chapter 4), a set of hardened prescriptions rooted in a distilled account of the Western economic past. Perhaps the most thorough refutation of Washington Consensus policies came with the Asian economic crisis of 1997, a financial meltdown in the state paragons of outward-oriented growth. Unregulated investment, loose credit, hot money fleeing financial panic—all of these suggested the need for economic regulation in a globalizing world.

In the face of criticism, Williamson was alternately defensive and conciliatory. In the late 1990s, he came to distinguish the "first-generation" policies of the original consensus, which stressed macro-economic reforms and state retrenchment, from "second-generation" institutional reforms such as anti-corruption, poverty reduction, social safety nets, and flexible labor markets.[13] This augmentation reflected perhaps the most prevalent aid trend of the decade: the turn toward governance as a focus of development policy.[14] The World Bank Report "Beyond the Washington Consensus" also rejected prevalent anti-government sentiments and argued instead that "institutions matter"; they could not simply be dismantled in the name of libertarian freedom.[15] More impactfully, World Bank economist David Dollar argued that aid worked in good policy environments, but failed otherwise; a country's governance and policy framework, not funding levels or program design, was the key variable.[16] Dollar's 2000 article with economist Craig Burnside provided intellectual ballast for George W. Bush's Millennium Challenge Corporation (MCC), a new agency that assisted countries who fulfilled conditions of good governance.[17]

This second-generation consensus—namely, that markets drive growth, but successful development also requires a political 'enabling environment' and country commitment—differed in emphasis from the free-market conditionality that preceded it. If the 1980s had prioritized macro-economic adjustment, at times tolerating authoritarian rulers who encouraged market growth, the new agenda stressed democratization—most dramatically in post-communist Eastern Europe, a test case for programs launched the globe over.[18] Good policy, Dollar and Burnside contended, not only combated corruption (a longstanding preoccupation), but also secured a flourishing civil society and widespread participation in decision-making, goals that were not central to Williamson's first-generation itinerary. Yet the governance turn maintained a disapprobation of state centralism inherited from the neoliberal 1980s, and it still touted private-sector efficiency and decentralization.[19] In this sense, a decade-old mistrust of the public sector, reinforced by the events of 1989, persisted in post–Cold War mandates.

For new varieties of historicism and ahistoricism, an influential example was the Peruvian economist Hernando de Soto. De Soto's work blended the close description and historicization of informal economies (in housing, business, transport) with action research designed to reproduce tasks faced by the poor (such as starting a business) and identify the obstacles they encountered. Working out of his Lima-based Institute for Liberty and Democracy, he not only focused his research on the livelihoods of the impoverished, but he also called for bottom-up programming that accommodated the informal practices of poor entrepreneurs who labored outside the legal system. His first book proposed a free-market alternative to development that countered both the Maoist Shining Path movement and (implicitly) the redistributive and dependency policies of Latin American populism. But it was his second work, *The Mystery of Capital* (2000), that made him an international celebrity.[20] Capitalism, de Soto insisted, was first and foremost a representational system whereby material assets were recognized as legal property that could be used for wealth generation. Across the globe, millions of poor people controlled vast resources, but they lacked the legal standing to turn these assets into transactional capital that could become collateral for a loan or evidence for a credit rating. As a result, they could not secure growth or development. De Soto's analysis of property rights drew on what he called the missing lessons of history: both the unacknowledged history of informal economies in

Peru—his laboratory—and the forgotten history of legal evolution in countries such as Germany, Switzerland, and the United States, where formal property law emerged gradually out of myriad local and unofficial precedents. This subaltern history of Western capitalism fell away in the transfer of markets abroad. Like Yunus, de Soto understood today's poor as entrepreneurs, but they labored without the tools that served businesspersons elsewhere. As a result, they could not improve their lot.

Yet de Soto practiced a different form of simplification: the rejection of a complex account of poverty in favor of a silver bullet. In his rendering, long-standing debates over planning, import substitution, and other state-led approaches were discounted as so many "redistributive regimes" that politicized societies by pitting interest groups against one another and casting economic actions in zero-sum terms. For all its manifold causes, poverty could be largely resolved, he argued, with the extension of property rights. Yet while this legal remedy would surely boost some enterprising poor, millions more would languish. For as Abhijit Banerjee and Esther Duflo remind us, the poor, like the rich, are not all born entrepreneurs.[21] Jeffrey Sachs was correct when he remarked that relying on a single explanatory factor for poverty—in de Soto's case, property rights—simply does not account for the "observed diversity of development experience."[22]

Amartya Sen's *Development as Freedom* provided another index of development's post–Cold War rethinking—and its continuities with the past.[23] The product of an elite Bengali background, Sen established his name as an Oxford don writing about the economics of famine and contributing with Mahbub ul Haq (Chapter 6) to the elaboration of the Human Development Index (HDI), designed to supplant GNP as the basic indicator of development. In addition to income, the HDI incorporated measures for education and life expectancy, offering a broad benchmark of country weal.[24] Underpinning the HDI was Sen's emerging conception of development not simply as growth (GNP, GNI, or other measures), but as increased individual capabilities that enabled the pursuit of personal desires and goals. While oppressive governments clearly limited development, so did extreme poverty and inequality. Conceived as freedom, development aligned substantially with liberalization, and Sen accepted liberal rights as essential components of human flourishing. But, like his 1970s-era cohort, he also stressed the inability of capitalist markets to resolve ills such as economic inequality and environmental degradation. Thus, proper development required some forms of state provision. Sen's earlier work on famine, which he had witnessed as a youth in Bengal and an adult in Bangladesh, informed this conception: For the most part, he observed, famines were not the result of unavailable food; instead, they grew from a lack of entitlements, an inability to command resources as a result of poverty and powerlessness.[25] In Ireland in the 1840s, India in the 1870s, and Bengal in the 1940s, food exports proceeded even as locals starved.[26] These laissez-faire catastrophes were political choices, not natural disasters. If Sen remained a liberal individualist to a large degree, he was nonetheless convinced of the need to counterbalance markets with a robust public sector, using each to mitigate the excesses of the other.[27]

Perhaps the most ardent cheerleader for aid's developmental mission was the economist Jeffrey Sachs, who gained renown as a purveyor of economic shock therapy before his experience in Russia convinced him of the importance of foreign aid to alleviate suffering.[28] His 2005 book *The End of Poverty* revived the goal of an aid-induced big push to end extreme poverty. Its publication was impeccably timed. The Millennium Development Goals announced in 2000 and the post-9/11 recognition that foreign poverty could have international consequences helped to revive aid funding that had declined in the 1990s. In this context, Sachs helped to fuel a new anti-poverty crusade by supplying both a policy framework for aid disbursements and large infusions of ethical zeal. As opposed to Rosenstein-Rodan's original big push, which focused on the industrial sector, Sachs's reprise encompassed economic *and* social development, including increased funding for agriculture, health, education, modern infrastructure, and sanitation to vault communities out of destitution and toward "take-off" (note the modernization terminology).[29] Since poverty prevented savings, Sachs saw it as a self-reinforcing trap from which the poor could not escape on their own—thus the economic and moral necessity of foreign aid. The primary failure of wealthy nations, accordingly, was miserliness: Sachs cited the example of USAID's West African Water Initiative, funded for three years at only $4.4 million, not even a penny per capita for the affected population.[30] Aid planners also needed more effective poverty diagnostics—a "clinical economics"—that addressed geography, health, and other fields. Based on his experience at the first Millennium Village in Sauri, Kenya—a project he launched to demonstrate what sufficient aid could accomplish—Sachs outlined a multisector package to lift the world's poorest toward self-sustaining growth.

Within a year, Sachs found his chief antagonist in former World Bank economist William Easterly, whose 2006 volume *The White Man's Burden* touched off a debate that captured aid industry attention.[31] For Easterly, the global poor suffered two tragedies. Not only were they afflicted by extreme poverty, but the millions of aid dollars spent by the West—he calculated $2.3 trillion over five decades—had failed in its uplift goal, sometimes deepening local impoverishment. This tragedy was the direct result of a misbegotten approach reiterated in various forms throughout aid history: an emphasis on top-down planning and a search for development panaceas. Sachs was the latest of these aid doctors, peddling a new infusion of the same old planner's potion. Easterly drew on the history of past Western interventions in "the Rest," from imperialism to foreign aid, to render an indictment of donor hubris. According to him, lasting growth and development required a bottom-up approach in which funds and assistance went to developing country "searchers" who set out *not* to end poverty—an impossibly grandiose goal—but to solve specific social and economic ills in particular locations. In their efforts, Easterly spied the workings of market incentives—profits above all—that drove local innovation. They were a kind of negative key to effective development policy, a set of economic and psychological signals that enforced accountability by requiring social entrepreneurs to attend to local needs.[32] Distant from local feedback, planners faced no such accountability when their programs went awry. Instead, they just moved on, implementing worn-out strategies in new countries and blaming disappointments on confounding factors. If Sachs argued that we know how to promote development but lack the will, Easterly maintained that there is no adequate plan: aid must accept uncertainty. Yet even he could not resist the allure of an answer.[33] If his book usefully challenged technocratic optimism about solving extreme poverty, its conclusion should be treated with some reserve. For surely one of the lessons of economic development history, as we saw in earlier chapters, is to maintain a healthy mistrust of market certitudes.

The Sachs-Easterly debate over aid effectiveness took place on both a moral and an empirical plane, yet ultimately it proved inconclusive. Was aid a moral calling or a moral travesty? Did the history of aid demonstrate success or failure? As we have seen, these are longstanding questions, and while Sachs and Easterly invigorated the debate, they did not invent its terms. Both acknowledged the mixed record of past foreign aid efforts, yet their argument left no clear victor, in part because its claims were so vast that well-curated historical examples could sustain either side. Indeed, to support their cases, both offered potted histories that read like travelogues of development high- and low-lights. Both called for diagnostic approaches modeled on health care.[34] And both echoed venerable development propositions: Sachs's plan read a lot like midcentury modernization (Chapter 2); and Easterly's incentives evoked the longstanding market rivals of aid planning (Chapter 6). Yet ultimately, one can wonder whether the markets-versus-planning dispute is really such an antithesis. Throughout development history, they have often gone hand in hand, with markets providing price and demand signals, and government regulation correcting for market failures.

In 2007, another widely read development diagnosis, this by the British economist Paul Collier, whose work we encountered in Zambia (Chapter 8), identified four traps ensnaring the world's poorest: the conflict trap; the natural resource trap; the "landlocked with bad neighbors" trap; and the bad governance trap. Collier was less certain of a solution than Sachs or Easterly, since each trap demanded a unique approach. Assisting the 'bottom billion,' he argued, required some combination of aid, trade, legal action, and peacekeeping, with the particular balance varying by sector and by problem.[35] Collier is one of the few economists to state what many imply by their practice: perhaps history has little value in helping us understand today's development needs.[36] He is surely correct to call out the opportunistic use of historical analogies to justify contemporary policy. Yet few historians would assent to so complete a dismissal of their field. Collier's remark rests on a simplified vision of history as supplying direct causal links for present circumstances or locking nations into conflict. If history were so narrow—seeking only mechanical explanations or perfect analogies, rather than wider contextual understanding—it is easy to see why it should be dismissed.

Randomized Control Trials

Indeed, one may wonder if the question of whether or not aid works lends itself to *any* conclusive answer. The advocates of randomized control trials

(RCTs), one of the most transformative post–Cold War innovations in development practice, doubt it: the question is too vast and aid's developmental record too mixed. Instead of such macro-problems, impact evaluators focus on the project and activity level: Did particular activities work in particular times and places? Pioneered by MIT's Abhijit Banerjee and Esther Duflo in the 1990s, development RCTs set out to determine the impact of aid initiatives by establishing a counterfactual control group: What would have happened if the intervention had not taken place? Adapting a methodology drawn from trials of new drugs, evaluators set up experiments based on randomly selected treatment and control groups within a target population. Treatment groups receive program support—for example, educational inputs such as textbooks or flip charts; agricultural inputs such as fertilizer—and then their results are compared against those in a control group, which, as a result of randomization, is assumed to be equal in all ways other than the treatment itself. In effect, the trials establish two different histories: one in which the program occurred, the other in which it did not. By using randomization to filter out confounding variables, one can be sure, according to proponents, that the results are caused by the program. Trials revealed that classroom cameras could decrease teacher absenteeism; pre-purchasing fertilizer could help to boost agricultural yields; and de-worming could improve school attendance. Their promise seemed infinite, for they could show—beyond reasonable doubt, it was claimed—what interventions succeeded. To use Banerjee's terms: "The beauty of randomized evaluations is that the results are what they are."[37]

By the new millennium, RCTs were widely hailed as the 'gold standard' of aid program evaluation, employed by the World Bank and other large development institutions. Their frequency increased from roughly 40 annual evaluations published in 2000 to over 350 in 2016.[38] This acceleration had salutary effects, challenging old certitudes—the universal recipes of modernization or the Washington Consensus—in favor of bottom-up experimentalism based on the frank admission that we do not know much about what promotes development.[39] Rodrik described this mindset well: "Relative ignorance calls for an approach that is explicitly *experimental,* and which is carried out using the tools of *diagnostics* and *evaluation.* Old dichotomies between states and markets play little role in this worldview and pragmatism reigns."[40] For Duflo, evaluation required a "plumbing" approach that moved beyond strategizing 'what to do' and toward the investigation of implementation logistics: how things work in the world.[41] Banerjee described it as a "new economics" from the ground up that needed constant conversation with the poor and drew its insights from empirical data rather than a "prior body of worked-out theory."[42] For even after more than fifty years of development programming, he explained, economists were still at "stage 1"—"gathering impressions" of what does and does not work. Some discoveries were surprising, such as the finding that decisions to take a small loan were influenced as much by the picture on the offer letter as by the interest rate. Others debunked common assumptions about textbooks, pedagogy, and other inputs. Perhaps most famously, impact evaluations challenged the efficacy of microcredit, revealing that, while they helped to sustain poor families, loans did not usually lift them from indigence.[43] These insights, Banerjee hoped, "would eventually allow us to build a set of new theories."[44] But the aim went well beyond economic modeling: As the website of MIT's Abdul Latif Jameel Poverty Action Lab (J-PAL) states, the chief goal was to "reduce poverty by ensuring that policy is informed by scientific evidence."[45]

How successful were RCTs at placing development knowledge on firm epistemological footing? Thoughtful advocates acknowledged that the new methodology was not appropriate for assessing all interventions. It was, for example, a poor fit for macro-economic policies such as exchange rate shifts or regulatory frameworks, the sorts imposed under SAPs. Furthermore, impact evaluators preferred project over program aid, not on the grounds of development effectiveness, but due to the fact that projects could be randomized, while larger programs could not. Of greater significance, RCT pioneers recognized that 'theory' was needed to inform evaluation design and interpret results. The word *theory* here denotes an interpretive framework that is not derived from experimental data, but is used to analyze them. It might designate anything from relevant social and economic models to detailed historical contextualization, though the latter was rarely applied.[46] Commonly, randomizers interpret findings through the lens of behavioral economics, which argues that humans are poor judges of their own interests and require policy "nudges" to do things that are good for them, such as saving money.[47] If on the one hand, the use of theory admits a range of valuable analytic perspectives, it also implies that experimental findings are not, as Banerjee declared, exactly "what they are." They instead require interpretation.

While few questioned the value of RCTs as tools for assessing project effectiveness, critics did point out that they often failed to meet the high bar touted by advocates. In the 1990s, James Heckman warned of potential biases induced by spillover between control and treatment groups and by randomization timing within a multistage project.[48] For philosopher Nancy Cartwright, the aspiration to "clinch" the validity of RCT findings came at the cost of severely restricting their relevance. In *this* time and place, for *this* experimental population, an RCT could prove that an activity had a particular effect. But it could not demonstrate that the same relationship would hold elsewhere. Other forms of evaluation, such as "qualitative comparative analysis," while less definitive, could canvas likely effects across a wider range of circumstances because they took stock of contextual variables. These methods could "vouch" but they could not clinch. There was a tradeoff between conclusiveness and broad relevance. For Cartwright, in sum, there was no methodological gold standard, and even rigorous RCTs relied on mixed methods: "[H]ow do [economists] decide what lessons to draw about target situations outside from conclusions rigorously derived inside the model?" she asked. They use "thought, discussion, debate; relatively secure knowledge; past practice; good bets"—in short, "theory," which lacks "the rigor demanded inside the models."[49] This does not gainsay the value of RCTs, though it does limit their reach.

In the new millennium, the World Bank's Michael Woolcock argued that proper evaluation requires an understanding of a project's "impact trajectory," the amount of time it takes for an activity to generate results. An RCT performed soon after a vaccination campaign might very well demonstrate effectiveness of uptake, but the impact of a primary education project could take years to manifest—and might appear different if one tests the knowledge of a recent project cohort, its later matriculation rate, or its employment rate when former students seek jobs. Multistage projects, moreover, are highly contextual; while the term *project* implies a fixed package, in fact projects entail a spectrum of activities over time and space, each determined by a range of factors. The mere "token genuflection to the importance of 'context,'" along with limited accounting for temporal evolution, can blinker even precise randomized trials.[50] There is, of course, no reason in principle, as Banerjee argues, why longer-term, multisequence impact evaluations cannot be done, although there may be logistical impediments.[51] Yet even still, the need to account for context and historical change suggests that, while RCTs can provide valuable insight, they must be supplemented by other tools.[52]

Perhaps the most persistent gadfly for RCTs is the question of 'external validity.' To what extent can rigorous statistical findings be extrapolated or generalized from their original setting to other times and places—either from the experimental subset to the population as a whole, or from the original location to a new country and community? Since temporal passage is also a kind of relocation, we can ask: To what degree will an intervention that succeeds at one time produce similar results later? The concern here, as voiced by economists such as Rodrik and Daron Acemoğlu, is not that RCTs do not generate accurate findings, but that they may not reveal much of a general policy nature.[53] If free bed nets effectively combat malaria in western Kenya, does that assure that a giveaway (rather than fee-based) program will work elsewhere? The typical response is that theory helps planners make the leap from local findings to generalizable policies. Yet even as RCT proponents concede the need for theory and other forms of 'less admissible' evidence, they also insist that "hard evidence," per Banerjee, is "evidence from a randomized experiment," that experimental results "are what they are." It is this seeming contradiction, coupled with the inflation of the method as a litmus test for scientific rigor, that led Angus Deaton to dub RCT advocates "randomistas," a term some proselytes embrace with relish.[54] Yet even the claim to conclusive knowledge within a single experiment—the insistence that "any difference in mean outcomes between treatment and control samples" must be attributed to the intervention—may be overoptimistic, since samples themselves can contain unknown variances from the overall population. Even "internal validity," Martin Ravallion thus warns, does not achieve real-world certitude as per the "ideal RCT."[55]

Another response to the external validity problem is to expand the number of RCTs. This is indeed happening. The more consistently evaluators find in favor of a particular intervention—in various settings—the more confident we can be in making general claims about its efficacy. It is perhaps this growth in the stock of RCT evidence that prompted Banerjee's exasperation with skeptics: We may not know in some ideal sense that RCT-certified successes in Kenya and India will work in Ghana, but in the real world we can be pretty sure of it.[56] Yet even if many would concede this point, RCTs still do a better job demonstrating *that* an intervention worked than they do in explaining *why*. And while it is tempting to dismiss the 'why' as long as one knows the 'that,' the former is essential to analyzing problems of scale and replicability—matters of considerable policy import. To put it another way, one cannot jump from 'it worked' (on this project) to 'it works' (elsewhere) unless one knows the reasons for success. Impact evaluators already rely on behavioral economics for this purpose. Historical awareness can add further insight, contributing to mixed-methods evaluations that combine rigorous data, social scientific theory, and contextual understanding.

But the hype surrounding RCTs militates against this hybridity. Both pioneers and acolytes, as we have seen, sometimes overreach, succumbing to overconfident assertions and mechanical notions of causality: Duflo's praise for economist-plumbers; Banerjee's insistence that results just "are what they are." In light of this bare-bones epistemology, several commentators have argued that impact evaluations work best for "tunnel"-type interventions with repetitive activities, a defined treatment group, clear outputs, and a "low causal density" (in which 'a' explicitly causes 'b').[57] For initiatives with more complex and circular causality (such as policy questions), it is hard to disaggregate project effects in a direct enough fashion to certify success or failure definitively.

Furthermore, commentators worry about "crowding-out" effects, with RCTs marginalizing other forms of evaluation that do not meet their inferential standards (or 'identification strategy'). Robert Picciotto, for example, complains of the loss of methodological diversity and the danger of a monistic positivism.[58] While many donors undertake mixed-methods evaluations, the rise of RCTs has indeed meant that numbers—good numbers, bad numbers, any numbers—often push out nonexperimental findings, particularly qualitative data that rarely afford easy conclusions. "Numbers," as Robert Chambers warned in 1997, "reassure by appearing to extend control, precision and knowledge beyond their real limits," and it is common for evaluation teams to be asked to quantify survey data that contain dubious assumptions.[59] RCT pioneers acknowledge these misuses and insist that randomized evaluations cannot be retrofitted onto ill-prepared projects.[60] But it is hard to deny that the enthusiasm for RCTs has sidelined other methods that offer valuable insights, even if their conclusions are not dispositive. Impact evaluation has, as Banerjee noted in 2005, turned development economics into a fashion—with the consequent irony that RCTs, in trying to end the quest for development panaceas, are often treated *as* a panacea, a promise of certain knowledge.[61] The problem, in the end, is not RCTs themselves, but the "hard sell" of RCTs as a gold standard whose results trump all others because they are seen as just "what they are."

In sum, when combined with historical and contextual analysis, RCTs can glean empirical information that gives us a better understanding of how development projects operate and of novel development prospects. But they can also work in the opposite direction, enforcing a new absolutism, an ahistorical gold standard that demands adherence and discounts historical and contextual insights that lack quantitative rigor. Which of these attitudes ultimately prevails has vital significance for future development programming.

History in Practice

Ultimately, the concerns and prospects raised by RCTs return us to one of the framing questions of this book: How can aid practitioners mobilize a useful past in an industry with such an accumulated prejudice against history? *Their Future* has discussed various types of ahistoricism that have informed development since the postwar era—historical ahistoricism, technical ahistoricism, quantitative ahistoricism, emotive ahistoricism, ethical ahistoricism, bureaucratic ahistoricism, ideological ahistoricism, and others. Yet as most historians will point out, it is equally easy to identify examples of simplified history used to justify ill-conceived policy. We have seen numerous examples in this book: the migration of an East European industrialization program to distant continents; modernization's elevation of a Eurocentric development template into a global model; the transference of U.S. cooperative experiences to highland Guatemala—each a historical template that trumped local understanding. The recent fad for civil society programming rests on a similarly shaky historical equation: that authoritarian regimes in Africa, the Middle East, and elsewhere would swoon before citizen groups and NGOs (flush with U.S. money) as they did in Eastern Europe.[62] The dashed hopes for Iraqi democratization after 2003 and the abortive Arab Spring put paid to that notion. Societies differ, and yesterday is not the same as today.

But if facile history lessons can support dubious policies, it is surely not appropriate to ignore the past altogether. Instead, the best antidote to misemployed history is more careful historicization—not to supplant policy analysis or technical expertise, but to supplement them with contextual awareness. Ahistoricism is, after all, a choice, one that makes decision-making easier by privileging simple formulas over nuanced perspective, project retreads over careful tailoring to time and place. It is also irresponsible—displaying indifference to the unique conditions in each country, to cultural knowledge and local development resources, and to past experience that may bear on present and future aspirations. History is, after all, a trove of human possibilities, and to ignore it is to cut off a vital source for imagining and planning the future. In a world of vast need and gross inequality, development in its broadest sense—that is, the promotion of prosperity and equity for all—requires both a sober assessment of the many legacies of the past and an expansive consideration of global prospects.

How can this be accomplished in a fast-paced, deadline-driven industry dominated by a sense of moral imperative? One answer might be to define techniques for incorporating historical analysis in planning sessions. In 1986, the political scientist Richard Neustadt and the historian Ernest May laid out strategies for using history to enrich policymaking, hoping to counter what they called the usual practice: "a plunge toward action; overdependence on fuzzy analogies . . . ; inattention to an issue's own past; failure to think a second time—sometimes even a first—about key presumptions; stereotyped suppositions about persons or organizations . . . ; and little or no effort to see choices as part of any historical sequence."[63] They put forward a set of heuristics—or "mini-methods"—for improving historical awareness:

- the careful interrogation of historical analogies (distinguishing "known" facts from the "unclear" and the "presumed"; probing likenesses and differences in analogous situations);
- placing events in a chronology or story that explicates origins and actors, and answers journalistic queries such as who, what, where, when, why, and how;
- subjecting characterizations (or stereotypes) of individuals, societies, and organizations to close scrutiny by fitting them into historical context and trying to understand their motives and perspectives;
- probing one's sources to isolate biases, insights, and blind spots; and
- understanding events and decisions as part of a long-term temporal process encompassing context, cause, and impact.

If these exercises were not specific to development, they might nonetheless have value around project design tables. One can imagine additional heuristics for analyzing sectoral trends (a project for bad but improving schools would differ from one for those that are bad and declining) and for mapping the relationships of key country stakeholders (what are the origins, allegiances, and constraints of potential public and private partners?). Each requires analysis over time and in context.

Yet development is more than a series of policy choices made in planning sessions. It transpires over decades and requires longstanding interaction among people from many cultures and socio-economic groups. It therefore offers a unique field for exploring the role that historical analysis and contextual awareness can play in intercultural policymaking and project collaboration. It is thus all the more regrettable that development, of all fields, has been largely treated as a technical exercise subject to checklist procedures. In challenging this tendency, we must go beyond heuristics to cultivate a more fundamental sense of history as a practice and mindset.[64] There are stages in a project when deliberate historicization can be incorporated. Project design and evaluation are obvious entry points, as is midcourse reappraisal. In these phases, practitioners might expand their usual concerns to encompass social, political, and economic contextualization, examining documents and querying experts who can situate sectoral trends in a broader awareness. This would of necessity go beyond factors that projects can manage or quantify, probing the interaction of aid activities with ongoing social and political affairs. But history is also borne in more daily engagements, as a form of interpersonal appreciation, an attitude of interest in and respect for local concerns, perspectives, and cultures. Even if one can never fully understand the lived experience of others or cancel the power dynamic inherent in donor–beneficiary relations, the effort to learn can partially bridge the distance between local and expatriate, and it can reveal new programming possibilities unimagined in donor headquarters. Since technical models habitually assume away much of the messy social world, the reminder that 'context matters' bears regular repeating.

Empowering this kind of awareness would require changes in professional culture: a slowing of the frenzied pace that rewards speed and privileges checklists; the decentralization of decision-making to practitioners and country representatives; the hiring and cultivation of staff with expertise in contextual modes of understanding. It would necessitate enlarging the decision-making table to invite participants with unorthodox perspectives, including those from beneficiary communities. One improvement is surely to heed Dan Honig's call for a relaxation of top-down mandates and the elevation of "judgment" among practitioners around the globe—those willing to buck formulaic approaches in favor of activities improvised in response to local need and feedback.[65] Another is to reject the understanding of projects as fixed packages or black boxes, as Erin Beck has argued, and to treat them instead as a set of ongoing interactions among agent-participants, each with their own histories and experiences to bring to the program.[66] Still further, it entails recognizing how the development efforts of the poor both engage with and extend beyond state and international programs.[67] Broadly speaking, change requires constant reference to local perspectives as a way to inform program design, tap new resources, and empower developing-country residents. This would not negate the value of technical models, but it would demand a readiness to adjust them in light of new insights, remaining flexible on all parameters of program implementation.

Although one cannot expect such change to occur overnight, the development industry is not immovable. In recent decades (to take the latest example), RCTs have transformed the culture of aid evaluation. Indeed, in private conversations, industry professionals exhibit a ready interest in the culture and history of the communities where they live and work, though few consider the practical implications of this knowledge for programming. Planners have talked about localization and participation for decades, though often without ceding real design or management control. In other words, the ideas put forth in this book already percolate among practitioners. The challenge is to implement them.

One of this book's main arguments is that the development—and hence the future—of Global South societies has been heavily shaped by donors outside its borders. It belongs, more properly, to them.[68] Yet ultimately, the dichotomy 'their future, our future' is rather artificial. Although Western ideas are disproportionately represented in the annals of development, Latin America, the Caribbean, East Asia, and South Asia have also supplied global templates. Poor and rich, South and North, East and West, peasant and elite—their future, our future—the border between 'them' and 'us' has always shifted, and it grows ever more porous in an age of climate change, global finance, mass migration, and pandemic. Nor, I hope it is clear, do past and future stand on either side of a strong divide. Surrendering the past means surrendering the future as well. And if we are to build a future that works for all the world's citizens and not just its elite percent, we need to draw on the experience of all communities and myriad pasts, returning development to what it is and always has been: history in the making.

ACKNOWLEDGMENTS

This book was conceived on Tuesday, August 26, 2003, at about 10 a.m.—my first day as a new proposal writer for a Washington, D.C.–based USAID education contractor. I was a recently minted history Ph.D. in a period of academic unemployment, and during my initial orientation at my new office I asked where, if I were assigned to write a proposal about schools in, say, Morocco, I might find information about the history of the local education sector. My interlocutor—now a good friend and one of the very best development professionals I know—laughed and pointed to a few online CIA reports. Although I was surprised by this casual dismissal, I too in the years before (and after) my return to academia wrote project proposals with hardly any attention to the history of the sectors and communities involved. I flew off to new countries knowing little about recent political trends, and wrote reports about education or civil society projects with only the briefest of internet research. Not only was there no time for deep contextualization, but I had no framework for giving historical analysis any recognizable value in the aid industry. And I was a trained historian. Ahistoricism, I came to understand, is built into the structure, schedules, and incentives of development practice, and there is no easy formula for overcoming it.

For a book born so suddenly, however, the gestation was extraordinarily long—more than twenty years. In great part, this was due to the fact that its topic and themes took me far from my academic fields of expertise. Not only did I have to educate myself in the field of development studies—with all of its interdisciplinary vocabulary and concepts—but I also had to rely heavily on the work of many brilliant scholars who know far more than I do about the specific countries and disciplines I studied. The endnotes in this book therefore double as a lengthy set of acknowledgments.

Along the way, this project received generous financial support at crucial junctures. Travel for case-study research to Guatemala, Zambia, and Bangladesh was supported by the History Department and the College of Arts and Letters at my home institution, James Madison University in Virginia. A well-timed Franklin Grant from the American Philosophical Society also supported my travel to Dhaka, allowing me to complete research for my final case study in the wake of the Covid pandemic. And the book would still be incomplete without a timely fellowship from the John Simon Guggenheim Foundation that gave me an uninterrupted year of research and writing. Without this assistance, a long project would have taken much longer.

I am also grateful to journals and volumes that published earlier versions of parts of these chapters: "The Presentist Bias: Ahistoricism, Equity, and International Development in the 1970s" appeared in the *Journal of Development Studies* 48 (2012), 1–14. Some arguments from Chapter 1 appeared in the Introduction to Jerrold Keilson and Michael Gubser, eds., *The Practice of International Development* (New York: Routledge, 2018), xv–xxv. And "Zambia's Missing Narrative of Structural Adjustment" was published open source in the *Zambia Social Science Journal* 9:1 (2023), 51–75, as part of a special issue on the legacy of Kenneth Kaunda. Some of my other publications on development and history are referenced in the endnotes of the present volume.

I also want to thank a range of practitioners and scholars—now friends—who read parts or all of this manuscript and with whom I engaged in conversations that helped to shape its arguments. Among the many who raised me from a novice proposal writer to a literate development practitioner, Kate Carpenter, Larry Lai, Mark Lynd, and Jon Silverstone stand out. Without them, this book would not exist. The case studies that inform it depended on the expertise and kindness of many others as well. Again the standouts: In Guatemala, Thelma Porres and J. T. Way; in Zambia, Caesar Cheelo, Marja Hinfelaar, Fred Kamanya, and Julie-Anne Savarit-Cosenza; in Bangladesh, Sakil Malik, Saifullah Sadeq, Saherah Luhnat Noor, Radia Tamim, and Sameeo Sheesh. I hope this book reflects at least some of the knowledge, trust, and generosity they shared. My research began not in the three countries listed above, but in Uganda and Nigeria, where Eugene Ssemakula, Nafisa Ado, and Ahmed Umar Jibrin provided guidance and friendship during the initial project stages. The immediate results of their work appeared in earlier articles, but their influence suffuses this book as well. Any errors and misrepresentations are, of course, my own.

To those listed above, I also need to add the following friends and colleagues, who contributed either through direct engagement with the book or in conversations and recommendations related to its themes: John Abromeit, Ojo Afolabi, Michele Alacevich, Neel Amin, Paige Arthur, Edward Baring, Julian Bourg, Heather Coltman, Samantha Constantine, Susannah Cramer-Greenbaum, Amy Czajkowski, Frank Dall, Etana Dinka, Alvis Dunn, David Evans, Suzanne Fiederlein, Susan Fitzpatrick-Behrens, Evan Friss, Nils Gilman, Shah Mahmoud Hanifi, Kevin Hardwick, Joseph Morgan Hodge, Terrence Jantzi, Melinda King, Penelope Kogan, Kristen McCleary, Colleen Moore, Samuel Moyn, Besi Mohonja, Sombo Muzata, Muna Ndulo, David Owusu-Ansah, Elizabeth Phelps, Delores Phillips, Golam Ahmed Rabbi, Mark Rankin, Steve Reich, Avi Rosenblum, Michael Seth, Amy Staples, Alain Thery, Robert Tignor, Bill Van Norman, Emek Uçarer, Godfrey Vincent, Ania Wertz, and Michael Woolcock; as well as numerous audience members and interlocutors in Lusaka, Dhaka, Antigua (Guatemala), and the United States. Last but not least are the many interviewees in multiple countries whose knowledge and experience enabled me to write this book but whose identities I am obliged to protect. They ranged from government officials and NGO staff members to professors, farmers, and students. Their names are indicated with letters in the relevant chapters, but their insights and experience permeate these pages.

Their Future is dedicated to my teachers and mentors, those who fostered my personal and professional development and who opened up new worlds for me. While I have had many excellent mentors, I single out six of them here whose impact still resonates today—two from my adolescence and four from adulthood. I met Victor Rohr and Rhea Lindstrom at Keene Mill Elementary School in Springfield, Virginia. Mr. Rohr was my trombone teacher from fifth grade through the end of high school. My dependency (to use a term employed in this book) on music for emotional and intellectual orientation owes much to his guidance. Even as I wrote this book, I felt his sense of tone and phrasing, rhythm and control, in its words and ideas. If everyone had experienced his lessons, arts education would be far more valued than it is. And Mrs. Lindstrom, my sixth-grade teacher, is quite possibly the greatest teacher in history. Among other memories: She dared to stage the musical *Oliver!* with our ornery class, letting me dodge not-so-artfully across the cafeteria stage for several packed houses. Although she passed away in 2020, one of many lost to the Covid pandemic, testimonies from my classmates showed the same lasting sense of awe and gratitude. She was, quite simply, magical.

In adulthood, the impact on my development—indeed, my life—of Martin Jay, Margaret Anderson, Jerrold Keilson, and Gwyn Osnos is also monumental. Without them, I would not be an intellectual historian, development practitioner, or musical theater writer (respectively). Martin Jay was my dissertation advisor and continues to guide and support my academic career. He is the chief reason I entered the endlessly varied and invigorating field of intellectual history. Margaret Anderson was an equally important guide to the riches of Central European history, as well as a mentor and champion of my efforts to move beyond Central Europe in my historical practice. Jerrold Keilson hired me into international development in 2003, changing the course of my life and research, and he has been a partner in many of my subsequent development projects. And Gwyn Osnos took a repressed home musician and shepherded me into musical theater, opening up a new field of experience and expression. All four made the transition from mentor to friend, showing me that development does not cease with the conclusion of formal education but continues throughout life.

I will not even try to list the many other friends who sustained me through the years of this project's development. But I do want to acknowledge two: Paolo Prandoni and Chris Vitiello did what best friends do best: provided hours, days, years of joy and deep wells of warmth and understanding. I hope I supplied them half as much.

Development, of course, attracts travel aficionados, and for that love, as for all my emotional and intellectual resources, I owe bottomless thanks to my two families: Mom, Dad, and Andrea introduced me to the joys and addictions of travel when I was a child, blazing the path for my future career when we spent my second-grade year in Zurich, Switzerland. Decades later, my wife, Elisa Oh, and my children, Theo and Mira, who tolerated my research trips for this project and now journey with me to many new places, have become my favorite travel companions. Without them, I am nowhere.

NOTES

Chapter 1. International Development and Historical Amnesia

1. William Easterly, *The White Man's Burden: Why the West's Efforts to Aid the Rest Have Done So Much Ill and So Little Good* (New York: Penguin, 2006), 200; Thomas Dichter, *Despite Good Intentions: Why Development Assistance to the Third World Has Failed* (Boston: University of Massachusetts Press, 2003), 9; Jeffrey Sachs, *The End of Poverty: Economic Possibilities for our Time* (New York: Penguin, 2005); Frederick Cooper and Randall Packard, eds., *International Development and the Social Sciences: Essays on the History and Politics of Knowledge* (Berkeley: University of California Press, 1997), viii.
2. James Ferguson, *The Anti-Politics Machine: Development, Depoliticization, and Bureaucratic Power in Lesotho* (Cambridge: Cambridge University Press, 1990). See also C. A. Bayly, Vijayendra Rao, Simon Szreter, and Michael Woolcock, eds., *History, Historians and Development Policy: A Necessary Dialogue* (Manchester: Manchester University Press, 2011).
3. The best summary of this literature is the two-part article by Joseph Morgan Hodge, "Writing the History of Development (Part 1: The First Wave)" and "Writing the History of Development (Part 2: Longer, Deeper, Wider)" in *Humanity* (Winter 2015/Spring 2016), 429–63/125–74.
4. Recent exceptions are David Mosse, *Cultivating Development: An Ethnography of Aid Policy and Practice* (London: Pluto, 2005); Daniel Immerwahr, *Thinking Small: The United States and the Lure of Community Development* (Cambridge: Harvard University Press, 2015); and David Engerman, *The Price of Aid: The Economic Cold War in India* (Cambridge: Harvard University Press, 2018).
5. Trouillot highlights the marginalization of the Haitian Revolution. Michel-Rolph Trouillot, *Silencing the Past: Power and the Production of History* (Boston: Beacon, 1995).
6. Dipesh Chakrabarty, *Provincializing Europe: Postcolonial Thought and Historical Difference* (Princeton: Princeton University Press, 2000)

7. Walter Mignolo, *The Darker Side of Modernity: Global Futures, Decolonial Options* (Durham: Duke, 2011), esp. Chap. 1. See also Mignolo and Catherine Walsh, *On Decoloniality: Concepts, Analytics, Praxis* (Durham: Duke University Press, 2018); and Mignolo, *The Politics of Decolonial Investigations* (Durham: Duke University Press, 2021).
8. While the terms *non-Western world, developing countries, Global South*, and others each come with historical freight—a point I discuss in the opening of Chapter 2—I sometimes interchange their use for linguistic variety.
9. Methodologically, I draw on the synoptic strategies of Martin Jay, who offers close textual analyses of concepts within and across time periods; and the cultural contextualization of Carl Schorske, whose "post-holing" approach to the study of fin-de-siècle Vienna tracked, excavated, and compared multiple fields of cultural production.
10. Nikole Hannah-Jones's 1619 Project is a clear example of this line of argument, as are the memoirs of Ta-Nehisi Coates and the op-eds of Jamelle Bouie. On the post-Obama shift in U.S. race politics, see Nils Gilman, "The Collapse of Racial Liberalism," *American Interest* 13:5 (March 2, 2018).
11. Thomas Piketty, *Capital in the Twenty-First Century* (Cambridge: Harvard University Press, 2014); Piketty, *Capital and Ideology* (Cambridge: Harvard University Press, 2020).
12. The 2022 COP21 meeting in Sharm al-Shaykh, Egypt, made this point adamantly. For historical outlooks on climate change, see Jo Guldi and David Armitage, *The History Manifesto* (Cambridge: Cambridge University Press, 2014); Naomi Oreskes and Erik Conway, *The Collapse of Western Civilization: A View from the Future* (New York: Columbia University Press, 2014).
13. The works of Timothy Snyder make this argument. For a debate over analogies to past authoritarianism, see Peter Gordon, "Why Historical Analogy Matters," *New York Review of Books* (January 7, 2020); Samuel Moyn, "The Trouble with Comparisons," *New York Review of Books* (May 19, 2020).
14. Arturo Escobar, *Encountering Development: The Making and Unmaking of the Third World* (Princeton: Princeton University Press, 1995); Gilbert Rist, *The History of Development: From Western Origins to Global Faith* (London: Zed, 1997); Wolfgang Sachs, ed., *The Development Dictionary: A Guide to Knowledge as Power* (London: Zed, 1992).
15. On this movement, see https://www.thenewhumanitarian.org/feature/2022/08/12/Decolonising-aid-a-reading-and-resource-list.
16. Joel Wainwright, *Decolonizing Development: Colonial Power and the Maya* (Malden, MA: Blackwell, 2008), 8–10.
17. See, inter alia, Gilman, *Mandarins of the Future: Modernization Theory in Cold War America* (Baltimore: Johns Hopkins University Press, 2007); David Ekbladh, *The Great American Mission: Modernization and the Construction of an American World Order* (Princeton: Princeton University Press, 2011); Michael Latham, *The Right Kind of Revolution: Modernization, Development, and U.S. Foreign Policy from the Cold War to the Present* (Ithaca: Cornell University Press, 2011); and Sara Loren-

zini, *Global Development: A Cold War History* (Princeton: Princeton University Press, 2019).

18. Guldi and Armitage, *The History Manifesto*, 1.
19. Jonathan Crush, "Introduction: Imagining Development," in Crush, ed., *Power of Development* (New York: Routledge, 1995), 9. For a similar complaint, see Douglas Porter, Bryant Allen, and Gaye Thompson, *Development in Practice: Paved with Good Intentions* (New York: Routledge, 1991), xv.
20. Eugene Staley, *The Future of Underdeveloped Countries: Political Implications of Economic Development* (New York: Harper, 1961), 79–81.
21. Paul Collier, *The Bottom Billion: Why the Poorest Countries Are Failing and What Can Be Done About It* (Oxford: Oxford University Press, 2007), 23.
22. "It is disturbing that the accepted development philosophies and fashions . . . owe very little to experience and thinking emerging from the developing countries themselves." Just Faaland, ed., *Aid and Influence: The Case of Bangladesh* (New York: St. Martin's, 1981), 182–83.
23. Michael Woolcock, *International Development: Navigating Humanity's Greatest Challenge* (Cambridge: Polity, 2023), 4.
24. This institutionalized oversight fits into the organizational ignorance described by Peter Burke in his history of agnatology: *Ignorance: A Global History* (New Haven: Yale University Press, 2023), 22–24.
25. Maia Green, "Calculating Compassion: Accounting for Some Categorical Practices in International Development," in David Mosse, ed., *Adventures in Aidland: The Anthropology of Professionals in International Development* (New York: Berghahn, 2011), 38.
26. Rosalind Eyben, "The Sociality of International Aid and Policy Convergence," in Mosse, ed., *Adventures in Aidland*, 139–60.
27. Marc Frey and Sönke Kunkel, "Writing the History of Development: A Review of the Recent Literature," *Contemporary European History* 20:2 (May 2011), 217.
28. Hla Myint, *The Economics of the Developing Countries* (London: Hutchinson, 1964), 21.
29. Mosse, *Cultivating*, 47. See also Mosse and David Lewis, eds., *The Aid Effect: Giving and Governing in International Development* (London: Pluto, 2005).
30. Tania Murray Li, *The Will to Improve: Governmentality, Development, and the Practice of Politics* (Durham: Duke University Press, 2007), 7.
31. Ferguson, *Machine*. See also Julie Livingston, *Self-Devouring Growth: A Planetary Parable as Told from Southern Africa* (Durham: Duke University Press, 2019), 21.
32. Timothy Mitchell, *Rule of Experts: Egypt, Techno-Politics, Modernity* (Berkeley: University of California Press, 2002), 41–42.
33. For a similar concern, see Joshua Muskin, "Sustainability in Development Projects: How Do We Do It, and Do We Really Want To?" in Jerrold Keilson and Michael Gubser, eds., *The Practice of International Development* (New York: Routledge, 2018), 65–93.
34. Michele Alacevich, "Planning Peace: The European Roots of the Post-War Global Development Challenge," *Past and Present* 239 (May 2018), 256, 262.

35. Nick Cullather, "Development? Its History," *Diplomatic History* 24:4 (Fall 2000), 645.
36. On the use of reductionist history in Indian colonialism, see Priya Satia, *Time's Monster: How History Makes History* (Cambridge: Harvard University Press, 2020); Nicholas Dirks, *Castes of Mind: Colonialism and the Making of Modern India* (Princeton: Princeton University Press, 2001); and Thomas Metcalf, *Ideologies of the Raj* (Cambridge: Cambridge University Press, 1994).
37. On debates regarding the use of history to understand the Trump era, see Daniel Steinmetz-Jenkins, "Beyond the End of History," *Chronicle of Higher Education* (August 14, 2020): https://www.chronicle.com/article/beyond-the-end-of-history?fbclid=IwAR2PfA4VbawH6APYfSTdKR1lqpTm4-IL-m6jzQbez8apzahesHfuRgHdsrs For an argument against public applications of history, see Allan Megill, *Historical Knowledge, Historical Error: A Contemporary Guide to Practice* (Chicago: University of Chicago Press, 2007), 36–37.
38. Sun Yat-Sen, *The International Development of China* (New York: Putnam, 1922); Amy Staples, *The Birth of Development: How the World Bank, Food and Agriculture Organization, and World Health Organization Changed the World, 1945–1965* (Kent: Kent State University Press, 2006); Eric Helleiner, *Forgotten Foundations of Bretton Woods: International Development and the Making of the Postwar World* (Ithaca: Cornell University Press, 2014); Frederick Cooper, *Citizenship between Empire and Nation: Remaking France and French Africa, 1945–1960* (Princeton: Princeton University Press, 2014); Odd Arne Westad, *The Global Cold War: Third World Interventions and the Making of Our Times* (Cambridge: Cambridge University Press, 2011); J. T. Way, *The Mayan in the Mall: Globalization, Development, and the Making of Modern Guatemala* (Durham: Duke University Press, 2012).
39. Quoted in Pankaj Mishra, *Bland Fanatics: Liberals, Race, and Empire* (New York: Farrar, Straus and Giroux, 2020), 101.
40. Cooper and Packard, *International Development and the Social Sciences*, 18.
41. Stephen Macekura and Erez Manela, *The Development Century: A Global History* (Cambridge: Cambridge University Press, 2018), 4, 3.
42. For these references, see, in order, David Apter, *Rethinking Development: Development, Modernization, and Postmodern Politics* (Newbury Park, CA: Sage, 1987), 7; M. P. Cowen and R. W. Shenton, *Doctrines of Development* (London: Routledge, 1996), 3; and H. W. Arndt, *Economic Development: The History of an Idea* (Chicago: University of Chicago Press, 1987), 1.
43. Alacevich draws attention this oversight and the ways that it distorts our understanding of development history in "Early Development Economics Debates Revisited," *Journal of the History of Economic Thought* 33:2 (2011), 145–71.
44. Anne-Meike Fechter and Heather Hindman, eds., *Inside the Everyday Lives of Development Workers: The Challenges and Futures of Aidland* (Boulder: Kumarian, 2014), 3–4.
45. Alacevich, "Theory and Practice in Development Economics," *History of Political Economy* 49 (Annual Supplement) (2017), 265. Development practitioners are examples of the "in-between figures" described by Jan-Werner Müller—project ex-

perts whose task was not so much to produce new ideas as to interpret policies through their own experiences. Müller, "European Intellectual History as Contemporary History," *Journal of Contemporary History* 46:3 (July 2011), 588.

46. In her evocative memoir of childhood in Communist and post-Communist Albania, Lea Ypi describes a coping mechanism common among development practitioners that also contributes to decontextualization: a tendency to compare characteristics in each new country of residence with those encountered elsewhere, ultimately reducing local distinctions and personal experiences to familiar categories. Ypi, *Free: Coming of Age at the End of History* (New York: Norton, 2021), 202–04.
47. Reinhart Kosellek, *Futures Past: On the Semantics of Historical Time* (Cambridge: MIT Press, 1985/1979), 92–104.
48. Peter Novick, *That Noble Dream: The 'Objectivity Question' and the American Historical Profession* (Cambridge: Cambridge University Press, 1988).
49. For surveys that stress this disciplinary fragmentation, see Georg Iggers, *Historiography in the Twentieth Century: From Scientific Objectivity to the Postmodern Challenge* (Middletown: Wesleyan University Press, 1997); Ernst Breisach, *On the Future of History: The Postmodernist Challenge and Its Aftermath* (Chicago: University of Chicago Press, 2003).
50. On the concept of 'historical experience,' see Martin Jay, *Songs of Experience: Modern American and European Variations on a Universal Theme* (Berkeley: University of California Press, 2005), Chap. 6.
51. Margaret MacMillan, *Dangerous Games: The Uses and Abuses of History* (New York: Modern Library, 2009), ix–x.
52. Much of twentieth-century philosophy, from Hegel to phenomenology, was preoccupied with the 'historicity' of human experience—its quality of being historical.
53. Piketty, *Capital and Ideology*, 12.
54. MacMillan, *Dangerous Games*, 144.

Chapter 2. The First Third Worlds

1. Nick Cullather, *The Hungry World: America's Cold War Battle Against Poverty in Asia* (Cambridge: Harvard University Press, 2010), 45.
2. Paul Streeten, "The Use and Abuse of Models in Development Planning," in Streeten, *The Frontiers of Development Studies* (London: Macmillan, 1972/1967), 52–70.
3. Timothy Mitchell, "Fixing the Economy," *Cultural Studies* 12:1 (1998), 82. For the ways that the newly coined national 'economy' shaped politics and development, see Mitchell, *Rule of Experts: Egypt, Techno-Politics, Modernity* (Berkeley: University of California Press, 2002); and Alden Young, *Transforming Sudan: Decolonization, Economic Development, and State Formation* (Cambridge: Cambridge University Press, 2018).
4. Marion Fourcade, cited in Matthias Schmelzer, *The Hegemony of Growth: The OECD and the Making of the Economic Growth Paradigm* (Cambridge: Cambridge

University Press, 2016), 23. On the prominence of economists in the West, see Fourcade, *Economists and Societies: Discipline and Profession in the United States, Britain, and France, 1890s to 1990s* (Princeton: Princeton University Press, 2009); and Stephanie Mudge, *Leftism Reinvented: Western Parties from Socialism to Neoliberalism* (Cambridge: Harvard University Press, 2018). On the century's quantophilia, see Theodore Porter, *Trust in Numbers: The Pursuit of Objectivity in Science and Public Life* (Princeton: Princeton University Press, 1995).

5. In addition to Schmelzer, *The Hegemony of Growth*, see Daniel Speich Chassé, *Die Erfindung des Bruttosozialprodukts: Globale Ungleichheit in der Wissenschaftsgeschichte der Ökonomie* (Göttingen: Vandenhoeck & Ruprecht, 2013); and Moshe Syrquin, "Quantifying Economic Development: Kuznets, Chenery, and the Quantitative Approach to Development Economics," *History of Political Economy* 50 (2018), 211–30. On the history of national accounts, see André Vanoli, *A History of National Accounting* (Amsterdam: IOS Press, 2005); Paul Studenski, *The Income of Nations: Theory, Measurement, and Analysis: Past and Present: A Study in Applied Economics and Statistics* (New York: NYU Press, 1958); and Zoltan Kenessey, "The Genesis of National Accounts: An Overview," in Kenessey, ed., *The Accounts of Nations* (Amsterdam: IOS Press, 1994), 1–15.

6. Keynesian theory typically emphasized short-term interventions to moderate economic business cycles. Harrod and Domar extended this framework to long-term growth by accounting for the savings and investment needed to promote capital expansion. For a still-valuable summary of the model and its significance, see Gerald Meier and Robert Baldwin, *Economic Development: Theory, History, Policy* (New York: John Wiley & Sons, 1957), 100–118. On its complex adoption by development economists, see Mauro Boianovsky, "Beyond Capital Fundamentalism: Harrod, Domar and the History of Development Economics," *Cambridge Journal of Economics* 42 (2018), 477–504. Hollis Chenery's two-gap model, a related formula, taught that development was impeded by gaps in the savings and foreign exchange rates, both of which foreign aid could fill. Chenery and Michael Bruno, "Development Alternatives in an Open Economy: The Case of Israel," *Economic Journal* 72:285 (1962), 79–103.

7. Preface to Hoselitz, ed., *The Progress of Underdeveloped Areas* (Chicago: University of Chicago Press, 1952), vii.

8. Schmelzer, *The Hegemony of Growth*, 97–98.

9. Marcel Boumans and Neil de Marchi. "Models, Measurement, and 'Universal Patterns': Jan Tinbergen and Development Planning without Theory," *History of Political Economy* 50 (2018), 233.

10. On similar recent problems, see Morton Jerven, *Poor Numbers: How We Are Misled by African Development Statistics and What to Do about It* (Ithaca: Cornell University Press, 2013).

11. Colin Clark, *The Conditions of Economic Progress* (London: Macmillan, 1940). On Clark's impact, see Chassé, *Erfindung*, 41–135. For his self-reflection, see Clark, "Development Economics: The Early Years," in Gerald Meier and Dudley Seers, eds., *Pioneers in Development* (New York: Oxford University Press, 1984), 57–77.

12. Phyllis Deane, *Colonial Social Accounting* (London: Cambridge University Press, 1953), 8–9. On Deane's time at the Rhodes-Livingstone Institute, see Lyn Schumaker, *Africanizing Anthropology: Fieldwork, Networks, and the Making of Cultural Knowledge in Central Africa* (Durham: Duke University Press, 2001), 104–07.
13. Deane, *Colonial Social Accounting,* 208–09.
14. Deane, *Colonial Social Accounting,* 2. On the fraught nature of Deane's project, see William O. Jones, "Colonial Social Accounting," *Journal of the American Statistical Association* 50:271 (September 1955), 665–76.
15. Judy Klein, *Statistical Visions in Time: A History of Time Series Analysis, 1662–1938* (Cambridge: Cambridge University Press, 1997), 1. In *Capital in the Twenty-First Century* (Cambridge: Harvard University Press, 2014), Thomas Piketty dismisses as "childish" the economist's "passion for mathematics and for purely theoretical and often highly ideological speculation, at the expense of historical research and collaboration with the other social sciences" (41).
16. Sun Yat-Sen, *The International Development of China* (New York: Putnam, 1922). See also Eric Helleiner, "Sun Yat-Sen as a Pioneer of International Development," *History of Political Economy* 50 (2018), 76–93.
17. H. W. Arndt, *Economic Development: The History of an Idea* (Chicago: University of Chicago Press, 1987), 16–17.
18. Michael Cowen and Robert Shenton, *Doctrines of Development* (London: Routledge, 1996); Cowen and Shenton, "The Invention of Development," in Jonathan Crush, ed., *Power of Development* (London: Routledge, 1995), 25–42.
19. Alfred Sauvy, "Trois mondes, une planète," *Observateur* 118 (August 14, 1952), 14. Sauvy's disciple Georges Balandier, director of the Institut National d'Études Démographiques, developed the concept further. See Balandier, ed., *Le "Tiers Monde": Sous-développement et développement* (Paris: Presses Universitaires de France, 1956).
20. Christoph Kalter, *The Discovery of the Third World: Decolonization and the Rise of the New Left in France* (Cambridge: Cambridge University Press, 2016), Chap. 2.
21. Christopher Lee, ed., *Making a World After Empire: The Bandung Moment and Its Political Afterlives* (Athens: Ohio University Press, 2010); Vijay Prashad, *The Darker Nations* (New York: New Press, 2008).
22. Even after 1989, East European economies were seen as distinctive: transition economies rather than developing economies.
23. On the ambiguous term *South-eastern Europe,* the locus classicus is Maria Todorova, *Imagining the Balkans* (New York: Oxford University Press, 1997), esp. 21–37.
24. Michele Alacevich makes a similar argument in his excellent essay "Planning Peace: The European Roots of the Post-War Global Development Challenge," *Past and Present* 239 (May 2018), 219–64. Robert E. Wood called Eastern Europe the "first Third World" in the context of intra-European trade relations. Wood, "From the Marshall Plan to the Third World," in Melvin P. Leffler and David S. Painter, eds., *The Origins of the Cold War: An International History* (New York: Routledge, 1994), 241. See also Wood, *From Marshall Plan to the Debt Crisis: Foreign Aid and Development Choices in the World Economy* (Berkeley: University of California Press, 1986), 31; Gavin Kitching, *Development and Underdevelopment in Historical Per-*

spective: Populism, Nationalism, and Industrialization (London: Routledge, 1982); Joseph Love, *Crafting the Third World: Theorizing Underdevelopment in Rumania and Brazil* (Palo Alto: Stanford University Press, 1996); James Warner and Kenneth Jameson, "The Role of Eastern Europe in Development Economics' History," *History of Economics Review* 39:1 (2004), 65–87; and Eric Helleiner, *Forgotten Foundations of Bretton Woods: International Development and the Making of the Postwar Order* (Ithaca: Cornell University Press, 2014).

25. Matthew Connelly, *Fatal Misconception: The Struggle to Control World Population* (Cambridge: Harvard University Press, 2008), Chap. 4.
26. Joseph Morgan Hodge, *Triumph of the Expert: Agrarian Doctrines of Development and the Legacies of British Colonialism* (Athens: Ohio University Press, 2009).
27. Arndt, "Development Economics before 1945," in Jagdish Bhagwati and Richard S. Eckaus, eds., *Development and Planning: Essays in Honour of Paul Rosenstein Rodan* (Cambridge: MIT Press, 1973), 17. For aid critic Harry Johnson, this Central European influence was baleful, bequeathing a legacy of protectionism and state intervention. Johnson, "The Ideology of Economic Policy in the New States," in Johnson, ed., *Economic Nationalism in Old and New States* (Chicago: University of Chicago Press, 1967), 124–41.
28. According to Walt Rostow, Rosenstein-Rodan kept his Viennese "style" throughout his life, long after becoming a British citizen at age twenty-eight. Rostow, *Theorists of Economic Growth from David Hume to the Present* (New York: Oxford University Press, 1990), 408. Some of this, Quinn Slobodian hazards, might speak to Central European nostalgia for Austria-Hungary, treating "Danubia" as a natural economic and cultural unit whose postimperial fragmentation had to be overcome. Slobodian, *Globalists: The End of Empire and the Birth of Neoliberalism* (Cambridge: Harvard University Press, 2018), 48, 68–69, 75, 93.
29. Connelly, *Fatal Misconception*, Chaps. 2 and 3. On the relation between refugees and concerns for Europe's population excess, see Mark Mazower, *No Enchanted Palace: The End of Empire and the Ideological Origins of the United Nations* (Princeton: Princeton University Press, 2009), 109–11.
30. John Connelly, *From Peoples into Nations: A History of Eastern Europe* (Princeton: Princeton University Press, 2020), Parts II and III.
31. Kitching, *Development and Underdevelopment in Historical Perspective*, 59–60.
32. Stanisław Szczepanowski, *Nędza Galicyi w cyfrach i program energicznego rozwoju gospodarstwa krajowego* (Lwów: Drukarnia Pillerów i Spólki, 1888). On Szczepanowski, see Alison Fleig Frank, *Oil Empire: Visions of Prosperity in Austrian Galicia* (Cambridge: Harvard University Press, 2005), 75–108.
33. In addition to Love, *Crafting the Third World*, see Tara Zahra, *Mass Migration from Eastern Europe and the Making of the Free World* (New York: Norton, 2017).
34. Jacek Kochanowicz, "La teoria de Chayanov y el punto de vista polaco respecto a la economia campesina," Manuscript, 1988. What distinguished Polish concerns from those of turn-of-the-century Russians was the question of population. Russian theorists, particularly Alexander Chayanov, proposed a distinctive model of peasant farming in thinly populated regions. Their Central European counterparts

were concerned about rural development in areas with surplus manpower. On Russian debates about agrarian reform, see Yanni Kotsonis, *Making Peasants Backward: Agricultural Cooperatives and the Agrarian Question in Russia, 1861–1914* (New York: St. Martin's, 1999); George Yaney, *The Urge to Mobilize: Agrarian Reform in Russia, 1861–1930* (Urbana: University of Illinois Press, 1982); Teodor Shanin, *The Awkward Class: Political Sociology of Peasantry in a Developing Society: Russia 1910–1925* (London: Oxford University Press, 1972); Shanin, *Russia as a 'Developing Society': The Roots of Otherness: Russia's Turn of the Century* (New Haven: Yale University Press, 1985); and Franco Venturi, *Roots of Revolution: A History of Populist and Socialist Movements in Nineteenth-Century Russia* (Chicago: University of Chicago Press, 1983). I thank Colleen Moore for directing me to this literature.

35. Józef Poniatowski, "Polska rolnicza czy przemysłowa?" *Gospodarka narodowa* 8 (1931), 115. The quotations come from Anna Jarosz-Nojszewska, "Józef Maria Poniatowski i 'Gospodarka Narodowa,'" *Gospodarka narodowa* 5–6 (2011), 123–39.
36. Poniatowski, *Przeludnienie wsi i rolnictwa* (Warsaw: Towarzystwo Oświaty Rolniczej, 1936), 76, 60.
37. Wincenty Styś, *Wpływ uprzemysłowienia na ustrój rolnej* (Lwów: Towarzystwo Naukowe, 1936). On Styś, see P. Skwarczyński, R. F. Leslie, and Doreen Warriner, "Wincenty Styś: A Memoir," *Slavonic and East European Review* 39:93 (1961), 313–26. See also the work of Jan Piekałkiewicz, Bohdan Dederko, Stanisław Antoniewski, and the economists connected with the journals *Gospodarka narodowa* and *Rolnictwa* (Agriculture); and the retrospective analysis by the interwar minister of rural reform, Witold Staniewicz, "The Agrarian Problem in Poland between the Two World Wars," *Slavonic and East European Review* 43:100 (December 1964), 23–33.
38. Małgorzata Mazurek, "Measuring Development: An Intellectual and Political History of Ludwik Landau's Scale of World Inequality," *Contemporary European History* 28:2 (2019), 2, 9; Landau, *Gospodarka światowa: Produkcja i dochód społeczny w liczbach* (Warsaw: Instytut Gospodarstwo Społecznego, 1939).
39. Mazurek, "Measuring Development," 14, 15.
40. Paul Lamartine Yates and Doreen Warriner, *Food and Farming in Post-War Europe* (London: Oxford University Press, 1943), 48, 52, 53. Her best-known work was *Economics of Peasant Farming* (London: Frank Cass, 1939).
41. Mazurek, "Measuring Development," 9.
42. Mazurek, "Polish Economists in Nehru's India: Making Science for the Third World in an Era of De-Stalinization and Decolonization," *Slavic Review* 77:3 (Fall 2018), 588–610. Kalecki's essays on development are compiled in English as Kalecki, *Essays on Developing Economies* (Sussex: Harvester, 1976; *The Collected Works of Michał Kalecki*, vol. 5 (Oxford: Clarendon Press, 1993). On Kalecki, see George R. Feiwel, *The Intellectual Capital of Michał Kalecki: A Study in Economic Theory and Policy* (Knoxville: University of Tennessee Press, 1975); Ignacy Sachs, "Kalecki and Development Planning," in Malcolm C. Sawyer, ed., *The Legacy of Michal Kalecki*, vol. 2 (Cheltenham, UK: Elgar, 1999); Zofia Dobrska, "M. Kalecki on the Developing Economies of the Third World," in *Collected Works*, vol. 5, 237–46; and Jan Toporowski's two-volume *Michał Kalecki: An Intellectual Biography* (London: Pal-

grave Macmillan, 2013/2018). In a parallel genealogy, Joseph Love (*Crafting the Third World*, 92–93) has shown how the Romanian Mihail Manoilescu's works influenced later Latin American structuralist economics.

43. Larry Wolff, *Inventing Eastern Europe* (Palo Alto: Stanford University Press, 1994), 9. The historian L. S. Stavrianos, also describing the early modern period, wrote: "The Third World is commonly thought of as comprising overseas territories, yet it made its first appearance in Eastern Europe." Stavrianos, *Global Rift: The Third World Comes of Age* (New York: William Morrow, 1981), 62.
44. Wallerstein, *The Modern World-System: Capitalist Agriculture and the Origins of the European World-Economy in the Sixteenth Century* (New York: Academic Press, 1974), esp. Chap. 2.
45. Nils Gilman, *Mandarins of the Future: Modernization Theory in Cold War America* (Baltimore: Johns Hopkins University Press, 2003), 30–31. Before Ataturk, Emily Greble shows, European concepts of modernization had an anti-Muslim inflection, with Balkan Muslims labeled as backward—an unhappy turnabout for a group considered elite in recent Ottoman times. Greble, *Muslims and the Making of Modern Europe* (New York: Oxford University Press, 2021).
46. Alexander Gerschenkron, *Bread and Democracy in Germany* (Ithaca: Cornell University Press, 1989/1943). See also Gerschenkron, "The Rate of Growth in Russia: The Rate of Industrial Growth in Russia since 1885," *Journal of Economic History* 7 (1947), 144–74.
47. The only scholarly biography to date is Alacevich, "Paul Rosenstein-Rodan and the Birth of Development Economics," *History of Political Economy* 53:5 (2021), 857–92.
48. Alacevich, "Planning Peace," 229–33. On Chatham House history, see Andrew Bosco and Cornelia Navari, eds., *Chatham House and British Foreign Policy: The Royal Institute of International Affairs during the Inter-War Period* (London: Lothian, 1994).
49. Helen Tilley, *Africa as a Living Laboratory: Empire, Development, and the Problem of Scientific Knowledge, 1870–1950* (Chicago: University of Chicago Press, 2011), 70, 72, 98–99.
50. On the various British institutes and think tanks concerned with East European development during the war, see Helleiner, *Forgotten Foundations*, 212–13, 236–43.
51. P. N. Rosenstein-Rodan, "Problems of Industrialisation in Eastern and South-Eastern Europe," *Economic Journal* 53:210/211 (June–September 1943), 202.
52. Rosenstein-Rodan, "Problems," 208.
53. David Engerman, *Modernization from the Other Shore: American Intellectuals and the Romance of Russian Development* (Cambridge: Harvard University Press, 2003).
54. Wood, "From the Marshall Plan to the Third World," 243–44.
55. The term came from a paper he delivered in Rio de Janeiro in 1957. Rosenstein-Rodan, "Notes on the Theory of the 'Big Push,'" in Howard Ellis and Henry Wallich, eds., *Economic Development for Latin America: Proceedings of a Conference Held by the International Economic Association* (London, Palgrave Macmillan, 1957), 57–81. An American economist who spent his last years at the London School of

Economics, Young delivered his most famous statement on increasing returns in 1928 as a presidential address before the British Association. Young, "Increasing Returns and Economic Progress," *Economic Journal* 38:152 (December 1928), 527–42. Although he died the following year, his idea circulated in the institutions that Rosenstein-Rodan later joined. For a biography, see Charles P. Blitch, *Allyn Young: The Peripatetic Economist* (New York: St. Martin's, 1995). For a contextualization of the increasing returns thesis, see Colin Clark, *Population Growth and Land Use* (London: Macmillan, 1967), 253–57.

56. Karl Polanyi, *The Great Transformation: The Political and Economic Origins of Our Time* (Boston: Beacon, 2001/1944).
57. Rosenstein-Rodan, "Problems," 210.
58. Rosenstein-Rodan, "Problems," 209. The example of cereals might have come straight from Poland's interwar crop register.
59. Rosenstein-Rodan, "Problems," 203.
60. Rosenstein-Rodan, "Problems," 206.
61. Rosenstein-Rodan, "Problems," 204.
62. Rosenstein-Rodan, "Problems," 206, 208.
63. Rosenstein-Rodan, "The International Development of Economically Backward Areas," *International Affairs* 20:2 (April 1944), 158–59.
64. Rosenstein-Rodan, "International Development," 159.
65. Rosenstein-Rodan, "International Development," 162–63.
66. Rosenstein-Rodan, "International Development," 164. In a 1984 retrospective, he insisted that "Eastern and Southeastern Europe were selected as a model not because of any special interest in those countries, but because their governments in exile were in London and because Eastern and Southeastern Europe . . . constitute a group of similar but not identical models." Rosenstein-Rodan, "Natura Facit Saltum: Analysis of the Disequilibrium Growth Process," in Meier and Seers, eds., *Pioneers in Development*, 207. As Alacevich, "Paul Rosenstein-Rodan," 866, notes, this demurral must be taken with a grain of salt.
67. Antonín Basch, "European Economic Regionalism," *American Economic Review* 33 (1943), 414. In exile from 1940, Basch was part of a University of California, Berkeley–based circle of thinkers (which also included Gerschenkron and Hirschman) surrounding the New Zealand economist John B. Condliffe. On Condliffe's circle, see Alacevich, *Albert O. Hirschman: An Intellectual Biography* (New York: Columbia University Press, 2021), 33–35. On Basch's life, see the obituary "Antonín Basch: World Bank Aide," *New York Times* (March 19, 1971), 43.
68. Basch, "European Economic Regionalism," 408, 410, 415 (italics in original). Basch also urged regional integration as a step toward "world trade." He was particularly troubled by the ill-fated experiments with "protectionism" and "autarchy," which made Eastern Europe an appendage of the German economy.
69. Political and Economic Planning (PEP), *Economic Development in S.E. Europe, including Poland, Czechoslovakia, Austria, Hungary, Roumania, Yugoslavia, Bulgaria, and Greece* (London: PEP, 1945).
70. On Mandelbaum, see "'I am the same but . . .': A Portrait of the Economist Kurt

Mandelbaum Based on an Interview with Matthias Greffrath," *Development and Change* 10:4 (1979), 506–07; and E. V. K. FitzGerald, "Kurt Mandelbaum and the Classical Tradition in Development Theory," in Kurt Martin, ed., *Strategies of Economic Development: Readings in the Political Economy of Industrialization* (New York: St. Martin's, 1991).

71. Martin Jay, "Kurt Mandelbaum: His Decade at the Institute of Social Research," *Development and Change* 10:4 (1979), 545–52.
72. Mandelbaum, *The Industrialisation of Backward Areas* (Oxford: Blackwell, 1945), 1. See also, Hans Singer, "A Generation Later: Kurt Mandelbaum's *The Industrialisation of Backward Areas* Revisited," *Development and Change* 10:4 (1979), 577–84.
73. Mandelbaum, *Industrialisation*, 1–2. In addition, Eastern Europe, China, and India all lacked natural resources commensurate with their population sizes.
74. Uniquely, Mandelbaum proposed four different models to accommodate regional variation.
75. The league was based in Geneva until 1940, then in Princeton, New Jersey. On Nurkse, see Rainer Kattel, Jan A. Kregel, and Erik S. Reinert, eds. *Ragnar Nurkse (1907–2007): Classical Development Economics and its Relevance for Today* (London: Anthem, 2009).
76. League of Nations, *International Currency Experience: Lessons of the Inter-War Period* (Geneva: League of Nations, 1944); Ragnar Nurkse, "Conditions of International Monetary Equilibrium," *Essays in International Finance,* No. 4 (Princeton: Princeton University Press, Spring 1945).
77. Patricia Clavin, *Securing the World Economy: The Reinvention of the League of Nations, 1920–1946* (Oxford: Oxford University Press, 2013), 313.
78. League of Nations, *International Currency Experience*, 198–99.
79. Nurkse, "Conditions," 16.
80. Nurkse, "Conditions," 17.
81. Nurkse, *Problems of Capital Formation in Underdeveloped Countries* (New York: Oxford University Press, 1955), 32. See also Nurkse, "Growth in Underdeveloped Countries [1952]," in Kattel et al., eds., *Ragnar Nurkse: Trade and Development* (London: Anthem, 2009), 85–97.
82. Nurkse, "Conditions," 12. For a reflection on the relation between balanced growth and comparative advantage, see Nurkse, "The Conflict between 'Balanced Growth' and International Specialization," in Nurkse, *Equilibrium and Growth in the World Economy: Economic Essays* (Cambridge: Harvard University Press, 1961), 241–59. The place of Ricardian comparative advantage in early development economics is complicated. While many economists agreed that Eastern Europe should focus on producing light manufactures, they also advocated for diversified domestic industries that could generate local demand, violating strict Ricardian advice to specialize based on comparative advantage. The importance for growth of a variegated industrial base necessitated the adjustment of classical economic principles.
83. Hirschman, *The Strategy of Economic Development* (New Haven: Yale University Press, 1958); and Alacevich, *The Political Economy of the World Bank: The Early*

Years (Stanford: Stanford University Press, 2009), 66–76. Two biographies of Hirschman have recently appeared: Jeremy Adelman, *Worldly Philosopher: The Odyssey of Albert O. Hirschman* (Princeton: Princeton University Press, 2013); and Alacevich, *Albert O. Hirschman: An Intellectual Biography* (New York: Columbia University Press, 2021).

84. Ignacy Sachs, *La découverte du Tiers Monde* (Paris: Flammarion, 1971), 132. Sachs made his mark in Brazil, where he lived from 1941 to 1953. On Sachs's Polish background and midcentury work in India, see Mazurek, "Polish Economists in Nehru's India," 600–604.
85. Greffrath, "'I am the same but . . . ,'" 511–12; FitzGerald, "Kurt Mandelbaum," 11.
86. Meier and Seers, eds., *Pioneers in Development*, 205–26.
87. Even as the Bank touted its apolitical credentials, it made clear its commitment to "economic development along capitalist lines, specifically following the model of the United States." Amy Staples, *The Birth of Development: How the World Bank, Food and Agriculture Organization, and World Health Organization Changed the World, 1945–1965* (Kent, OH: Kent State University Press, 2006), 8, 38, Chap. 3. On the evolution of Bank thinking, see Edward Mason and Robert Asher, *The World Bank since Bretton Woods* (Washington, DC: Brookings Institution Press, 1973). For a more critical account, see Alacevich, *The Political Economy of the World Bank: The Early Years* (Stanford: Stanford University Press, 2009).
88. Rosenstein-Rodan, "International Aid for Underdeveloped Countries," *Review of Economics and Statistics* 43:2 (May 1961), 108–09; Gilman, *Mandarins*, 164–65.
89. Alacevich, "Theory and Practice in Development Economics," in Roger E. Backhouse and Béatrice Cherrier, eds., *The Age of the Applied Economist: The Transformation of Economics since the 1970s* (Durham: Duke University Press, 2017), 269.
90. Corinna Unger, *International Development: A Postwar History* (London: Bloomsbury, 2018), 84.
91. Alacevich, "Paul Rosenstein-Rodan," 869–72.
92. Rosenstein-Rodan, "Disguised Unemployment and Under-Employment."
93. Alacevich, "Planning Peace," 224–25, 246.
94. For two recent biographies, see Robert Tignor, *W. Arthur Lewis and the Birth of Development Economics* (Princeton: Princeton University Press, 2006); and Barbara Ingham and Paul Mosley, *Sir Arthur Lewis: A Biography* (Hampshire: Palgrave Macmillan, 2013). See also Denis M. Benn, *The Caribbean: An Intellectual History, 1774–2003* (Kingston: Ian Randle, 2004), Chap. 4; and Gerald Meier, *Biography of a Subject: An Evolution of Development Economics* (Oxford: Oxford University Press, 2005), Chaps. 4 and 5 and Appendix A.
95. W. A. Lewis, "Economic Development with Unlimited Supplies of Labour," *The Manchester School* 22:2 (May 1954), 140.
96. Lewis, "Unlimited Supplies," 145, 152.
97. Lewis, "Unlimited Supplies," 157. On the classical foundations of this model, see Boianovsky, "When the History of Ideas Meets Theory: Arthur Lewis and the Classical Economists on Development," *History of Political Economy* 50 (2018), 172–

90; Boianovsky, "Arthur Lewis and the Classical Foundations of Development Economics," *Research in the History of Economic Thought and Methodology* 37 (2019), 1–57.

98. Lewis, "Unlimited Supplies," 155, 157, 175, 190.
99. For retrospective assessments, see Colin Kirkpatrick and Armando Barrientos, "The Lewis Model after 50 Years," *The Manchester School* 72:6 (December 2004), 679–90; Gary S. Fields, "Dualism in the Labor Market: A Perspective on the Lewis Model after a Half a Century," *The Manchester School* 72:6 (December 2004), 724–35; and Douglas Gollin, "The Lewis Model: A 60-Year Retrospective," *Journal of Economic Perspectives* 28:3 (Summer 2014), 71–88. For a textbook rendering, see Michael Todaro and Stephen Smith, *Economic Development*, 8th ed. (Boston: Addison Wesley, 2003), 116–21.
100. Mark Figueroa, "W. Arthur Lewis versus the Lewis Model: Agricultural or Industrial Development?" *The Manchester School* 72:6 (December 2004), 736–50.
101. Lewis, "Unlimited Supplies," 175.
102. Lewis, "Unlimited Supplies," 183, 189.
103. Yoichi Mine, "The Political Element in the Works of W. Arthur Lewis: The 1954 Lewis Model and African Development," *Developing Economies* XLIV-3 (September 2006), 329–55.
104. Andrew Downes, "Arthur Lewis and Industrial Development in the Caribbean: An Assessment," Conference Presentation, University of Manchester, July 6–7, 2004: https://laprimaradice.myblog.it/media/02/02/776508438.pdf, 3. See also Ray Kiely, *The Politics of Labour and Development in Trinidad* (Kingston: University of the West Indies, 1996), 6.
105. Cowen and Shenton, "The Origin and Course of Fabian Colonialism in Africa," *Journal of Historical Sociology* 4:2 (June 1991), 143–74.
106. *West India Royal Commission Report* (London: Her Majesty's Stationery Office, 1945), 426. The Moyne Commission report was published in full in 1945, but an abridged version of its initial findings appeared in 1939.
107. Eric Williams, *The Negro in the Caribbean* (Buffalo, NY: EWorld, 2012/1942), 46–56. On Williams, see Colin A. Palmer, *Eric Williams and the Making of the Modern Caribbean* (Chapel Hill: University of North Carolina Press, 2006); and Maurice St. Pierre, *Eric Williams and the Anticolonial Tradition* (Charlottesville: University of Virginia Press, 2015).
108. Tignor, *W. Arthur Lewis*, 45.
109. Lewis, *Labour in the West Indies: The Birth of a Workers' Movement* (London: New Beacon, 1977/1939), 46. On Lewis's responses to the Moyne Commission report, see Tignor, *W. Arthur Lewis*, 44–47.
110. Susan Craig, "The Germs of an Idea," in Lewis, *Labour in the West Indies*, 69. Craig meant this critically, arguing that Lewis's model masked its regional and ideological origins in the "value neutrality" of economic analysis. She accused him of perpetuating a neocolonial development program for the Caribbean, in which "international capital" became the "fundamental determinant of the major social and political formations" (81). For other critical accounts by Trinidadian

economists, see Edwin Carrington, "The Post-War Political Economy of Trinidad and Tobago," *New World Quarterly* 4:1 (1967), 130–45; Carrington, "Industrialization by Invitation in Trinidad and Tobago since 1950," in Norman Girvan and O. Jefferson, eds., *Readings in the Political Economy of the Caribbean* (Mona: New World Associates, 1971), 143–50; and Carl Parris, "Capital or Labour? The Decision to Introduce the Industrial Stabilization Act in Trinidad and Tobago," Working Paper No. 11, Institute of Social and Economic Research, University of the West Indies, Jamaica (1976). For a more favorable analysis, see Terrence Farrell, "Arthur Lewis and the Case for Caribbean Industrialisation," *Social and Economic Studies* 29:4 (December 1980), 52–75.

111. Lewis, "An Economic Plan for Jamaica," *Agenda* 3:4 (1944), 155, 161–62. For the report, see "Report of the Economic Policy Committee" (Kingston: Government Printer, 1945). Report writers felt that "further industrialization will make very little contribution towards solving the employment problem" (31).
112. This anti-imperialism was complicated by numerous factors. While opposing imperialism publicly, the United States recognized that Europe's colonies might help rebuild the continent; thus, it channeled Marshall Plan monies to the imperial peripheries. The USSR was rhetorically anti-imperialist even while claiming European colonies.
113. Tony Martin, "Eric Williams and the Anglo-American Caribbean Commission, 1942–1944," in E. Franklin Frazier and Eric Williams, eds., *The Economic Future of the Caribbean* (Dover, MA, and Washington, DC: Majority Press/Howard University, 2004/1944).
114. Lewis, "The Industrialisation of the British West Indies," *Caribbean Economic Review* 2:1 (1950), 6–7.
115. Lewis, "British West Indies," 16.
116. A. W. Maldonado, *Teodoro Moscoso and Puerto Rico's Operation Bootstrap* (Gainesville: University Press of Florida, 1997). For a summary, see Jan Rogoziński, *A Brief History of the Caribbean* (New York: Plume, 1999), 284–93.
117. Sabine Clarke, *Science at the End of Empire: Experts and the Development of the British Caribbean, 1940–1962* (Manchester: Manchester University Press, 2018), 82–84.
118. Lewis, "Industrial Development in Puerto Rico," *Caribbean Economic Review* 1:1 and 2 (1949), 164–65.
119. Lewis, "Puerto Rico," 175.
120. Lewis, "British West Indies," 34, 36, 40–41, 44–45, 52–53; Clarke, *Science*, 87.
121. Clarke *Science*, 147–49; Williams, *Inward Hunger: The Education of a Prime Minister* (Chicago: University of Chicago Press, 1969), 246. See also St. Pierre, *Eric Williams*, 118–20. Williams led Trinidad and Tobago to full independence in 1962.
122. United Nations, Department of Economic Affairs, "Measures for the Economic Development of Under-Developed Countries" (May 1951), 7, 9.
123. United Nations, "Measures," 59.
124. Lewis, *Aspects of Industrialisation* (Cairo: National Bank of Egypt, 1953), 9–10.

125. Lewis, "Reflections on South-East Asia," *District Bank Review* 104 (December 1952), 11.
126. Lewis, "A Policy for Colonial Africa," in Lewis, Michael Scott, Martin Wight, and Colin Legum, *Attitude to Africa* (Harmondsworth: Penguin, 1951), 70–104. Underpopulated Northern Rhodesia (later Zambia) also required careful planning to boost agriculture *and* develop its copper mines. Lewis, *The Principles of Economic Planning*, 3d ed. (London: Allen & Unwin, 1949/1969), 127.
127. Lewis, *Report on Industrialisation and the Gold Coast* (Accra: Government Printing Department, 1953), 22.
128. Lewis, *Gold Coast*, 2.
129. Tignor, *W. Arthur Lewis*, 123–27.
130. Lewis, "Unlimited Labour: Further Notes," *The Manchester School* 26:1 (1958), 1–32; Lewis, "Reflections on Unlimited Labour," Discussion Paper No. 5, Woodrow Wilson Center, Princeton University (October 1969), 1–47.
131. Lewis, "Unlimited Labour: Further Notes," 23.
132. P. T. Bauer, "Lewis' Theory of Economic Growth," in Bauer, *Dissent on Development: Studies and Debates in Development Economics* (Cambridge: Harvard University Press, 1972/1956), 436–37.
133. John Fei and Gustav Ranis, "Innovation, Capital Accumulation, and Economic Development," *American Economic Review* 53:3 (June 1963), 283–313; Fei and Ranis, *Development of the Labor Surplus Economy: Theory and Policy* (Homewood, IL: Richard D. Irwin, 1964). See also Gustav Ranis, "Arthur Lewis's Contribution to Development Thinking and Policy," *The Manchester School* 72:6 (December 2004), 712–23. They did state that their work pertained to only one, albeit quite prevalent, type of economy—the "labor surplus type." *Development of the Labor Surplus Economy*, vii, 3.
134. P. T. Bauer and Basil Yamey, *The Economics of Under-developed Countries* (Chicago: University of Chicago Press, 1957); Bauer and Yamey, "Economic Progress and Occupational Distribution," *Economic Journal* 61:244 (December 1951), 741–55. See also Bauer, *The Rubber Industry: A Study in Competition and Monopoly* (Cambridge: Harvard University Press, 1948); Bauer, *West African Trade: A Study of Competition, Oligopoly and Monopoly in a Changing Economy* (London: Routledge and Kegan Paul, 1954). For a retrospective on his early studies, see Bauer, "Remembrance of Studies Past: Retracing First Steps," in Bauer, *Reality and Rhetoric: Studies in the Economics of Development* (Cambridge: Harvard University Press, 1984), 1–18. On Bauer's early career, see Keith Tribe, "The Colonial Office and British Development Economics, 1940–60," *History of Political Economy* 50 (2018), 97–113.
135. Sol Tax, *Penny Capitalism: A Guatemalan Indian Economy* (Chicago: University of Chicago Press, 1963/1953), x. The book helped to pioneer economic anthropology; on this subfield, see Robert Hinshaw, ed., *Currents in Anthropology: Essays in Honor of Sol Tax* (The Hague: Mouton, 1979).
136. Tax, *Penny Capitalism*, ix.
137. Ironically, the two men went on to share the 1979 Nobel Prize in Economics.

138. Schultz, *Transforming Traditional Agriculture* (New Haven: Yale University Press, 1964), 57–59.
139. Schultz (*Transforming Traditional Agriculture,* 48–49) cited Bauer for this claim. Schultz's analysis of Senapur drew on the agricultural economist W. David Hopper's analysis in "The Economic Organization of a Village in North-Central India," Ph.D. diss., Cornell University (June 1957). See the interview with W. Dennis Hopper, World Bank Group Archives, Oral History Program (Washington, DC, April 2 and May 12, 2004), 5–13.
140. Schultz, *Transforming Traditional Agriculture,* 49.
141. Schultz, *Transforming Traditional Agriculture,* 131.
142. Schultz, *Transforming Traditional Agriculture,* 176. See also, Schultz, *Investment in Human Capital: The Role of Education and of Research* (New York: Free Press, 1971).
143. Hla Myint, *The Economics of Developing Countries* (London: Hutchinson, 1964), 91. On Myint, see Sean Turnell, "Sayagyi and Sage: Hla Myint, Myanmar's 'Classical' Economist," *Sojourn: Journal of Social Issues in Southeast Asia* 29:3 (November 2014), 691–720.
144. Myint, *Economics,* 92–101.
145. Myint, *Economics,* 14.
146. Myint, "The "Classical Theory" of International Trade and the Underdeveloped Countries," *Economic Journal* 68:270 (June 1958), 317–37.
147. Myint, *Economics,* 51 (italics in original). Myint cited rice production in his own homeland and the cocoa exports described in Lewis's Gold Coast report.
148. Myint, *Economic Theory and the Underdeveloped Countries* (London: Oxford University Press, 1971), 21, 26. See also Myint, *Economics,* 21.
149. Myint, *Economic Theory,* 22–24.
150. For his own self-assessment, see Myint, "The Neoclassical Resurgence in Development Economics: Its Strength and Limitations," in Meier, ed., *Pioneers in Development,* 2d ser. (Washington, DC: World Bank, 1987), 107–36.
151. This generalization was paired with an equally dubious leap from Western experience. John Kenneth Galbraith, *Economic Development in Perspective* (Cambridge: Harvard University Press, 1962), 10–12.
152. Edward Mason, *Economic Planning in Underdeveloped Countries: Government and Business* (New York: Fordham University Press, 1958), esp. 5–7. See also Mason and Robert Asher, *The World Bank since Bretton Woods* (Washington, DC: Brookings Institution Press, 1973).

Chapter 3. A Thousand Valleys

1. For another marker of size, Charles Maier noted that the ERP comprised about 2% of U.S. GNP, making it the largest "voluntary transfer of resources from one country to another since World War II." Maier, ed., *The Marshall Plan and Germany: West German Development within the Framework of the European Recovery Program* (New York: Berg, 1991), 36. Whether the Marshall Plan rescued Europe or played a lesser role in its recovery is a debate of long standing.

2. See, for example, Vernon Ruttan, *United States Development Assistance Policy: The Domestic Politics of Foreign Economic Aid* (Baltimore: Johns Hopkins University Press, 1996); Sara Lorenzini, *Global Development: A Cold War History* (Princeton: Princeton University Press, 2019); and Corinna Unger, *International Development: A Postwar History* (London: Bloomsbury, 2018).
3. Michael Hogan, *The Marshall Plan: America, Britain, and the Reconstruction of Western Europe, 1947–1952* (Cambridge: Cambridge University Press, 1987), 19.
4. Michael Holm, *The Marshall Plan: A New Deal For Europe* (New York: Routledge, 2017), xxvii.
5. Charles Maier, "The Politics of Productivity: Foundations of American International Economic Policy after World War II," *International Organization* 43:4 (Autumn 1977), 607–33.
6. Stephen Rabe, "Controlling Revolutions: Latin America, the Alliance for Progress, and Cold War Anti-Communism," in Thomas Peterson, ed., *Kennedy's Quest for Victory: American Foreign Policy, 1961–1963* (Oxford: Oxford University Press, 1989), 112.
7. Barbara Ward, *The Rich Nations and the Poor Nations* (New York: Norton, 1962), 149.
8. For recent invocations, see Benn Steil, *The Marshall Plan: Dawn of the Cold War* (New York: Simon & Schuster, 2018), 373–74.
9. John Chasteen, *Born of Blood and Fire: A Concise History of Latin America*, 2nd ed. (New York: Norton, 2006), 257, 281. On U.S.–Latin America wartime collaboration, see Eric Helleiner, *Forgotten Foundations of Bretton Woods: International Development and the Making of the Postwar Order* (Ithaca: Cornell University Press, 2014). When the 1960s Alliance for Progress failed to lift the region, social democrats called for a Latin American Marshall Plan in 1981. David Johnson Lee, *The Ends of Modernization: Nicaragua and the United States in the Cold War Era* (Ithaca: Cornell University Press, 2021), 116.
10. Cited in Michele Alacevich, *The Political Economy of the World Bank: The Early Years* (Palo Alto: Stanford University Press, 2009), 12–13.
11. Joseph Morgan Hodge, *Triumph of the Expert: Agrarian Doctrines of Development and the Legacies of British Colonialism* (Athens: Ohio University Press, 2007); Monica van Beusekom, *Negotiating Development: African Farmers and Colonial Experts at the Office du Niger, 1920–1960* (Portsmouth, NH: Heinemann, 2002).
12. The term is from Frederick Lugard, *The Dual Mandate in British Tropical Africa* (London: Frank Cass, 1922). On the use of science and indigenous knowledge to justify colonialism, see Florian Wagner, *Colonial Internationalism and the Governmentality of Empire, 1893–1982* (Cambridge: Cambridge University Press, 2022).
13. Hodge, *Triumph of the Expert*, 256–62; Uma Kothari, "From Colonialism to Development: Reflections of Former Colonial Officers," *Commonwealth & Comparative Politics* 44:1 (March 2006), 118–36.
14. For the phrase "know his natives," see Hodge, *Triumph of the Expert*, 12.
15. James Scott, *Seeing Like a State: How Certain Schemes to Improve the Human Condition Have Failed* (New Haven: Yale University Press, 1998), 228–29; Hodge, *Triumph of the Expert*, 209–14.

16. For the House of Commons inquiry, see https://hansard.millbanksystems.com/commons/1951/mar/13/gambia-poultry-scheme.
17. Grace Carswell, *Cultivating Success in Uganda: Kigezi Farmers and Colonial Policies* (Oxford: James Currey, 2007).
18. Helen Tilley, *Africa as a Living Laboratory: Empire, Development, and the Problem of Scientific Knowledge, 1870–1950* (Chicago: University of Chicago Press, 2011), 5.
19. Van Beusekam, *Negotiating Development.*
20. Hodge, *Triumph of the Expert.*
21. On the Rhodes-Livingstone Institute, see Lyn Schumaker, *Africanizing Anthropology: Fieldwork, Networks, and the Making of Cultural Knowledge in Central Africa* (Durham: Duke University Press, 2001).
22. Suzanne Moon, *Technology and Ethical Idealism: A History of Development in the Netherlands East Indies* (Leiden: CNWS Publications, 2007), 6.
23. Eric Worby, "'Discipline without Oppression': Sequence, Timing, and Marginality in Southern Rhodesia's Post-War Development Regime," *Journal of African History* 41:1 (2000), 101–25.
24. A. Adu Boahen, *African Perspectives on Colonialism* (Baltimore: Johns Hopkins University Press, 1987), 105–06.
25. Van Beusekom and Dorothy Hodgson, "Lessons Learned? Development Experiences in the Late Colonial Period," *Journal of African History* 41:1 (2000), 32.
26. Henry R. Luce, *The American Century* (New York: Farrar & Rinehart, 1941), 77. Writing on the eve of America's entry into war, Luce wondered whether his country would rise to the occasion as the world's "Good Samaritan." Postwar development ambassadors exhibited little doubt.
27. Ever since the Depression, historians have debated the relative impact of various New Deal programs. "Find out what a historian thinks about the New Deal," writes historian Michael Kazin, "and you will quickly find out what they think about the virtues and failures of the liberal state writ large." Kazin, "The Cornerstone: What Is Living and What Is Dead in the New Deal?" *Nation* 313:3 (August 9–16, 2021), 32. In the vast literature on the New Deal, I found Kiran Klaus Patel, *The New Deal: A Global History* (Princeton: Princeton University Press, 2016) particularly useful.
28. On the U.S. decision to embrace global leadership, see Stephen Wertheim, *Tomorrow, the World: The Birth of U.S. Global Supremacy* (Cambridge: Harvard University Press, 2020).
29. Daniel Immerwahr, *Thinking Small: The United States and the Lure of Community Development* (Cambridge: Harvard University Press, 2015), 52–54. On America's smaller, less carefully tended empire, see Immerwahr, *How to Hide an Empire: A History of the Greater United States* (New York: Picador, 2019).
30. Norman Vincent Peale, *Three Complete Books: The Power of Positive Thinking; The Positive Principle Today; Enthusiasm Makes the Difference* (New York: Wings Books, 1994), 414–15, 417, 420–33. Donald Trump is a professed disciple.
31. Peale, *Three Complete Books*, 527, 566, 571.
32. Beth Blum, *The Self-Help Compulsion: Searching for Advice in Modern Literature* (New York: Columbia University Press, 2020), 78–79.

33. Riesman, *The Lonely Crowd: A Study of the Changing American Character* (New Haven: Yale University Press, 1950), 196–99.
34. The era's other sociological classic, similarly anxious, was William Whyte, *The Organization Man* (New York: Simon and Schuster, 1956). For an account of Cold War liberalism as glum and fearful, rather than enthusiastic, see Samuel Moyn, *Liberalism against Itself: Cold War Intellectuals and the Making of our Time* (New Haven: Yale University Press, 2023).
35. David Lilienthal, *T.V.A.: Democracy on the March* (New York: Pocket Books, 1944), x–xi.
36. Lilienthal was chosen by chairman Arthur Morgan. The third member, Harcourt Morgan (no relation), was an agriculturalist.
37. Quoted in David Ekbladh, *The Great American Mission: Modernization and the Construction of an American World Order* (Princeton: Princeton University Press, 2011), 49.
38. Ekbladh, *The Great American Mission*, 53.
39. Ekbladh, *The Great American Mission*, 8.
40. Lilienthal, *T.V.A.*, ix–x, 2–3, 222–24.
41. Lilienthal, *T.V.A.*, 3–6.
42. Herman Pritchett, *The Tennessee Valley Authority: A Study in Public Administration* (Chapel Hill: University of North Carolina Press, 1943), 314, 321–22; Pritchett, "The Power and the Glory," *Virginia Quarterly Review* 20:4 (1944), 621.
43. Lilienthal, *T.V.A.*, 156, 19, 37.
44. *The Journals of David E. Lilienthal*, vol. 1: *The TVA Years, 1939–1945* (New York: Harper & Row, 1964), 471, entry of April 14, 1942. Cited in Maier, "The Politics of Productivity," 615.
45. Lilienthal, *T.V.A.*, 47, 124.
46. Lilienthal, *T.V.A.*, 150, 152, 204.
47. Lilienthal, *T.V.A.*, 80, 82.
48. Lilienthal, *T.V.A.*, 185, 193.
49. Lilienthal, *T.V.A.*, 51, 60, 177.
50. Lilienthal, *T.V.A.*, 209–11.
51. Lilienthal, *T.V.A.*, 227, 231.
52. Daniel Klingensmith, *One Valley in a Thousand: Dams, Nationalism, and Development* (New Delhi: Oxford University Press, 2007), 88.
53. Lilienthal, *T.V.A.*, 223–24.
54. Patel, *The New Deal*, 295.
55. Amy C. Offner, *Sorting Out the Mixed Economy: The Rise and Fall of Welfare and Developmental States in the Americas* (Princeton: Princeton University Press, 2019), Chap. 1.
56. Ekbladh, *The Great American Mission*, 230–34; and James Bill, *The Eagle and the Lion: The Tragedy of American-Iranian Relations* (New Haven: Yale University Press, 1988), Chap. 9. For an ethnography of the Khuzestan Development Program and the Dez Irrigation Project, see Grace Goodell, *The Elementary Structures of Political Life: Rural Development in Pahlavi Iran* (Oxford: Oxford University Press, 1966).

57. Ekbladh, *The Great American Mission*, 212–20.
58. On the Danube hopes, see Julian Huxley, *TVA: Adventure in Planning* (London: Architectural Press, 1943), 135–36. On the TVA as a global reference, see Patel, *The New Deal*, 294–300; and Jordan Schwarz, *The New Dealers: Power Politics in the Age of Roosevelt* (New York: Vintage, 1993), 337–38. For the Helmand quotation, see Patel, *The New Deal*, 295. On the Helmand initiative, see Timothy Nunan, *Humanitarian Invasion: Global Development in Cold War Afghanistan* (Cambridge: Cambridge University Press, 2016), 82–92. On the Kariba Dam, see Julia Tischler, *Light and Power for a Multiracial Nation: The Kariba Dam Scheme in the Central African Federation* (London: Palgrave Macmillan, 2013). See page 216 for the TVA reference. For a Zimbabwean perspective, see Joann McGregor, *Crossing the Zambezi: The Politics of Landscape on a Central African Frontier* (Suffolk: James Currey, 2009), Chap. 6.
59. Christopher Sneddon, *Concrete Revolution: Large Dams, Cold War Geopolitics, and the US Bureau of Reclamation* (Chicago: University of Chicago Press, 2015).
60. The *Cassa*-TVA reference is found in Rita Mascolo, "Tennessee Valley in Southern Italy: How the ENSI project Was the First and Only World Bank Loan for Nuclear Power," *Business History* 10.1080/00076791.2020.1819984 (2020), 5. For a discussion of the Cassa, see Alacevich, "Postwar Development in the Italian Mezzogiorno: Analyses and Policies," *Journal of Modern Italian Studies* 18:1 (2013), 90–112.
61. Wilson Whitman, *God's Valley: People and Power along the Tennessee River* (New York: Viking, 1939). The Dutch journalist Odette Keun, in *A Foreigner Looks at the TVA* (New York: Longmans, Green, 1937), depicted the TVA as a developmental alternative to both left and right totalitarianism. See also the eclectic economist Stuart Chase, author of laudatory works about Soviet planning and Mexican peasant traditions, *Rich Land, Poor Land: A Study of Waste in the Natural Resources of America* (New York: McGraw-Hill, 1936); and G. V. Jacks and R. O. Whyte, *Rape of the Earth: A World Survey of Soil Erosion* (London: Faber and Faber, 1939), 237, which praised the TVA for cultivating a new "blossom" in the Tennessee Valley "desert." For a deflationary fiftieth-anniversary review, see William Chandler, *The Myth of TVA: Conservation and Development in the Tennessee Valley, 1933–1983* (Cambridge, MA: Ballinger, 1984).
62. Herman Finer, *Theory and Practice of Modern Government* (New York: Dial Press, 1932); Finer, *Road to Reaction* (Boston: Little, Brown, 1945).
63. Finer, *The T.V.A.: Lessons for International Application* (Montreal: ILO, 1944), ii.
64. Finer, *T.V.A.*, 18, 113–16, 216–36.
65. Stephen Macekura, "The Point Four Program and U.S. International Development Policy," *Political Science Quarterly* 128:1 (2013), 132–33. The Commager quotation appears in Thomas McCraw, *Morgan vs. Lilienthal: The Feud within the TVA* (Chicago: Loyola University Press, 1970), ix.
66. Schwarz, *The New Dealers*, 337.
67. See the Colonial Development Act of 1940; and financial advisor Sidney Caine's August 16, 1943 memo reproduced in S. R. Ashton and S. E. Stockwell, eds., *Im-*

*perial Policy and Colonial Practice, 1925–1945*mpart 2: *Economic Policy, Social Policies and Colonial Research* (London: HMSO, 1996), 166–71. For the minutes of a 1939 meeting of British colonial officials, in which the TVA was proposed as a model that incorporated local organizations but maintained central oversight, see Ashton and Stockwell, eds., *Imperial Policy and Colonial Practice, 1925–1945*, part 1: *Metropolitan Reorganisation, Defence and International Relations, Political Change and Constitutional Reform* (London: HMSO, 1996), 300–301.

68. Julian Huxley, *TVA: Adventure in Planning*, 7.
69. James Dahir, *Region Building: Community Development Lessons from the Tennessee Valley* (New York: Harper & Brothers, 1955), 158.
70. Immerwahr, *Thinking Small*, 43.
71. Dahir, *Region Building*, 1, 159, 175.
72. Truman Second Inaugural (1949) https://avalon.law.yale.edu/20th_century/truman asp. The literature on Point Four remains rather sparse. The best recent analysis is Stephen Macekura, "The Point Four Program and U.S. International Development Policy," *Political Science Quarterly* 128:1 (2013). See also Sergei Shenin, *The United States and the Third World: The Origins of Postwar Relations and the Point Four Program* (Huntington, NY: Nova Science Publishers, 2000); Vernon Ruttan, *United States Development Assistance Policy: The Domestic Politics of Foreign Economic Aid* (Baltimore: Johns Hopkins University Press, 1996), 49–68; Robert Packenham, *Liberal America and the Third World: Political Development Ideas in Foreign Aid and Social Science* (Princeton: Princeton University Press, 1973), 43–49; and Tarun C. Bose, "The Point Four Programme: A Critical Study," *International Studies* 7:1 (1965), 66–97.
73. Some historians have dismissed this anti-imperial credo, noting that Point Four boosted U.S. policy and economic interests. Gilbert Rist, *The History of Development: From Western Origins to Global Faith* (London: Zed, 2006), Chap. 4.
74. Truman, "Remarks at the Women's National Democratic Club Dinner," November 8 1949, quoted in Ekbladh, *The Great American Mission*, 99. Others, too, saw the TVA as "custom-made for Point Four use." Morris Llewellyn Clerk, "Down to Earth with Point Four," *New Republic* 121 (July 11, 1949), 18–21; cited in Walter M. Daniels, ed., *The Point Four Program* (New York: Wilson, 1951), 114.
75. Macekura, "The Point Four Program," 129, 135–36, 142–43.
76. Douglas Ensminger, the Ford Foundation's India representative, observed that the arrival of former ERP staff shifted Point Four from its small-scale beginnings toward bigger projects. Ensminger, Oral History Interview, 1976: https://www.trumanlibrary.gov/library/oral-histories/esmingr.
77. The funding was even tighter than suggested here: Although Truman requested $45 million and Congress authorized $35 million for FY 1950–51, only $26.9 million was appropriated. In FY 1951/52, the authorization was raised to $125 million; in 1952–53, $155.6 million. Bose, "The Point Four Programme," 85n86. By contrast, the Marshall Plan received $2.25 billion in FY 1950–51, and more than $15 billion over its duration. Paterson, "Foreign Aid under Wraps," 122. For the con-

gressional debates, see Jeffrey Taffet, *Against Aid: A History of Opposition to U.S. Foreign Aid Spending* (New York: Routledge, 2022), 71–77.

78. Macekura, "The Point Four Program," 129.
79. For a longer history of American technical assistance missions, see Merle Curti and Kendall Birr, *Prelude to Point Four: American Technical Missions Overseas, 1838–1938* (Madison: University of Wisconsin Press, 1954).
80. Bose, "The Point Four Programme," 86.
81. Taffet, *Against Aid,* 83–90.
82. For a range of contemporary viewpoints, see Daniels, ed., *The Point Four Program;* and the essays compiled in "Formulating a Point Four Program," *Annals of the American Academy of Political and Social Science* 270 (July 1950).
83. Henry Hazlitt, *Illusions of Point Four* (Irvington-on-Hudson, NY: Foundation for Economic Education, 1950), 7.
84. Herman Olden and Paul Phillips, "The Point Four Program: Promise or Menace," *Science & Society* 16:3 (Summer 1952), 245–46.
85. Thomas Paterson, "Foreign Aid under Wraps," *Wisconsin Magazine of History* 56:2 (1972–73), 123–24.
86. Espy, *Bold New Program* (New York: Bantam, 1950), 3, 17.
87. Espy, *Bold New Program,* 9, and Chaps. 3 and 13. In the 1950s, *Reader's Digest* "regularly promoted private capitalist investment in the developing world as an alternative to taxpayer-funded foreign aid." Christina Klein, "Musicals and Modernization: Rodgers and Hammerstein's *The King and I,*" in David Engerman, Nils Gilman, Mark Haefele, and Michael Latham, eds., *Staging Growth: Modernization, Development, and the Global Cold War* (Amherst: University of Massachusetts Press, 2003), 156–57.
88. Espy, *Bold New Program,* 255.
89. Jonathan Bingham, *Shirt-Sleeve Diplomacy: Point 4 in Action* (New York: John Day, 1953), 3–4, 12, 16. On the last point he seconded historian Arnold Toynbee. "[O]ur age," Toynbee wrote in the "Not the Age of Atoms but of Welfare for All" (*New York Times Magazine* [October 21, 1951], 15, 38, 40), "will be remembered chiefly . . . for its having been the first age since the dawn of civilization . . . in which people dared to think it practicable to make the benefits of civilization available for the whole human race." The essay charts rising aspirations for a better material life and espouses technology as the resource to meet them. "Mankind's hope of better things," Toynbee announces, "lies in a permanent industrial revolution." Despite shared enthusiasm, Bingham chided Toynbee for oversimplifying the complexities of development.
90. Bingham, *Shirt-Sleeve Diplomacy,* Chap. 5.
91. Bingham, *Shirt-Sleeve Diplomacy,* 6. This virtue is embodied in Harry Truman, "an ex-haberdasher from Independence, MO" (15), who launched a program to better the world.
92. Bingham, *Shirt-Sleeve Diplomacy,* 26, 47.
93. Bingham, *Shirt-Sleeve Diplomacy,* 99–100, 202–07.

94. María Josefina Saldaña-Portillo, *The Revolutionary Imagination in the Americas and the Age of Development* (Durham: Duke University Press, 2003), 29.
95. For this traditional Ghanaian quote, see Robert Chambers, ed., *The Volta Resettlement Experience* (New York: Praeger, 1970), 76.
96. Gary Wilder, *Freedom Time: Negritude, Decolonization, and the Future of the World* (Durham: Duke University Press, 2015).
97. Farrell, "Arthur Lewis and the Case for Caribbean Industrialisation," *Social and Economic Studies* 29:4 (December 1980), 52–75.
98. Lewis, "Report on Industrialisation and the Gold Coast" (Accra: Gold Coast Government, 1953).
99. Barbara Ingham and Paul Mosley, *Sir Arthur Lewis: A Biography* (Hampshire: Palgrave Macmillan, 2013), 152. Nkrumah, too, was alert to the need for agricultural reform, establishing Workers' Brigades to provide youth employment and labor for state farms.
100. "In 1951," writes Barbara Ingham, "the Gold Coast produced about one third of the total world output of cocoa, and cocoa constituted two-thirds of the value of total Gold Coast exports." Ingham, "Dudley Seers as a Development Advisor in Ghana and Malta," *IDS Bulletin* 20:3 (1989), 46. On cocoa prices and policies in the 1950s, see Douglas Rimmer, *Staying Poor: Ghana's Political Economy, 1950–1990* (London: Pergamon, 1992), 53–59.
101. Ingham, "Dudley Seers," 43–52.
102. Rimmer, *Staying Poor,* 87.
103. Robert Tignor, *W. Arthur Lewis and the Birth of Development Economics* (Princeton: Princeton University Press, 2006), 169–73; Ingham and Mosley, *Sir Arthur Lewis,* 158–60.
104. Lewis joined a star-studded roster of international economists, which by 1963 including Józef Bognár, Dudley Seers, Albert Hirschman, Nicholas Kaldor, and Osvaldo Sunkel—a key reason why Killick, *Development Economics in Action* (New York: St. Martin's, 1978), saw Ghana's economic failure as an indictment of development economics *tout court.* See also Seers, "Why Visiting Economists Fail," *Journal of Political Economy* 70:4 (August 1962), 325–38, which diagnosed this problem, likely with Lewis in mind.
105. Nkrumah, *Africa Must Unite* (New York: Praeger, 1963), 167. Quoted in Ebere Nwaubani, *The United States and Decolonization in West Africa, 1950–1960* (Rochester: University of Rochester Press, 2001), 164.
106. The quotations are from Nwaubani, *The United States and Decolonization,* 165; and Stephan Miescher and Dzodzi Tsikata, "Hydro-Power and the Promise of Modernity and Development in Ghana: Comparing the Akosombo and Bui Dam Projects," *Ghana Studies* 12–13 (2009–10), 21.
107. Quoted in Tignor, *W. Arthur Lewis,* 199; Ingham and Mosley, *Sir Arthur Lewis,* 153. Nkrumah's advisor Geoffrey Bing, in *Reap the Whirlwind: An Account of Kwame Nkrumah's Ghana from 1950–1966* (London: MacGibbon & Kee, 1968), 392, 442, points out that Nkrumah tended to favor the United States over the former master, Britain. Nwaubani, Chap. 6, details the negotiations that went into building

the dam. On the magnate Henry Kaiser, see Schwarz, *The New Dealers,* Chap. 14. For a criticism of the dam's Preparatory Commission report—as well as Lewis's wariness over rapid industrialization—see the Hungarian-born economist Thomas Balogh, "Time and the Volta—Once More," *West Africa* 40 (September 29–October 6, 1956), 753–54, 775–76.

108. Ingham and Mosley, *Sir Arthur Lewis,* 155, 159.
109. Lewis, "On Assessing a Development Plan," *Economic Bulletin of Ghana* 3:6/7 (July 1959), 6, 8. Quoted in Apter, *Ghana in Transition* (Princeton: Princeton University Press, 1972/1955), 358n42.
110. Lewis, *Politics in West Africa* (New York: Oxford University Press, 1965), 65, 78.
111. Lewis, "On Assessing a Development Plan," 3.
112. As Robert Tignor put it, Nkrumah's leadership has become a "veritable morality play" (*W. Arthur Lewis,* 145). Immediately after the 1966 coup, Bob Fitch and Mary Oppenheimer, *Ghana: End of an Illusion* (New York: Monthly Review Press, 1966), condemned him for not taking a harder socialist line, for adhering to the Lewis plan until 1961, and for failing to break with a colonial development model. Henry Bretton, *Power and Politics in Africa* (Chicago: Aldine, 1973) and Victor Le Vine, *Political Corruption: The Ghana Case* (Stanford: Hoover Institution, 1975) attacked Nkrumah's cronyism and authoritarianism, while Maxwell Owusu, *Uses and Abuses of Political Power: A Case Study of Continuity and Change in the Politics of Ghana* (Chicago: University of Chicago Press, 1970) contended that the one-party state demanded too much economic sacrifice. By contrast, Bing, in *Reap the Whirlwind,* argued that expectations for Ghana were too high and Western financing paltry. He blamed the colonial policy of political and economic balkanization, which Nkrumah tried to reverse, for setting up continental failure. As a reference throughout, I have relied on conversations with David Owusu-Ansah as well as his *Historical Dictionary of Ghana,* 3d ed. (Lanham, MD: Scarecrow, 2005).
113. The best account of the Volta Dam's complex and ambivalent meanings is Stephan Miescher, *A Dam for Africa: Akosombo Stories from Ghana* (Bloomington: Indiana University Press, 2022). For another study of the entwinement of dam-building and African independence, see Allen and Barbara Isaacman, *Dams, Displacement, and the Delusion of Development: Cahora Bassa and Its Legacies in Mozambique, 1965–2007* (Athens: Ohio University Press, 2013).
114. On the workings of this plan, see Killick, *Development Economics in Action,* and Rimmer, *Staying Poor.* Bognár was one of several Soviet bloc economists who worked in the country. On Soviet development efforts, see Alessandro Iandolo, *Arrested Development: The Soviet Union in Ghana, Guinea, and Mali, 1955–68* (Ithaca: Cornell University Press, 2022).
115. The consortium comprised two U.S. firms: the Kaiser Corporation (90% shareholder) and the Reynolds Company (10%). On Kaiser's influence, see Miescher, *A Dam for Africa,* Chap. 3; Stephanie Decker, "Corporate Political Activity in Less Developed Countries: The Volta River Project in Ghana, 1958–66," *Business History* 53:7 (December 2011), 993–1017.

116. W. A. Hance, *The Proposed Volta River Project: A Study in Industrial Development* (New York: Harper, 1958), 67; quoted in Tsikata, *Living in the Shadow of the Large Dams: Long Term Responses of Down Stream and Lakeside Communities of Ghana's Volta River Project* (Leiden: Brill, 2006), 62.
117. Killick, "The Volta River Project," in Walter Birmingham, I. Neustadt, and E. N. Omaboe, eds., *A Study of Contemporary Ghana*, vol. 2 (London: Allen and Unwin, 1967), 391–410.
118. David Hart, *The Volta River Project: A Case Study in Politics and Technology* (Edinburgh: Edinburgh University Press, 1980), 29–30. Of this money, £47 million was earmarked for the Volta Project: £13 for power and £34 for the smelter. James Moxon, *Volta—Man's Greatest Lake: The Story of Ghana's Akosombo Dam* (London: Andre Deutsch, 1969), 114. On U.S. administration debates over funding, including concerns over Nkrumah's criticism of U.S. Congo policy, see Thomas Noer, "The New Frontier and African Neutralism: Kennedy, Nkrumah, and the Volta River Project," *Diplomatic History* 8:1 (Winter 1984), 61–79. For a breakdown of the financing, see Killick, "The Volta River Project," 396.
119. Tsikata, *Living in the Shadow*, 48.
120. Nkrumah, *Neo-Colonialism: The Last Stage of Imperialism* (London: Panaf, 1970/1965), 242.
121. Hart, The *Volta River Project*, 59, 67–68.
122. Rod Sims, "The Volta Aluminium Company Agreements in Ghana," in Vincent Cable and Bishnodat Persaud, eds., *Developing with Foreign Investment* (London: Routledge, 1987), 178–90; Zeki Ergas, *Le Projet de la Volta* (Geneva: Éditions Médecine et Hygiène, 1972).
123. Miescher and Tsikata, "Hydro-Power," 31; Miescher, *A Dam for Africa*, Chap. 8. While the Volta Lake had been fitted with floodgates, droughts went unanticipated.
124. Côte d'Ivoire diversified its power supply more rapidly than Ghana. In 1984, Ghana's drought grew so acute that the dropping water levels, printed on the front page of the *People's Daily Graphic*, came to symbolize the country's sinking fortunes. "How the Aluminum Deal Foiled Ghana," *Washington Post*, December 14, 1980: https://www.washingtonpost.com/archive/opinions/1980/12/14/how-the-aluminum-deal-foiled-ghana/f8bc342e-8ecc-48bf-b5e1–456d2e92c8df/.
125. Tsikata, *Living in the Shadow*, 389.
126. Elizabeth Colson, *The Social Consequences of Resettlement: The Impact of the Kariba Resettlement on the Gwembe Tonga* (Manchester: Manchester University Press, 1971), 1. The Gwembe Tonga straddled the Zambezi River in what today are Zambia and Zimbabwe.
127. Tsikata, *Living in the Shadow*, 137–44. For a summary of the experience, see Miescher, *A Dam for Africa*, Chap. 5. For an early evaluation that highlighted the extensive planning, see W. Dean Boyle and Buford Kuhns, "Evaluations, and Suggestions and Recommendations on The Program of The Volta River Authority for Resettlement of the People in the Area to be Inundated by Construction of the Volta River Dam, Ghana," U.S. Department of the Interior, Bureau of Land Reclamation, November 1963.

128. Miescher and Tsikata, "Hydro-Power," 23–25. For an edited collection of papers delivered at a Kumasi on March 23–27, 1965, many by managers involved in the resettlement, see Robert Chambers, ed., *The Volta Resettlement Experience* (New York: Praeger, 1970). The original mimeographed papers can be found in *Volta Resettlement Symposium Papers* (Accra: Volta River Authority, 1965). Downstream communities, once reliant on seasonal floods for their livelihoods, also faced out-migration, but they did not receive compensation.
129. Tsikata, *Living in the Shadow*, Chap. 4; Hart, *The Volta River Project*, 88–89.
130. Scott, *Seeing Like a State*, 6. If the TVA was the grandfather, then the great-grandfather was the Aswan Dam in Egypt, built between 1898 and 1902. Mitchell, *Rule of Experts: Egypt, Techno-Politics, Modernity* (Berkeley: University of California Press, 2002), Chap. 1. Twentieth-century dam blueprints also came from the USSR, China, and the British Empire.
131. World Commission on Dams, "Dams and Development: A New Framework for Decision-Making" (London: Earthscan, 2000), xxix; Sanjeev Khagram, *Dams and Development: Transnational Struggles for Water and Power* (Ithaca: Cornell University Press, 2004).
132. For prior critical studies, see the three-volume study *The Social and Environmental Effects of Large Dams*, ed. Edward Goldsmith and Nicholas Hildyard (San Francisco: Sierra Club Books, 1986); and Patrick McCully, *Silenced Rivers: The Ecology and Politics of Large Dams* (London: Zed, 1996). On the report, see Klingensmith, Introduction to *One Valley;* and Sneddon, *Concrete Revolution*, which describes it as "remarkably ahistorical" (2).
133. Immerwahr, *Thinking Small;* for a review of U.S. CD programs, see Lane Holdcroft, "The Rise and Fall of Community Development in Developing Countries, 1950–65: A Critical Analysis and Bibliography," *Michigan State University Rural Development Paper No. 2* (East Lansing: Michigan State University, 1978).
134. Robert Redfield, *Tepoztlán, a Mexican Village: A Study of Folk Life* (Chicago: University of Chicago Press, 1930). During World War II, Redfield worked in the Japanese internment camps, helping to set up their internal 'democratic' system. For an account, see David Price, *Anthropological Intelligence: The Deployment and Neglect of American Anthropology in the Second World War* (Durham: Duke University Press, 2008), Chap. 7.
135. Chase, *Mexico: A Study of Two Americas* (New York: Macmillan 1935/1931), 318. The full passage is a paean to traditional folkways.
136. Redfield, *Tepoztlán*, 217.
137. Redfield, *Tepoztlán*, 219 and all of Chap. 13.
138. Redfield, "Culture Contact without Conflict," *American Anthropologist* 41:3 (July–September 1939), 515–16. In Mexico, Redfield also found a model in the Yucatan village of Chan Kom, which he studied three times. Redfield and Alfonso Villa Rojas, *Chan Kom: A Maya Village* (Chicago: University of Chicago Press, 1934); Redfield, *The Folk Culture of Yucatan* (Chicago: University of Chicago Press, 1941); and Redfield *A Village that Chose Progress: Chan Kom Revisited* (Chicago: University of Chicago Press, 1950). In the last, he described Chan Kom's decision

to become a pueblo, embracing Spanish ways and opening to the outside world. He ascribed its internal cohesion to a practical ethic that sustained industry without immediate reward, a "Protestant ethic before ever they heard of Protestantism" (157).

139. Although the attitude was foundational for modern anthropology, the term *ethnographic present* did not come into currency until the second half of the twentieth century, peaking in anthropological self-criticism during the 1980s. For a touchstone critique, see Johannes Fabian, *Time and the Other: How Anthropology Makes Its Object* (New York: Columbia University Press, 2014/1983). For an attempt to reconstruct the history of the term, see John W. Burton, "A Note on History and the Ethnographic Present," *Proceedings of the American Philosophical Society* 132:4 (December 1988), 420–33.
140. George Marcus, *Anthropology as Cultural Critique: An Experimental Moment in the Human Sciences* (Chicago: University of Chicago Press, 1986), 95.
141. Redfield, "The Natural History of Folk Society," *Social Forces* 31:3 (1953), 224–28; Redfield, *The Little Community* (Chicago: University of Chicago Press, 1955); Redfield, *Peasant Society and Culture: An Anthropological Approach to Civilization* (Chicago: University of Chicago Press, 1956). On Redfield, see Nicole Sackley, "Cosmopolitanism and the Uses of Tradition: Robert Redfield and Alternative Visions of Modernization during the Cold War," *Modern Intellectual History* 9:3 (2012), 565–95.
142. Immerwahr, *Thinking Small*, 60–61; Sackley, "Cosmopolitanism,′ 583–84.
143. M. N. Srinivas, ed., *India's Villages* (Bombay: Asia Publishing House, 1955/1960), 23. See also Srinivas, "The Social System of a Mysore Village," in McKim Marriot, ed., *Village India: Studies in the Little Community* (Chicago: University of Chicago Press, 1955), 1–35. The latter volume appeared in Redfield's *Comparative Studies of Culture and Civilizations* series.
144. Srinivas, *India's Villages*, 6; "The Social Structure," 27.
145. Srinivas's most famous articulation of the Sanskritization thesis is in *The Remembered Village* (Oxford: Oxford University Press, 1978).
146. Sackley, "Cosmopolitanism," 586.
147. On the widespread idea of the 'awakening' Asian peasant, which ignored peasant activism in the 1930s and before, see Sackley, "The Village as Cold War Site: Experts, Development, and the History of Rural Reconstruction," *Journal of Global History* 6 (2011), 490. Indians, too, deployed the metaphor: see *The Awakening: The Story of Twelve Villages in the Community Development Programme* (New Delhi: Ministry of Community Development and Cooperation, 1959).
148. Albert Mayer, *Pilot Project, India: The Story of Rural Development at Etawah, Uttar Pradesh* (Westport: Greenwood, 1958), 31–34, 37.
149. Redfield, *Tepoztlán*, 222, 223; Mayer, *Pilot Project, India*, 132–34.
150. Mayer, *Pilot Project, India*, 87, 173–74, 177–78.
151. Bingham, *Shirt-Sleeve Diplomacy*, 44. On Etawah, see Immerwahr, *Thinking Small*, 71–77; Nick Cullather, "'The Target Is the People': Representations of the Village

in Modernization and U.S. National Security Doctrine," *Cultural Politics* 2:1 (2006), 29–48.

152. Mayer, *Pilot Project, India*, 64–66.

153. For a description of these structures, see S. K. Dey, *Power to the People? A Chronicle of India, 1947–67* (Bombay: Orient Longmans, 1969), 22–25.

154. Cited in Sackley, "Foundation in the Field: The Ford Foundation's New Delhi Office and the Construction of Development Knowledge, 1951–1970," in John Krige and Helke Rausch, eds., *American Foundations and the Coproduction of World Order in the Twentieth Century* (Göttingen: Vandenhoeck & Ruprecht, 2012), 240.

155. Mayer, *Pilot Project, India*, 7.

156. Mayer, *Pilot Project, India*, 14, 37, 224–27.

157. Mayer, *Pilot Project, India*, 65, 68, 71; more generally, Chap. 3.

158. Mayer, *Pilot Project, India*, 77, 93–102, 105. Among other strategies, he encouraged "night halts" and "bull sessions" with local villagers in order to stir excitement and raise awareness (107).

159. For even earlier interest, see Henry Sumner Maine, *Village-Communities in the East and West* (New York: Henry Holt, 1889).

160. F. L. Brayne, *Village Uplift in India* (Allahabad: Pioneer, 1927); Brayne, *The Remaking of Village India* (London: Oxford University Press, 1929); Brayne, *Socrates in an Indian Village (Dehati Socrat)* (London: Oxford University Press, 1929). In the latter, Brayne casts himself as the Greek philosopher gadding villagers to root out bad traditions. Mayer, *Pilot Project, India*, 17–22, defined his Etawah program partly against colonial models; for his tragicomic description of the colonial development agent, see p. 58.

161. Subir Sinha, "Lineages of the Developmentalist State: Transnationality and Village India, 1900–1965," *Comparative Studies in Society and History* 50:1 (January 2008), 61–65; V. P. Pande, *Village Community Projects in India: Origin, Development and Problems* (Bombay: Asia Publishing House, 1967).

162. S. K. Dey, *Nilokheri* (Bombay: Asia Publishing House, 1962); Dey, *Power to the People?*, Part I, Chaps. 1 and 2.

163. On U.S. assistance, see Howard Schaffer, *Chester Bowles: New Dealer in the Cold War* (Cambridge: Harvard University Press, 1993), 64–65. On the Ford Foundation, see Sackley, "Foundation in the Field"; and George Rosen, *Western Economists and Eastern Societies: Agents of Change in South Asia, 1950–1970* (Baltimore: Johns Hopkins University Press, 1985).

164. Dey, *Community Development: A Bird's-Eye View* (Bombay: Asia Publishing House, 1964), 42–44.

165. Immerwahr, *Thinking Small*, 77–78; Garvin Karunaratne, "The Failure of the Community Development Programme in India," *Community Development Journal* 11:2 (1976), 95; "A Decade of C.D. Programme at a Glance," *Kurukshetra* (October 2, 1962), 97; S. C. Jain with B. V. Krishnamurty and P. M. Tripathi, *Grass without Roots: Rural Development under Government Auspices* (New Delhi: Sage, 1985), Chap. 1.

166. S. C. Dube, *India's Changing Villages: Human Factors in Community Development* (London: Routledge and Kegan Paul, 1958), 19–21.
167. Dey, *Panchayat-i-Raj: A Synthesis* (London: Asia Publishing House, 1961), 97; *Community Development through Sahakari Samaj* (Delhi: Ministry of Community Development and Cooperation, 1962); *Sahakari Samaj: The Cooperative Commonwealth* (London: Asia Publishing House, 1967).
168. Dey, *Community Development*, 26.
169. B. Mukerji, *Community Development in India* (Bombay: Orient Longmans, 1961), 84–85.
170. Dey, *Community Development*, 27. For a discussion of some of organizational challenges in otherwise ecstatic accounts, see Dey, *Panchayat-i-Raj;* and Dey, *Community Development*, Chap. 15.
171. Quoted in Henry Maddick, *Panchayati Raj: A Study of Rural Local Government in India* (London: Longman, 1970), 53–54.
172. Mukerji, *Community Development*, 27–31.
173. Quoted from the Mehta Committee Report in Jain et al., *Grass without Roots*, 31.
174. Dey, *Power to the People?* Chap 11; Dey, *Community Development*, 42–59.
175. Dey, *Power to the People?* 287.
176. Cited in Jain et al., *Grass without Roots*, 28, 30.
177. Kusum Nair, *Blossoms in the Dust: The Human Element in Indian Development* (London: Duckworth, 1961), Chaps. 11 and 12. See also Dube, *India's Changing Villages*, 114.
178. Dey, *Community Development through Sahakari Samaj*, 3. Similarly, the economist V. P. Pande cited a 1960 survey indicating that "people look upon the programme as a government scheme for rural welfare and feel that the government should do everything without seeking any contribution from them." Pande, *Village Community Projects*, 182.
179. Ensminger, "What Future for Community Development?" *Kurukshetra* (October 2, 1960), 14.
180. Dey, *Community Development*, 47.
181. Mukerji, *Community Development*, 38; on "felt needs," 60–63.
182. Dube, *India's Changing Villages*, 157, 159, Appendix II. See also *The Gram Sevak's Guide for Increasing Agricultural Production* (New Delhi: Ministry of Community Development, October 1958), notably Part I, Chap. 2, 'Why the Gram Sevak Must Emphasise Increased Agricultural Production.'
183. Dube, *India's Changing Villages*, 166–68, 173–74, 179.
184. Here I use the 1962 revised guide: *A Guide to Community Development (Revised)* (Calcutta: Ministry of Community Development and Co-operation, 1962). The 1957 guide is similar, if slightly less assertive.
185. Ensminger, *Guide*, 12, 18.
186. Ensminger, *Guide*, 3, 15.
187. Ensminger, *Guide*, 2, 84.
188. Ensminger, *Guide*, Chaps. 7 and 8.

189. Ensminger, *Guide*, 20.
190. Ensminger, "What Future for Community Development?" 13.
191. Rosen, *Western Economists*, 74–75; Maddick, *Panchayati Raj*, 7.
192. The Ford Foundation, "Report on India's Food Crisis and Steps to Meet It," Government of India (April 1959), 1, 6, 11 (italics in original). Ensminger insisted that "the food problem" was India's number one concern. Ensminger, "What Future for Community Development?" 15.
193. Jain et al., *Grass without Roots*, 215. For a Marxist and dependency-inspired account of the "negligible" gains of community development and its gradual replacement by capitalist agriculture, see Ranjit Sau, *India's Economic Development: Aspects of Class Relations* (New Delhi: Orient Longman, 1981).

Chapter 4. The History Wars

1. Nils Gilman, "Modernization Theory Never Dies," *History of Political Economy* 50 (2018), 133–51. "Everyone and no one believes in modernization," adds Michael Woolcock, rejecting modernization theory but embracing political and economic modernization. Woolcock, *International Development: Navigating Humanity's Greatest Challenge* (Cambridge: Polity, 2023), 69.
2. Gilman, *Mandarins of the Future: Modernization Theory in Cold War America* (Baltimore: Johns Hopkins University Press, 2003); Michael Latham, *Modernization as Ideology: American Social Science and 'Nation Building' in the Kennedy Era* (Chapel Hill: University of North Carolina Press, 2000); David Engerman, Gilman, Mark Haefele, and Latham, eds., *Modernization, Development, and the Global Cold War* (Amherst: University of Massachusetts Press, 2003); David Ekbladh, *The Great American Mission: Modernization and the Construction of an American World Order* (Princeton: Princeton University Press, 2010); Latham, *The Right Kind of Revolution: Modernization, Development, and U.S. Foreign Policy from the Cold War to the Present* (Ithaca: Cornell University Press, 2011). There is also a growing literature on modernization programs in various countries: Roland Popp, "An Application of Modernization during the Cold War? The Case of Pahlavi Iran," *International History Review* 30:1 (2008), 76–98; Bradley Simpson, *Economists with Guns: Authoritarian Development and U.S.-Indonesian Relations, 1960–1968* (Palo Alto: Stanford University Press, 2008); Thomas C. Field, *From Development to Dictatorship: Bolivia and the Alliance for Progress in the Kennedy Era* (Ithaca: Cornell University Press, 2014); Timothy Nunan, *Humanitarian Invasion: Global Development in Cold War Afghanistan* (Cambridge: Cambridge University Press, 2016); Engerman, *The Price of Aid: The Economic Cold War in India* (Cambridge: Harvard University Press, 2018); Alden Young, *Transforming Sudan: Decolonization, Economic Development, and State Formation* (Cambridge: Cambridge University Press, 2018); Amy Offner, *Sorting Out the Mixed Economy: The Rise and Fall of Welfare and Developmental States in the Americas* (Princeton: Princeton University Press, 2019).

3. Both passages are cited in Gilman, *Mandarins,* 27–28. The first is from *Capital,* vol. 1, Preface to the First German Edition (Moscow: Progress, 1887), 6–7; the second from "The Future Results of British Rule in India" in *The Marx-Engels Reader,* 2nd ed., Robert Tucker, ed. (New York: Norton, 1978), 659.
4. M. P. Cowen and R. W. Shenton, *Doctrines of Development* (Routledge: London, 1996).
5. Inderjeet Parmar, *Foundations of the American Century: The Ford, Carnegie, and Rockefeller Foundations in the Rise of American Power* (New York: Columbia University Press, 2012); Nicolas Guilhot, *The Democracy Makers: Human Rights and International Order* (New York: Columbia University Press, 2005), Chap. 3; Edward Berman, *The Ideology of Philanthropy: The Influence of the Carnegie, Ford, and Rockefeller Foundations on American Foreign Policy* (Albany: SUNY Press, 1983), Chap. 4. On the nexus among philanthropy, modernization, and area studies, see Zachary Lockman, *Field Notes: The Making of Middle East Studies in the United States* (Stanford: Stanford University Press, 2016).
6. Amanda Kay McVety, *Enlightened Aid: U.S. Development as Foreign Policy in Ethiopia* (New York: Oxford University Press, 2012), 112–16, 151–52.
7. On Rosenstein-Rodan's time at CENIS, see Michele Alacevich, "Paul Rosenstein-Rodan and the Birth of Development Economics," *History of Political Economy* 53:5 (2021), 871–75. Rosenstein-Rodan's 1961 article on developing-country absorptive capacity is "International Aid for Underdeveloped Countries," *Review of Economics and Statistics* 43:2 (May 1961), 107–38.
8. W. W. Rostow, *The Process of Economic Growth* (New York: Norton, 1952).
9. Harold Lasswell's Freudian theory of politics, which attributed radicalism to the psychological disturbances of its purveyors, was a particularly fertile source. Lasswell, *Psychopathology and Politics* (Chicago: University of Chicago Press, 1930); and Gilman, *Mandarins of the Future,* 160–74. Though Lasswell was not a modernizer, he influenced card-carrying adherents such as Lucian Pye and Daniel Lerner. Pye's seminal work *Guerilla Communism in Malaya: Its Social and Political Meaning* (Princeton: Princeton University Press, 1956) traced Communist sympathies back to social and psychological dislocation.
10. Jeffrey Alexander, *Fin de Siècle Social Theory: Relativism, Reduction, and the Problem of Reason* (London: Verso, 1995), 13.
11. Daniel Lerner, *The Passing of Traditional Society: Modernizing the Middle East* (New York: Free Press, 1958), 438.
12. Robert Packenham, *Liberal America and the Third World: Political Development Ideas in Foreign Aid and Social Science* (Princeton: Princeton University Press, 1973), 123–29. Skeptic Samuel Huntington attributed this sanguine belief to the United States' "happy history." Huntington, *Political Order in Changing Societies* (New Haven: Yale University Press, 1968), 5.
13. Edward Shils, "Political Development in the New States," *Comparative Studies in Society and History* 2:3 (April 1960), 267.
14. S. N. Eisenstadt, *Modernization: Protest and Change* (Englewood Cliffs: Prentice-Hall, 1966). 1.
15. Gilman, *Mandarins,* 24.

16. On German sociology's tragic-*cum*-utopian outlook, see Harry Liebersohn, *Fate and Utopia in German Sociology, 1870–1923* (Cambridge: MIT Press, 1988).
17. Talcott Parsons, *The Structure of Social Action* (New York: McGraw Hill, 1937), 51. See also Parsons's Preface to the Second Edition (Glencoe, IL: Free Press, 1949), B. For sympathetic readings of Parsons's masterpiece, see Uta Gerhardt, *Talcott Parsons: An Intellectual Biography* (Cambridge: Cambridge University Press, 2002), Chap. 1; and Guy Rocher, *Talcott Parsons and American Sociology* (New York: Barnes & Noble, 1975). Parsonian sociology has also been variously criticized. See Robert Bierstedt, *American Sociological Theory: A Critical History* (New York: Academic Press, 1981), 389–442; and the thoughtful analysis in Stephen Savage, *The Theories of Talcott Parsons: The Social Relations of Action* (New York: St. Martin's, 1981).
18. Jürgen Habermas, *The Theory of Communicative Action*, vol. 2: *Lifeworld and System: A Critique of Functionalist Reason* (Boston: Beacon, 1985/1982), 203.
19. Parsons and Edward Shils, *Toward a General Theory of Action: Theoretical Foundations for the Social Sciences* (New York: Harper & Row, 1951), 77, 76–98.
20. Parsons, *Societies: Evolutionary and Comparative Perspectives* (Englewood Cliffs: Prentice-Hall, 1966); and Parsons, *The System of Modern Societies* (Englewood Cliffs: Prentice-Hall, 1971), both written for the Foundations of Modern Sociology series edited by Alex Inkeles.
21. Rostow, *The Stages of Economic Growth: A Non-Communist Manifesto* (Cambridge: Cambridge University Press, 1960), 1. This caveat echoed earlier warnings: While theoretical models provide useful guides, he wrote in 1952, "the historian's loyalty must remain to his perception of the facts." Rostow, *The Process of Economic Growth*, 1–2. And in his student days, Rostow recalled, he recognized the "complexities of history and the inadequacy of any simple theory of causation, including economic causation." Rostow, "Development: The Political Economy of the Marshallian Long Period," in Gerald Meier and Dudley Seers, eds., *Pioneers in Development* (New York: Oxford University Press, 1984), 229–30.
22. Arthur D. Gayer, Rostow, and Anna Jacobson Schwartz, *The Growth and Fluctuation of the British Economy 1790–1850* (Sussex: Harvester, 1975/1953). U.S. history, presented in a decidedly sunny light, was another source. See Rostow, "The National Style," in Elting E. Morison, ed., *The American Style: Essays in Value and Performance* (New York: Harper & Brothers, 1958), 246–313; Rostow, *The United States in the World Arena: An Essay in Recent History* (New York: Harper & Row, 1960); and the unpublished manuscript "The Making of Modern America, 1776–1940: An Essay on Three Themes" (1960), https://dspace.mit.edu/handle/1721.1/82961.
23. Rostow, *Stages*, 12–13.
24. Rostow, "The Take-Off into Self-Sustaining Growth," *Economic Journal* 66 (1956), 25, 33.
25. Beyond this stage, Rostow abjured prediction, though he glimpsed in the United States a turn away from consumption to other forms of well-being, such as larger families and leisure pursuits, a trend he called the Buddenbrooks dynamic, after Thomas Mann's famous novel. Kimber Charles Pearce, *Rostow, Kennedy, and the Rhetoric of Foreign Aid* (East Lansing: Michigan State University Press, 2001).

26. Simon Kuznets, "Notes on the Take-Off," in Rostow, ed., *The Economics of Take-Off into Sustained Growth* (New York: St. Martin's, 1968), 22–43.
27. Alexander Gerschenkron, "The Early Phases of Industrialization in Russia: Afterthoughts and Counterthoughts," in Rostow, ed., *The Economics of Take-Off,* 151–69.
28. Gerschenkron, *Economic Backwardness in Historical Perspective* (Cambridge: Harvard University Press, 1962).
29. Karl Deutsch, "Social Mobilization and Political Development," *American Political Science Review* 55:3 (September 1961), 493–513.
30. Pye, *Politics, Personality, and Nation Building: Burma's Search for Identity* (New Haven: Yale University Press, 1962), 5, 295–98. Eisenstadt, too, warned that transitional social movements had to be absorbed politically or they could prompt turmoil. Eisenstadt, *Modernization: Protest and Change* (Englewood Cliffs: Prentice-Hall, 1966).
31. Pye, *Aspects of Political Development* (Boston: Little, Brown, 1966), 49, 71, 75, 79, 102, 117, 120.
32. Marion Levy, *The Family Revolution in China* (Cambridge: Harvard University Press, 1949). In the 1950s and 1960s, Levy developed an abstract model of modernization for sociological comparison in *The Structure of Society* (Princeton: Princeton University Press, 1952); and *Modernization and the Structure of Societies* (Princeton: Princeton University Press, 1966).
33. Gabriel Almond and James Coleman, eds., *The Politics of Developing Areas* (Princeton: Princeton University Press, 1960).
34. David Apter, *Ghana in Transition* (New York: Atheneum, 1966/1955), 83, 87. Some modernizers dissented from this colonial boosterism. The comparativist Rupert Emerson saw imperial rule as a violation of basic human aspirations. Emerson, *From Empire to Nation: The Rise to Self-Assertion of Asian and African Peoples* (Cambridge: Harvard University Press, 1960), 41–43.
35. Apter, *Ghana,* 19–20.
36. Apter, *Ghana,* 120, 274.
37. Apter later described the reliance on "political religion" as a problem in many new nations. Apter, *Some Conceptual Approaches to the Study of Modernization* (Englewood Cliffs: Prentice Hall, 1968), 193–232. On Nkrumah's consolidation process, see Apter, "The Politics of Solidarity in Ghana" in the same volume, 136–92. For a critique of Apter's emphasis on 'charisma,' see Maxwell Owusu, *Uses and Abuses of Political Power* (Chicago: University of Chicago Press, 1970).
38. Dzodzi Tsikata, *Living in the Shadow of Large Dams: Long Term Responses of Downstream and Lakeside Communities of Ghana's Volta River Project* (Leiden: Brill, 2006), 47–8.
39. Apter, *Ghana,* 241, 285, 303–08.
40. Apter, "The Role of Traditionalism in the Political Modernization of Ghana and Uganda," *World Politics* 13:1 (October 1960), 67.
41. Apter, *Ghana,* 2nd ed. (1972), 358–59.
42. Apter, *The Political Kingdom of Uganda: A Study of Bureaucratic Nationalism* (Prince-

ton: Princeton University Press, 1961), vii. In the language of Luganda, Buganda is the place and Baganda (or Ganda) the people.

43. Apter, "Traditionalism and Political Modernization of Ghana and Uganda," in Apter, *Some Conceptual Approaches*, 125, 129. The traditional parliament, or Lukiiko, he wrote, could function as a modern parliament because it "was regarded as an age-old institution." In Ghana, by contrast, the government sought "to drive people toward a new way of life."
44. Apter, *Uganda*, 4–5. Elsewhere, Apter described his tripartite system as mobilization (Ghana); reconciliation (Nigerian federalism); and modernizing autocracy (Buganda). Apter, "System, Process, and the Politics of Economic Development," in Apter, *Some Conceptual Approaches*, 277–78.
45. Apter, *Uganda*, 26–27, 21.
46. Apter, *Uganda*, vii.
47. Apter, *Uganda*, 108–17. For a recent history, see Richard Reid, *A History of Modern Uganda* (Cambridge: Cambridge University Press, 2017).
48. Apolo Kagwa, *The Kings of Buganda* (Nairobi: East African Publishing House, 1971); Kagwa, *The Tales of Sir Apolo: Uganda Folklore and Proverbs* (London: Religious Tract Society, 1928); and Kagwa, *The Customs of the Baganda* (New York: Columbia University Press, 1934).
49. Mahmood Mamdani, *Citizen and Subject: Contemporary Africa and the Legacy of Late Colonialism* (Princeton: Princeton University Press, 1996).
50. Apter himself viewed this book as an attempt to enlarge modernization. Apter, *The Politics of Modernization* (Chicago: University of Chicago Press, 1965).
51. On the 'truthiness' of modernization, see Gilman, "Modernization Theory Never Dies."
52. Robert Nisbet, *Social Change and History: Aspects of the Western Theory of Development* (New York: Oxford University Press, 1969), 251–67. See also economist Harvey Leibenstein, *Economic Backwardness and Economic Growth* (New York: Wiley & Sons, 1957), viii.
53. The title was conferred by State Department official Averell Harriman. On Rostow as modern Svengali, see David Milne, *America's Rasputin: Walt Rostow and the Vietnam War* (New York: Hill and Wang, 2008).
54. Pye, *Aspects of Political Development*, Chap. 9; Pye, "Armies in the Process of Political Modernization," in John Johnson, ed., *The Role of the Military in Under-Developed Countries* (Princeton: Princeton University Press, 1962), 88–89.
55. Deutsch, "Social Mobilization and Political Development," 494. On modernization's affinity for the military, see Irene Gendzier, *Managing Political Change: Social Scientists and the Third World* (Boulder: Westview, 1985), 63–69.
56. Edgar Dosman, *The Life and Times of Raul Prebisch, 1901–1986* (Montreal: McGill-Queens University Press, 2008), Chap. 16.
57. Joseph Love, *Crafting the Third World: Theorizing Underdevelopment in Rumania and Brazil* (Stanford: Stanford University Press, 1996), 120.
58. On Prebisch's life, see Dosman, *Raúl Prebisch;* Prebisch, "Five Stages in My Thinking on Development," in Meier and Seers, eds., *Pioneers in Development*, 175–91.

59. ECLA, *Economic Survey of Latin America, 1949* (New York: United Nations Department of Economic Affairs, 1951).
60. C. P. Kindleberger, "Planning for Foreign Investment," *American Economic Review* 33:1, Part 2 (March 1943), 347–54; Kindleberger, "International Monetary Stabilization," in Seymour Harris, ed., *Postwar Economic Problems* (New York: McGraw Hill, 1943), 375–95.
61. While noting that both economists arrived at the thesis separately, Love gives priority to Prebisch. John and Richard Toye, by contrast, argue not only that Singer got there first but that his formulation influenced Prebisch. Toye and Toye, "The Origins and Interpretation of the Prebisch-Singer Thesis," *History of Political Economy* 35 (2003). A German-Jewish student of Joseph Schumpeter, Singer arrived at his thesis when the UN asked him to explore the problem of underdeveloped countries that had run trade surpluses during the war yet faced poor postwar terms for purchasing capital goods. His declension thesis appeared in the December 1949 UN report, several months after the appearance of Prebisch's ECLA Manifesto. United Nations, *Relative Prices of Exports and Imports of Under-Developed Countries: A Study of Post-war Terms of trade between Under-developed and Industrialized Countries* (Lake Success, NT: UN Department of Economic Affairs, 1949), 7, 16. In a later brief, he claimed that trade trends only emerge when considering the "flow of history of a country," not in the stationary analyses of neoclassical economists. Singer, "The Distribution of Gains between Investing and Borrowing Countries," *American Economic Review* 40:2 (May 1950), 477, 479.
62. ECLA, "The Economic Development of Latin America and Its Principal Problems" (Lake Success, NY: United Nations Department of Economic Affairs, 1950/1949), 1. This was not the first time Prebisch employed the center-periphery concepts or the decline thesis. Love (*Crafting the Third World,* 126–30) finds them in lectures, texts, and meeting notes from the mid-1940s. Mauro Boianovsky and Ricardo Solis ("The Origins and Development of the Latin American Structuralist Approach to the Balance of Payments, 1944–1964," *Review of Political Economy* 26:1 [2014], 25) point to Prebisch's 1944 lectures at the Colegio de Mexico. Dosman (243) identifies the secular decline thesis in Prebisch's 1943 book *Rhythm of Economic Activity.*
63. ECLA, "Economic Development," 3, 17.
64. ECLA, "Economic Development," 37.
65. ECLA, "Economic Development," 10.
66. ECLA, "Economic Development," 13.
67. ECLA, "Economic Development," 15–18.
68. ECLA, "Economic Development," Chaps. 6 and 7.
69. United Nations, "Towards a Dynamic Development Policy for Latin America" (New York: United Nations, 1963). For the "nostrums" quotation, see p. 14.
70. For a prescient analysis by an ECLA associate that anticipates later dependency concerns, see Octavio Rodríguez, *La teoría del subdesarrollo de la CEPAL* (Mexico City: Siglo Veintiuno, 1980).
71. Osvaldo Sunkel, "The Pattern of Latin American Dependence," in Victor Urquidi

and Rosemary Thorp, eds., *Latin America in the International Economy* (London: Palgrave Macmillan, 1973), 3–25.

72. Gauhar and Prebisch, "Raul Prebisch"; Prebisch, "Five Stages of My Thinking," 181–91.

73. Love, "The Origins of Dependency Analysis," *Journal of Latin American Studies* 22:1 (February 1990), 143–68. For *dependentistas,* the American Paul Baran, the Brazilian Caio Prado, and the Argentinian Sergio Bagú were particularly influential. Marxism had a Latin American pedigree dating to the turn of the century, though it did not become a common tool of social analysis until the 1960s. Sheldon Liss, *Marxist Thought in Latin America* (Berkeley: University of California Press, 1984), 36–38, 277; Michael Löwy, Introduction to *Marxism in Latin America from 1909 to the Present* (New Jersey: Humanities Press, 1992), xlvi.

74. On Furtado, see Mauro Boianovsky, "Furtado, Celso (1920–2004)," in Steven Durlauf and Lawrence Blume, eds., *The New Palgrave Dictionary of Economics,* 2nd ed. (London: Palgrave, 2008), 517–21; Boianovsky, "A View from the Tropics: Celso Furtado and the Theory of Economic Development in the 1950s," *History of Political Economy* 42:2 (2010), 221–66; Boianovsky, "Furtado, North, and the New Economic History," *Revista economia* 10 (December 2009), 849–66; and Love, *Crafting the Third World,* Chap. 10.

75. Cited in Boianovsky, "Furtado," 518.

76. Furtado, *Development and Underdevelopment: A Structural View of the Problems of Developed and Underdeveloped Economies* (Berkeley: University of California Press, 1964), 76, 4. Though the economist, he wrote elsewhere, had developed tools for studying "conditions of equilibrium based on immediate functional relationships, he rendered himself mentally incapable of grasping economic phenomena *in development* as one aspect of a wider process of social change" (italics in original). Furtado, *Diagnosis of the Brazilian Crisis* (Berkeley: University of California Press, 1965/1964), 13.

77. Furtado, *Development and Underdevelopment,* 5.

78. Furtado, *Development and Underdevelopment,* 1–2.

79. Furtado, *Development and Underdevelopment,* 47, 3–4, 75.

80. For a condensed summary, see Furtado, "Development and Stagnation in Latin America," *Studies in Comparative International Development* 1 (1965), 159–75. See also Furtado, *Uma economía dependente* (Rio de Janeiro: Ministerio da Educação e Cultura, 1956)

81. Furtado, *The Economic Growth of Brazil* (Berkeley: University of California Press, 1963/1959), 37, 52–53.

82. Furtado, *The Economic Growth of Brazil,* 106–14. Furtado also acknowledged effective American domestic policies, singling out Hamilton's debt and credit policies.

83. Furtado, "Development and Stagnation in Latin America," *Studies in Comparative International Development* 1 (1965), 174. His Brazilian colleague Francisco Weffort argued that the country's political struggles grew from this economic condition. Since industrialization was dependent on external factors, none of the contend-

ing internal groups was able to establish effective control over the state. The result was a compromised democracy and economy. Weffort, "State and Mass in Brazil," *Studies in Comparative International Development* 2:12 (1966), 187–96.

84. Furtado, *Diagnosis of the Brazilian Crisis*, 17, 47, 63.
85. Furtado, "Underdevelopment: To Conform or Reform," in Gerald Meier, ed., *Pioneers of Development*, 2d ser. (New York: Oxford University Press, 1987), 205.
86. Furtado, *Diagnosis of the Brazilian Crisis*, 61; Furtado, *Development and Underdevelopment*, 132.
87. Furtado, *The Economic Growth of Brazil*, 165.
88. Furtado, "Underdevelopment: To Conform or Reform," 207.
89. Furtado, *Development and Underdevelopment*, 83. On his Keynesian influences, see Furtado, "Adventures of Brazilian Economist," *International Social Science Journal* 25:1–2 (1973), 34. Boianovsky notes that Furtado sometimes echoed mainstream economic doctrines. Boianovsky, "A View from the Tropics," 235, 238–39; Boianovsky, "Furtado," 519.
90. Furtado, *Development and Underdevelopment*, 64.
91. Furtado, *Diagnosis of the Brazilian Crisis*, 107–08. For Frank's critique, see Frank, *Capitalism and Underdevelopment in Latin America: Historical Studies of Chile and Brazil* (New York: Monthly Review Press, 1967), 201.
92. Furtado, "Underdevelopment: To Conform or Reform," 224. See also Furtado, *Economic Development of Latin America: A Survey from Colonial Times to the Cuban Revolution* (Cambridge: Cambridge University Press, 1970), 187. In 1973, a chastened Furtado had come to question the planning impulse. "I regarded planning as a social technique of the first importance," he wrote, and "the idea that man can take reasoned action to affect the course of history became rooted in my mind. Today, I am inclined to wonder whether there isn't a great deal of presumption in the attitude of those who imagine that we can give history a meaning." Furtado, "Adventures of a Brazilian Economist," 32.
93. Sunkel, "La inflación chilena: Un enfoque heterodoxo," *Trimestre económico* 25:4 (1958), 570–99. See also Sunkel, G. Maynard, D. Seers, and J. G. Olivera, *Inflacion y estructura economica* (Buenos Aires: Paidos, 1967). For an account of the debate, see Cristóbal Kay, *Latin American Theories of Development and Underdevelopment* (London: Routledge, 1989), 47–57.
94. Sunkel, "The Structural Background of Development Problems in Latin America," in Charles Nisbet, ed., *Latin America: Problems in Economic Development* (New York: Free Press, 1969), 13.
95. Sunkel and Pedro Paz, *El subdesarollo latinoamericano y la teoría del desarollo* (Mexico City: Siglo Veintiuno Editores, 1970). For summaries of the dependency school, see Gary Gereffi, *The Pharmaceutical Industry and Dependency in the Third World* (Princeton: Princeton University Press, 1983), 3–49; Peter Evans, *Dependent Development: The Alliance of Multinational, State, and Local Capital in Brazil* (Princeton: Princeton University Press, 1979), 14–54; Gabriel Palma, "Dependency and Development: A Critical Overview," in Dudley Seers, *Dependency Theory: A Critical Reassessment* (London: Frances Pinter, 1981), 20–78; Cristóbal Kay, *Latin Ameri-*

can Theories of Development and Underdevelopment (London: Routledge, 1989); Robert Packenham, *The Dependency Movement: Scholarship and Politics in Development Studies* (Cambridge: Harvard University Press, 1992).

96. Gereffi, *The Pharmaceutical Industry*, 6–7.
97. Fernando Henrique Cardoso and Enzo Faletto, *Dependency and Development in Latin America* (Berkeley: University of California Press, 1979/1969), xvi, 13; Cardoso, "'Teoria da dependência' ou análises concretas de situações de dependência?" in Cardoso, *O modelo político brasileiro e outros ensaios* (Sao Paulo: Difel, 1972), 123–39.
98. Packenham, *The Dependency Movement*, 130.
99. Cardoso and Faletto, *Dependency and Development*, 22.
100. Cardoso and Faletto, *Dependency and Development*, 132f.
101. Cardoso and Faletto, *Dependency and Development*, 174.
102. Joseph Kahl, *Modernization, Exploitation and Dependency in Latin America: Germani, González Casanova and Cardoso* (New Brunswick: Transaction, 1976), 167–69. Some of the most fruitful work of second-generation *dependentistas* focused on the nature of the relations between multinationals and local capital. See Evans, *Dependent Development*, 1979; Gereffi, *The Pharmaceutical Industry*, 1983.
103. For a sympathetic biography, see Ted Goertzel, *Fernando Henrique Cardoso: Reinventing Democracy in Brazil* (Boulder: Lynne Rienner, 1999). Cardoso's flexible dependency also contributed to the postrevolutionary transition paradigm of social change that arose in Latin America and Eastern Europe in the late 1980s. James Mark, Bogdan Iacob, Tobias Rupprecht, and Ljubica Spaskivska, *1989: A Global History of Eastern Europe* (Cambridge: Cambridge University Press, 2019), 91.
104. Cardoso, *The Accidental President of Brazil: A Memoir* (New York: Public Affairs, 2006), 97.
105. Baran's 1957 work *The Political Economic of Growth* (New York: Modern Reader, 1957) was particularly influential not only in criticizing Western economics but also in challenging a "vulgar" Marxism that wrote off everything to imperialism and external dominance. See also Baran and Sweezy, *Monopoly Capital: An Essay on the American Economic and Social Order* (New York: Monthly Review Press, 1966).
106. Cited in Kay, *Latin American Theories of Development and Underdevelopment*, 156.
107. There was some evolution: In the 1980s he turned his attention to the global debt crisis. And at the end of his life he turned to Asia and global economic reorientation.
108. Tulio Halperín-Donghi, "'Dependency Theory' and Latin American Historiography," *Latin American Research Review* 17:1 (1982), 116–17, quoted in Packenham, *The Dependency Movement*, 189.
109. Gereffi, *The Pharmaceutical Industry*, Chap. 1; Thandika Mkandawire, "The Crisis in Economic Development Theory," *Africa Development* 15:3–4 (1990), 223.
110. Cardoso, "The Consumption of Dependency Theory in the United States," *Latin American Research Review* 12:3 (1977), 7–24.

111. Frank, *Latin America: Underdevelopment or Revolution: Essays on Underdevelopment and the Immediate Enemy* (New York: Modern Reader, 1969), 21. Surprisingly, Frank also studied under Milton Friedman.
112. Frank, *Latin America*, 24, 56.
113. Hoselitz, "Social Structure and Economic Growth," *Economia internazionale* 6:3 (1953), 52–77.
114. *Dependentistas* termed these types 'compradors'—Third World agents of the capitalist West.
115. Frank, *Latin America*, 30.
116. Frank, *Latin America*, 40.
117. Frank, *Latin America*, 73.
118. Frank, *Latin America*, 44–45.
119. Frank, *Latin America*, xii, 3.
120. Frank, *Latin America*, 5. Interestingly, Frank drew on Robert Redfield to argue that "there are no peasants without the city to which they are tied" and "no city without its peasants" (65). On the dualism of Furtado, see Frank, "Capitalism and the Myth of Feudalism in Brazilian Agriculture," in Frank, *Capitalism and Underdevelopment in Latin America*, 221–318.
121. Frank, *Latin America*, x.
122. This point was developed further by world systems theorist Immanuel Wallerstein, who dismissed modernization theory as ahistorical: "We do not live in a modernizing world," he scoffed, "but in a capitalist world." Wallerstein, "Modernization: Requiescat in Pace," in Lewis Coser and Otto Larsen, eds., *The Uses of Controversy in Sociology* (New York: Free Press, 1976), 132.
123. See the Preface and introductory chapters of Frank, *Dependent Accumulation and Underdevelopment* (New York: Monthly Review Press, 1979).
124. Frank, *Latin America*, 8–9. At the same time, he condemned the selective application of supposedly universal economic principles. Even as developed countries pushed open trade and comparative advantage for satellite states, they employed heavy doses of protection for themselves (48–61).
125. Thomas Skidmore, Peter Smith, and James Green, *Modern Latin America*, 8th ed. (New York: Oxford University Press, 2014), 357.
126. His stint as head of UNCTAD left few specific proposals, and he departed in 1969 complaining of bureaucratic stasis (Prebisch, "Five Stages in my Thinking," 182–83). Altaf Gauhar and Raul Prebisch, "Raul Prebisch," *Third World Quarterly* 2:1 (January 1980), 14–20. For recent reconsiderations of the NIEO, see the articles collected in *Humanity* 6:1 (Spring 2015). On the Third World as project, see Vijay Prasad, *The Darker Nations: A People's History of the Third World* (New York: New Press, 2007), 62–74; Adom Getachew, *Worldmaking after Empire: The Rise and Fall of Self-Determination* (Princeton: Princeton University Press, 2019), 161; and Gilbert Rist, *The History of Development: From Western Origins to Global Faith* (London: Zed, 2006), 110.
127. Samir Amin, *Delinking: Towards a Polycentric World* (London: Zed, 1990). His most notable West African examination is *Le développement du capitalisme en Côte d'Ivoire* (Paris: Minuit, 1967).

128. Getachew, *Worldmaking after Empire*, 152–53.
129. Tanya Harmer, *Allende's Chile and the Inter-American Cold War* (Chapel Hill: University of North Carolina Press, 2011), 44.
130. Salvador Allende, "Inaugural Address in the National Stadium, November 5, 1970," repr. in James Cockcroft, ed., *Salvador Allende Reader* (Melbourne: Ocean Press, 2000), 53.
131. Allende, "Address to the Third United Nations Conference on Trade and Development UNCTAD," April 13, 1972, in Cockcroft, ed., *Salvador Allende Reader*, 156–75.
132. David Johnson Lee, *The Ends of Modernization: Nicaragua and the United States in the Cold War Era* (Ithaca: Cornell University Press, 2021), 103. On Sandinista thinking about the local bourgeoisie and broader dependency, see Jorge Castañeda, *Nicaragua: Contradicciones en la revolucion* (Mexico City: Tiempo Extra, 1980), 71–87. Although Harry Vanden and Gary Prevost (*Democracy and Socialism in Sandinista Nicaragua* [Boulder: Lynne Rienner, 1993], 44) argue that dependency influenced only the most traditionally Marxist faction, the texts of Sandinista official Jaime Wheelock Román suggest that it became pervasive in those quarters. Wheelock, *Inperialismo y dictadura: Crisis de una formación social* (Mexico City: Siglo Veintiuno Editores, 1975); Wheelock, *On the Nicaraguan Revolution* (San Francisco: Center for the Study of American Militarism, 1984), 34.
133. Statement of the Conference of Latin American Bishops, 1968: https://www.geraldschlabach.net/misc/medellin-1968-excerpts/.
134. Gustavo Gutiérrez, *A Theology of Liberation: History, Politics and Salvation* (Maryknoll, NY: Orbis Books, 1973), Chap. 6.
135. Apter, *Rethinking Development: Modernization, Dependency, and Postmodern Politics* (Newbury Park, CA: Sage, 1987), 16–17.

Chapter 5. Playing Both Sides of the War

1. J. T. Way, *The Mayan in the Mall: Globalization, Development, and the Making of Modern Guatemala* (Durham: Duke University Press, 2012), 134–37.
2. Betsy Konefal, *For Every Indio Who Falls: A History of Maya Activism in Guatemala* (Albuquerque: University of New Mexico Press, 2010), 68–72.
3. Shelton Davis, "Introduction: Sowing the Seeds of Violence," in Robert Carmack, ed., *Harvest of Violence: The Maya Indians and the Guatemalan Crisis* (Norman: University of Oklahoma Press, 1988), 21–22.
4. Creative Associates International, Inc., "A Retrospective of A.I.D.'s Experience in Strengthening Democratic Institutions in Latin America," September 1987, V-10.
5. Stephen Streeter, "Nation-Building in the Land of Eternal Counter-Insurgency: Guatemala and the Contradictions of the Alliance for Progress," *Third World Quarterly* 27:1 (2006), 57–68. Streeter's article sparked my own interest in this topic. See also Susan Fitzpatrick-Behrens and Catherine C. LeGrand, "Canadian and US Catholic Promotion of Co-operatives in Central America and the Caribbean and Their Political Implications," in Mary Hilson, Silke Neunsinger, and

Greg Patmore, eds., *A Global History of Consumer Co-operation since 1850: Movements and Businesses* (Leiden: Brill, 2017), 172.

6. Way, *Mayan*, 92. Way focuses on Guatemala City, where the story is somewhat different from the highlands—less one of purportedly apolitical Mayans victimized by a terror state, and more one of state agencies and death squads targeting politically active unions and parties.
7. This sentence is a nod to Greg Grandin's turn of phrase in the Introduction to *The Last Colonial Massacre: Latin America in the Cold War* (Chicago: University of Chicago Press, 2004), where he described the narrowing of democracy as *the* story of the twentieth century. On the role of development in forging Latin American subjectivities, see María Josefina Saldaña-Portillo, *The Revolutionary Imagination in the Americas and the Age of Development* (Durham: Duke University Press, 2003).
8. Jack Shaffer, *Historical Dictionary of the Cooperative Movement* (Lanham, MD: Scarecrow, 1999), 189.
9. Margaret Digby, *The World Co-operative Movement* (London: Hutchinson's University Library, 1948), 8.
10. George Jacob Holyoake, *Self-Help by the People: The History of the Rochdale Pioneers* (London: Swan Sonnenschein, 1893). The seven principles were: "voluntary and open membership; democratic member control; member economic participation; autonomy and independence; education, training and information; cooperation among cooperators; and concern for community." Shaffer, *Historical Dictionary*, 196.
11. Alex Gourevitch, *From Slavery to the Cooperative Commonwealth: Labor and Republican Liberty in the Nineteenth Century* (New York: Cambridge University Press, 2015), esp. Chap. 5.
12. On this, see former California congressman Jerry Voorhis, *American Cooperatives: Where They Came From, What They Do, Where They Are Going* (New York: Harper, 1961), 115–16. Filene also took inspiration from travels in India and Germany.
13. Digby, *The World Co-operative Movement*, 148. See also Nicole Sackley, "The Village as a Cold War Site: Experts, Development, and the History of Rural Reconstruction," *Journal of Global History* 6 (2011), 481–504.
14. Digby, *The World Co-operative Movement*, 149–50.
15. Stephen Yeo, "Looking Forward: Cooperative Politics or Can Owen Still Help?" in Noel Thompson and Chris Williams, eds., *Robert Owen and his Legacy* (Cardiff: University of Wales Press, 2011), 239–58; and Bruno Jossa, "Marx, Marxism, and the Cooperative Movement," *Cambridge Journal of Economics* 29 (2005), 3–18.
16. For a fascinating account of how cooperativist internationalism fit into the modernization of a small socialist country, see Elidor Mëhilli, *From Stalin to Mao: Albania and the Socialist World* (Ithaca: Cornell University Press, 2017). On cooperatives within wider socialist property regimes, see Katherine Verdery, *The Vanishing Hectare: Property and Value in Postsocialist Transylvania* (Ithaca: Cornell University Press, 2003), Chap. 1.
17. Moshe Lewin, *Russian Peasants and Soviet Power: A Study of Collectivization* (New York: Norton, 1968), 93–94.

18. A. V. Chayanov, *The Theory of Peasant Economy* (Madison: University of Wisconsin Press, 1986/1966); Chayanov, *The Theory of Peasant Co-operatives* (London: I. B. Taurus, 1991). For introductions to his thought, see the essays by Shanin, Daniel Thorner, and Basile Kerblay in *The Theory of Peasant Economy;* and Jacek Kochanowicz, "La teoria de Chayanov y el punto de visto polaco respecto a la economia campesina," *Areas* 11 (1989), 109–22. Chayanov emerged out of wide-ranging Russian debates over the peasantry that ran from the 1861 abolition of serfdom through Pyotr Stolypin's 1906 agrarian reforms. On cooperatives' role in these debates, see Yanni Kotsonis, *Making Peasants Backward: Agricultural Cooperatives and the Agrarian Question in Russia, 1861–1914* (New York: St. Martin's, 1999).
19. Via the interwar Romanian economist Mihail Manoilescu, Chayanov's model influenced structuralist ideas in midcentury Brazil. Joseph Love, *Crafting the Third World: Theorizing Underdevelopment in Rumania and Brazil* (Stanford: Stanford University Press, 1996).
20. On Chayanov's significance for midcentury rural development ideas, see Shanin's Introduction to *The Theory of Peasant Economy;* Viktor Danilov's Introduction to *The Theory of Peasant Co-operatives;* and Gavin Kitching, *Development and Underdevelopment in Historical Perspective: Populism, Nationalism, and Industrialization* (London: Routledge, 1982).
21. Wallace Campbell and Richard Giles, *Helping People Help Themselves* (Washington, DC: Public Affairs Institute, 1950), 6.
22. Albert Hirschman, *Getting Ahead Collectively: Grassroots Experiences in Latin America* (New York: Pergamon, 1984), 59, 61 (italics in original).
23. Susan Berger, *Political and Agrarian Development in Guatemala* (Boulder: Westview, 1992), 26–39; Rachel May, *Terror in the Countryside: Campesino Responses to Political Violence in Guatemala, 1954–1985* (Athens: Ohio University Press, 2001), 4.
24. Jim Handy, *Revolution in the Countryside: Rural Conflict and Agrarian Reform in Guatemala, 1944–1954* (Chapel Hill: University of North Carolina Press, 1994), 26.
25. Piero Gleijeses, *Shattered Hope: The Guatemalan Revolution and the United States, 1944–1954* (Princeton: Princeton University Press, 1991), 150.
26. Berger, *Political and Agrarian Development*, 64.
27. The sociologist and former guerilla Gustavo Porras Castejón called CALs "embryo[s] of local power . . . the most democratic institutions that have ever existed in the Guatemalan countryside." "Analisis Estructural y Recomposicion Clasista de la Sociedad Guatemalteca de 1954–1980," in Centro de Estudios Integrados de Desarrollo Comunal, ed., *Seminario estado, clases sociales y cuestión etnico-nacional* (Mexico City: Praxis, 1992), 88; cited in Grandin, *The Blood of Guatemala: A History of Race and Nation* (Durham: Duke University Press, 2000), 201.
28. Coffee production experienced an initial dip, but then, along with corn, rice, and wheat, began to grow.
29. José Luis Paredes Moreira, *Reforma agraria: Una experiencia en Guatemala* (Guatemala: Imprenta Universitaria, 1963), 80; Handy, *Revolution in the Countryside,* 121, 95–96. The national *fincas* were expropriated from Germans during World War II.

30. Grandin, "To End with All These Evils: Ethnic Transformation and Community Mobilization in Guatemala's Western Highlands, 1954–1980," *Latin American Perspectives* 24:2 (1997), 14.
31. Fortuny, quoted in Gleijeses, *Shattered Hope*, 152, said this in 1980. See also Handy, *Revolution in the Countryside*, Chap. 4; Way, *Mayan*, 61–63; Berger, *Political and Agrarian Development*, 64–71.
32. Roberto Barillas Izaguirre, *Legislación cooperativa: Comentarios al Decreto 643 del Congreso* (Guatemala: Departamento de Fomento Cooperativo, 1950), 28. I thank J. T. Way for this citation.
33. On the history of United Fruit, see Stephen Schlesinger and Stephen Kinzer, *Bitter Fruit: The Story of the American Coup in Guatemala* (Cambridge: Harvard University Press, 2005).
34. On the European history of Catholic Action, see Klaus Große Kracht, *Die Stunde der Laien? Katholische Aktion in Deutschland im europäischen Kontext* (Paderborn: Ferdinand Schöningh, 2017).
35. See the subsection "Artisans and Co-operative Enterprises" in Section 2 of *Mater et Magistra*, 1961.
36. This process has been the subject of abundant anthropological research. Ricardo Falla's *Quiché rebelde: Religious Conversion, Politics, and Ethnic Identity in Guatemala* (Austin: University of Texas Press, 2001) is a touchstone source. See also Matilda González, dir., *Se cambió el tiempo: Conflict y poder en territorio K'iché, 1880–1996* (Guatemala: AVANCSO, 2002); Douglas Brintnall, *Revolt against the Dead: The Modernization of a Mayan Community in the Highlands of Guatemala* (New York: Gordon & Breach, 1979); Robert Carmack, *Rebels of Highland Guatemala: The Quiche-Mayas of Momostenango* (Norman: University of Oklahoma Press, 1995); Richard Wilson, *Maya Resurgence in Guatemala: Q'eqchi' Experiences* (Norman: University of Oklahoma Press, 1995); Laura Hurtado Paz y Paz, *Dinámicas agrarias y reproducción campesina en la globalización: El caso de Alta Verapaz, 1970–2007* (Guatemala: F&G Editores, 2008); Kay B. Warren, *The Symbolism of Subordination: Indian Identity in a Guatemalan Town* (Austin: University of Texas Press, 1978); John Watanabe, *Maya Saints and Souls in a Changing World* (Austin: University of Texas Press, 1992); and Karen Ponciano, "Iglesia y campesinos: Construyendo un imaginario de lucha campesina en Guatemala," in *Aproximación a los imaginarios sobre organización campesina en Guatemala* (Guatemala: AVANCSO, 2007), 71–114.
37. Bruce J. Calder, "Interwoven Histories: The Catholic Church and the Maya, 1940 to the Present," in Edward Cleary and Timothy Steigenga, eds., *Resurgent Voices in Latin America: Indigenous People, Political Mobilization, and Religious Change* (New Brunswick: Rutgers University Press, 2004), 94.
38. Grandin, "To End with All These Evils," 9.
39. On the Church's anti-revolutionary credentials and the archbishop's avowed conservatism, see Warren, *Symbolism*, 87–94.
40. Calder, "Interwoven Histories," 97.
41. Initially urban-focused, Maryknolls founded an elite girls' school, Colegio Monte María, in 1953. Amanda Izzo, *Liberal Christianity and Women's Global Activism:*

The YWCA of the USA and the Maryknoll Sisters (New Brunswick: Rutgers University Press, 2018), 148–49.

42. Falla, *Quiché rebelde*, 170–78.
43. Thomas and Marjorie Melville, expelled from the Guatemala in 1968 for association with the FAR, tell their story in *Whose Heaven, Whose Earth?* (New York: Knopf, 1971); and *Guatemala—Another Vietnam?* (Middlesex: Penguin, 1971).
44. Konefal, *Indio*, 34–35, 49–51.
45. Quoted in Susan Fitzpatrick-Behrens, *The Maryknoll Catholic Mission in Peru, 1943–1989* (Notre Dame: University of Notre Dame Press, 2012), 92.
46. Proceedings of the Lima Methods Conference of the Maryknoll Fathers, Lima, Peru, August 23–28, 1954 (Maryknoll, NY: Maryknoll Fathers, 1954), 161.
47. Lima Methods Conference, 285.
48. Quoted in Warren, *Symbolism*, 140.
49. Wilson, *Maya Resurgence*, 174–75.
50. Warren, *Symbolism*, 141.
51. Ponciano, "Iglesia y campesinos," 94.
52. Arturo Arias, "Changing Indian Identity: Guatemala's Violent Transition to Modernity," in Carol A. Smith and Marilyn M. Moors, eds., *Guatemalan Indians and the State, 1540–1988* (Austin: University of Texas Press, 1990), 233. See also Brintnall, *Revolt against the Dead*, 155.
53. Brintnall, *Revolt against the Dead*, 155.
54. Clause 14 (Rural Transformation) of the Medellín Declaration.
55. According to the 1952 census, Guatemala had 1,674,521 rural inhabitants; by 1973, this number had doubled. Berger, *Political and Agrarian Development*, 130.
56. Richard Adams, *Crucifixion by Power: Essays on Guatemalan National Social Structure, 1944–1966* (Austin: University of Texas Press, 1970), 200–201.
57. Jonathan Bingham, *Shirt-Sleeve Diplomacy: Point 4 in Action* (New York: John Day, 1954), 249–50.
58. Streeter, *Managing the Counterrevolution: The United States and Guatemala, 1954–1961* (Athens: Ohio University Press, 2000), 110.
59. International Development Services, Inc. (IDS), "The Rural Development Program in Guatemala: New Lands and Lives for Farmers—An Interim Report, 1959" (New York: IDS, April 1960), 1, 8.
60. IDS, "Rural Development Program: Final Report, 1955–63," (Washington, DC: IDS, August 1963), 1–2, 10; IDS, "Interim Report," 6.
61. IDS, "Final Report," 8. See also Streeter, *Managing the Revolution*, 151–52.
62. IDS, "Final Report," 7.
63. IDS, "Final Report," 5.
64. IDS, "Interim Report," 24, 25.
65. Cited in Streeter, "Nation-Building in the Land of Eternal Counter-Insurgency," 59; see the 1962 "Assessment of Communism in Guatemala," Airgram A-28 (July 18, 1962). Available at Centro de Investigaciones Regionales de Mesoamerica (CIRMA), DES, No. 405.
66. On official Guatemalan views of cooperatives, see Tirso Constantino Escobar

Loarca, "Cooperativismo agrario en el occidente de Guatemala" (master's thesis, University of San Carlos, Guatemala, 1974), 39–40; and Bernardo López and Alberto Mora, "Visión panorámica del sector cooperativo en Guatemala: Un mecanismo de promoción del desarrollo y lucha contra la pobreza" (La Paz: Organización Internacional del Trabajo, 2012), 32.

67. On the origins of the Development Loan Fund, see David Engerman, *The Price of Aid: The Economic Cold War in India* (Cambridge: Harvard University Press, 2018), 170–76.

68. Ian MacPherson, *Hands Around the Globe: A History of the International Credit Union Movement and the Role and Development of World Council of Credit Unions, Inc.* (Madison: World Council of Credit Unions, 1999), 60–61; Fitzpatrick-Behrens, *The Maryknoll Catholic Mission*, 124–26.

69. OAS, "1960 Annual Report of the Secretary General to the Council of the Organization" (Washington, DC: Pan American Union, 1961), 42.

70. Judy Hilkey, *Character as Capital: Success Manuals and Manhood in Gilded Age America* (Chapel Hill: University of North Carolina Press, 1997), 96. The term *self-help* dates earlier to the Scottish writer Samuel Smiles, whose 1859 book of the same name sold well in the United States. That year also saw the American publication of George Holyoake's *Self-Help by the People*. John Curl, *For All the People: Uncovering the Hidden History of Cooperation, Cooperative Movements, and Communalism in America* (Oakland: PM Press, 2009), 57–58. For a recent account of Smiles's international appeal, see Beth Blum, *The Self-Help Compulsion: Searching for Advice in Modern Literature* (New York: Columbia University Press, 2020), Introduction and Chap. 1.

71. For a detailed history, see Joseph G. Knapp, *The Rise of American Cooperative Enterprise, 1620–1920* and *The Advance of American Cooperative Enterprise, 1920–1945* (Danville, IL: Interstate Printers & Publishers, 1973). See also Florence E. Parker, *The First 125 Years: A History of Distributive and Service Cooperation in the United States, 1829–1954* (Superior, WI: Cooperative Publishing Association, 1956).

72. Curl, *For All the People*, 190–91. Not all cooperative sectors suffered: credit unions saw increasing numbers and membership in the early 1950s. MacPherson, *Hands Around the Globe*, 39–40.

73. Truman wrote this in his 1955–56 memoirs. Quoted in Sara Lorenzini, *Global Development: A Cold War History* (Princeton: Princeton University Press, 2019), 28–29.

74. According to USAID's Greenbook of overseas loans and grants, the United States obligated over $141 million in economic and military assistance to Guatemala during the 1960s, equivalent to over $870 million in constant 2018 dollars. The dataset is available at https://data.usaid.gov/Administration-and-Oversight/U-S-Overseas-Loans-and-Grants-Greenbook-Data/7cnw-pw8v.

75. The talk was delivered in Madison, WI, headquarters of CUNA. Kennedy, "Strengthening of Farm Cooperatives," Papers of John F. Kennedy, September 1959, p. 2. Digital Identifier: JFKCAMP1960-1028-018-p0001. Available at https://www.jfklibrary.org/asset-viewer/archives/JFKCAMP1960/1028/JFKCAMP1960-1028-018.

76. Jeffrey Taffet, *Foreign Aid as Foreign Policy: The Alliance for Progress in Latin America* (New York: Routledge, 2007); L. Ronald Scheman, ed., *The Alliance for Progress: A Retrospective* (New York: Praeger, 1988).
77. USAID and Department of State, "Implementation of the Humphrey Amendment to the Foreign Assistance Act of 1961" (Washington, DC: Government Printing Office, 1962), 1–2; Congressional Quarterly Almanac, 1961 https://library.cqpress.com/cqalmanac/document.php?id=cqal61-1373202.
78. "AID Cooperative Report," ICATO Circular A-127, December 13, 1961, NARA RG 286, Entry P367, Box 2, Folder Cooperatives.
79. AID/DOS, "Implementation of the Humphrey Amendment," III.
80. Special Advisory Committee on Cooperatives to the Administrator of the Agency for International Development, "Cooperatives: Democratic Institutions for Economic and Social Development" (1961), 2.
81. Special Advisory Committee, "Cooperatives," 6.
82. Cited in Thomas Carothers, *Development Aid Confronts Politics: The Almost Revolution* (Washington, DC: Carnegie Endowment for International Peace, 2013), 30. See also USAID, "Development of Cooperative Enterprises 1966: Implementation of the Humphrey Amendment to the Foreign Assistance Act of 1961," Fifth Annual Report to Congress (1966).
83. See the document marked MOSS AMENDMENT, n.d.; AID Circular A-193, May 8, 1970; and the handwritten note entitled *Moss Amendment* (from which the above quotation comes) in NARA RG 286, Entry P397, Box 2, Folder Coop: Moss Amendment FY-71.
84. For reviews of USAID's cooperative support from 1962 to 1980, see "Assessment of Cooperative Development Organizations," Washington, DC: Development Associates, October 1980; "Evaluation of Cooperative Development Projects: Summary Analysis of Selected Aid Evaluations," Washington, DC: Development Associates, October 1980.
85. For the charter, see Appendix B of Jerome Levinson and Juan de Onís, eds., *The Alliance That Lost Its Way: A Critical Report on the Alliance for Progress* (Chicago: Quadrangle, 1970), 352–71—in particular Title II, Chaps. 1, 2, and 4.
86. On colonization and development in Petén, see Norman B. Schwartz, *Forest Society: A Social History of Petén, Guatemala* (Philadelphia: University of Pennsylvania Press, 1990); and Falla's unpublished manuscript series *Al atardecer de la vida . . . Escritos de Ricardo Falla, sj*, especially the third volume, *Ixcán: El campesino indígena se levanta: Guatemala 1966–1982* (Guatemala: AVANCSO, 2015).
87. James Morrissey, "A Missionary Directed Resettlement Project among the Highland Maya of Western Guatemala" (Ph.D. diss., Stanford University, May 1978), 77–78. Despite concern over the haste with which the law passed and the lack of judicial recourse for land decisions, the American ambassador to Guatemala found things to appreciate: the preservation of private property, the commitment to address land tenure, and the resistance to forced expropriation and redistribution. Department of State Memo A-134, "Agrarian Reform Policy" (September 8, 1962). Available at CIRMA, DES, No. 712. United Fruit and numerous elite agri-

culturalists supported the reform out of concern for communism, though they too feared the restrictions on judicial review. See the May 5, 1961, May 25, 1961, and June 6, 1961 letters from John Muccio, as well as Airgram A-280, "Summary of Agrarian Reform Law" (November 8, 1962). All available at CIRMA, DES, Nos. 663, 665, 666, 725.

88. Manuel Roberto Yurrita Elgueta, "Agriculture," in *Historia general de Guatemala,* vol. 4: *Época contemporánea: De 1945 a la actualidad* (Guatemala: Fundación para la Cultura y el Desarollo, 1997), 388–90.

89. In 1959, Ydígoras had to legalize two squatter settlements in Guatemala City after more than 11,000 migrants arrived from the peripheries. Way, *Mayan,* 105.

90. "La importancia de las cooperativas en el mercado agricola," *Informador agricola* 174 (March 15, 1962), 4–5, NARA RG 286, Entry P367, Box 2, Folder Informador Agricola.

91. See David Carey, "Guatemala's Green Revolution: Synthetic Fertilizer, Public Health, and Economic Autonomy in the Mayan Highland," *Agricultural History* 83:3 (2009), 283–322.

92. They were nonetheless hampered by a lack of appropriate personnel since "Guatemalans trained prior to 1952 cannot be used . . . because of their political orientation." "Cooperatives," ICATO Circular 37, June 20, 1961, pp. 1–3, NARA RG 286, Entry P367, Box 2, Folder Cooperatives. The "Syndicate" model presumably refers to syndicalism, a movement for worker production and redistribution through labor unions. The term was sometimes applied to organizations such as the Industrial Workers of the World, although they did not use it themselves.

93. "Research Memorandum from the Director of the Bureau of Intelligence and Research (Hughes) to the Assistant Secretary of State for Inter-American Affairs (Woodward)," January 19, 1962, in *Foreign Relations of the United States, 1961–1963,* vol. 12 (Washington, DC: U.S. Government Printing Office, 1996), 90. On unions in Guatemala, see Deborah Levenson-Estrada, *Trade Unionists Against Terror: Guatemala City, 1954–1985* (Chapel Hill: University of North Carolina Press, 1994).

94. "Feasibility Study of Cooperative Banks," Airgram Circular with reference to AIDTO CIRC LA-76, May 18, 1962, p. 1, NARA RG 286, Entry P367, Box 2, Folder Cooperatives.

95. Department of State Memorandum, "U.S. Missionaries Have Own Aid Program in Guatemalan Indian Area," Airgram A-296 (November 15, 1962). Available at CIRMA, DES, No. 730.

96. "Research Memorandum from the Director of the Bureau of Intelligence and Research (Hughes)," January 19, 1962, 87.

97. In 1968, USAID introduced a fifth component, contracting IDF to establish farmer associations—"pre-cooperatives"—on formerly government-owned coastland. These were never successful, and in 1970 they were terminated. John R. Davidson, "The Rural Credit and Cooperative Development Project in Guatemala," PN-AAD-300 (1976), 5–6. Available at DEC.

98. USAID Project Appraisal Report "Rural Community Leadership & Modernization—

Credit Union Development/CUNA," PD-AAA-894-A1 (1969), 2. Available at DEC.

99. "Federación Nacional de Cooperativas de Ahorro y Credito: Plan de trabajo para el año 1970," 2, NARA RG 286, Entry P397, Box 2, Folder Coop/F: FENACOAC Plan of Action CY-1970/FY-71.

100. José Miguel Gaitán Alvarez, "El movimiento cooperativista de Guatemala: Desarrollo de la Federacion Nacional de Cooperativas de Ahorro y Credito," *Estudios sociales* 7 (August 1972), 39–40.

101. Project Appraisal Report, "Rural Community Leadership & Modernization—Agricultural Cooperative School," PD-AAA-893-G1 (1969), 2–3. Available at DEC.

102. Project Appraisal Report, "Rural Community Leadership & Modernization Center for Training Social Promoters (CAPS), Rafael Landivar University" (July 16, 1970), 1; Non-Capital Project Paper (PROP), PD-AAA-893-C1 (December 14, 1970), 6 (both available at DEC). CAPS was based on a Loyola University program that trained Latin American community organizers.

103. Federación Nacional de Cooperativas de Ahorro y Credito: Plan de trabajo para el año 1970, 1.

104. USAID Project Appraisal Report, "Rural Community Leadership & Modernization—Credit Union Development/CUNA" (1969), 3–4. Available at DEC.

105. Oficina de Derechos Humanos del Arzobispado de Guatemala, *Guatemala: Nunca más, Informe Proyecto Interdiocesano de Recuperación de la Memoria Histórica*, vol. 3 (Guatemala: ODHAG, 1998). Quoted in Konefal, *Indio*, 36.

106. Furthermore, rising prices meant that peasants who had grown dependent on modern inputs were increasingly unable to afford them. May, *Terror*, 121.

107. Berger, *Political and Agrarian Development*, 125, 143–44.

108. On *Operación Limpieza*, see Grandin, *The Last Colonial Massacre*, 73–74, 96–99. According to one estimate, the United States contributed over $23 million to the Guatemalan military and police between 1964 and 1972, with USAID channeling over $4 million of that sum. Carlos Figueroa Ibarra, Guillermo Paz Cárcamo, and Arturo Taracena Arriola, "El primer ciclo de la insurgencia revolucionaria en Guatemala (1954–1972)," in Virgilio Álvarez Aragón, Carlos Figueroa Ibarra, Arturo Taracen Arriola, Sergio Tischler Visquerra, and Edmundo Urrutia García, eds., *Guatemala: Historia reciente (1954–1996)*, vol. 2: *La dimensión revolucionaria* (Guatemala: FLACSO, 2013), 82.

109. Thomas C. Field, Jr., *From Development to Dictatorship: Bolivia and the Alliance for Progress in the Kennedy Era* (Ithaca: Cornell University Press, 2014), 81, 36. On civic action under the Alliance for Progress, see Stephen Rabe, "Controlling Revolutions: Latin America, the Alliance for Progress, and Cold War Anti-Communism," in Thomas Peterson, ed., *Kennedy's Quest for Victory: American Foreign Policy, 1961–1963* (Oxford: Oxford University Press, 1989), 105–22. On its use in Indonesia, see Bradley Simpson, *Economists with Guns: Authoritarian Development and U.S.-Indonesian Relations, 1960–1968* (Palo Alto: Stanford University Press, 2008), esp. Chap. 2.

110. In addition to Grandin, see Susanne Jonas, *The Battle for Guatemala: Rebels, Death*

Squads and U.S. Power (Boulder: Westview, 1991); and Kirsten Weld, *Paper Cadavers: The Archives of Dictatorship in Guatemala* (Durham: Duke University Press, 2014), Chap. 4.

111. Davidson, "Rural Credit," 14. For a list of the agencies, see Way, *Mayan*, 126–27, 251.
112. Gustavo Porras Castejón, *Las huellas de Guatemala* (Guatemala City: F&G Editores, 2009), 6.
113. In particular, USAID commissioned evaluations of three components of the Rural Community Leadership and Modernization Program: credit union development and the agricultural cooperative school (both in 1969), and CAPS (1970). For a more general assessment led by an Iowa State University team, see Lehman Fletcher, Eric Graber, William Merrill, and Erik Thorbecke, *Guatemala's Economic Development: The Role of Agriculture* (Ames: Iowa State University Press, 1970).
114. USAID Project Appraisal Report, "Rural Community Leadership & Modernization Project—Credit Union Development/CUNA" (1969), 14, 15. Available at DEC.
115. Davidson, "Rural Credit," 5.
116. William H. Rusch, Fred L. Mann, and Eugene Braun, "Rural Cooperatives in Guatemala: A Study of their Development and Evaluation of A.I.D. Programs in their Support," Volume I, PN-AAB-6s6 (McLean, VA: American Technical Assistance Corporation, 1976), 22. Available at DEC.
117. Cited in Morrissey, "A Missionary Directed Resettlement Project," 75–76.
118. Until 1971, CUNA remained in an advisory role, moving out of most Latin American countries and concentrating on the development of a regional credit union confederation. USAID, "Support for Credit Union Development by the Agency for International Development," PN-AAJ-604 (May 1, 1980), 7–8. Available at DEC.
119. David Fledderjohn, "Terminal Report: Agricultural Cooperative Project in Guatemala," ACDI (October 1976), 45 (available at DEC); Davidson, "Rural Credit," 14. The shift had begun under CUNA's watch.
120. ACDI Monthly Report, March 8, 1971, NARA RG 286, Entry P397, Box 1, Folder Coop: ACDI Monthly Reports FY/71, 1.
121. Davidson, "Rural Credit," 7, 11.
122. Fledderjohn, "Regional Cooperatives in Guatemala," *Development Digest* 12:2 (1974), 15–16.
123. Davidson, "Rural Credit," 23. Older cooperatives "complained bitterly about these norms," reported Fledderjohn in "Terminal Report: Agricultural Cooperative Project in Guatemala" (ACDI/USAID: 1976), 27. Available at DEC.
124. Fledderjohn, "Terminal Report," 26–27.
125. Fledderjohn, "Terminal Report," 28.
126. Davidson, "Rural Credit," 25.
127. See EACA's termination notice, NARA RG 286, Entry P397, Box 1, Folder CCOP/E A.C.A. (Contracts) FY-71.
128. The longstanding association of cooperatives with the opposition Christian Dem-

ocratic Party also recommended a policy of compensatory apoliticism. Davidson, "Rural Credit," 15.

129. Fledderjohn, *Building Small Farmer Cooperatives: A Central American Experience* (Washington, DC: ACDI, 1990), 12.
130. May, *Terror,* 87.
131. Fledderjohn, "Terminal Report," 12–13.
132. May, *Terror,* 124.
133. Way, *Mayan,* 133.
134. "Laugerud: 'El campesino tiene derecho a vivir mejor,'" *Diario grafico* (December 7, 1974), 1; "Texto del discurso presidencial," *Imparcial* (July 1, 1975), 2. Both available at CIRMA.
135. "Institucionalizado el movimiento cooperativista," *Diario de Centro America* (January 14, 1975), 1. Available at CIRMA.
136. Baltasar Morales de la Cruz, "La Accion Cooperativista (I)," *Diaria Prensa Libre* (December 5, 1974), n.p. Available at CIRMA. The *economia popular* typically designates those sectors beyond the formal labor market.
137. "El cooperativismo (I)," *Diario grafico,* December 9, 1974, n.p. Available at CIRMA.
138. For an account of the EGP's rise by one if its founders, see Mario Payeras, *Days of the Jungle: The Testimony of a Guatemalan Guerrillero, 1972–76* (New York: Monthly Review Press, 1983/1981).
139. Berger, *Political and Agrarian Development,* 176–77.
140. For a particularly vicious 1975 threat published in the paper *La tarde,* see Michael McClintock, *The American Connection,* vol. 2: *State Terror and Popular Resistance in Guatemala* (London: Zed, 1985), 134. Another vivid account of military violence is the Maryknoll Victor Montejo's *Testimony: Death of a Guatemalan Village* (Willimantic, CT: Curbstone, 1987).
141. Quoted in McClintock, *American Connection,* 133.
142. Cited in Jennifer Schirmer, *The Guatemalan Military Project: A Violence Called Democracy* (Philadelphia: University of Pennsylvania Press, 1998), 75.
143. On the project, see Morrissey, "A Missionary Directed Resettlement Project"; Sarah Foss, *On Our Own Terms: Development and Indigeneity in Cold War Guatemala* (Chapel Hill: University of North Carolina Press, 2022), Chap. 6. A similar migration, organized by Gurriarán, moved in from Santa Cruz del Quiché. On this community, see Beatriz Manz, *Paradise in Ashes: A Guatemalan Journey of Courage, Terror, and Hope* (Berkeley: University of California Press, 2004). On Gurriarán's cooperative efforts in Santa Cruz, see Luisa Frank and Philip Wheaton, *Indian Guatemala: Path to Liberation* (Washington, DC: EPICA, 1984), 33; and Carmack, "The Story of Santa Cruz Quiché," in Carmack, ed., *Harvest of Violence,* 39–69.
144. Foss, *On Our Own Terms,* 6.
145. Falla, *Ixcan,* 126, 123.
146. Manz, *Paradise in Ashes,* 66, 20.
147. Manz, "The Transformation of La Esperanza, an Ixcán Village," in Carmack, ed., *Harvest of Violence,* 72, 75–76.

148. Falla, *Ixcán: El campesino indígena se levanta: Guatemala 1966–1982* (Guatemala: AVANCSO, 2015), 57.
149. Morrissey, "A Missionary Directed Resettlement Project," 460. Woods was killed in a mysterious 1976 plane crash.
150. Konefal, *Indio,* 69.
151. "Operacion Ixcan," *Revista militar* (July–August 1977), 25, 41–42 (available at CIRMA, Col. E, No. 72). The journal *Revista militar* was founded by Laugerud.
152. Falla, *Ixcan,* 89.
153. The original INACOP proposal dated to the Laugerud years. The new administrative architecture also included INGECOP (Inspección General de Cooperativas) and CONACO (Coordinadora General de Cooperativas), later absorbed into INACOP.
154. "Total apoliticidad en cooperatives afiliadas al INACOP: Castillo R." *Prensa libre* (October 1981), n.p. Available at CIRMA.
155. "Cancelan inscripción de 200 cooperatives," *Prensa libre* (October 13, 1981); "Nuevos centros cooperativistas se van a creer en los areas conflictivas," *Imparcial* (October 6, 1982), n.p.; "INACOP asume desafío para demostrar rentabilidad de las cooperativas," *Noticias del INACOP* (September and October 1983), 13. All available at CIRMA.
156. Gustavo Barascout Ramás, "Resumen historico del movimiento cooperativo de Guatemala" (Guatemala City: INACOP, July 1983), 1–2. Available at CIRMA, Código 10–01–05 (Cooperativas), Cartapacio 112.
157. "El movimiento cooperativo guatemalteco," *Grafico* (November 18, 1981), 47. Available at CIRMA.
158. "An den Leiter der Menchschenrechtsabteilung des Vereinten Nationen," unpublished report (April 16, 1982), 2. Available at CIRMA, Código 10–01–05 (Cooperativas), Cartapacio 112. For other grisly accounts of military violence, see Foss, *On Our Own Terms,* 194–98.
159. "MCG: 'Una estrategia creativa de organizacion . . . ,'" unpublished brochure (Guatemala: MCG, August 1991), 5. Available at CIRMA, CAS, 002–1075.
160. May, *Terror,* 125.
161. "El mito del cooperativismo," *Pulso rural* 2:1 (1994), 9–12. Available at CIRMA, CAS, 002–1125.
162. "Zusammenfassende Übersetzung eines Artikels der exilguatemaltekischen Hilfsorganisation—Instancia Obrero Campesina de Emergencia," unpublished report (August 1985), 2. Available at CIRMA, Código 10–01–05 (Cooperativas), Cartapacio 112.
163. The signal event of the intensifying violence was the Panzós massacre of 1978, detailed by Grandin in *The Last Colonial Massacre.* In Ixcán, the 1975 rebel execution of the notorious landowner Luis Arenas, whose cruelty to laborers earned him the nickname "the Tiger of the Ixcan," is also cited.
164. Philip Dennis, Gary Elbow, and Peter Heller, "Development under Fire: The Playa Grande Colonization Project in Guatemala," *Human Organization* 47:1 (Spring 1988), 71.

165. Dennis, Elbow, and Heller/USAID, "Evaluation of the Ixcan Colonization Project (520-T-026) Guatemala" (Texas Tech, January 1984), 11. Available at DEC.
166. Fledderjohn and Thompson, "Final Report: Northern Transversal Strip Land Resettlement Project" (1982), 19. Available at DEC.
167. Fledderjohn and Thompson, "Final Report," 15. Grandin, too, in *The Last Colonial Massacre,* noted this continued belief in the necessity of government services, perhaps a residue of the October Revolution.
168. Fledderjohn and Thompson, "Final Report," 3.
169. Fledderjohn and Thompson, "Final Report," 24.
170. Fledderjohn and Thompson, "Final Report," 3–4. On the self-help goal, see Dennis et al./USAID, "Evaluation of the Ixcan Colonization Project," 5.
171. Fledderjohn and Thompson, "Final Report," 10, 28.
172. Fledderjohn and Thompson, "Final Report," 7. What J. T. Way writes about twenty-first-century Guatemala applies, *mutatis mutandis,* to earlier eras and many impoverished countries: Guatemala "escapes both the control and the gaze of the state. There are no accurate population statistics or up-to-date maps; place-names are wrong on Google Earth. . . . [O]verlapping layers of authority and opaque structures of power make it difficult to know who, if anyone, is in charge." Way, *Agrotopolis: Youth, Street, and Nation in the New Urban Guatemala* (Berkeley: University of California Press, 2021), 1–2.
173. Fledderjohn and Thompson, "Final Report," 17, 24.
174. Dennis et al./USAID, "Evaluation of the Ixcan Colonization Project (520-T-026) Guatemala" (Texas Tech, January 1984), 4.
175. Fledderjohn and Thompson, "Final Report," 10.
176. Dennis et al./USAID, "Evaluation," 11. According to project managers, federation attitudes "ranged from lukewarm interest to outright opposition," with one advertising its withdrawal in a newspaper, saying that project rules "would condemn settlers to poverty." Fledderjohn and Thompson, "Final Report," 9.
177. Fledderjohn and Thompson, "Final Report," 12, 18–19.
178. Fledderjohn and Thompson, "Final Report," 7.
179. Dennis et al., "Development under Fire," 72.
180. "Frequently questions were raised such as 'Is it true that the government wants us to go there so that the large landowners can have a supply of labor?' 'Is there a guerrilla war going on there?' 'What sort of surveying and title can we expect so that our lands won't be taken away once we get them into production?'" Fledderjohn and Thompson, "Final Report," 21.
181. Fledderjohn and Thompson, "Final Report," 30; Falla, *Ixcán,* 148.
182. Fledderjohn and Thompson, "Final Report," 43.
183. Fledderjohn and Thompson, "Final Report," 28–29.
184. Dennis et al./USAID, "Evaluation," 16.
185. Fledderjohn and Thompson, "Final Report," 39.
186. Dennis et al./USAID, "Evaluation," 26–27.
187. Dennis et al., "Development under Fire," 75.
188. Dennis et al./USAID, "Evaluation," 8, 27.

189. "Land and Labor in Guatemala: An Assessment," USAID/DAI, 38. See also Fledderjohn and Thompson, "Final Report," 31.
190. USAID support for military rebuilding of the despoiled regions continued into the mid-1980s. Schirmer, *Guatemalan Military Project*, 67–68. For Rios-Montt's later conviction, see the *Sentencia por genocidio y delitos contra los deberes de humanidad contra el pueblo Maya Ixil* (Guatemala: Asociación para la Justicia y Reconciliación and the Centro para la Acción Legal en Derechos Humanos, 2013).
191. Compare Dennis et al./USAID, "Evaluation" (1984) with Dennis et al., "Development under Fire" (1988).
192. Foss, *On Our Own Terms*, 183.
193. Dennis et al., "Development under Fire," 73–75.
194. Manz, *Paradise in Ashes*, 27.
195. The economist Dudley Seers used this phrase to describe the jargon of the United Nations. Cited in Arturo Escobar, "Dudley Seers," in David Simon, ed., *Fifty Key Thinkers on Development* (London: Routledge, 2006), 228.
196. Other USAID cooperative projects foundered during the early 1980s as well. See, for example, Peter Kolar, "Project Evaluation Summary, Small Farmer Marketing Systems" (Project 520–0238) (September 10, 1982), 7. Available at DEC.
197. David Stoll, *Between Two Armies in the Ixil Towns of Guatemala* (New York: Columbia University Press, 1994), 284–86.
198. Interview with Oswaldo Oliva, head of MICOOPE (the renamed FENACOAC), Guatemala's leading cooperative federation, July 23, 2018, Guatemala City. Even in 2018, he remarked, the advocates of cooperativism had to fend off accusations of socialism.
199. Konefal, *Indio*, Chap. 7.

Chapter 6. The Presentist Bias

1. Robert Chambers, *Revolutions in Development Inquiry* (London: Earthscan, 2008), 68.
2. Hans Singer, "Poverty, Income Distribution, and Levels of Living: Thirty Years of Changing Thought on Development Problems," in C. H. H. Rao and P. C. Joshi, eds., *Reflections on Economic Development and Social Change: Essays in Honour of V. K. R. V. Rao* (Oxford: Martin Robertson, 1979), 29–40.
3. Patrick Allan Sharma, *Robert McNamara's Other War: The World Bank and International Development* (Philadelphia: University of Pennsylvania Press, 2017); Joanne Meyerowitz, *A War on Global Poverty: The Lost Promise of Redistribution and the Rise of Microcredit* (Princeton: Princeton University Press, 2021).
4. Dharam Ghai, "Basic Needs and its Critics," *IDS Bulletin* 9:4 (June 1978), 16.
5. John Cole, *The Poor of the Earth* (London: Macmillan, 1976).
6. Denis Goulet, *The Cruel Choice: A New Concept in the Theory of Development* (New York: Atheneum, 1975), vii.
7. Alex Inkeles and David Smith, *Becoming Modern: Individual Change in Six Developing Countries* (Cambridge: Harvard University Press, 1972).

8. Colin Leys, *The Rise and Fall of Development Theory* (Bloomington: Indiana University Press, 1996); Nils Gilman, *Mandarins of the Future: Modernization Theory in Cold War America* (Baltimore: Johns Hopkins University Press, 2003); David Ekbladh, *The Great American Mission: Modernization and the Construction of an American World Order* (Princeton: Princeton University Press, 2010); and Michael E. Latham, *The Right Kind of Revolution: Modernization, Development, and U.S. Foreign Policy from the Cold War to the Present* (Ithaca: Cornell University Press, 2011).
9. Nick Cullather, *The Hungry World: America's Cold War Battle against Poverty in Asia* (Cambridge: Harvard University Press, 2010), 205–31.
10. Colin Clark, *Growthmanship: A Study in the Mythology of Investment* (London: Barrie and Rockliff, 1961). On challenges to the growth paradigm, see Matthias Schmelzer, *The Hegemony of Growth: The Making and Remaking of the Economic Growth Paradigm and the OECD, 1948–2010* (Cambridge: Cambridge, 2016); and Stephen Macekura, *The Mismeasure of Progress: Economic Growth and its Critics* (Chicago: University of Chicago Press, 2020).
11. Gunnar Myrdal, *Asian Drama: An Inquiry in the Poverty of Nations* (3 volumes) (New York: Pantheon, 1968).
12. Myrdal, *An American Dilemma: The Negro Problem and Modern Democracy* (New York: Harper, 1944). For his international welfare proposals, see Myrdal, *An International Economy: Problems and Prospects* (New York: Harper & Brothers, 1956); and Myrdal, *Rich Lands and Poor: The Road to World Prosperity* (published in Britain as *Economic Theory and Under-Developed Regions*) (New York: Harper & Row, 1957). On his hopes for global welfare, see Samuel Moyn, "Welfare World," *Humanity* 8:1 (Spring 2017), 175–83.
13. For an account of the project, see William J. Barber, *Gunnar Myrdal: An Intellectual Biography* (New York: Palgrave Macmillan, 2008), Chap. 9.
14. Benjamin Siegel, "Asian Drama Revisited," *Humanity* 8:1 (Spring 2017), 195–205. The Naxalite rebellion in West Bengal proved particularly stubborn.
15. Myrdal, *Asian Drama*, 565–66.
16. Two years later, he issued the same warning in Myrdal, *The Challenge of World Poverty: A World Anti-Poverty Program in Outline* (New York: Pantheon, 1970), Chap. 1.
17. Richard Jolly, "Dudley Seers (1920–1983)," in Philip Arestis and Malcolm Sawyer, eds., *A Biographical Dictionary of Dissenting Economists* (Aldershot: Elgar, 1992), 491–99; Arturo Escobar, "Dudley Seers," in David Simon, ed., *Fifty Key Thinkers on Development* (London: Routledge, 2006), 224–30. The *IDS Bulletin* 20:3 presents a set of essays on his work.
18. Dudley Seers, "What Are We Trying to Measure?" *Journal of Development Studies* 8:3 (1972), 24. In the late 1970s, he added self-reliance as another goal. Seers, "The New Meaning of Development," *International Development Review* 19:3 (1977), 2–7.
19. At ECLA, Seers was involved in debates over the causes of developing-country inflation. Seers, "A Theory of Inflation and Growth in Under-Developed Countries Based on the Experience of Latin America," *Oxford Economic Papers* 14:2 (June

1962), 173–95. For later works that reflect his continuing collaboration with ECLA thinkers, see Osvaldo Sunkel, G. Maynard, D. Seers, and J. G. Olivera, *Inflación y estructura economica* (Buenos Aires: Paidos, 1967); and Seers, ed., *Dependency Theory: A Critical Reassessment* (London: Frances Pinter, 1981). He retained an abiding interest in Chile, participating in conferences organized by the Allende government and helping to resettle economists-in-exile after the 1973 coup—including Osvaldo Sunkel at IDS. Jolly, "Dudley Seers," 27–28.

20. "Report of the UN/ECA/FAO Economic Survey Mission on the Economic Development of Zambia" (Ndola: Falcon Press, 1964). On the impact of the Seers report, see Miles Larmer, "Historical Perspectives on Zambia's Mining Booms and Busts," in Alastair Fraser and Larmer, eds., *Zambia, Mining, and Neoliberalism: Boom and Bust on the Globalized Copper Belt* (New York: Palgrave Macmillan, 2010), 35. See also Seers, "The Use of a Modified Input-Output System for an Economic Program in Zambia" (Sussex: IDS, 1967).
21. On Seers's time at the ministry, see Paul Streeten, "Dudley Seers: An Appreciation," *IDS Bulletin* 20:3 (1989), 26–30.
22. Seers, "Why Visiting Economists Fail," *Journal of Political Economy* 70:4 (August 1962), 325–38; Seers, "The Limitations of the Special Case," *Oxford Bulletin of Economics and Statistics* 25:2 (May 1963), 77–98. For a house history, see Richard Jolly, "A Short History of IDS: A Personal Reflection," IDS Discussion Paper 388 (Institute for Development Studies, January 2008).
23. ILO, *Towards Full Employment, A Programme for Colombia Prepared by an Inter-agency Team Organised by the International Labour Office* (Geneva: ILO, 1970).
24. He "had a knack for getting his ideas and visions translated into practice." Quoted in Arturo Escobar, "Dudley Seers," 228. For Jolly, Seers "was at his best analyzing real-life situations." Jolly, "Dudley Seers," *IDS Bulletin* 20:3 (1989), 33.
25. Seers, "Limitations," 79, 93.
26. Seers, "The Political Economy of National Accounting," in Alec Cairncross and Mohinder Puri, eds., *Employment, Income Distribution and Development Strategy: Problems of the Developing Countries—Essays in Honour of H. W. Singer* (New York: Holmes and Meier, 1976), 193, 200. For a critique of Seers's views on national accounting, see John Toye, *Dilemmas of Development: Reflections on the Counter-Revolution in Development Theory and Policy* (Oxford: Basil Blackwell, 1987), 35–41; and Toye, "Nationalism and Structuralism: Two Themes in the Work of Dudley Seers," *IDS Bulletin* 20:3 (1989), 55–57.
27. Seers, "Limitations," 79, 93–96.
28. Seers, "The Cultural Lag in Economics," in Jozef Pajestka and C. H. Feinstein, eds., *The Relevance of Economic Theories* (London: Macmillan, 1980), 6 (italics in original).
29. Seers, "Measure," 22.
30. Seers, "Why Visiting Economists Fail," 329–30.
31. Seers, "Measure," 32.
32. "The Coyococ Declaration," *International Organization* 29:3 (Summer 1975), 896–97. See also Meyerowitz, *A War on Global Poverty*, 68–70.

33. Louis Lefeber, "On the Paradigm for Economic Development," *World Development* 2:1 (January 1974), 1.
34. Michael Lipton, *Why Poor People Stay Poor: Urban Bias in World Development* (Cambridge: Harvard University Press, 1977), 32–43.
35. See Streeten, "Single Barrier Theories of Development" and "How Poor Are the Poor Countries and Why?" in Streeten, *The Frontiers of Development Studies* (London: Macmillan, 1972), 13–37. For a churlish review of Lipton, see T. J. Byres, "Of Neo-Populist Pipedreams: Daedalus in the Third World and the Myth of Urban Bias," *Journal of Peasant Studies* 6:2 (1979), 210–44. For a more recent critique of the hard division between urban and rural, see James Ferguson, *Expectations of Modernity: Myths and Meanings of Urban Life on the Zambian Copperbelt* (Berkeley: University of California Press, 1999).
36. Hans Singer, *Technologies for Basic Need* (Geneva: ILO, 1977), 5, 11–27.
37. Edgar Owens and Robert Shaw, *Development Reconsidered* (Lexington, MA: Heath, 1974), xix–xx; Woods quoted in Barbara Ward, Lenore d'Anjou, and J. D. Runnalls, eds., *The Widening Gap: Development in the 1970s* (New York: Columbia University Press, 1971), 2–3.
38. Robert McNamara, "Speech to the World Bank Board of Governors, September 21, 1970," in *The McNamara Years at the World Bank: Major Policy Addresses of Robert S. McNamara, 1968–1981* (Baltimore: Johns Hopkins University Press, 1981), 128.
39. Chambers, *Rural Development: Putting the Last First* (Essex: Longman, 1983), 25; see the full chapter for the discussion of biases.
40. Paul Bairoch, *The Economic Development of the Third World since 1900* (Berkeley: University of California Press, 1975/1970); Richard Weisskoff, "Income Distribution and Economic Growth in Puerto Rico, Argentina, and Mexico," *Review of Income and Wealth* 16:4 (1970); V. M. Dandekar and Nilakantha Rath, "Poverty in India—I: Dimensions and Trends," *Economic and Political Weekly* 6:1 (January 2, 1971); ILO, *Employment, Incomes, and Equity: A Strategy for Increasing Productive Employment in Kenya* (Geneva: ILO, 1972); Albert Fishlow, "Brazilian Size Distribution of Income," *American Economic Review* 62:1–2 (March 1, 1972); Irma Adelman and Cynthia Taft Morris, *Economic Growth and Social Equity in Developing Countries* (Stanford: Stanford University Press, 1973); Hollis Chenery and Moises Syrquin, *Patterns of Development, 1950–1970* (Washington, DC: World Bank, 1975); ILO, *Poverty and Landlessness in Rural Asia* (Geneva: ILO, 1977); David Morawetz, *Twenty-five Years of Economic Development, 1950–1975* (Baltimore: Johns Hopkins University Press, 1977); John McHale and Magda Cordell McHale, *Basic Human Needs: A Framework for Action* (New Brunswick, NJ: Transaction, 1977); Montek Ahluwalia, N. G. Carter, and Hollis Chenery, "Growth and Poverty in Developing Countries," *Journal of Development Economics* 6 (1979), 299–341.
41. Quoted in Goulet, "Strategies for Meeting Human Needs," in *Growth with Equity: Strategies for Meeting Human Needs* (New York: Paulist, 1979), 60.
42. Morawetz, *Twenty-five Years of Economic Development*, 7–10.
43. See Lester Brown, the chief of the USDA's International Agricultural Develop-

ment Service, *Seeds of Change: The Green Revolution and Development in the 1970's* (New York: Praeger, 1970); Cullather, *The Hungry World.*

44. Branko Milanovic, *Visions of Inequality from the French Revolution to the End of the Cold War* (Cambridge: Harvard University Press, 2023), 189. The other was John Maynard Keynes. On Kuznets, see the whole of Chap. 6.
45. Simon Kuznets, "Economic Growth and Income Inequality," *American Economic Review* 45:1 (March 1955), 25, 26, 28. See also the series of articles entitled "Quantitative Aspects of the Economic Growth of Nations" that Kuznets published in the journal *Economic Development and Cultural Change* in the late 1950s and early 1960s.
46. Kuznets, "The Gap: Concept, Measurement, Trends," in Gustav Ranis, ed., *The Gap between Rich and Poor Nations: Proceedings of a Conference Held by the International Economic Association at Bled, Yugoslavia* (London: Macmillan, 1972), 3–41. By the time the Bled proceedings were published, Kuznets had won the Nobel Prize.
47. Dandekar and Rath, "Poverty in India—I," 25.
48. Dandekar and Rath, "Poverty in India—I," 46, 40. Since they focused on the relation between the earnings of the top 40 percent of the population and the second lowest decile, their projected thirty-five-year horizon did not even account for the very poorest. Their study's second installment is "Poverty in India—II: Policies and Programmes," *Economic and Political Weekly* 6:2 (January 9, 1971), 106–46.
49. Weisskoff, "Income Distribution and Economic Growth," 304–05, 327.
50. Fishlow, "Brazilian Size Distribution of Income," 391, 402.
51. Chenery and Syrquin, *Patterns of Development,* 3–4.
52. Montek Ahluwalia, "Inequality, Poverty and Development," *Journal of Development Economics* 3 (1976), 307–08; Chenery and Syrquin, *Patterns of Development,* 63.
53. Morawetz, *Twenty-five Years of Economic Development,* 39.
54. Lewis, "Development and Distribution," in Cairncross and Puri, eds., *Employment, Income Distribution and Development Strategy,* eds., 26–42.
55. See, for example, Jeffrey B. Nugent and Pan A. Yotopoulos, "What Has Orthodox Development Economics Learned from Recent Experience?" in Charles Wilber, ed., *The Political Economy of Development and Under-Development,* 3d ed. (New York: Random House, 1984), 26–44.
56. For her use of East Asian examples, see Adelman, "Growth, Income Distribution and Equity-oriented Development Strategies," *World Development* 3:2 and 3 (1975), 67–76; and Adelman, ed., *Practical Approaches to Development Planning: Korea's Second Five-Year Plan* (Baltimore: Johns Hopkins University Press, 1969).
57. Adelman and Morris, "Growth and Impoverishment in the Middle of the Nineteenth Century," *World Development* 6:3 (1978), 256.
58. Adelman, "Development Economics—A Reassessment of Goals," *American Economic Review* 65:2 (1975), 306–08.
59. Adelman and Morris, *Economic Growth and Social Equity,* 192–93, 199, 201–02.
60. Mahbub ul Haq, *The Poverty Curtain: Choices for the Third World* (New York: Columbia University Press, 1976), xv. On Haq, see Marcus Power, "Mahbub ul Haq,"

in Simon, ed., *Fifty Key Thinkers*, 264–70; Meyerowitz, *A War on Global Poverty*, 45–46, 72–76; Samuel Moyn, *Not Enough: Human Rights in an Unequal World* (Cambridge: Harvard University Press, 2018), 127–32, 139–41.

61. Haq, *The Strategy of Economic Planning: A Case Study of Pakistan* (Karachi: Oxford University Press, 1963). In a 1982 oral history, he described Pakistani development in the 1960s as "warped." Interview with Robert Asher, The World Bank/IFC Archives—Oral History Program (December 3, 1982), 2: https://documents1.worldbank.org/curated/en/538481468338976295/pdf/790280TRN0Haq00iew0December03001982.pdf. See also Haq, "The Crisis in Development Strategies" (1973), in Wilber, ed., *The Political Economy of Development and Underdevelopment* (New York: Random House, 1973), 367–72, which criticized poor economic decision-making in developing countries.
62. Quoted in Power, "Mahbub ul Haq," 268.
63. Haq, *The Poverty Curtain: Choices for the Third World* (New York: Columbia University Press, 1976), Chap. 1, 204.
64. Quoted in Power, "Mahbub ul Haq," 265. Contra Adelman, Haq argued that Israel and the Tigers were too exceptional to serve as models. The better archetype was China, just emerging from two decades of isolation with a remarkably egalitarian wealth scale, modest growth rates, and full employment—and without "the worst forms of poverty." Haq, *Poverty Curtain*, 37, 61, 73. For an alternate reading of Chinese success as part of a revised basic needs program, see Ajit Singh, "The 'Basic Needs' Approach to Development vs. the New International Economic Order: The Significance of Third World Industrialization," *World Development* 7 (1979), 585–606.
65. James Grant, "Development: The End of Trickle Down?" *Foreign Policy* 12 (Autumn 1973), 62. His title was interrogative, not declarative.
66. Cited in Grant, "Development," 43. On New Directions, see Samuel Hale Butterfield, *U.S. Development Aid—An Historic First: Achievements and Failures in the Twentieth Century* (Westport, CT: Praeger, 2004), 175–96.
67. John Norris, *The Enduring Struggle: The History of the U.S. Agency for International Development and America's Uneasy Transformation of the World* (Lanham: Rowman & Littlefield, 2021), 102–03.
68. McNamara invoked the term poorest 40% in several policy speeches before the Bank's Board of Governors. On these years, see Sharma, *Robert McNamara's Other War;* Finnemore, "Redefining Development at the World Bank"; and Robert L. Ayres, *Banking on the Poor: The World Bank and Poverty* (Cambridge: MIT Press, 1985). McNamara's speeches are collected in *The McNamara Years at the World Bank: Major Policy Addresses of Robert S. McNamara, 1968–1981* (Baltimore: Johns Hopkins University Press, 1981).
69. McNamara, *The McNamara Years*, xi, xiii. At the same time, he was a strong defender of past development efforts. See his September 26, 1977, "Speech to the Bank's Board of Governors" in McNamara, *The McNamara Years*, 435–75.
70. Quoted in Sharma, *Robert McNamara's Other War*, 57.
71. The Pearson Commission, *Partners in Development: Report of the Commission on*

International Development (New York: Praeger, 1969). See also Pearson, *The Crisis of Development* (New York: Praeger, 1970).

72. Conference Declaration quoted in Ward et al., eds., *The Widening Gap*, 10–13.
73. ILO teams went to Colombia, Ceylon, Kenya, Iran, the Philippines, the Dominican Republic, and Sudan. For reviews of the early missions, see Singer and Jolly, "Unemployment in an African Setting: Lessons of the Employment Strategy Mission to Kenya"; Jolly, Seers, and Singer, "The Pilot Missions under the World Employment Programme," *IDS Communication 111* (1973); and Erik Thorbecke, "The Employment Problem: A Critical Evaluation of Four ILO Comprehensive Country Reports," *International Labour Review* 107:5 (May 1973), 393–423.
74. ILO, *Employment, Incomes, and Equality*, 98.
75. ILO, *Employment, Incomes, and Equality*, 325–27.
76. ILO, *Employment, Incomes, and Equality*, 12.
77. The new movement produced a reader: Chenery, Ahluwalia, C. L. G. Bell, John H. Duloy, and Richard Jolly, *Redistribution with Growth* (London: Oxford University Press, 1974). For competing growth and equity models, see James H. Weaver, Kenneth P. Jameson, and Richard N. Blue, "Growth and Equity: Can They Be Happy Together?" *International Development Review* 20:1 (1978), 20–27; and Mary Evelyn Jegen and Charles K. Wilber, eds., *Growth with Equity*.
78. ILO, *Employment, Growth, and Basic Needs: A One-World Problem* (New York: Praeger, 1977).
79. Moyn, *Not Enough*, Chap. 5.
80. Veteran diplomat Harlan Cleveland's Introduction to John and Magda Cordell McHale, *Basic Human Needs* (New Brunswick: Transaction, 1977) provides a good review of the strategy.
81. Francis Wilson, "Paul Patrick Streeten," in Simon, ed., *Fifty Key Thinkers*, 252–58.
82. Streeten, *Frontiers*, Part 1. See also Streeten, *Aid to Africa: A Policy Outline for the 1970's* (New York: Praeger, 1972).
83. Frances Stewart and Streeten, "New Strategies for Development: Poverty, Income Distribution, and Growth," *Oxford Economic Papers* 28:3 (November 1976), 403–04.
84. Meyerowitz, *A War on Global Poverty*, 72–76.
85. Streeten and Shahid Javed Burki, "Basic Needs: Some Issues," *World Development* 6:3 (1978), 412, 413, 414. See also Streeten, "Development Ideas in Historical Perspective," in *Toward a New Strategy for Development: A Rothko Chapel Colloquium* (New York: Pergamon, 1979), 21–52.
86. Streeten, *First Things First: Meeting Basic Needs in Developing Countries* (Oxford: Oxford University Press, 1981), 192. See also Streeten's lectures on human development in *Thinking about Development* (Cambridge: Cambridge University Press, 1995). The rights equation also appears in Ghai, A. R. Khan, E. L. H. Lee, and T. Alfthan, *The Basic Needs Approach to Development: Some Issues Regarding Concepts and Methodology* (Geneva: ILO, 1977); and ILO, *Employment, Growth, and Basic Needs.*
87. Stewart and Streeten, "New Strategies," 388, 394; Streeten and Nurki, "Basic Needs," 416.
88. Stewart, *Planning to Meet Basic Needs* (London: Macmillan, 1985), 4.

89. Stewart, *Planning to Meet Basic Needs*, 4–6.
90. Reported in Jolly, "A Short History of the IDS," 40n39. Streeten, *First Things First*, 34, swatted aside this complaint as simplistic.
91. Jolly, "The World Employment Conference: The Enthronement of Basic Needs," *ODI Review* 2 (1976), 31–44; Benjamin Higgins, "The Disenthronement of Basic Needs? Twenty Questions," *Regional Development Dialogue* 1:1 (1980), 79–128.
92. Quoted in Wilson, "Paul Patrick Streeten," 255.
93. Streeten, "Basic Needs: Some Unsettled Questions," *World Development* 12:9 (1984), 973–78. Today, behavioral economists argue that humans are poor judges of their interests and should be 'nudged' by benevolent public policy.
94. Anne Hope and Sally Timmel, *Training for Transformation: A Handbook for Community Workers*, Book 1 (Zimbabwe: Mambo Press, 1984), 8.
95. On this domesticating reception, see Stanley Aronowitz, "Paulo Freire's Radical Democratic Humanism," in *Paulo Freire: A Critical Encounter* (London: Routledge, 1993), 8–24; and Donald Macedo, Introduction to *Freire, Pedagogy of the Oppressed: 50th Anniversary Edition* (New York: Bloomsbury, 2018), 1–33; as well as the "Interviews with Contemporary Scholars" in the same volume, 191–213.
96. Human capital models continued to exert influence. See George Psacharopoulos, *Returns to Education: An International Comparison* (Amsterdam: Elsevier, 1972).
97. E. F. Schumacher, *Small Is Beautiful: Economics as if People Mattered* (London: Blond and Briggs, 1973). On Schumacher, see Stephen Macekura, *Of Limits and Growth: The Rise of Global Sustainable Development in the Twentieth Century* (Cambridge: Cambridge University Press, 2015), Chap. 4; Robert Leonard, "E. F. Schumacher and Intermediate Technology," *History of Political Economy* 50 (2018), 249–65; and Tony Binns, "E. F. (Fritz) Schumacher," in Simon, ed., *Fifty Development Thinkers*, 218–23.
98. For a critique of localism à la Schumacher, see Trevor Latimer, *Small Isn't Beautiful: The Case against Localism* (Washington, DC: Brookings Institution Press, 2023).
99. Chambers, *Rural Development*; as well as *Managing Rural Development: Ideas and Experience from East Africa* (West Hartford: Kumarian, 1985); *Challenging the Processions: Frontiers for Rural Development* (London: Intermediate Technology, 1993); *Whose Reality Counts? Putting the First Last* (London: Intermediate Technology Publications, 1997); and *Revolutions in Development Inquiry* (2008). On Chambers, see Michael Parnwell, "Robert Chambers," in Simon, ed., *Fifty Development Thinkers*, 73–78.
100. On the Freirian inspiration, see Chambers, *Rural Development*, 73; and Chambers, *Whose Reality Counts?* 106. For a discussion of some of the contradictions of participation in a different time and place, see Kari Henquinet, "Reformulating Participation in Nigerien Development Programs: An Examination of Conflicting Messages Concerning Gender and Class," in Nana Akua Amponsah, ed., *Beyond the Boundaries: Toyin Falola and the Art of Genre-Bending* (Trenton: Africa World, 2014), 647–74. According to one of Henquinet's Nigerienne respondents, participation actually meant "'What they tell us to do, we do'" (659), a definition I heard repeated almost verbatim by a colleague in Bangladesh.

101. The issue was complex, since economists also expected a certain amount of population increase to fuel overall economic growth.
102. Vandana Desai, "Ester Boserup," in Simon, ed., *Fifty Key Thinkers*, 50–51.
103. Ester Boserup, *The Conditions of Agricultural Growth: The Economics of Agrarian Change under Population Pressure* (Chicago: Aldine, 1965), 121. James Scott, *Against the Grain: A Deep History of the Earliest States* (New Haven: Yale University Press, 2017), has recently taken inspiration from Boserup's early work.
104. Boserup, *Woman's Role in Economic Development* (London: Earthscan, 2007/1970), 179.
105. Boserup, *Woman's Role*, 184.
106. For a later instantiation of the Women in Development paradigm, see the work of Diane Elson, notably *Male Bias in the Development Process* (Manchester: Manchester University Press, 1991).
107. For a history of the movement, see Macekura, *Of Limits and Growth.*
108. Moyn, *Not Enough;* and Moyn, *The Last Utopia: Human Rights in History* (Cambridge: Harvard University Press, 2012).
109. Ghai et al., *The Basic-Needs Approach to Development*, 16.
110. "If they appear to have no economic history, it is mostly because it has yet to be written." IDS, "Myths about the Development Process," *IDS Bulletin* 1:4 (1969), 14–15.
111. Haq, *The Poverty Curtain*, 21.
112. The most thorough investigation of the classical resurgence is John Toye, *Dilemmas of Development.*
113. Peter Bauer, *Economic Analysis and Policy in Underdeveloped Countries* (Durham: Duke University Press, 1957), 15, 37.
114. Bauer, *Dissent on Development: Studies and Debates in Development Economics* (Cambridge: Harvard University Press, 1972), 78–79; Bauer, "Remembrance of Studies Past: Retracing First Steps," in Gerald Meier and Dudley Seers, eds., *Pioneers in Development* (New York: World Bank, 1984), 33–34.
115. Bauer, *Equality, the Third World, and Economic Delusion* (Cambridge: Harvard University Press, 1981), 205; Shiva Naipaul, *North of South: An African Journey* (New York: Simon & Schuster, 1978), 323.
116. Bauer, *Dissent*, 149.
117. Bauer, *Dissent*, 33–34.
118. Bauer, *Dissent*, 17, 18, 20, 21, 24, 147.
119. Bauer, *Dissent*, 89, 92, 94, 173, 204, 221, 320. Myrdal was the bête noir, the stand-in for the general problems of the field.
120. On this point, see T. N. Srinivasan in his comment on Bauer's essay in Meier and Seers, eds., *Pioneers*, 54.
121. Gottfried Haberler, *International Trade and Economic Development* (Cairo: National Bank of Egypt, 1959). Interestingly, Haberler's influential 1958 report for GATT found declining terms of trade for primary products from 1955 to 1957, though he refused, unlike Prebisch, to extrapolate this into a long-term trend necessitating import substitution. GATT Panel of Experts, "Trends in Interna-

tional Trade" (Geneva: General Agreement on Tariffs and Trade, October 1958). On Haberler's LIEO, see Janek Wasserman, *The Marginal Revolutionaries: How Austrian Economists Fought the War of Ideas* (New Haven: Yale University Press, 2019), 223–27. On the NIEO as a target of neoliberal attacks, see Jennifer Bair, "Taking Aim at the New International Economic Order," in Philip Mirowski and Dieter Plehwe, eds., *The Road from Mont Pèlerin: The Making of the Neoliberal Thought Collective* (Cambridge: Harvard University Press, 2009), 347–85.

122. Milton Friedman, "A Memorandum to the Government of India, 1955," in Friedman, *Friedman on India* (New Delhi: Centre for Civil Society, 2000), 22–25.

123. Friedman, "Indian Economic Planning," in *Friedman on India*, 10–11.

124. Friedman, "Foreign Economic Aid: Means and Objectives," *Yale Review* (Summer 1958), 508–09, 516.

125. Harry G. Johnson, "The Ideology of Economic Policy in the New States," in Johnson, ed., *Economic Nationalism in Old and New States* (Chicago: University of Chicago Press, 1967), 137. See also David Wall, ed., *Chicago Essays in Economic Development* (Chicago: University of Chicago Press, 1972).

126. Bauer appeared in Meier and Seers, eds., *Pioneers*, 25–55.

127. The innovation grew out of welfare economics, a branch of economics that examines resource allocation and social welfare, commonly using micro-economic tools to analyze macro-economic aggregates such as national income. Little, *A Critique of Welfare Economics* (Oxford: Clarendon, 1950. For a justification, see Little and Mirrlees, *Project Appraisal and Planning for Developing Countries* (New York: Basic Books, 1974), Chap. 19. For a discussion of welfare economics in the context of Cold War rational choice theory, see S. M. Amadae, *Rationalizing Capitalist Democracy: The Cold War Origins of Rational Choice Liberalism* (Chicago: University of Chicago Press, 2003).

128. Little and Mirrlees, *Manual of Industrial Project Analysis in Developing Countries*, vol. 2 (Paris: OECD, 1968), 23–24; rewritten as Little and Mirrlees, *Project Appraisal and Planning for Developing Countries* (1974). See also Little and Mirrlees, "Further Reflections on the OECD Manual of Project Analysis in Developing Countries," in Jagdish Bhagwati and Richard Eckaus, eds., *Development and Planning: Essays in Honour of Paul Rosenstein Rodan* (Cambridge: MIT Press, 1973), 257–80. For a review, see Streeten, "The Little-Mirrlees Method and Project Appraisal," in Streeten, *Frontiers*, 347–66.

129. For examples of its use, see Deepak Lal, *Appraising Foreign Investment in Developing Countries* (London: Heinemann, 1975); Little and Maurice Scott, eds., *Using Shadow Prices* (London: Heinemann, 1976); M. F. G. Scott, J. D. MacArthur, and D. M. G. Newbery, *Project Appraisal in Practice: The Little-Mirrlees Method Applied in Kenya* (London: Heinemann, 1976); Lal with A. Heap, H. Boisen, B. Nilsson, and L. Karlsson, *Men or Machines: A Study of Labour-Capital Substitution in Road Construction in the Philippines* (Geneva: International Labour Organisation, 1978); and Lal, *Prices for Planning: Towards the Reform of Indian Planning* (London: Heinemann, 1980). For review of cost-benefit analysis, see Lal, *Methods of Project Analysis: A Review* (Baltimore: International Bank for Reconstruction and Devel-

opment, 1974). See also Janos Kornai, "Appraisal of Project Appraisal," in Michael Biskin, ed., *Economics and Human Welfare: Essays in Honor of Tibor Scitovsky* (New York: Academic Press, 1979), 75–99.

130. Thandika Mkandawire, "The Crisis in Economic Development Theory," *Africa Development* 15:3–4 (1990), 219–20.

131. Little, *Economic Development: Theory, Policy, and International Relations* (New York: Basic Books, 1982), 380.

132. Little, Scitovsky, and Scott, *Industry and Trade in Some Development Countries* (London: Oxford University Press, 1970), 28–29.

133. Little, *Economic Development,* 372–73. Little subsumed mainstream economics and dependency under the label of structuralism, which he contrasted to neoclassical economics. The structuralist, he wrote, does not trust the "price mechanism" since he "sees the world as inflexible . . . inhibited by obstacles, bottlenecks, and constraints" (20–21).

134. Balassa, "My Life Philosophy," *American Economist* 33:1 (1989), 16. On the debate over planning in socialism, see Balassa, *The Hungarian Experience in Economic Planning: A Theoretical and Empirical Study* (New Haven: Yale University Press, 1959); Balassa, "The Economic Reform in Hungary," *Economica* 37:145 (February 1970), 1–22. The socialist planning debates, which occurred in more open states such as Hungary and Yugoslavia, sought to determine how the price mechanism could enhance central planning by providing information needed to rationalize economic decision-making.

135. Balassa, *The Hungarian Experience,* 24; Balassa, "Growth Strategies in Semi-Industrial Countries," *The Quarterly Journal of Economics* 84:1 (February 1970), 45.

136. Balassa and Associates, *The Structure of Protection in Developing Countries* (Baltimore: Johns Hopkins University Press, 1971).

137. "With the exception of Britain at the time of the Industrial Revolution and Hong Kong more recently, all present-day industrial and developing countries protected their incipient manufacturing industries producing for domestic markets," Balassa remarked in "The Process of Industrial Development and Alternative Development Strategies," *Essays on International Finance* 141, Princeton Department of Economics, International Finance Section (December 1980), 5. He favored tariffs over quotas and subsidies over tariffs as less market-disruptive. See also Balassa, *Policy Reform in Developing Countries* (Oxford: Pergamon, 1977).

138. Balassa, "The Process of Industrial Development and Alternative Development Strategies," 18–19; and Balassa, "The Lessons of East Asian Development: An Overview," *Economic Development and Cultural Change* 36:3 (April 1988), 273–90.

139. Balassa, "Growth Strategies in Semi-Industrial Countries," *Quarterly Journal of Economics* 84:1 (February 1970), 45.

140. Balassa, "Reforming the System of Incentives in Developing Countries," *World Development* 3:6 (June 1975), 365–82; Bhagwati, *Protectionism* (Cambridge: MIT Press, 1988), Chap. 5. On East Asian growth and its economic reception, see

Takatoshi Ito and Anne Krueger, eds., *Growth Theories in Light of the East Asian Experience* (Chicago: University of Chicago Press, 1995).

141. On South Korean development, see Jung-en Woo, *State and Finance in Korean Industrialization* (New York: Columbia University Press, 1991); John Lie, *Han Unbound: The Political Economy of South Korea* (Stanford: Stanford University Press, 1998); Michael Seth, *A Concise History of Korea: From Antiquity to the Present* (New York: Rowman & Littlefield, 2019), Chap. 13.

142. Balassa and Associates, *Development Strategies in Semi-Industrial Economies* (Baltimore: John Hopkins University Press, 1982); Balassa, "The 'New Protectionism' and the International Economy," *Journal of World Trade Law* 12:5 (1978), 409–36; Balassa, "The Tokyo Round and the Developing Countries," *Journal of World Trade Law* 14 (1980).

143. Balassa, "Structural Adjustment Policies in Developing Countries," Staff Working Paper No. 464, World Bank, Washington, DC (June 20, 1981).

144. Krueger, *Foreign Trade Regimes and Economic Development: Liberalization Attempts and Consequences* (New York: National Bureau of Economic Research, 1978); and Bhagwati, *Foreign Trade Regimes and Economic Development: Anatomy and Consequences of Exchange Control Regimes* (New York: National Bureau of Economic Research, 1978).

145. Krueger, "The Political Economy of the Rent-Seeking Society," *American Economic Review* 64:3 (June 1974), 291–303. On public choice, the classic text is James Buchanan and Gordon Tullock, *The Calculus of Consent: Logical Foundations of Constitutional Democracy* (Ann Arbor: University of Michigan Press, 1962). For an account of public choice within the wider rational choice movement, see S. M. Amadae, *Rationalizing Capitalist Democracy*, 133–55. For a scathing critique, see Nancy MacLean, *Democracy in Chains: The Deep History of the Radical Right's Stealth Plan for America* (New York: Viking, 2017).

146. Bauer, *Indian Economic Policy and Development* (New York: Praeger, 1961); Krueger, *The Benefits and Costs of Import Substitution in India: A Microeconomic Study* (Minneapolis: University of Minnesota Press, 1975). Little offered a more moderate analysis in "The Strategy of Indian Development," *National Institute Economic Review* 9 (May 1960), 20–29.

147. In 2000, he wrote the Foreword to an Indian compilation of Friedman's writings: *Friedman on India*.

148. Lal, *Prices for Planning*, xvi–xvii; Lal, *The Poverty of 'Development Economics'* (Cambridge: MIT Press, 2000/1983), 46.

149. Lal, *Poverty*, 7, 72–75.

150. In addition to *Poverty*, see Lal, *Against Dirigisme: The Case for Unshackling Economic Markets* (San Francisco: ICS Press, 1994).

151. Lal, *Poverty*, 9–11, 20–26.

152. Lal, *Poverty*, 8, 31–33, 46, 109.

153. Lal, *In Praise of Empires: Globalization and Order* (New York: Palgrave Macmillan, 2004).

154. Lal, "Poverty, Power and Prejudice: The North-South Confrontation," *Quadrant* 23:1–2 (January–February 1979), 17, 19. Lal's fellow Indian liberal economist, Jagdish Bhagwati, was more accepting of Third World concerns. See the Introduction to Bhagwati, ed., *The New International Economic Order: The North-South Debate* (Cambridge: MIT Press, 1977). Yet even he worried about the rise of nontariff protectionism. See Bhagwati, *Protectionism* (Cambridge: MIT Press, 1988).
155. Naomi Klein, *The Shock Doctrine: The Rise of Disaster Capitalism* (New York: Picador, 2007). In addition to Friedman and Schultz, Rosenstein-Rodan, once a proponent of government-managed uplift, spoke repeatedly in favor of Chile's coup. Michele Alacevich, "Paul Rosenstein-Rodan and the Birth of Development Economics," *History of Political Economy* 53:5 (2021), 880–83.
156. Sebastian Edwards, *The Chile Project: The Story of the Chicago Boys and the Downfall of Neoliberalism* (Princeton: Princeton University Press, 2023).
157. Juan Gabriel Valdés, *Pinochet's Economists: The Chicago School in Chile* (Cambridge: Cambridge University Press, 1995), 6, 277.
158. Charles Gore, "The Rise and Fall of the Washington Consensus as a Paradigm for Developing Countries," *World Development* 28:5 (2000), 789–804.
159. Keith Griffin and Azizur Rahman Khan, "Poverty in the Third World: Ugly Facts and Fancy Models," *World Development* 6:3 (1978). 295, 302–03. For the Bangladeshi intellectual context from which this class critique emerged, see Chap. 7.
160. Miles Kahler, "Orthodoxy and Its Alternatives: Explaining Approaches to Stabilization and Adjustment," in Joan M. Nelson, ed., *Economic Crisis and Policy Choice: The Politics of Adjustment in the Third World* (Princeton: Princeton University Press, 1990), 35.
161. Giovanni Andrea Cornia, Richard Jolly, and Frances Stewart, *Adjustment with a Human Face: Protecting the Vulnerable and Promoting Growth* (Oxford: Clarendon, 1987).
162. Meyerowitz, *A War on Global Poverty*, 190–92.
163. Albert Hirschman, "The Rise and Decline of Development Economics," in Hirschman, *Essays in Trespassing: Economic to Politics and Beyond* (Cambridge: Cambridge University Press, 1981), 1, 6.
164. Seers, "The Birth, Life and Death of Development Economics (Revisiting a Manchester Conference)," *Development and Change* 10 (1979), 710–12.
165. In the mid-1990s, two further post mortems appeared. Colin Leys argued that pressing problems faced by developing countries after 1973—and the disparate trajectories of each country—rendered much of development theory irrelevant. And Paul Krugman contended that development economists were never able to formalize their insights in the mathematical models that were increasingly de rigueur in economics. Leys, *The Rise and Fall of Development Theory* (Oxford: James Curry, 1996), Chap 1; Krugman, "The Fall and Rise of Development Economics," in Krugman, *Development, Geography, and Economic Theory* (Cambridge: MIT Press, 1995), Chap. 1. The re-rise to which Krugman refers is the rediscovery and formalization of some development theorems in the 1990s. For an analysis of Krugman's argument—in particular, his argument about Hirschman's role in

the decline of development theory—see Michael Woolcock, *International Development: Navigating Humanity's Greatest Challenge* (Cambridge: Polity, 2023), 117–20. See also the Swedish scholar Björn Hettne, whose *Development Theory and the Third World* (New York: Longman, 1990) tracked the development theory crisis through the 1980s and highlighted the reliance on Eurocentric models.

Chapter 7. Touching Distance

1. Joanne Meyerowitz, *A War on Global Poverty: The Lost Promise of Redistribution and the Rise of Microcredit* (Princeton: Princeton University Press, 2021).
2. Ben Rogaly, "Micro-finance Evangelism, 'Destitute Women,' and the Hard Selling of a New Anti-poverty Formula," *Development in Practice* 6:2 (2010), 100–112. For a related argument, see Geoffrey Wood and Iffath Sharif, eds., *Who Needs Credit? Poverty and Finance in Bangladesh* (Dhaka: University Press, 1997), 27–58.
3. Jessica Matthews, "Power Shift," *Foreign Affairs* 76:1 (January–February 1997), 50–66; Akira Iriye, *Global Community: The Role of International Institutions in the Making of the Contemporary World* (Berkeley: University of California Press, 2002), Chap. 5.
4. Manzurul Mannan, *BRAC, Global Policy Language, and Women in Bangladesh* (Albany: SUNY Press, 2015), Chap. 1. See also Sajjad Zohir, "NGO Sector in Bangladesh: An Overview," in K. A. S. Murshid, Minhaj Mahmud, and Kazi Iqbal, eds., *Readings in Bangladesh Development*, vol. 2 (Dhaka: BIDS, 2021), 193–208.
5. Gunnar Myrdal, *The Challenge of World Poverty: A World Anti-Poverty Program in Outline* (New York: Pantheon, 1970), Chap. 7.
6. Wood, *Bangladesh: Whose Ideas, Whose Interests?* (London: Intermediate Technology, 1994), Chap. 22.
7. Willem van Schendel, *A History of Bangladesh* (Cambridge: Cambridge University Press, 2009), 136.
8. On the intriguing 'Red Maulana' Bhashani, see Nurul Kabir, *The Red Maulana: An Essay on Bhashani's Ever-Oppositional Spirit* (Dhaka: Samhati, 2012); Dewan Arefin, *Bhashani, The Moulana Bhashani, The Comrade* (Xlibris, 2019); Peter Custers, "Maulana Bhashani and the Transition to Secular Politics in East Bengal," *Indian Economic and Social History Review* 47:2 (2010), 231–59.
9. On the scroll, entitled *Monpura '70*, see Sanjukta Sunderason, "Shadow Lines: Zainul Abedin and the After-Lives of the Bengal Famine of 1943," *Third Text* 31 (2017), 239–59.
10. BRAC was preceded by Abed's post-Bhola relief organization HELP (Hatiya/Heartland Emergency Livelihood Project), and then two London-based organizations, Action Bangladesh and Help Bangladesh, that operated during the Liberation War. Hatiya was one of the hard-hit islands in the Bay of Bengal.
11. On BRAC history, in addition to Mannan, *BRAC*, see BRAC Institute of Governance and Development (BiGD), "Formation of BRAC: A Historical Account," BiGD Monograph 1 (the first of a series of forthcoming accounts of BRAC History) (April 2022); Mahabub Hossain, Shib Narayan Kairy, and Abdul Bayes, eds.,

Driving Development: The Story of BRAC's Evolution and Effectiveness (Dhaka: University Press, 2016); Ian Smillie, *Freedom from Want: The Remarkable Success Story of BRAC, the Global Grassroots Organization That's Winning the Fight against Poverty* (Sterling, VA: Kumarian, 2009); and Scott MacMillan, *Hope over Fate: Fazle Hasan Abed and the Science of Ending Global Poverty* (Lanham, MD: Rowman & Littlefield, 2022).

12. On solidarity activism, see Christian Smith, *Resisting Reagan: The U.S. Central America Peace Movement* (Chicago: University of Chicago Press, 1996), Chap. 10.
13. For a later, postindependence account of elite attitudes toward the poor, see Naomi Hossain, *Elite Perceptions of Poverty in Bangladesh* (Dhaka: University Press, 2005).
14. Rounaq Jahan, *Pakistan: Failure in National Integration* (New York: Columbia University Press, 1972).
15. On the Liberation War, see Nurul Kabir, *Birth of Bangladesh: The Politics of History and the History of Politics* (Dhaka: Samhati, 2022); Srinath Raghavan, *1971: A Global History of the Creation of Bangladesh* (Cambridge: Harvard University Press, 2013); and Abdus Samad, *History of Liberation War in Bangladesh* (Dhaka: Aparajeyo Bangla Prakashani, 2019). Kabir's bulky new book is intriguing for its criticism of the ways that war history is enlisted to support political and class interests in Bangladesh. The genocide is a particularly fraught chapter of the war. Enshrined in official Bangladeshi war memory is the number of 3 million killed. The most credible scholarly estimates range between 500,000 and 1.5 million. Rudolph J. Rummel, *Statistics of Democide: Genocide and Mass Murder since 1900* (New Brunswick: Transaction, 1997), 153–63. Pakistan denies the genocide, advancing estimates as (ludicrously) low as 26,000.
16. Interview, May 2022, Dhaka. On GK's history and programs, see Ashish Bose, *Women's Empowerment through Capacity Building: Enduring Efforts in Bangladesh* (Dhaka: Gonoprokashani, 2004); Rafiqul Huda Chowdhury and Zafrullah Chowdhury, *Achieving the Millennium Development Goal on Maternal Mortality: Gonshasthaya Kendra's Experience in Rural Bangladesh* (Dhaka: Gonoprokashani, 2007); Jayanta Kumar Ray, *Organizing Villagers for Self-Reliance: A Study of Gonoshasthaya Kendra in Bangladesh* (Hyderabad: Orient Longman, 1986); *Gonoshasthaya Kendra: Challenges of the First 40 Years and Beyond* (Dhaka: Gonoprokashani, 2012); *Publications of Gonoshasthaya Kendra,* available in Bangladesh Institute for Development Studies (BIDS) Library, Dhaka, Bangladesh.
17. Ray, *Organizing Villagers,* 5–13.
18. For his complaints about expensive private health care in the 1980s, he was physically targeted, and he was known until his 2023 death as someone who could be dangerously outspoken. On his criticism of neocolonialism in international drug policy and advocacy of local production, see Chowdhury, *The Politics of Essential Drugs: The Makings of a Successful Health Strategy: Lessons from Bangladesh* (Dhaka: Gonoprokashani, 2010). On the international impact of the Bangladesh campaign for a local pharmaceutical industry, see Paul Adler, *No Globalization Without Representation: U.S. Activists and World Inequality* (Philadelphia: University of Pennsylvania Press, 2021), 70–71.

19. The reference, usually credited to Henry Kissinger, originated with one of his aides. See Gary Bass, *The Blood Telegram: Nixon, Kissinger, and a Forgotten Genocide* (New York: Vintage, 2013).
20. Sheikh Mujibur Rahman, *The Unfinished Memoirs* (Dhaka: University Press, 2012), 237. See also Jahan, "Political Philosophy of Bangabandhu Sheikh Mujibur Rahman," in Jahan and Rehman Sobhan, *Bangabandhu Sheikh Mujibur Rahman: Philosophy, Politics and Policies* (Dhaka: Prothoma Prokashan, 2022), 49–68.
21. Talukder Maniruzzaman, *The Bangladesh Revolution and Its Aftermath* (Dhaka: University Press, 1980). Maniruzzaman argues that the revolution ultimately went unfinished, throttled by India and by conservative elements in Bangladeshi society.
22. Naomi Hossain, *The Aid Lab: Understanding Bangladesh's Unexpected Success* (Oxford: Oxford University Press, 2017).
23. Mannan, *BRAC*, Chap. 3.
24. Purdah was a flexible instrument, as BRAC employee Martha Alter Chen noticed; it was relaxed in cases of influence or need. Chen, *A Quiet Revolution: Women in Transition in Rural Bangladesh* (Dhaka: BRAC, 1986), 73.
25. On the ways that Bangladeshi women have reshaped the institution of purdah, see Elora Shehabuddin, *Reshaping the Holy: Democracy, Development, and Muslim Women in Bangladesh* (New York: Columbia University Press, 2008).
26. Tahrunessa Abdullah, *Village Women as I Saw Them* (Dacca: Ford Foundation, 1974); Abdullah and Sondra Zeidenstein, *Village Women of Bangladesh: Prospects for Change* (Oxford: Pergamon, 1982); Rounaq Jahan, *Women in Bangladesh* (Dacca: Ford Foundation, 1973); Jahan and Hanna Papanek, eds., *Women and Development: Perspectives from South and Southeast Asia* (Dacca: Bangladesh Institute of Law and International Affairs, 1979).
27. Jahan, *The Elusive Agenda: Mainstreaming Women in Development* (London: Zed, 1995), 8–9.
28. Abdullah, *Village Women of Bangladesh*, 7, 23, 110, 203.
29. Donald McHenry and Kai Bird, "Food Bungle in Bangladesh," *Foreign Policy* 27 (Summer 1977), 72–88.
30. Amartya Sen, *Poverty and Famines: An Essay in Entitlement and Deprivation* (Oxford: Clarendon, 1981). For a critique, see Caf Dowlah, "The Politics and Economics of Food and Famine in Bangladesh in the Early 1970s—with Special Reference to Amartya Sen's Interpretation of the 1974 Famine," *International Journal of Social Welfare* 15 (2006), 344–56.
31. For a brisk description of the last gasp of leftism in the months between Mujib's assassination and Zia's consolidation, see journalist Lawrence Lifschultz's *Bangladesh: The Unfinished Revolution* (London: Zed, 1977).
32. Since South Korea had reached its trade quota under the 1974 Multi Fibre Agreement, Bangladesh served as a quota-free manufacturing outlet.
33. Rehman Sobhan, *From Two Economies to Two Nations: My Journey to Bangladesh* (Dhaka: Daily Star, 2015); Nurul Islam, *Making of a Nation, Bangladesh: An Economist's Tale* (Dhaka: University Press, 2021/2003). Both have published autobiographies: Islam, *Making of a Nation;* Rehman Sobhan, *Untranquil Reflections: The*

Years of Fulfillment (Los Angeles: SAGE, 2016); Sobhan, *Untranquil Reflections: From Dawn to Darkness* (Dhaka: University Press, 2022).

34. Sobhan and Ahmad, *Public Enterprise in an Intermediate Regime: A Study in the Political Economy of Bangladesh* (Dhaka: BIDS, 1983). See also Peter Bertocci, "Bangladesh in the Early 1980s: Praetorian Politics in an Intermediate Regime" *Asian Survey* 22:10 (October 1982), 988–1008; S. M. Shamsul Alam, *The State, Class Formation, and Development in Bangladesh* (Lanham: University Press of America, 1995). One of the scholarly debates of this era was whether rural Bangladesh fit into a class model or if cross-cutting patron–client relations made it too fragmented for such a framework. See Bertocci, "Community Structure and Social Rank in Two Villages in Bangladesh," *Contributions to Indian Sociology*, n.s. 6 (1972), 19–52; Bertocci, "Structural Fragmentation and Peasant Classes in Bangladesh," *Journal of Social Studies* 5 (1979), 43–59; Burhannudin Khan Jahangir, *Differentiation, Polarisation, and Confrontation in Rural Bangladesh* (Dacca: Centre for Social Studies, 1979); Wood, *Bangladesh: Whose Ideas, Whose Interests?* Chap. 2. For an argument against the thesis of a capitalist rural Bangladesh, see Shakeeb Khan, *The State and Village Society: The Political Economy of Agricultural Development in Bangladesh* (Dhaka: University Press, 1989).
35. On Abed's embrace of Freire, see MacMillan, *Hope over Fate*, Chaps. 9, 10, and 13.
36. BRAC, "Report on Jamalpur Women's Programme, January to December 1976," 7. Available at: http://dspace.bracu.ac.bd/xmlui/handle/10361/5804.
37. BRAC, "Jamalpur Women's Programme: Annual Report—1978," 7–8, http://dspace.bracu.ac.bd/xmlui/handle/10361/5826.
38. Chen, *A Quiet Revolution*; Smillie, *Freedom from Want*, Chap. 5.
39. BRAC, *The Net: Power Structure in Ten Villages* (Dacca: BRAC, 1980). See also BRAC, *Peasant Perceptions: Famine* (Dacca: BRAC, 1979), which advocated food-for-work programs since they gave the poor a claim or entitlement to food. These writings continued in the Peasant Perceptions series in the mid-1980s.
40. Betsy Hartmann and James Boyce, *A Quiet Violence: View from a Bangladesh Village* (London: Zed, 1983), Chap. 9.
41. MacMillan, *Hope over Fate*, 121–26, 135–36; Smillie, *Freedom from Want*, 60–61. For an appraisal of the NGO target-group approach, see Aditee Nag Chowdhury, *Let Grassroots Speak: People's Participation Self-Help Groups and NGOs in Bangladesh* (Dhaka: University Press, 1989).
42. Interview, Nijera Kori staff, May 2022.
43. Naila Kabeer, "'We Don't Do Credit': Nijera Kori, Social Mobilisation and the Collective Capabilities of the Poor in Rural Bangladesh" (Dhaka: Nijera Kori, 2002). Available at BIDS.
44. Interview, Nijera Kori staff, May 2022.
45. The few studies of Nijera Kori are openly sympathetic and tend to find significant impact on civic engagement, community participation, and economic progress among group members. Kabeer, Simeen Mahmud, and Jairo G. Isaza Castro, "NGOs and the Political Empowerment of Poor People in Rural Bangladesh: Cultivating the Habits of Democracy?" *World Development* 40:10 (2012), 2060; Abul

Barkat, Sadeka Halim, Avijit Poddar, Asmar Osman, and Md. Badiuzzaman, *Development as Conscientization: The Case of Nijera Kori in Bangladesh* (Dhaka: Pathak Shamabesh, 2008).

46. On Proshika, see David Lewis, "Organising and Representing the Poor in a Clientelistic Democracy: The Decline of Radical NGOs in Bangladesh," *Journal of Development Studies* 53:10 (2017), 1551; Smillie and John Hailey, *Managing for Change: Leadership, Strategy and Management in Asian NGOs* (London: Earthscan, 2001).
47. Mannan, *BRAC*, 90–94, 265–70, 275–76.
48. Quoted in Stuart Rutherford, *The Pledge: ASA, Peasant Politics, and Microfinance in the Development of Bangladesh* (Oxford: Oxford University Press, 2009), 97.
49. ASA's publications continued to use the old language, describing income generation as a form of empowerment and social justice. See ASA, "ASA in Transition" (1994); ASA, "One Step Forward" (1995); ASA, "An Evaluation of ASA" (1994), all available at BIDS.
50. The term *aid lab* is from Naomi Hossain. Among the NGOs from the period, we should also note Rangpur—Dinajpur Rural Service (RDRS), which operated in northern Bangladesh as a refugee and rehabilitation organization and then as a multisectoral service provider. Created partly at the behest of Lutheran World Service, it received funding from international donors RDRS, "The Comprehensive Project Policy Paper" (1989). Available at BIDS.
51. These are rough calculations, but they give an idea of the magnitude of international investment. Sobhan, *The Crisis of External Dependence: The Political Economy of Foreign Aid in Bangladesh* (Dhaka: University Press, 1982), 8–10, 239–40. See also Just Faaland, ed., *Aid and Influence: The Case of Bangladesh* (New York: St. Martin's, 1981).
52. Sobhan, *The Crisis of External Dependence* (London: Zed, 1982), 7; Sobhan, ed., *From Aid Dependence to Self-Reliance: Development Options for Bangladesh* (Dhaka: BIDS, 1990); Sobhan, *The Political Economy of Malgovernance in Bangladesh*, in *The Collected Works of Rehman Sobhan*, vol. 3 (Dhaka: Centre for Policy Dialogue, 2007).
53. Islam, *Making of a Nation*, 259, 298, 409.
54. Faaland and J. R. Parkinson, *Bangladesh: The Test Case of Development* (Boulder: Westview, 1976). Only Rwanda, according to the 1974 World Bank Atlas, was poorer. Faaland and Parkinson, *Bangladesh*, 3. According to Abed's sources, Upper Volta saved Bangladesh from last-place dishonor. MacMillan, *Hope over Fate*, 2.
55. Milan Kundera, *The Book of Laughter and Forgetting* (New York: Harper, 1996/1978), 9–10.
56. On this history, see Stuart Rutherford, *The Pledge*, Chap. 2.
57. On the historical distinctiveness of the delta region, see Akbar Ali Khan, *Discovery of Bangladesh: Explorations into Dynamics of a Hidden Nation* (Dhaka: University Press, 1996); Richard Eaton, *The Rise of Islam and the Bengal Frontier* (Berkeley: University of California Press, 1993); and Sugata Bose, *Agrarian Bengal: Economy, Social Structure, and Politics, 1919–1947* (Cambridge: Cambridge University Press, 1986).
58. On the jute industry as part of global capitalist networks, see Tariq Omar Ali, *A*

Local History of Global Capital: Jute and Peasant Life in the Bengal Delta (Princeton: Princeton University Press, 2018).

59. On V-AID, see Zaker Hussain, "Village Agricultural and Industrial Development (V-AID) Programme," in Abdul Quddus, ed., *Rural Development in Bangladesh: Strategies and Experiences* (Comilla: BARD, 1993), 97–112; Arthur Raper, *Rural Development in Action: The Comprehensive Experiment at Comilla, East Pakistan* (Ithaca: Cornell University Press, 1970), Chaps. 1 and 2.
60. Khan, "Redesigning the Village-AID Programme," in *The Works of Akhter Hameed Khan*, Vol. 2: *Rural Development Approaches and the Comilla Model* (Comilla: BARD, 1983), 3–9.
61. Abul Hossain Ahmed Bhuiyan, Aminul Haque Faraizi, and Jim McAllister, "Developmentalism as a Disciplinary Strategy in Bangladesh," *Modern Asian Studies* 39:2 (2005), 349–68.
62. In 1982, *thanas* were renamed *upazilas.*
63. Sobhan, *Basic Democracies Works Programme and Rural Development in East Pakistan* (Dacca: Bureau of Economic Research, University of Dacca, 1968); Raper, *Rural Development,* 99–104.
64. Sobhan, *Basic Democracies,* 89.
65. In addition to the laudatory Arthur Raper, see Azizur Rahman Khan, "The Comilla Model and the Integrated Rural Development Programme in Bangladesh: An Experiment in 'Cooperative Capitalism,'" *World Development* 7 (1979), 397–422; Harry Blair, "Rural Development, Class Structure, and Bureaucracy in Bangladesh," *World Development* 6:1 (1978), 65–82; and M. Ghulam Sattar, "Comilla Models of Rural Development: Significance and Relevance," in Quddus, ed., *Rural Development in Bangladesh,* 113–30.
66. Tariq Omar Ali, "Technologies of Peasant Production and Reproduction: The Post-Colonial State and Cold War Empire in Comilla, East Pakistan, 1960–70," *Journal of South Asian Studies* 42:3 (2019), 435–51. Khan drew partly on ideas learned in his U.K. education and at Michigan State.
67. Khan, "The Rural Development Programme at Comilla," in *The Works of Akhter Hameed Khan*, vol. 2: *Rural Development Approaches and the Comilla Model* (Comilla: BARD, 1983), 72–73.
68. For indicators of this success, see Azizur Rahman Khan and Robert Stevens, "Comilla Rural Development Programs in 1971," in Robert Stevens, Hamza Alavi, and Bertocci, eds., *Rural Development in Bangladesh and Pakistan* (Honolulu: University Press of Hawaii, 1976), 95–128.
69. As we saw in Chapter 3, this was a common charge lodged against community development. That PARD/BARD was alert to rural inequality is clear from publications such as M. Ameerul Huq, ed., *Exploitation and the Rural Poor—A Working Paper on the Rural Power Structure in Bangladesh* (Comilla: BARD, 1976).
70. On Comilla's relative egalitarianism (reinforced by the refusal of some large landowners to participate), see Harry Blair, *The Elusiveness of Equity: Institutional Approaches to Rural Development in Bangladesh* (Ithaca: Center for International Studies, Rural Development Committee, 1974), 16, 38. See also Bertocci, "Social Organi-

zation and Agricultural Development in Bangladesh," in Stevens et al., *Rural Development*, 157–84.

71. Starting in 1988, BRDB ran its own targeted credit program, the Rural Development (RD-12) project. Shahidur Khandker, Zahed Khan, and Baqui Khalily, "Sustainability of a Government-Targeted Credit Programme: The Bangladesh Rural Development Board Rural Development 12 Project in Bangladesh," *World Bank Discussion Paper* 316 (1994).
72. Azizur Rahman Khan, "The Comilla Model," 414–17; Hasnat Abdul Hye, "IRDP: Replication of an Experimental Project," in Quddus, ed., *Rural Development in Bangladesh*, 131–73.
73. Raper, *Rural Development*, 64–65; Hye, "IRDP," 163.
74. Khan, "Review of the Functions of IRDP National Office and the TCCA's," in *The Works of Akhter Hameed Khan*, vol. 3: *Rural Works and the Comilla Cooperative* (Comilla: BARD, 1983), 186–202.
75. Yunus, "Rural/Agricultural Credit Operations in Bangladesh," available in Grameen Bank Library (May 1981), 14–15, 20.
76. M. Mahabub-ul Islam, Abu N. M. Wahid, and Zahed Khan, "The Grameen Bank: Peer Monitoring in Dual Credit Market," in Abu Wahid, ed., *The Grameen Bank: Poverty Relief in Bangladesh* (Boulder: Westview, 1993), 28. Yunus and some of his staff, for example, attended a government-funded conference at BARD in 1978. Interview, Grameen staff member, May 2022.
77. A. K. M. Obaidullah, "Comprehensive Village Development Programme: An Approach to Rural Development," in Quddus, ed., *Rural Development in Bangladesh*, 267, 270, 271.
78. On the SFDP/SFP, see Kazi Bazlul Karun, "A Case Study of the Small Farmers Group Action" (n.d., late 1970s); Fazlul Bari, Zahirul Alam, and Zainul Abedin, eds., "Small Farmers and Landless Labourers Development Project" (1978); Zainul Abedin, "Experiences of the SFDP in Generating Employment and Income for the Rural Poor in Bangladesh" (1980); Fazlul Bari, "Small Efforts by Small Farmers" (1987); Mihir Kumar Roy, "An Introduction to the Small Farmers' Development Project" (1999); Rezaul Karim, Abdul Mannan, Ataur Rahman, and Jannatun Ara Begum, "Small Farmers and Landless Labourers Development Project" (1994); Ministry of Local Government, "An Evaluation of Small Farmers and Landless Labourers Development Project" (1991); and Mihir Kumar Roy and Jahangir Alam Nuruzzaman, "Generation of Employment through Small Farmers Development Project" (1999)—all available at the BARD library, Comilla, Bangladesh.
79. M. A. Chashi, "Self-Reliant Rural Bangladesh: Problems and Prospects," *Political Economy* 2:1 (1976), 172–73.
80. Sajjad Zohir, "A Study of Swanirvar Bangladesh," unpublished manuscript printed by BIDS (October 1990), 136; available at BIDS. See also Rita Afsar, "Swanirvar: Being Self Reliant—Experiment with Community Level Development in Bangladesh," RUSHSAP Series on Monographs and Occasional Papers (Bangkok: UNESCO, 1988); and Atiur Rahman, "Swanirwar Movement: An Experiment in Local Level Planning" (1987)—both available at BIDS; Mahabub Hossain, Raisul

Awal Mahmood, and Qazi Kholiquzzaman Ahmad, "'Participatory' Development Efforts in Rural Bangladesh: A Case Study of Experiences in Three Areas," in Amit Bhaduri and Anisur Rahman, eds., *Studies in Rural Participation* (New Delhi: Oxford University Press, 1982), 90–115; and Blair, *The Elusiveness of Equity*, 62–68, for an early appraisal of Chashi's efforts in Rangunia, Chittagong District.

81. Afsar, "Swanirvar," 20.
82. Zohir, *Swanirvar Bangladesh*, 52.
83. For a survey of poverty's dynamic state, see Hossain Zillur Rahman, "Crisis and Insecurity: The 'Other' Face of Poverty," in Zillur Rahman and Mahabub Hossain, eds., *Rethinking Rural Poverty: Bangladesh as a Case Study* (New Delhi: Sage, 1995), 113–31.
84. Shamsul Bari, ed., *Bangladesh Newsletter: A Chronicle of Bangladesh Movement in North America* (Dhaka: Liberation War Museum, 2001). On Yunus's biography, see Alex Counts, *Give Us Credit: How Muhammad Yunus's Micro-Lending Revolution Is Empowering Women from Bangladesh to Chicago* (New York: Times Books, 1996), 9–13.
85. The most famous and useful telling is Yunus's autobiography, *Banker to the Poor: Micro-Lending and the Battle against World Poverty* (New York: Public Affairs, 1999).
86. David Bornstein, *The Price of a Dream: The Story of Grameen Bank and the Idea That Is Helping the Poor to Change Their Lives* (New York: Simon & Schuster, 1996); Phil Smith and Eric Thurman, *A Billion Bootstraps: Microcredit, Barefoot Banking, and the Business Solution for Ending Poverty* (New York: McGraw-Hill, 2007).
87. Yunus, *Banker*, 142–44.
88. Quoted in Counts, *Give Us Credit*, 183. In fact, the World Bank had recently made a loan to Grameen Bank when Yunus made this statement in 1993. On Bangladesh's uneven structural adjustment experience, see K. M. Matin, "Structural Adjustment under the Extended Fund Facility: The Case of Bangladesh," in K. A. S. Murshid, Minhaj Mahmud, and Kazi Iqbal, eds., *Readings in Bangladesh Development*, vol. 1 (Dhaka: BIDS, 2021), 549–82.
89. Yunus, "Planning in Bangladesh: Format, Technique, and Priority," unpublished manuscript, BIDS Library, Dhaka, Bangladesh (March 1974), 7–16.
90. Yunus, "Rural/Agricultural Credit Operations in Bangladesh," available in Grameen Bank Library (May 1981), 14–15, 20.
91. Yunus, "Grameen Bank in Bangladesh—A Poverty-Focused Rural Development Programme," available in Grameen Bank Library (1982), 3–5; Yunus, *Banker*, 37–39; Counts, *Give Us Credit*, 26; M. Khalid Shams, "Raising Productivity of the Poor: Grameen Bank Experience in Managing New Technologies," available in Grameen Bank Library (1997), 10–12.
92. Interview with Grameen Bank staff, May 2022, Dhaka.
93. Quoted in Norman MacIsaac and Abu N. M. Wahid, "The Grameen Bank: Its Institutional Lessons for Rural Financing," in Wahid, ed., *The Grameen Bank*, 196; Yunus, "Rural Development: A New Development Strategy, Not a New Priority," available in Grameen Bank Library (1978).

94. By law, the state retained a small ownership stake, though Yunus regularly expressed a desire to turn it over to clients.
95. Yunus, *Banker,* 209–10, Chap. 11. In the 2000s, analysts associated with the impact evaluation movement would take issue with the contention that all (or most) people are born entrepreneurs. See Chap. 9.
96. The dissertation was published as Rahman, *Peasants and Classes: A Study in Differentiation in Bangladesh* (London: Zed, 1986). It compared a populist (Chayanovian), noncapitalist understanding of peasant social structure to a Leninist, capitalist one, arguing that the latter more aptly explained developments in his country. At BIDS, see Rahman, "Differentiation of the Peasantry in Bangladesh.—The Leninist Approach" (1985); Rahman, "Where Do the Poor Stand in the Process of Nation-Building" (1985); and Rahman, "Rural Power Structure and Development: A Review Study" (1989).
97. Rahman, *Rural Power Structure: A Study of the Local Level Leaders in Bangladesh* (Dacca: Bangladesh Books International, 1981), 53.
98. In addition to those mentioned earlier, see the favorable reviews in Rahman, "Demand and Marketing Aspects of Grameen" (1985); "Alleviation of Rural Poverty: Replicability of Grameen Bank Model" (1987); and "Rural Development from Below: Lessons Learned from Grameen Bank Experience in Bangladesh" (1992), all available at BIDS. See also Rahman, Rushidan Islam Rahman, Mahabub Hossain, and Shahabuddin Mosherraf Hossain, *Early Impact of Grameen* (Dhaka: Grameen Trust, 2002).
99. The 16 Decisions are reproduced in many places. I used Bornstein, *The Price of a Dream,* 97.
100. Atiur Rahman made this point as well. See Rahman, "Consciousness-Raising Efforts of Grameen Bank," Working Paper No. 3, Grameen Bank Evaluation Project (Dhaka: BIDS, July 1986); and Rahman, "Impact of Grameen Bank Intervention on the Rural Power Structure," Working Paper No. 2, Grameen Bank Evaluation Project (Dhaka: BIDS, July 1986). Both available at BIDS.
101. Lamia Karim, *Microfinance and Its Discontents* (Minneapolis: University of Minnesota Press, 2011), 40–41.
102. David Lewis, "Organising and Representing the Poor in a Clientelistic Democracy: The Decline of Radical NGOs in Bangladesh," *Journal of Development Studies* 53:10 (2017).
103. Mannan, *BRAC,* Chap. 9.
104. In addition to Atiur Rahman, see Mahabub Hossain, "Credit for Alleviation of Rural Poverty: The Grameen Bank in Bangladesh," *International Food Policy Research Institute, Research Report* 65 (February 1988); David Gibbons, "Replication of Grameen Bank Financial System" (Dhaka: Grameen, 1990); Gibbons, ed., *The Grameen Reader: Training Materials for International Replication of the Grameen Bank Financial System for Reduction of Rural Poverty* (Dhaka: Grameen Bank, 1994/1992); and Wahid, ed., *The Grameen Bank,* Chaps. 11, 12, 13, and 14.
105. Meyerowitz, *A War on Global Poverty,* 216–19. For a thoughtful recent account of

the rise of microfinance and its subsequent turmoil, see Mara Kardas-Nelson, *We Are Not Able to Live in the Sky: The Seductive Promise of Microfinance* (New York: Metropolitan Books, 2024).

106. Khandker, "Microfinance and Poverty: Evidence Using Panel Data from Bangladesh," *World Bank Economic Review* 19:2 (2005), 285. Among the many positive assessments of Grameen by Khandker and Mark M. Pitt, see "Household and Intrahousehold Impact of the Grameen Bank and Similar Targeted Credit Programs in Bangladesh," *World Bank Discussion Papers* 320 (1996); and "The Impact of Group-Based Credit Programs on Poor Households in Bangladesh: Does the Gender of Participants Matter?" *Journal of Political Economy* 106:5 (1998); Khandker, *Fighting Poverty with Microcredit: Experience in Bangladesh* (Oxford: Oxford University Press, 1998); Rushidan Islam Rahman and Khandker, "Role of Targeted Credit Programmes in Promoting Employment and Productivity of the Poor in Bangladesh," in Murshid et al., eds., *Readings*, vol. 1, 665–712. Khandker recognized that microfinance did not reach all the rural poor, required heavy subsidies, and could not address all facets of poverty; but he felt that credit for the landless could nonetheless facilitate rural growth.

107. Susan Holcombe, *Managing to Empower: The Grameen Bank's Experience of Poverty Alleviation* (London: Zed, 1995).

108. Yunus, ed., *Jorimon and Others: Faces of Poverty* (Dhaka: University Press, 1982/1984).

109. Gibbons, ed., *The Grameen Reader*. For a typology of attitudes toward Grameen replication, see David Hulme, "Can the Grameen Bank Be Replicated? Recent Experiments in Malaysia, Malawi, and Sri Lanka," *Development Policy Review* 8 (1990), 287–300.

110. For an explicit statement of these assumptions, see Counts, *Give Us Credit*, 97, 318.

111. Rogaly, "Microfinance Evangelism," 105.

112. For some indications of the reach of microcredit, see K. P. Padmanabhan, *Rural Credit: Lessons for Rural Bankers and Policy Makers* (New York: St. Martins, 1988); and Sam Daley-Harris, ed., *Pathways Out of Poverty: Innovations in Microfinance for the Poorest Families* (West Hartford: Kumarian, 2002).

113. Asok Rai and Tomas Sjöström, "Is Grameen Lending Efficient? Repayment Incentives and Insurance," *Review of Economic Studies* 71 (2004), 217–34.

114. For a sample of this type of attack, see Parminder Bahra, "Microfinance: Is Grameen Founder Muhammad Yunus a Bloodsucker of the Poor?" *Wall Street Journal*, December 6, 2010 https://www.wsj.com/articles/BL-SOURCEB-16792. Much of the criticism from Bangladeshi prime minister Sheikh Hasina seems to have derived from Yunus's flirtation with a run for political office between 2006 and 2008. For Grameen's rejoinders, see Yunus Centre, "Questions by Critics on Grameen bank and the Facts," available at https://www.muhammadyunus.org/news/1616/questions-by-critics-on-grameen-bank-and-the-facts-n and http://www.yunuscentre.org/. In 2024, Sheikh Hasina's AL government was driven from power by popular protests and a Yunus-led caretaker government took over.

115. Jonathan Morduch, "Does Microfinance Really Help the Poor? New Evidence from Flagship Programs in Bangladesh" (June 1998), available at https://wagner.nyu.edu/files/faculty/publications/1998-Does-MF-really-help-the-poor.pdf; and Morduch, "The Microfinance Promise," *Journal of Economic Literature* 37 (December 1999), 1569–1614.
116. Abhijit Banerjee, Esther Duflo, Rachel Glennerster, and Cynthia Kinnan, "The Miracle of Microfinance? Evidence from a Randomized Evaluation" (2009), available at https://economics.mit.edu/files/5993; republished as part of a special issue of the *American Economic Journal: Applied Economics* 7:1 (January 2015) that presented six randomized evaluations of microcredit programs around the globe, with similarly mixed verdicts. See also Erica Field, Rohini Pande, John Papp, and Natalia Rigol, "Does Classic Microfinance Discourage Entrepreneurship among the Poor? Experimental Evidence from India," *American Economic Review* 103:6 (2013), 2196–2226, which suggested that the repayment plans of the original Grameen model discouraged the risky investment needed to produce growth.
117. Morduch, "The Role of Subsidies in Microfinance: Evidence from the Grameen Bank," *Journal of Development Economics* 60 (1999), 229–48.
118. Hulme and Paul Mosley, *Finance against Poverty*, vol. 2 (London: Routledge, 1996), 176. See also Kabeer, "Is Microfinance a 'Magic Bullet' for Women's Empowerment? Analysis of Findings from South Asia," *Economic and Political Weekly* (October 29, 2005), 4711; Atiur Rahman and Abdur Razzaque, "On Reaching the Hardcore Poor: Some Evidence on Social Exclusion in NGO Programmes," in Murshid et al., eds., *Readings*, vol. 2, 1–38. Hulme and Mosley base their conclusion on an analysis of BRAC's Rural Development Programme and the government's Thana Resource and Development Programme, both of which were late-1980s initiatives. On rural inequality in the 1980s, see Mustafa Mujeri and Salehuddin, "Poverty and Human Resource Development," in M. G. Quibria, ed., *The Bangladesh Economy in Transition* (Delhi: Oxford University Press, 1997), 117–20; and Mahabub Hossain, "Structure and Distribution of Household Income and Income Dimensions of Poverty," in Hossain Zillur Rahman and Mahabub Hossain, eds., *Rethinking Rural Poverty*, 57–73. But cf. Omar Haider Chowdhury's essay "Nutritional Dimensions of Poverty" in the same volume (74–98), which shows that per capita food consumption, declining from the 1960s until the early 1980s, began to rise thereafter, albeit with temporal and regional variations.
119. Ananya Roy, *Poverty Capital: Microfinance and the Making of Development* (New York: Routledge, 2010), 132. In Roy's view, BRAC succeeds best as a wraparound services provider, not a minimalist microfinance program.
120. Sobhan, "The Political Economy of Micro-credit," in Wood and Sharif, eds., *Who Needs Credit?* Chap 4.
121. Hossain, *The Aid Lab*, 193.
122. Zillur Rahman, "Poverty: The Challenges of Graduation," in Murshid et al., *Readings*, vol. 2, 65–90. Iffath Sharif and Geoffrey Wood call for microfinance to move from poverty alleviation to poverty eradication. If subsequent studies raise

doubts about whether it can make that transition, their work is nonetheless powerful in suggesting the many possible roles for microfinance—from savings to insurance to multiple loans formulations. Sharif and Wood, *Challenges for Second Generation Microfinance: Regulation, Supervision and Resource Mobilization* (Dhaka: University Press, 2001). In a later volume, Wood calls for a new political settlement to boost resilience among the poor. Wood, Zulfiqar Ali, Mathilde Maitrot, and Joe Devine, eds., *Aiding Resilience among the Extreme Poor in Bangladesh* (Dhaka: University Press, 2018), 61.

123. On borrower suicides in Andhra Pradesh, see Sohini Kar, *Financializing Poverty: Labour and Risk in Indian Microfinance* (Stanford: Stanford University Press, 2018), Chap. 6. For an essay that challenges the view that microcredit produces debt traps, see S. R. Osmani, "Is Microcredit a Debt Trap for the Poor? Sifting Reality from Myth," in K. A. S. Murshid and Atiqur Rahman, *Agricultural Transformation and Rural Poverty in Bangladesh: Essays in Memory of Dr. Mahabub Hossain* (Dhaka: University Press, 2021), 193–236.

124. Aminur Rahman, *Women and Microcredit in Bangladesh: Anthropological Study of the Rhetoric and Realities of Grameen Bank Lending* (Boulder: Westview, 1999), 3. Others found that interest rates were sometimes higher than stated, with NGOs overly strict in their payment regimen. Qazi Kholiquzzaman Ahmad, ed., *Socio-Economic and Indebtedness-Related Impact of Micro-credit in Bangladesh* (Dhaka: University Press, 2007). See also Thomas Dichter and Malcolm Harper, eds., *What's Wrong with Microfinance?* (Rugby, UK: Practical Action, 2007).

125. Karim, *Microfinance and Its Discontents*. For the original use of "hidden and public transcripts," see James Scott, *Domination and the Arts of Resistance: Hidden Transcripts* (New Haven: Yale University Press, 1990).

126. Helen Todd, *Women at the Center: Grameen Bank Borrowers after One Decade* (Boulder: Westview, 1996), 223. Development economist Judith Tendler also praised "minimalistic" programs that focus on one area or activity because they were easier to manage and concentrated scarce resources. Cited in MacIsaac and Wahid, "The Grameen Bank," in Wahid, ed., *The Grameen Bank*, 196.

127. Anne Marie Goetz and Rin Sen Gupta, "Who Takes the Credit? Gender, Power, and Control over Loan Use in Rural Credit Programs in Bangladesh," *World Development* 24: 1 (1996), 45–63; Kabeer, "Conflicts over Credit: Re-Evaluating the Empowerment Potential of Loans to Women in Rural Bangladesh," *World Development* 29:1 (2001), 63–84; Beatriz Armendáriz and Jonathan Morduch, *The Economics of Microfinance*, 2nd ed. (Cambridge: MIT Press, 2010), 227–31.

128. Simeen Mahmud, "Actually How Empowering Is Microcredit?" in Murshid et al., eds., *Readings*, vol. 2, 91–126.

129. For sharp critiques of neocolonial forces in development and academic policy, see Hossen, *Water Policy and Governance in South Asian: Empowering Rural Communities* (London: Routledge, 2017); and "Decolonizing Sociology for Social Justice in Bangladesh: Delta Scholarship Matters," *Critical Sociology* 25:1 (2022), 1–17.

130. Stuart Rutherford has charted these around Dhaka. Rutherford, *The Poor and the Money* (Oxford: Oxford University Press, 2000), 90; Rutherford, "Informal Fi-

nancial Services in Dhaka's Slums," in Wood and Sharif, eds., *Who Needs Credit?* Chap. 16. See also the influential later study: Daryl Collins, Jonathan Morduch, Stuart Rutherford, and Orlanda Ruthven, *Portfolios of the Poor: How the World's Poor Live on $2 a Day* (Princeton: Princeton University Press, 2009).

131. Shakhawat Ali, পরার্থপরতার আনন্দদর্শন: কাজী রফিকুল আলম ও ঢাকা আহ্ছানিয়া মিশন [*Kazi Rafiqul Alam and Dhaka Ahsania Mission in Development Advancement*] (Dhaka: Batighar, 2022); interview with author, May 2022. The Dhaka Mission, which did not accept external funds until Alam took over, focused on health, education, and rural development. Though based in Muslim Sufi teachings, it stressed religious tolerance.

132. Shelley Feldman, "NGOs and Civil Society: (Un)stated Contradictions," in Rounaq Jahan, ed., *Bangladesh: Promise and Performance* (London: Zed, 2000), 237–38. "NGOs act as brokers speaking on behalf of their members," Feldman writes elsewhere, "rather than mobilizing people to speak on their own behalf." Feldman, "Paradoxes of Institutionalisation: The Depoliticisation of Bangladeshi NGOs," *Development in Practice* 13:1 (February 2003), 22.

133. For this micro–macro disconnect, see Zillur Rahman, "Poverty: The Challenges of Graduation," in Murshid et al., eds., *Readings*, vol. 2, 65–90; James Surowiecki, "What Microloans Miss," *New Yorker* (March 10, 2008), available at https://www.newyorker.com/magazine/2008/03/17/what-microloans-miss.

134. Roy, *Poverty Capital*, 132. More extreme criticism described microfinance as a form of "local neoliberalism," in which NGOs take over services and enforce modes of discipline on their subject-clients. Milford Bateman, *Why Doesn't Microfinance Work? The Destructive Rise of Local Neoliberalism* (London: Zed, 2010).

135. Wood, *Bangladesh*, Chap. 22; Mannan, *BRAC*, Chap. 8.

136. For a discussion of how the floods affected rural borrowers and microcredit NGOs, see Zillur Rahman and Khandaker Shakhawat Ali, eds., *Researching Poverty from the Bottom Up: Reflections on the Experience of the Programme for Research on Poverty Alleviation 1994–2002* (Dhaka: Grameen Trust, 2007), 97, 103–04, 107, 111–13.

137. For a summary of Grameen II changes, see Asif Dowla and Dipal Barua, *The Poor Always Pay Back: The Grameen II Story* (Bloomfield: Kumarian, 2006); Collins et al., *Portfolios*, Chap. 6.

138. For an evaluation of BRAC's Targeting the Ultra-Poor Program, see M. Shahe Emran, Virginia Robani, and Stephen Smith, "Assessing the Frontiers of Ultra-Poverty Reduction: Evidence from CFPR/TUP, an Innovative Program in Bangladesh," Department of Economics, George Washington University (March 2009).

139. Kabeer, Simeen Mahmud, and Jairo G. Isaza Castro, "NGOs and the Political Empowerment of Poor People in Rural Bangladesh: Cultivating the Habits of Democracy?" *World Development* 40:10 (2012), 2060. See also Michael Woolcock, "Learning from Failures in Microfinance: What Unsuccessful Cases Tell Us about How Group-Based Programs Work," *American Journal of Economics and Sociology* 58:1 (January 1999), 17–42.

140. Kabeer, "Citizenship Narratives in the Face of Bad Governance: The Voices of

the Working Poor in Bangladesh," *Journal of Peasant Studies* 38:2 (March 2011), 352.

141. For these numbers, see Stefan Dercon, *Gambling on Development: Why Some Countries Win and Others Lose* (London: Hurst, 2022), 219–20. For a judicious assessment of the role of garments, remittances, and microcredit in the Bangladesh economy, see Hossain, *The Aid Lab*, Chap. 8.
142. Sobhan, "Bangladesh's Permanent Liberation Struggle: Constructing an Inclusive Democratic State," in Sobhan, *An Inclusive Democracy for a Just Society: Reigniting the Spirit of the Liberation Struggle* (Dhaka: Prothoma Prokashan, 2021), 49–81. See also David Lewis, *Bangladesh: Politics, Economy and Civil Society* (Cambridge: Cambridge University Press, 2011).
143. Ali Riaz, *More Than Meets the Eye: Essays in Bangladeshi Politics* (Dhaka: University Press, 2022).
144. Although one Indian journalist, noting the rise of fundamentalism, warned in 2006 that it could become the "next Afghanistan." Hiranmey Karlekar, *Bangladesh: The Next Afghanistan?* (New Delhi: Sage, 2005).
145. Binayak Sen, "Drivers of Escape and Descent: Changing Household Fortunes in Rural Bangladesh," in Murshid et al., eds., *Readings*, vol. 2, 129.

Chapter 8. "Until Lions Have Their Own Historians"

1. Interview with Joseph F. Stepanek, The Association for Diplomatic Studies and Training Foreign Affairs Oral History Project, Foreign Assistance Series (1998), 61.
2. Chilombo Mwondela, "Bilateral Donors Withholding Aid," *Post* (August 7, 1996), 4.
3. In the *Weekly Post*, see the articles "Pot-holes on the Road to Reform" (March 5–11, 1993), 10–11; "Everything Seems Wrong in Public Sector" (March 11–18, 1993), 8–9; "What People Think about the MMD" (June 18–24, 1993), n.p.; and "What People Think about Chiluba" (June 25–July 1, 1993), n.p.
4. See the analysis by Chilean economist and post-Pinochet finance minister Alejandro Foxley, *Latin American Experiments in Neo-Conservative Economics* (Berkeley: University of California Press, 1983).
5. John Toye, "Structural Adjustment: Context, Assumptions, Origin and Diversity," in Rolph van der Hoeven and Fred van der Kraaij, *Structural Adjustment and Beyond in Sub-Saharan Africa* (London: James Currey, 1994), 18–19.
6. Patrick Sharma, *Robert McNamara's Other War: The World Bank and International Development* (Philadelphia: University of Pennsylvania Press, 2017).
7. For a summary of the Bretton Woods institutions, see Michael Todaro and Stephen Smith, *Economic Development*, 8th ed. (Boston: Addison Wesley, 2003), 626–33. On an earlier debate over program vs. project loans, see Michele Alacevich, "Early Development Economics Debates Revisited," *Journal of the History of Economic Thought* 33:2 (2011), 151–55.
8. Paul Mosley, Jane Harrigan, and John Toye, *Aid and Power: The World Bank and*

Policy-based Lending, vol. 1 (London: Routledge, 1991), 7–29; David Engerman, *The Price of Aid: The Economic Cold War in India* (Cambridge: Harvard University Press, 2018), Chap. 7; and Sharma, *Robert McNamara's Other War*, 147–50. A similar program occurred in Indonesia, reports Bradley Simpson in *Economists with Guns: Authoritarian Development and U.S.–Indonesian Relations, 1960–1968* (Palo Alto: Stanford University Press, 2008), Chap. 4.

9. Sharma, *Robert McNamara's Other War*, 41. Rather than managing projects or hiring implementers directly, the World Bank typically provides loans to host countries and then assists them with project oversight.
10. For accounts of this history, see Todaro and Smith, *Economic Development*, 605–19; Alfred B. Zack-Williams, Ed Brown, and Giles Mohan, "The Long Road to Structural Adjustment"; and Bob Milward, "What Is Structural Adjustment?" in Mohan, Brown, Milward, and Zack-Williams, *Structural Adjustment: Theory, Practice, and Impacts* (London: Routledge, 2000), 3–38. See also Sharma, *Robert McNamara's Other War*, Chaps. 4, 5, and 7.
11. Sharma, *Robert McNamara's Other War*, 138.
12. Olivier Blanchard, Rudiger Dornbusch, Paul Krugman, Richard Layard, and Lawrence Summers, *Reform in Eastern Europe* (Cambridge: MIT Press, 1991), 1. For a discussion, see Kristen Ghodsee and Mitchell Orenstein, *Taking Stock of Shock: Social Consequences of the 1989 Revolutions* (Oxford: Oxford University Press, 2021), Chap. 1.
13. For a list of loans, see Ralph van der Hoeven and Fred van der Kraaij, *Structural Adjustment and Beyond in Sub-Saharan Africa* (London: James Currey, 1994), 255. See also Eva Jespersen, "External Shocks, Adjustment Policies and Economic and Social Performance," in Giovanni Andrea Cornia, van der Hoeven, and Thandika Mkandawire, eds., *Africa's Recovery in the 1990s: From Stagnation and Adjustment to Human Development* (New York: St. Martin's, 1992), 9–50.
14. The literature on structural adjustment is vast. For useful analyses and definitions of key terms, see Tony Killick, ed., *The Quest for Economic Stabilization: The IMF and the Third World* (London: Heinemann, 1984); Killick, ed., *The IMF and Stabilisation: Developing Country Experiences;* and Killick, *IMF Programmes in Developing Countries* (London: Routledge, 1995).
15. From a "positive flow of nearly $43 billion," reported the UNDP's 1990 Human Development Report, transfers reversed "to a negative flow of nearly $33 billion in 1988." United Nations Development Programme, *Human Development Report* (New York: Oxford University Press, 1990), 78.
16. The longstanding equation of development with "producers increasing output by intensifying their use of standardized inputs manufactured in developed countries," wrote three critics, was entirely compatible with adjusters' "promotion of an 'enabling environment.'" Peter Gibbon, Kjell Havnevik, and Kenneth Hermele, *A Blighted Harvest: The World Bank and African Agriculture in the 1980s* (Trenton: Africa World, 1993).
17. Cornia, Richard Jolly, and Frances Stewart, eds., *Adjustment with a Human Face* (Oxford: Clarendon, 1987). See also the pamphlet by the Debt Crisis Network,

From Debt to Development: Alternatives to the International Debt Crisis (Washington, DC: Institute for Policy Studies, 1985). On the 1970s background to these works, see Joanne Meyerowitz, *A War on Global Poverty: The Lost Promise of Redistribution and the Rise of Microcredit* (Princeton: Princeton University Press, 2021), 184–93.

18. Stewart, Sanjaya Lall, and Samiel Wangwe, eds., *Alternative Development Strategies in Sub-Saharan Africa* (New York: St. Martin's, 1992).
19. Robert Lensink, *Structural Adjustment in Sub-Saharan Africa* (London: Longman, 1996); and Sarah Babb, *Behind the Development Banks: Washington Politics, World Poverty, and the Wealth of Nations* (Chicago: University of Chicago Press, 2009), 155–60.
20. Lawrence H. Summers and Lant H. Pritchett, "The Structural-Adjustment Debate," *American Economic Review* 83:2 (May 1993), 384. For a summary from the same era, see Killick, "Structural Adjustment and Poverty Alleviation: An Interpretive Survey," *Development and Change* 26 (1995), 305–31.
21. Summers and Pritchett, "The Structural-Adjustment Debate," 385.
22. Summers and Pritchett, "The Structural-Adjustment Debate," 384.
23. Matthew Martin, *The Crumbling Façade of African Debt Negotiations* (New York: St. Martin's, 1991), 275. On Adedeji, see Adebayo Adedeji, *Towards a Dynamic African Economy: Selected Speeches and Lectures, 1975–1986* (London: Frank Cass, 1989); Adedeji, Owodunni Teriba, and Patrick Bugembe, eds., *The Challenge of African Economic Recovery and Development* (London: Frank Cass, 1991); and S. K. B. Asante, *African Development: Adebayo Adedeji's Alternative Strategies* (London: Hans Zell, 1991). For a series of contemporary and often censorious analyses of both the Lagos Plan and World Bank policy, see John Ravenhill, ed., *Africa in Economic Crisis* (New York: Columbia University Press, 1986). For later volumes on African viewpoints, see Mkandawire and Charles Soludo, *Our Continent, Our Future: African Perspectives on Structural Adjustment* (Trenton: Africa World, 1999); and Mkandawire and Soludo, eds., *African Voices on Structural Adjustment* (Trenton: Africa World, 2003).
24. Asante, *African Development*, 146–49. For a critical review of APPER and UNPAAERD, see Adrien Ratsimbaharison, *The Failure of the United Nations Development Programs for Africa* (Dallas: University Press of America, 2003).
25. For a volume co-edited by a Zambian economist who would later join the MMD, see Samir Amin, Derrick Chitala, and Ibbo Mandaza, eds., *SADCC: Prospects for Disengagement and Development in Southern Africa* (London: Zed, 1987).
26. Lise Rakner, *Political and Economic Liberalisation in Zambia, 1991–2001* (Stockholm: Nordic Africa Institute, 2003), 56.
27. Respondent A, August 20, 2019, Washington, DC.
28. Respondent J, June 4, 2019.
29. Mosley, Harrigan, and Toye, *Aid and Power*.
30. Respondent D, May 25, 2019.
31. John Ravenhill, "A Second Decade of Adjustment: Greater Complexity, Greater Uncertainty," in Thomas Callaghy and Ravenhill, eds., *Hemmed In: Responses to*

Africa's Economic Decline (New York: Columbia University Press, 1993), 21. In addition, Robert H. Bates, *Markets and States in Tropical Africa: The Political Basis of Agricultural Policy* (Berkeley: University of California Press, 2005/1981) played an important role in establishing this new consensus. Bates's experience was rooted in Zambia.

32. Ravenhill, "A Second Decade of Adjustment," 20–24.
33. Countries should not be seen as single units, uniformly rejecting or embracing SAPs. As Caesar Cheelo and Marja Hinfelaar recently showed, the Bank of Zambia aligned itself closely with IFIs and had the relative autonomy to pursue its mandate. Other agencies—the Ministry of Finance or the Zambia Revenue Service, for example—exhibited greater diffidence. Cheelo and Hinfelaar, "Bank of Zambia's Autonomy amidst Political Turnovers in Zambia," Effective States and Inclusive Development Working Paper No. 153, University of Manchester (September 2020), 1–37.
34. Morton Jerven, *Poor Numbers: How We Are Misled by African Development Statistics and What to Do about It* (Ithaca: Cornell University Press, 2013), 45–47.
35. For these figures, see Miles Larmer, "Reaction and Resistance to Neo-Liberalism in Zambia," *Review of African Political Economy* 32:103 (March 2005), 32; Chukwuma Obidegwu and Mudziviri Nziramasanga, *Copper and Zambia: An Econometric Analysis* (Lexington, MA: Lexington Books, 1981), 14. On the modern history of Zambia, see Andrew Roberts, *A History of Zambia* (New York: Africana, 1976); Bizeck Jube Phiri, *A Political History of Zambia* (Trenton, NJ: Africa World, 2006); and Andrew Sardanis, *Zambia: The First 50 Years* (London: I. B. Tauris, 2014). Roberts was influenced by the Dar es Salaam School of historiography, which produced unified national histories to support independent African nations. For a critical assessment of the school, see Donald Denoon and Adam Kuper, "Nationalist Historians in Search of a Nation: The 'New Historiography' in Dar es Salaam," *African Affairs* 69:277 (October 1970), 329–49. For a later volume that reflects a more fractured understanding of the Zambian past, see Jan-Bart Gewald, Marja Hinfelaar, and Giacomo Macola, eds., *One Zambia, Many Histories: Towards a Post-Colonial History of Zambia* (Leiden: Brill, 2008).
36. Calculated from a chart on pp. 19–20 of Raymond F. Mikesell, *The Global Copper Industry: Problems and Prospects* (London: Croom Helm, 1988). For a history of Zambia's copper mining industry, see Christopher Adam and Anthony M. Simpasa, "Copper Mining in Zambia: From Collapse to Recovery," in Paul Collier and Anthony J. Venables, eds., *Plundered Nations? Successes and Failures in Natural Resource Extraction* (London: Palgrave Macmillan, 2011), 304–48. On the Zambian mining economy, see Alastair Fraser and Larmer, eds., *Zambia, Mining, and Neoliberalism: Boom and Bust on the Globalized Copperbelt* (New York: Palgrave Macmillan, 2010).
37. Catherine Hill and Malcolm McPherson, eds., *Promoting and Sustaining Economic Reform in Zambia* (Cambridge: Harvard University Press, 2004), 2n2, 3. For the GNP figure, see Ravi Gulhati, "Impasse in Zambia: The Economics and Politics of Reform," *Economic Development Institute Development Policy Case Series*, Analytical

Case Studies No. 2 (Washington, DC: World Bank, 1989), 3. See also Bates and Collier, "The Politics and Economics of Policy Reform in Zambia," in Bates and A. O. Krueger, eds., *Political and Economic Interactions in Economic Policy Reform: Evidence from Eight Countries* (London: Blackwell, 1993), 388.

38. Manenga Ndulo, "Planning in Zambia: An Analysis of the Third Five-Year Plan," in Kwaku Osei-Hwedie and Muna Ndulo, eds., *Issues in Zambian Development* (Nyangwe, Zaire: Omenana, 1985), 14–27.
39. On rural development under UNIP, see Michael Bratton, *The Local Politics of Rural Development: Peasant and Party-State in Zambia* (Hanover: University Press of New England, 1980).
40. To quote Richard Jolly, who participated in the 1964 UN mission led by Dudley Seers that laid out a development program for newly independent Zambia: the "inequalities in Zambia were some of the major and extreme challenges for economic policy which the government would face—inequalities, of course, between the mining and the nonmining sector, inequalities between the rural and urban areas, and of course enormous inequalities between white and black." Interview of Richard Jolly, United Nations Intellectual History Project (July 20, 2005), 31. See also the *Report of the UN/ECA/FAO Economic Survey Mission on the Economic Development of Zambia* (Ndola: Falcon Press, 1964). For critiques of the Seers report, see Larmer, "Historical Perspectives on Zambia's Mining Booms and Busts," in Fraser and Larmer, eds., *Zambia, Mining, and Neoliberalism*, 35; and Jolly, "The Seers Report in Retrospect," *African Social Research* 11 (June 1971), 1–26.
41. Bates and Collier, "The Politics and Economics of Policy Reform in Zambia," *Journal of African Economies* 4:1 (1993), 118. Bates broadened this theme into a general development theory in *Prosperity and Violence: The Political Economy of Development* (New York: Norton, 2001). Since these factions often had support from particular regions or populations, the dominance of one group could sow ethnic discord. See Eve Nan Sandberg, "International Foreign Aid, Donor Cohesion, and Donor Bounded Decision-Making in Zambia's Agricultural Sector" (Ph.D. diss., Yale University, 1990).
42. Respondent C, May 30, 2019. See also the memoir by Ng'andu Peter Magande, *The Depth of My Footprints: From the Hills of Namaila to the Global Stage* (Atlanta: Maleendo, 2018), 186.
43. See, for example, Kristen Ghodsee, *Second World, Second Sex: Socialist Women's Activism and Global Solidarity during the Cold War* (Durham: Duke University Press, 2018).
44. James Ferguson, *Global Shadows: Africa in the Neoliberal World Order* (Durham: Duke University Press, 2006), 76; Kenneth Kaunda, *Humanism in Zambia and a Guide to Its Implementation*, Part 1I (Lusaka: Zambian Information Services, 1968). For a recent discussion of African socialism in Zambia and Tanzania, see Priya Lal, "Decolonization and the Gendered Politics of Developmental Labor in Southeastern Africa," in Stephen Macekura and Erez Manela, eds., *The Development Century: A Global History* (Cambridge: Cambridge University Press, 2018), 173–93.

See also Lal, *African Socialism in Postcolonial Tanzania: Between the Village and the World* (New York: Cambridge University Press, 2015), esp. Chap. 1.

45. Guy Scott, *Adventures in Zambian Politics: A Story in Black and White* (Boulder: Lynne Rienner, 2019), 72.
46. Respondent C. The state held 60.3 percent of shares in ZCCM, while Anglo American controlled 27.3 percent. John Craig, "Putting Privatisation into Practice: The Case of Zambia Consolidated Copper Mines Limited," *Journal of Modern African Studies* 39:3 (September 2001), 391.
47. Carolyn Baylies and Morris Szeftel, "The Rise of a Zambian Capitalist Class in the 1970s," *Journal of Southern African Studies* 8:2 (April 1982), 187–213. See also Jeffrey J. Hawkins, Jr., "Understanding the Failure of IMF reform: The Zambian Case," *World Development* 19:7 (1991), 839–49.
48. Alastair Fraser, "Introduction: Boom and Bust on the Zambian Copperbelt," in Fraser and Larmer, eds., *Zambia, Mining, and Neoliberalism*, 6.
49. See Kaunda's Foreword to Adedeji, *Towards a Dynamic African Economy*, xvii–xx.
50. For a list of the loans, see Fundanga, "The Role of the IMF and World Bank in Zambia," in Bade Onimode, ed., *The IMF, the World Bank, and the African Debt*, vol 1: *The Economic Impact* (London: Zed, 1989), 143. On Zambia's interactions with the IMF, see Manenga Ndulo and Martin Sakala, "Stabilisation Policies in Zambia: 1976–85," World Employment Programme Research Working Paper 13, May 1987; and Roger Young and John Loxley, *Zambia: An Assessment of Zambia's Structural Adjustment Experience* (Ottawa: North-South Institute, 1990).
51. Sandberg, "International Foreign Aid," 256. For the GDP figures, see https://tradingeconomics.com/zambia/gdp.
52. Manenga Ndulo and Martin Sakala, "Stabilisation Policies in Zambia: 1976–85," World Employment Programme Research Working Paper 13, May 1987, 31.
53. Caleb Fundanga, "The Role of the IMF and World Bank in Zambia," 144.
54. Akashambatwa Mbikusita-Lewanika, *Zambia: Broken Promises, Betrayed Trust and a Case for Re-Decolonisation* (Mongu, Zambia: Barotse National Library, 2017).
55. Van de Walle describes these as ahistorical summaries that present structural adjustment as largely ineluctable. See *African Economies and the Politics of Permanent Crisis, 1979–1999* (Cambridge: Cambridge University Press, 2001), 13. For an analysis by Zambia experts of Africa's democratic transitions, see Bratton and Van de Walle, *Democratic Experiments in Africa: Regime Transitions in Comparative Perspective* (Cambridge: Cambridge University Press, 1997).
56. I use the term *civil society* advisedly since Zambia did not have a robust nonstate sector in the late 1980s and early 1990s. For a reflection on the concept applied in Africa, see Callaghy, "Civil Society, Democracy, and Economic Change in Africa: A Dissenting Opinion about Resurgent Societies," in John W. Harbeson, Donald Rothchild, and Naomi Chazan, eds., *Civil Society and the State in Africa* (Boulder: Lynne Rienner, 1994), 231–53.
57. These have been the subject of a considerable literature. Robert Bates's classic study *Union, Parties, and Political Development: A Study of Mineworkers in Zambia*

(New Haven: Yale University Press, 1971) argued that unions struggled to balance the specific needs of their members with the long-term needs of national development. On mines and Zambianization, see Michael Burawoy, *The Colour of Class on the Copper Mines: From African Advancement to Zambianization* (Lusaka: Manchester University Press, 1972). A recent revisionist account—Larmer, *Mineworkers in Zambia: Labour and Political Change in Post-Colonial Africa* (London: Tauris, 2007)—finds union militancy and willingness to confront UNIP from the time of Zambian independence. In the background of the debate over union activism lurks the suspicion that Copperbelt mineworkers held back national development by demanding food subsidies to sustain a modern urban lifestyle. Ferguson, *Expectations of Modernity: Myths and Meanings of Urban Life on the Zambian Copperbelt* (Berkeley: University of California Press, 1999), disputes the thesis of a stark rural-urban divide. And Deborah Potts, "Counter-urbanisation on the Zambian Copperbelt? Interpretations and Implications," *Urban Studies* 42:4 (April 2005), 583–609, shows a trend toward reverse urban to rural migration between the mid-1980s and 2005.

58. Larmer, "Historical Perspectives on Zambia's Mining Booms and Busts," 47.
59. David M. C. Bartlett, "Civil Society and Democracy: A Zambian Case Study," *Journal of Southern African Studies* 26:3 (2000), 435.
60. Bartlett, "Civil Society and Democracy," 435–36.
61. Larmer, *Rethinking African Politics: A History of Opposition in Zambia* (Oxfordshire: Routledge, 2016/2011), 245.
62. Bartlett, "Civil Society and Democracy," 432, 439–40; John Mwanakatwe, *End of Kaunda Era* (Lusaka: Multimedia, 1994), 218–23.
63. Bates and Collier, "The Politics and Economics of Policy Reform in Zambia," 119.
64. For an account of these shifts in the late 1970s and early 1980s, see Sandberg, "International Foreign Aid," Chap. 4.
65. Baylies and Szeftel, "The Fall and Rise of Multi-Party Politics," *Review of African Political Economy* 54 (July 1992), 83–84.
66. Respondent H. The Friedrich Ebert Foundation, based for four years (1985–89) in an office at the Institute of African Studies, ran a program designed to promote dialogue between researchers (in academics or the parastatal sector) and the public sector, which generally meant the government. It also worked with the Zambian Bar Association, Chiluba's ZCTU, and the Farmer's Association of Zambia. Respondent B.
67. Mbikusita-Lewanika, *Milk in a Basket: The Political-Economic Malaise in Zambia* (Lusaka: Zambia Research Foundation, 1990), 53, 86, 134–35, 142.
68. Interview, May 2019.
69. Musokotwane, "Financing of Health Services in Zambia," unpublished paper, Institute for African Studies. Cited in Katele Kalumba and Paul Freund, "The Eclipse of Idealism: Health Planning in Zambia," *Health Policy and Planning* 4:3 (1989), 225–27.
70. Respondent F, May 28, 2019.

71. Kalumba and Freund, "The Eclipse of Idealism,"225–27.
72. See, e.g., the article "IMF Programmes Have Failed, Says Kalumba," *Post* (June 13, 2001), 1, 3.
73. Gilbert Mudenda, "Dangers Lurk behind Sale of Public Enterprises," *Weekly Post* (July 26–August 1, 1991), 5.
74. Mudenda, "Why Zambia Is Failing to Lure Foreign Investors," *Weekly Post* (August 2–8, 1991), 5; Mudenda, "Third Republic Needs to Revamp Economy," *Weekly Post* (November 2–7, 1991), 9; Mudenda, "Parastatal Firms' Monopoly Retards Development," *Weekly Post* (December 20–26, 1991), 5.
75. Mudenda, "Excessive Belief in Market Forces, a False God," *Weekly Post* (February 28–March 5, 1992), 9.
76. Mudenda, "New Budget Should Be a Tool for Welfare," *Weekly Post* (November 13 University Press 19, 1992), 7.
77. John Clark (with Caroline Allison), *Zambia: Debt and Poverty* (Oxford: Oxfam, 1989), 8.
78. "The MMD coalition," wrote van de Walle and Dennis Chiwele, "never enjoyed a consensus on some aspects of the reform program, often the ones that are stalled today, such as privatization." Van de Walle and Chiwele, "Democratization and Economic Reform in Zambia," USAID/Zambia (November 4, 1994), 43.
79. Although IAS researchers focused on social and cultural topics, Saasa's interests brought it into the economic debates of the day, and the institute's pedigree and international standing lent weight to the opposition. For a history of the institute—née Rhodes-Livingstone Institute, now Institute for Social and Economic Research (INESOR)—see Schumaker, *Africanizing Anthropology: Fieldwork, Networks, and the Making of Cultural Knowledge in Central Africa* (Durham: Duke University Press, 2001).
80. Respondent C, Lusaka, May 30, 2019.
81. Respondent H, Lusaka, May 28, 2019. V. J. Mwaanga describes this juxtaposition at work in the March 1990 UNIP Convention, where delegates embraced economic restructuring even while rejecting political reform. Mwaanga, "Can the Party Reform Itself? Multi-Party Options and Prospects," in Mbikusita-Lewanika and Chitala, eds., *The Hour Has Come! Proceedings of the National Conference on the Multi-Party Option Held at the Garden House Hotel, Lusaka, Zambia, 20–21 July, 1990* (Lusaka: Zambia Research Foundation, 1990–91), 78–83. According to one respondent, unless there was a direct attack on Kaunda, there was no problem airing oppositional views of government policy. Respondent B. Yet Kaunda's liberality should not be overstated. For a prominent political jailing, see Mwaanga, *The Other Society: A Detainee's Diary* (Lusaka: Fleetfoot, 1987).
82. Numerous respondents told me that Chiluba named his children after socialist leaders: Tito, Castro, and Mikoyan. For a recollection of Chiluba's pre-1990s socialism, see Scott, *Adventures in Zambian Politics*, 81.
83. Magande, *Depth*, 189.
84. Respondent B.

85. Chitala, *Not Yet Democracy: The Transition of the Twin Process of Political and Economic Reform in Zambia (1991–2001)* (Lusaka: Zambia Research Foundation, 2002), 26–29.
86. The Garden House was a last-minute change of venue, since other hotels refused to host the meeting.
87. Mbikusita-Lewanika and Chitala, eds., *The Hour Has Come!* 12, 17, 45–47, 49, 55–58, 64, 76, 97, 98.
88. In this regard, Kaunda's Humanism left as its legacy a moral vision of political economy that even opponents imbibed. As in Eastern Europe after communism, post-1991 complaints about inequality and impoverishment—not to mention nostalgia for the country's first leader—suggest that Humanist aspirations had not vanished, despite rhetorical condemnation.
89. Baylies and Szeftel, "The Fall and Rise," 81. See also Magande, *Depth*, 193.
90. Respondent I.
91. For a list of the reforms through 1995, see McPherson, Annex D of "The Sequencing of Economic Reforms: Lessons from Zambia," Harvard Institute for International Development, Discussion Paper No. 516 (November 1995), 41–46.
92. Oliver Saasa and Jerker Carlsson, *The Aid Relationship in Zambia: A Conflict Scenario* (IAS: Lusaka, 1996), 48. For a fifty-year chart of Zambia's official development assistance (ODA) as a percentage of Gross Domestic Income, see the charts compiled by Trading Economics from World Bank data: https://tradingeconomics.com/zambia/net-oda-received-percent-of-gni-wb-data.html.
93. Lise Rakner, Nicolas van de Walle, and Dominic Mulaisho, "Zambia," in Shantayanan Devarajan, David Dollar, and Torgney Holmgren, eds., *Aid and Reform in Africa: Lessons from Ten Case Studies* (Washington, DC: World Bank, 2001), 537, 539–40, 548.
94. The figure comes from Flora Musonda and Christopher Adam, "Trade Liberalization in Zambia, 1970–95," in Ademola Oyejide, Benno Ndulu, and Jan Willem Gunning, eds., *Regional Integration and Trade Liberalization in Sub-Saharan Africa*, vol. 2: *Country Case-Studies* (London: Palgrave Macmillan, 1999), 451–52. For reference, the U.S. debt in 2020 was just over 100 percent of GDP and a cause of considerable concern. With growth in the mid-2000s and debt cancellation under the Heavily Indebted Poor Countries (HIPC) program, which Zambia completed in 2005, donor contributions to revenue dropped from around 40 percent to less than 2 percent. Marja Hinfelaar and Justine Sichone, "The Challenge of Sustaining a Professional Civil Service amidst Shifting Political Coalitions—The Case of the Ministry of Finance in Zambia, 1991–2018," Global Development Institute Working Paper Series esid-122–19, GDI, University of Manchester (2019), 4.
95. Richard Sakala, *Difficult Decisions: Changing a Nation* (Lusaka: Sentor Publishing, 2001), 69, 72, 69–91. The inevitability of neoliberalism was a common rhetorical trope: recall Margaret Thatcher's insistence that "there is no alternative" to a market economy, a slogan that earned the acronym TINA.
96. Martin, *Crumbling Façade*, 92, 149. Martin criticizes the Paris Club debt rescheduling negotiations in particular. For sympathetic histories of the Paris Club, see

Alexis Rieffel, "The Paris Club, 1978–1983," *Columbia Journal of Transnational Law* 23 (1984), 83–110; and Rieffel, "The Role of the Paris Club in Managing Debt Problems," Essays in International Finance No. 161, International Finance Section, Department of Economics, Princeton (December 1985). For a comparison of Ghana's and Zambia's experience with reform negotiations, see Martin, "Neither Phoenix nor Icarus: Negotiating Economic Reform in Ghana and Zambia, 1983–1992," in Callaghy and Ravenhill, eds., *Hemmed In*, 130–79.

97. Larmer, "Reaction and Resistance," 30.
98. Respondent I.
99. Respondent J, June 4, 2019.
100. Larmer, "Reaction and Resistance," 31; see the discussion on pp. 29–32.
101. Deborah Hoover and McPherson, "Capacity Building in the Ministry of Finance, Zambia," in Hill and McPherson, eds., *Promoting and Sustaining Economic Reform in Zambia*, 389. Though marginalized, the EAZ continues to operate today.
102. Respondent E, June 5, 2019. For accounts of these years by the Harvard advisors, see the essays collected in Hill and McPherson, eds., *Promoting and Sustaining Economic Reform in Zambia*. The volume is striking for the degree to which it lays the blame for economic failure on the Zambian government.
103. Fundanga, "Practical Effects of Economic and Political Conditionality in the Recipient Administration," in Kjell Havnevik and Brian van Arkadie, eds., *Domination or Dialogue? Experiences and Prospects for African Development Cooperation* (Sweden: Nordiska Afrikainstitutet, 1996), 92–93.
104. Respondent I.
105. On these advantages, see Chitala, Preface, in Mbikusita-Lewanika and Chitala, eds., *The Hour Has Come!* vii–viii.
106. Respondent L.
107. Baylies and Szeftel, "The Fall and Rise," 89.
108. Saasa and Simutanyi, "Zambia: Power and Change Analysis—Underlying Factors Explaining Governance Issues and Implications for Policy Change," Report Commissioned by the Embassy of the Netherlands (Lusaka, 2007), 20–21.
109. Respondents M and I.
110. MMD Manifesto (1991), 1. Economic issues occupied the largest portion of the ten-page manifesto; Respondent P interview, June 5, 2019.
111. Quoted in Larmer, "Reaction and Resistance," 38.
112. Chiluba, "Workers' Challenge: The Pursuit of the Rule of Law and Enabling Environment for Economic Recovery," in Mbikusita-Lewanika and Chitala, eds., *The Hour Has Come!* 95, 98.
113. Quoted in Larmer, "Reaction and Resistance," 38. One interviewee (Respondent D) dubbed Chiluba "Mr. Liberalization." On the discrepant views of the business class and organized labor, see Simutanyi, "The Politics of Structural Adjustment in Zambia," *Third World Quarterly* 17:4 (1996), 825.
114. Reports of the drought appeared in March, and the cuts listed were either introduced or continued thereafter.
115. Magande, *Depth*, 200–206.

116. For an account of the economic hardships, see Saasa, "Structural Adjustment and Governance Capacity in Zambia: 1983–1994," paper commissioned by Private Sector Development Department (Washington, DC: World Bank, June 1994), 23–31. See also "Out Goes 'Humanism,' in Comes 'Nyu Katcha,'" *Weekly Post* (February 26—March 4, 1993), 17.
117. Aidan Cox and John Healey, *European Development Cooperation and the Poor* (London: Palgrave Macmillan, 2000), 4–5, 9, 15–16. The statistics are found on pp. 4–5. See also Austin N. Isamah, "Labour Response to Structural Adjustment in Nigeria and Zambia," in Thandika Mkandawire and Adebayo Olukoshi, *Between Liberalisation and Oppression: The Politics of Structural Adjustment in Africa* (Dakar: Codesria, 1995), 324–44.
118. Callaghy, "Civil Society, Democracy, and Economic Change in Africa," 243. See also Bratton and Beatrice Liatto-Katundu, "A Focus Group Assessment of Political Attitudes in Zambia," *African Affairs* 93:373 (October 1994), 535–63, esp. 536–37, 542, 544, 548–49.
119. On the belt-tightening required in agricultural funding, see the memoir by the former minister of agriculture, Simon Zukas, *Into Exile and Back* (Lusaka: Bookworld, 2002), Chap. 13. On the broader challenges to agriculture, see Saasa, "Policy Reforms and Structural Adjustment in Zambia: The Case of Agriculture and Trade," Technical Paper No. 35, SD Publication Series, Office of Sustainable Development, USAID Bureau for Africa (October 1996).
120. Respondent N, Chanyanya, June 1, 2019.
121. Peter Dwyer and Leo Zeilig, *African Struggles Today: Social Movements since Independence* (Chicago: Haymarket, 2012), 141. On the range of public views on structural adjustment, see Venkatesh Seshamani and E. C. Kaunga, "Employment and Labour Markets during Adjustment: The Case of Zambia," International Labour Organization report (February 1996), 16–25.
122. On disappointments in the Copperbelt, see Ferguson, *Expectations of Modernity*. On labor union marginalization, see Felix Kani, "Structural Adjustment and Economic Reform Programmes, Labour Market Institutions, Employment and the Role of Social Partners: The Zambian Experience," Structural Adjustment Programme and Social Dialogue Discussion Paper Series No. 5 (Harare: International Labour Organization, February 2000). On the weakness of opposition to MMD liberalization, see Arne Bigsten and Steve Kayizzi-Mugerwa, "The Political Economy of Policy Failure in Zambia," Working Paper in Economics No. 23, Department of Economics, Göteborg University, Sweden (2000), 15.
123. Larmer, "Historical Perspectives on Zambia's Mining Booms and Busts," 48.
124. Before launching his weekly column in the *Post*, Father Joe Komakoma was arrested for protesting the 1995 constitutional changes that barred those without dual Zambian parentage from competing in elections. Komakoma, *The Best of Fr. Joe Komakoma's Ruminations (1999–2004)*, ed. Hinfelaar (Ndola: Mission Press, 2008), 7.
125. Bartlett, "Civil Society and Democracy," 431n15. His departure drew a lot of press attention.

126. Chitala, *Not Yet Democracy,* 50, 59.
127. Magande, *Depth,* Chaps. 16–18.
128. Respondent O; Rakner, van de Walle, and Mulaisho, "Zambia," 536.
129. Binwell Sinyangwe, *A Cowrie of Hope* (Oxford: Heinemann, 2000), 122.
130. Respondent J, June 4, 2019.
131. Christopher Adam, "Fiscal Adjustment, Financial Liberalization, and the Dynamics of Inflation: Some Evidence from Zambia," *World Development* 23:5 (1995), 735–50; and Saasa, "Policy Reforms and Structural Adjustment in Zambia: The Case of Agriculture and Trade," Technical Paper No. 35, SD Publication Series, Office of Sustainable Development, USAID Bureau for Africa (October 1996).
132. Respondents F and H. Against donor wishes, the sale of such an important asset to a foreign company—there was no Zambian firm capable of buying it—was deferred until the decade's end. Part of the problem was technical: whether to sell the mines as a whole or "unbundle" them for separate sales. Eventually, the latter was undertaken. For a description of the privatization process by the chairman of the ZCCM Privatisation Negotiating Team (and former ZCCM head), see Francis Kaunda, *Selling the Family Silver* (KwaZulu-Natal: Interpak, 2002). For a case study of mine privatization, see Craig, "Putting Privatisation into Practice." For an influential critique, see Alastair Fraser and John Lungu, *For Whom the Windfalls? Winners and Losers in the Privatisation of Zambia's Copper Mines* (Lusaka: Civil Society Trade Network of Zambia, 2007).
133. Respondent Q, interview, Chanyanya.
134. Sinyangwe, *Cowrie,* 147.
135. World Bank estimate, http://www.indexmundi.com/facts/zambia/gini-index, CSO (1996, 2006, 2010, 2015). Cited in Cheelo, Hinfelaar, and Manenga Ndulo, eds., *Inequality in Zambia* (New York: Routledge, 2022), 2. See also Chrispin Mphuka, Oliver Kaonga, and Mike Tembo, "Economic Growth, Inequality, and Poverty: Estimating the Growth Elasticity of Poverty in Zambia, 2006–2015," in the same volume, 83–119.
136. Cheelo, Hinfelaar, and Ndulo, eds., *Inequality,* 2, 24.
137. Seshamani and Obrian Ndhlovu, "Poverty, Inequality, Growth, and Empowerment: Reflections on a Continuing Debate," in Cheelo, Hinfelaar, and Ndulo, eds., *Inequality,* 22–23.
138. African proverb, quoted in Chammah J. Kaunda and Maria Hinfelaar, eds., *Competing for Caesar: Religions and Politics in Postcolonial Zambia* (Minneapolis: Fortress Press, 2020), 3.
139. I thank Caesar Cheelo, in a 2019 conversation, for this phrase.

Chapter 9. Conclusion

1. Joel Clark and Mark West, "Downsizing in a Laboratory: Federal Staff Cuts at USAID during the Government Reinvention Movement," https://pdf.usaid.gov/pdf_docs/pcaac535.pdf, 10; Carol Lancaster, *George Bush's Foreign Aid: Transformation or Chaos?* (Washington, DC: Center for Global Development, 2008), 14–15.

2. John Norris, *The Enduring Struggle: The History of the U.S. Agency for International Development and America's Uneasy Transformation of the World* (Lanham: Rowman & Littlefield, 2021), 184; see Chap. 9 for much of this information.
3. There was even a move to close the agency in the mid-1990s.
4. Francis Fukuyama, *The End of History and the Last Man* (New York: Macmillan, 1992). For the original article, see Fukuyama, "The End of History?" *The National Interest* 16 (1989), 3–18. The concept of posthistory is as old as Hegel in the early nineteenth century.
5. If Fukuyama spent considerable ink disputing simplifications of his thesis in the decades to follow, Putin's 2022 invasion of Ukraine found him once again hazarding the imminent end of history and the possible overcoming of populist authoritarianism. Fukuyama, "More Proof That This Really Is the End of History," *Atlantic* (October 17, 2022), https://www.theatlantic.com/ideas/archive/2022/10/francis-fukuyama-still-end-history/671761/.
6. Several interviewees told me that American aid practitioners went to Eastern Europe with Tocqueville's *Democracy in America* tucked in their suitcases. The image of Americans as vibrant community "joiners" was famously questioned by Robert Putnam in *Bowling Alone: The Collapsed and Revival of American Community* (2000), who warned of a decline in American community involvement.
7. John Williamson, "What Washington Means by Policy Reform," in Williamson, ed., *Latin American Adjustment: How Much Has Happened?* (Washington, DC: Institute for International Economics, 1990), 7–20. The occasion for Williamson's essay was a review of Latin American growth after a decade of adjustment. Ironically, the continent's poor performance encouraged a redoubling of market reform.
8. Williamson, "Democracy and the 'Washington Consensus,'" *World Development* 21:8 (1993), 1329.
9. He condemned the early Reaganomics of supply-side economics, monetarism, trickle down, and minimal government. Williamson, "What Should the World Bank Think of the Washington Consensus?" *World Bank Research Observer* 15:2 (2000), 251–64; Williamson, "A Short History of the Washington Consensus," in Narcís Serra and Joseph Stiglitz, eds., *The Washington Consensus Reconsidered: Towards a New Global Governance* (Oxford: Oxford University Press, 2008), 14–30. For an account of the Washington Consensus as a neoliberal annex, see David Harvey, "Neoliberalism as Creative Destruction," *Annals of the American Academy of Political and Social Science* 610:1 (2007), 22–44.
10. Joseph Stiglitz, "More Instruments and Broader Goals: Moving Toward the Post–Washington Consensus," *Brazilian Journal of Political Economy* 19:1 (1999), 101–28; Stiglitz, "Is There a Post–Washington Consensus?" in Serra and Stiglitz, eds., *The Washington Consensus Reconsidered*, 41–56. For a fuller exposition, see Stiglitz, *Globalization and Its Discontents* (New York: Norton, 2002).
11. Nancy Birdsall and Augusto de la Torre, with Rachel Menezes, "Washington Contentious: Economic Policies for Social Equity in Latin America" (Washington, DC: Carnegie Endowment for International Peace, 2001).
12. Dani Rodrik, "After Neoliberalism, What?"; paper presented at the Alternatives to

Neoliberalism Conference sponsored by the New Rules for Global Finance Coalition (May 23–24, 2002): https://drodrik.scholar.harvard.edu/links/after-neoliberalism-what. For a summary of these critiques, see Robin Broad and John Cavanagh, "The Death of the Washington Consensus?" *World Policy Journal* 16:3 (Fall 1999), 79–88.

13. In 2003, Williamson argued that Latin America's crisis-laden 1990s was due to the region's skewed income distribution. Williamson, "An Agenda for Restarting Growth and Reform" and "Summing Up" in Pedro-Pablo Kuczynski and Williamson, eds., *After the Washington Consensus: Restarting Growth and Reform in Latin America* (Washington, DC: Institute for International Economics, 2003), 1–19, 305–21.
14. John Marangos, *International Development and the Washington Consensus: A Pluralist Perspective* (New York: Routledge, 2021). For the augmented consensus, see pp. 80–99.
15. Shahid Javed Burki and Guillermo E. Perry, "Beyond the Washington Consensus: Institutions Matter" (Washington, DC: World Bank, 1998).
16. World Bank, *Assessing Aid: What Works, What Doesn't, and Why* (Oxford: Oxford University Press, 1998).
17. Craig Burnside and David Dollar, "Aid, Policies, and Growth," *American Economic Review* 90:4 (2000), 847–68. On the MCC, see Lancaster, *George Bush's Foreign Aid*, 16–22, 48–54. This certitude was challenged when William Easterly, Ross Levine, and David Roodman reexamined Dollar and Burnside's findings with an expanded data set: The benefits of aid in a good policy environment, they found, had vanished. Easterly, Levine, and Roodman, "New Data, New Doubts: A Comment of Burnside and Dollar's 'Aid, Policies, and Growth' (2000)," NBER Working Paper 9846 (July 2003).
18. For a study of a representative USAID democracy program, see Thomas Carothers, *Assessing Democracy Assistance: The Case of Romania* (Washington: Carnegie Endowment for International Peace, 1996).
19. For a study of decentralization in Uganda, see Michael Gubser "The View from Le Château: USAID's Recent Decentralisation Programming in Uganda," *Development Policy Review* 29:1 (2011), 23–46. In an analysis with provocative implications, Judith Tendler, a veteran of 1970s aid debates, argued that the dismissal of the public sector in developing countries was counterproductive. There were, she wrote, examples of "good government in the tropics" that provided services for poor constituents. She focused on effective state government in Ceará, northeastern Brazil. *Good Government in the Tropics* (Baltimore: John Hopkins University Press, 1997).
20. Hernando de Soto, *The Other Path: The Economic Answer to Terrorism* (New York: Basic Books, 1989); de Soto, *The Mystery of Capital: Why Capitalism Triumphs in the West and Fails Everywhere Else* (New York: Basic Books, 2000). On his influence in Washington, D.C., see Norris, *The Enduring Struggle*, 244.
21. Abhijit Banerjee and Esther Duflo, *Poor Economics: A Radical Rethinking of the Way to Fight Poverty* (New York: Public Affairs, 2011), Chap. 9.
22. Jeffrey Sachs, *The End of Poverty: Economic Possibilities for Our Time* (New York: Penguin, 2005), 321–22.

23. Amartya Sen, *Development as Freedom* (Oxford: Oxford University Press, 1999).
24. Mahbub ul Haq, *Reflections on Human Development* (New York: Oxford University Press, 1995).
25. Sen, *Poverty and Famines: An Essay on Entitlement and Deprivation* (Oxford: Oxford University Press, 1981). Famine also helped launch the career of ethicist Peter Singer. See "Famine, Affluence and Morality," *Philosophy and Public Affairs* 1:1 (Spring 1972), 229–43.
26. For a scathing account of system-induced famines in the late nineteenth century, see Mike Davis, *Late Victorian Holocausts: El Niño Famines and the Making of the Third World* (London: Verso, 2001).
27. Sen also criticized cultural restrictions on freedom, rejecting Singaporean president Lee Kwan Yew's assertion that "Asian values" did not enable democracy and that a Confucian legacy necessitated authoritarian rule. For key interventions in this debate, see Fareed Zakaria, "Culture Is Destiny: A Conversation with Lee Kwan Yew," *Foreign Affairs* 73 (March–April 1994); and Kim Dae Jung, "Is Culture Destiny? The Myth of Asia's Anti-Democratic Values," *Foreign Affairs* 73 (November–December 1973).
28. And of the insufficiency of Western assistance. He demanded a "glasnost for the IMF." Sachs, "Toward Glasnost in the IMF," *Challenge* 37:3 (1994), 4–11.
29. Sachs, *End of Poverty*, 31.
30. Sachs, *End of Poverty*, 266–67.
31. William Easterly, *The White Man's Burden: Why the West's Efforts to Aid the Rest Have Done So Much Ill and So Little Good* (New York: Penguin, 2006).
32. Easterly, *The Elusive Quest for Growth: Economists' Adventures and Misadventures in the Tropics* (Cambridge: MIT Press, 2001), 143.
33. Though he claimed that incentives were not another panacea. Easterly, *Elusive Quest*, 143.
34. Sachs cited his wife's pediatric practice as inspiration; Easterly guardedly endorsed randomized impact evaluations that assess projects using an approach derived from drug testing, an endorsement he later qualified. Sachs, *End of Poverty*, Chap. 4; Easterly, *White Man's Burden*, 326–28. To this day, Sachs contends that his shock therapy prescriptions in the 1980s and 1990s were based not on neoliberal standards but on a clinical evaluation of the needs of the Bolivian and East European economies. A clinical approach, Sachs argues, dispenses with economic orthodoxy and simply addresses the needs of the patient. "Entrevista com Jeffrey Sachs: 'Em tempo de guerra a Europa não é nada,'" *Publico P2* (Lisbon) (June 16, 2024), 4–9.
35. Paul Collier, *The Bottom Billion: Why the Poorest Countries Are Failing and What Can Be Done about It* (Oxford: Oxford University Press, 2007).
36. Collier, *Bottom Billion*, 23. This passage focuses on the roots of conflict.
37. Banerjee, cited in Florent Bédécarrats, Isabelle Guérin, and François Roubaud, eds., *Randomized Control Trials in the Field of Development: A Critical Perspective* (Oxford: Oxford University Press, 2020), 211.
38. See the chart in Martin Ravallion, "Should the Randomistas (Continue to) Rule?"

Center for Global Development Working Paper 492 (August 2018), 2. For a database of evaluations and meta-evaluations, see the International Initiative for Impact Evaluation website www.3ieimpact.org.

39. It also broadened the field of economic topics, encouraging new applications that treat economics not simply as the study of economies but also of rational, incentive-based decision-making more generally. See, for example, Ray Fisman and Edward Miguel, *Economic Gangsters: Corruption, Violence, and the Poverty of Nations* (Princeton: Princeton University Press, 2010).
40. Rodrik, "The New Development Economics: We Shall Experiment, but How Shall We Learn?" in Jessica Cohen and William Easterly, eds., *What Works in Development? Thinking Big and Thinking Small* (Washington, DC: Brookings Institution Press, 2009), 25.
41. Duflo, "The Economist as Plumber," *American Economic Review* 107:5 (May 2017), 1–26.
42. Banerjee, *Making Aid Work* (Cambridge: MIT Press, 2007), 165; Banerjee and Duflo, *Poor Economics,* 265. See also Dean Karlan and Jacob Appel, *More than Good Intentions: How a New Economics Is Helping to Solve Global Poverty* (New York: Dutton, 2011); Duflo and Michael Kremer, "Use of Randomization in the Evaluation of Development Effectiveness," in O. Feinstein, G. K. Ingram, and G. K. Pitman, eds., *Evaluating Development Effectiveness* (New Brunswick: Transaction, 2005); Duflo, Rachel Glennerster, and Kremer, "Using Randomization in Development Economics Research: A Toolkit," Center for Economic Policy Research Discussion Paper 6059 (January 2007); Banerjee and Duflo, "The Experimental Approach to Development Economics," *Annual Review of Economics* 1 (September 2009), 151–78.
43. In addition to Jonathan Morduch, "Does Microfinance Really Help the Poor?" and "The Microfinance Promise" (See Chap., note 115), see Banerjee, Duflo, Rachel Glennerster, and Cynthia Kinnan, "The Miracle of Microfinance? Evidence from a Randomized Evaluation," *American Economic Journal: Applied Economics* 7:1 (January 2015/May 2009), 22–53; M. Shahe Emran, Virginia Robano, and Stephen Smith, "Assessing the Frontiers of Ultra-Poverty Reduction: Evidence from CFPR/TUP, an Innovative Program in Bangladesh" (March 2009), available at SSRN: https://ssrn.com/abstract=1354158 or http://dx.doi.org/10.2139/ssrn.1354158. More generally, behavioral economists have reminded us that the poor, like the rich, are not all entrepreneurs. In a 2007 article, Banerjee and Duflo argue that the middle class tends to be characterized more by employment than by entrepreneurship. Banerjee and Duflo, "What Is Middle Class about the Middle Classes around the Globe?" Massachusetts Institute of Technology Working Paper 07–29 (December 11, 2007). And in 2008, they asked to what degree the poor even want to take charge of their own development. Banerjee and Duflo, "Mandated Empowerment: Handing Anti-Poverty Policy Bank to the Poor?" *Annals of the New York Academy of Sciences* 1136 (2008), 333–41.
44. Banerjee, "'New Development Economics' and the Challenge to Theory," *Economic and Political Weekly* 40:40 (October 1–7, 2005), 4343.

45. https://www.povertyactionlab.org/. The Poverty Action Lab—later J-PAL—was founded in 2003 as an online hub for impact evaluation.
46. A few economists have applied RCTs—or related methods, such as natural experiments—to examine questions from the past. Banerjee, Lakshmi Iyer, and Rohini Somanathan, "History, Social Divisions and Public Goods in Rural India," *Journal of the European Economic Association* 3:2–3 (May 2005), 639–47; and Banerjee and Iyer, "History, Institutions, and Economic Performance: The Legacy of Colonial Land Tenure Systems in India," *American Economic Review* 95:4 (September 2015), 1190–1213.
47. Richard Thaler and Cass Sunstein, *Nudge: Improving Decisions about Health, Wealth, and Happiness* (New York: Penguin, 2008). Behavioral economics, in turn, was based on the behavioral psychology of Daniel Kahnemann and Amos Tversky.
48. James Heckman, "Randomization and Social Policy Evaluation," in Charles Manski and Irv Garfinkel, eds., *Evaluating Welfare and Training Programs* (Cambridge: Harvard University Press, 1992), 201–30.
49. Nancy Cartwright, "Are RCTs the Gold Standard?" *Biosocieties* 2:1 (March 2007), 18; Cartwright, "What Are Randomised Controlled Trials Good For?" *Philosophical Studies* 147 (2010), 59–70.
50. Michael Woolcock, "Toward a Plurality of Methods in Project Evaluation: A Contextualised Approach to Understanding Impact Trajectories and Efficacy," *Journal of Development Effectiveness* 1:1 (March 2009), 9.
51. Banerjee, "'New Development Economics,'" 4341.
52. For recent deflationary accounts of RCTs, see the articles collected in *American Economic Journal: Applied Economics* 7:1 (January 2015/May 2009); and Timothy Ogden, ed., *Experimental Conversations: Perspectives on Randomized Trials in Development Economics* (Cambridge: MIT Press, 2016); and Bédécarrats et al., eds., *Randomized Control Trials.*
53. Rodrik, "The New Development Economics"; Daron Acemoğlu, "Theory, General Equilibrium and Political Economy in Development," *Journal of Economic Perspectives* 24:3 (Summer 2010), 17–32.
54. Banerjee, *Making Aid Work,* 12. Angus Deaton, in Banerjee, *Making Aid Work,* 56.
55. Ravallion, "Randomistas," 4–6.
56. Banerjee, "'New Development Economics,'" 4341.
57. Tanguy Bernard, Jocelyne Delarue, and Jean-David Naudet, "Impact Evaluations: A Tool for Accountability? Lessons from Experience at Agence Française de Développement," *Journal of Development Effectiveness* 4:2 (2012), 314–27; Woolcock, "Using Case Studies to Explore the External Validity of 'Complex' Development Interventions," *Evaluation* 19:3 (2013), 229–48.
58. Robert Picciotto, "Are the 'Randomistas' Evaluators?" in Bédécarrats et al., eds., *Randomized Control Trials,* 256–79.
59. Chambers, *Whose Reality Counts? Putting the First Last* (London: Intermediate Technology Publications, 1997), 41. This author has been told to do just such questionable quantification in a project evaluation.
60. One example of this inability is the troubled effort to evaluate Jeffrey Sachs's Mil-

lennium Villages Project. See Michael Clemens and Gabriel Demombynes, "When Does Rigorous Impact Evaluation Make a Difference? The Case of the Millennium Villages," Center for Global Development Working Paper 225 (October 2010).

61. Banerjee, "'New Development Economics,'" 4340.
62. Barbara Falk discusses several dubious lessons drawn from 1989 in "From Berlin to Baghdad: Learning the 'Wrong' Lessons from the Collapse of Communism," in George Lawson, Chris Armbruster, and Michael Cox, eds., *The Global 1989: Continuity and Change in World Politics* (Cambridge: Cambridge University Press, 2010), 243–70. For civil society lessons misapplied in Azerbaijan, see Michael Gubser and Jerrold Keilson, "Retrieving the Past: The Study of History and the Practice of International Development," *Monday Developments* 28:10 (October 2010), 27–28, 32.
63. Richard Neustadt and Ernest May, *Thinking in Time: The Uses of History for Decision Makers* (New York: Free Press, 1986), 32–33.
64. In earlier drafts, I called this *historiopraxis*.
65. Dan Honig, *Navigation by Judgment: Why and When Top-Down Management of Foreign Aid Doesn't Work* (New York: Oxford University Press, 2018).
66. Erin Beck, *How Development Projects Persist: Everyday Negotiations with Guatemalan NGOs* (Durham: Duke University Press, 2017).
67. Sarah Foss, *On Their Own Terms: Development and Indigeneity in Cold War Guatemala* (Chapel Hill: University of North Carolina Press, 2022).
68. For a relevant reflection by Global South practitioners and scholars on the ways development perpetuates longstanding neocolonial influence, as well as ideas for overcoming these tendencies, see Jessi Hanson-DeFusco, Sakil Malik, Rosine Assamoi, Antony Chiromba, Decontee Davis, Fidèle Marc Hounnouvi, Furqan B. Irfan, Patrick Faley, Djo Dieudonne Matangwa, Tambu Muzenda, Hanifa Nakiryowa, Andiwo Obondoh, S. Parveen, Ana Julia Pinales, and Rugare Zimunya, "Unethical Issues in Twenty-First Century International Development and Global Health Policy," *International Studies Perspectives* 25:1 (2024), 60–85.

INDEX